ÉMILE DURKHEIM AND THE BIRTH OF THE GODS

The *Birth of the Gods* is dedicated to Durkheim's effort to understand the basis of social integration. Unlike most social scientists, then and now, Durkheim concluded that humans are naturally more individualistic than collectivistic, that the primal social unit for humans is the macro-level unit ('the horde'), rather than the family, and that social cohesion is easily disrupted by human self-interest. Hence, for Durkheim, one of the "gravest" problems facing sociology is how to mold these human proclivities to serve the collective good. The analysis of elementary religions, Durkheim believed, would allow social scientists to see the fundamental basis of solidarity in human societies, built around collective representations, totems marking sacred forces, and emotion-arousing rituals directed at these totems.

The first half of the book traces the key influences and events that led Durkheim to embrace such novel generalizations. The second part makes a significant contribution to sociological theory with an analysis that essentially "tests" Durkheim's core assumptions using cladistic analysis, social network tools and theory, and data on humans closest living relatives—the great apes. Maryanski marshals hard data from primatology, paleontology, archaeology, genetics, and neuroscience that enlightens and, surprisingly, confirms many of Durkheim's speculations. These data show that integration among both humans and great apes is not so much group or kin oriented, per se, but orientation to a community standing outside each individual that includes a sense of self, but also encompassing a cognitive awareness of a "sense of community" or a connectedness that transcends sensory reality and concrete social relations. This "community complex," as Maryanski terms it, is what Durkheim was beginning to see, although he did not have the data to buttress his arguments as Maryanski is able to do.

Alexandra Maryanski is Professor of the Graduate Division at the University of California, Riverside, Emerita Professor of Sociology at UCR, and a founding member of the Institute for Theoretical Social Science. She holds advanced degrees in anthropology, network analysis, and interdisciplinary social science. She has co-authored six books, *Functionalism*, *The Social Cage*, *Incest: Origin of the Taboo*, *On the Evolution of Societies by Means of Natural Selection*, *Handbook on Evolution and Society*, and *The Emergence and Evolution of Religion*. She has written dozens of articles demonstrating the utility of network analysis, cladistics, and evolutionary theory in sociological analysis and has been at the forefront of two intellectual movements in sociology: evolutionary sociology and neurosociology.

Maryanski has undertaken to critically review accumulated data from various sources, including evolutionary biology, primatology, and comparative history... as she methodically retraces Durkheim shedding light on the origin of the mysterious force that transforms human individualism into a collective community... Readers of *Émile Durkheim and the Birth of the Gods* will find it an essential new, must sociological reading.

Edward A. Tiryakian, Professor Emeritus of Sociology,
Duke University

This is an important book. Maryanski shows that the evolutionary record of human ancestors and relatives needed a mechanism that would turn very loosely organized, in many respects individualistic and a-social apes, into the strong-yet-flexible ties that have made up the history of human societies. It could not have happened by building on ape family structures, since these lacked strong ties across and within the generations. Humans took a different route by developing emotional rituals that generate symbols of membership, thus providing a flexible tool for building societies of many different kinds. Maryanski uses evidence of biology and animal researchers in a new and impressive way to show how humans interact emotionally and cognitively to create socially shared institutions. This is an important theoretical broadening of human evolution, beyond the slow mechanism of genetic selection, and the usual focus on individual psychology: how humans acting together developed a mechanism to create and change social structure.

Randall Collins, Emeritus Professor of Sociology,
University of Pennsylvania

This is a brilliant, original, and challenging contribution to the sociology of religion and to our understanding of social life. It is essential reading for scholars and graduate students in sociology, anthropology, and religion. Using convincing data Maryanski sheds fresh light on Durkheim's quest to provide a scientific explanation of the roots of religion and the central part it plays in the roots of human sociality.

Kenneth Thompson, Emeritus Professor,
The Open University

A scintillating effort to put Durkheim into conversation with contemporary knowledge from paleoanthropology, primatology, evolutionary biology, and sociobiology. Maryanski proves there is still gold to be mined in the oeuvre of this venerable founding father.

Alexander Riley, Professor of Sociology,
Bucknell University

Émile Durkheim and the Birth of the Gods

Clans, Incest, Totems, Phratries,
Hordes, Mana, Taboos, Corroborees, Sodalities,
Menstrual Blood, Apes, Churingas, Cairns,
and Other Mysterious Things

Alexandra Maryanski

First published 2018
by Routledge
711 Third Avenue, New York, NY 10017

and by Routledge
2 Park Square, Milton Park, Abingdon, Oxon, OX14 4RN

Routledge is an imprint of the Taylor & Francis Group, an informa business

© 2018 Taylor & Francis

The right of Alexandra Maryanski to be identified as author of this work has been asserted by her in accordance with sections 77 and 78 of the Copyright, Designs and Patents Act 1988.

All rights reserved. No part of this book may be reprinted or reproduced or utilised in any form or by any electronic, mechanical, or other means, now known or hereafter invented, including photocopying and recording, or in any information storage or retrieval system, without permission in writing from the publishers.

Trademark notice: Product or corporate names may be trademarks or registered trademarks, and are used only for identification and explanation without intent to infringe.

Library of Congress Cataloging-in-Publication Data
A catalog record for this title has been requested

ISBN: 978-1-138-58093-0 (hbk)
ISBN: 978-1-138-58736-6 (pbk)
ISBN: 978-0-429-50399-3 (ebk)

Typeset in Minion
by Florence Production Ltd, Stoodleigh, Devon, UK

FOR PROFESSOR JONATHAN H. TURNER
MY PERSON OF VALOR

Contents

Foreword		ix
Acknowledgments		xii
Introduction: Why Write Another Book on Durkheim?		xiv
1	A Matter of Time	1
2	Points of Departure	26
3	Networks	42
4	The Young Sociology Professor	54
5	The Révélation	63
6	W. Robertson Smith and the Scottish School of Totemism	83
7	A Turn to Religion	102
8	A Blueprint for Religion	111
9	Smashing Totemic Blows	128
10	The Great Totemic March	141
11	Totemism: The Elementary Religion	163
12	Under the Microscope	194
13	The Hominoid Social Legacy	211
14	A Sense of Community	231
15	The Hominoid Mind and the Self	246
16	The Community Complex	258
17	Secrets of the Totem	274
Bibliography		305
Index		337

Foreword

Durkheim returned to Paris in 1902 in an era of renewed multi-modernity that has been characterized as "La Belle Époque". Following the "Long Depression" that marked the economic life of industrial countries, progress resumed in many forms. In France, slowly recovering from the humiliating 1870 defeat by Germany and an ensuing period of political instability, which climaxed from 1894–1899 with an undeclared civil war pitting various elements of the left against various elements of the right, a return to normalcy occurred in centripetal centers of attraction. Political life became institutionalized with the presidency of republican Émile Loubet (1899–1906), who resolved the Dreyfus crisis, made possible the start of a long-lasting Anglo–French *entente,* and inaugurated the greatest international exhibition in history, the Paris Universal Exposition of 1900, which made Paris in the age of electricity, "The City of Lights".

Marcel Fournier, the faithful chronicler of Durkheim, makes little of the latter's involvement at the Exposition, even though "solidarity" (his doctoral thesis) was feted by Léon Bourgeois as the social philosophy of the great Exposition. Durkheim was in the midst of arduously preparing for successive volumes of the *Année Sociologique.* Nevertheless, he found it timely to attend one of the many distinguished intellectual conferences (or "congresses") held that summer: the International Congress of Social Education, limiting his participation to reading a paper "devoted to the use of the education system to promote solidarist ideas" (Marcel Fournier, *Émile Durkheim,* p. 341).

Tying together some strands of thought, Durkheim argued in his presentation that sociology should have a major role to play in all the universities, that beliefs and moral rules are social formations, and that solidarity is society's very condition of existence and the essential law of humanity (Fournier, p. 342). Complementing the panache of outer luxury available on **the right bank** of Paris, and the electricity that transformed the entire city through technology, Durkheim had become a prized "scholastic" of what Albert Thibaudet later aptly called **the left bank's** "Republic of the Professors" (Thibaudet, *La République des Professeurs,*

1927, p. 155). This is echoed in the present study by Maryanski noting that Durkheim "was also a living icon in French intellectual life" (17–13).

Committed to the presupposition of the merit of a democratic republican form of government, Durkheim turned to his abiding concern over social cohesion and its moral foundation. He had an epiphanic moment when his nephew Marcel Mauss introduced him to the work of Robertson Smith, *Lectures on the Religion of the Semites*. Durkheim used his keen insight to search in totemism the basic "stuff" of religion, sensing that religion has the elements of the social force for social integration. To find the facticity of this primal force, generated in emotional gatherings of "collective effervescence", led Durkheim to a close reading and interpretation of the recently published ethnographic accounts of "primitive" tribes of Central Australia.

A major tenet of Durkheim's ensuing *Elementary Forms of the Religious Life*—the sacred/profane dichotomy—quickly found its way in the discourse of the Anglo–Franco public. However, two generations ago the empirical materials on totemism tended to be glossed over or even ridiculed by anthropologists (and by traditional religionists) refusing to see totemic religion as a matrix of primitives' social life and key access to modern religious systems.

A century later, Alexandra Maryanski has undertaken to critically review accumulated data from various sources, including evolutionary biology, primatology, and comparative history (e.g., in her presentation of Ralph Linton's discussion of the totemic aspects of the 42nd Infantry Rainbow Division) to investigate the claims of Durkheim for totemism, past and present.

Just as Paris became bathed in light in the Universal Exposition, so can we follow Maryanski as she methodically retraces Durkheim shedding light on the origins of the mysterious force that transforms human individualism into a collective community. In the first page of the oft-neglected Introduction to what became his magnum opus, *The Elementary Forms of Religious Life*, Durkheim narrates Sociology as a positive science which arrives at knowledge through systematic observation. Stumbling in the caverns of Ethnography, Durkheim found a lodestone of data which he enriched with his insights on the primacy of rituals that he recognized in the proto-religious system of totemism, rituals which on certain occasions activate the group's *collective effervescence* and the successive remembrance (often symbolic) of this extraordinary condition.

Maryanski does not only take us through various stages of Durkheim's research on The Baldwin Spencer and Francis Gillen rich ethnographic data of *The Native Tribes of Central Australia* and their companion piece,

The Northern Tribes of Central Australia,, she also in her ultimate chapter discusses the harsh criticism levelled at totemism, and at Durkheim's advocacy of totemism as expressing the fundamentals of religion.

Readers of *Émile Durkheim and the Birth of the Gods* will find it an essential new, must sociological reading of a "classic", as Karen Fields set the stage with her 1995 translation of *The Elementary Forms,* and as Robert Bellah and Hans Joas found it in preparing their magistral volume on evolutionary culture in *The Axial Age and its Consequences* (2012). The fundamental problem of individualism and social integration faced by higher apes, which occupy so much of Alexandra Maryanski's attention, as well as by us humans, is one that still remains at the heart of sociological inquiry.

Edward A. Tiryakian
Professor Emeritus of Sociology
Duke University

Acknowledgments

I am indebted to many individuals and institutions that contributed directly or indirectly to the writing of this book and for their generous support, encouragement, guidance, and friendship. At the University of California in Riverside, the Academic Senate provided funds to help support my research and travel expenses, indeed all my research over the years. I am greatly indebted to Maria Mendoza, Kimberly Noon, Debbie Snow, Bernice Ridgeway, Esther Barraza, and especially to Janet Moores in UCR's Interlibrary loan. Thanks to their efforts to locate books, manuscripts, and journal articles literally around the globe, I was able to incorporate the rich nineteenth-century materials I needed for my analysis. I also want to thank the library staff at the University of California at Santa Barbara for their courteous and helpful service in locating some critical works for me. I am also indebted to the generous help given to me by the staff at the Alice Springs Library in the Northern Territory, Australia when I visited Alice Springs for archival research. I am also very grateful to my wonderful UCR undergraduates and graduate students in my theory courses over the years who read, and pointed out errors on some of the early drafts. Their comments helped to make the text more readable and I believe, a more enjoyable book to read.

A special acknowledgment is due to Vartan Messier and Patricia Turner who helped me with the translations of Durkheim's materials as well as works by his colleagues and the scholars that influenced him. This book greatly benefited from their contributions. As Vartan Messier is a native French speaker with a specialization in literature and Patricia Turner is a French historian and an expert on nineteenth-century France, both lent a deep-reaching expertise by translating materials in the light of what they implied in the context of a nineteenth-century Western worldview.

Portions of this manuscript were written during my stay in Australia, France, and Denmark. A special appreciation to Aarhus University in Denmark in the Department for The Study of Religion where I had the leisure to read and write in such a stimulating atmosphere. My warmest thanks for the helpful suggestions and thoughtful critiques of the Aarhus faculty, especially Anders Klostergaard Peterson, Armin Geertz, Marianne Schleicher, and Hans Jøgen Lundager Jensen.

I would like to offer my deep appreciation to Randall Collins, Kenneth Thompson, Alexander Riley and Ghislaine Roelant, who generously gave their time reviewing the manuscript. And, to Edward Tiryakian for his thoughtful and perceptive foreword to the book. I hope that the project will prove to be worthy of all their effort. I was very fortunate to have Dean Birkenkamp as my editor and his assistant Tyler Bay. Not only were they wonderfully accomplished in getting the book into production, and providing sound advice, but they walked the extra mile by evaluating bookjacket colors, totem faces (we chose a totem pole from Victoria, BC, Canada) and other design features, assuring that hard to reproduce photographs were given a facelift for the book, and assisting me in numerous other ways. My thanks also go to Tamsyn Hopkins who has been most cooperative during the last hurdles. Finally, this book is dedicated to my husband, Jonathan Turner who heroically supported, prodded, and cheered me on during some rough times in completing this project. I greatly value his insight, counsel, and patience both personally and professionally.

Introduction
Why Write Another Book on Durkheim?

A Note to the Reader

After visiting the old Alice Springs telegraph station in Central Australia, and the sacred grounds where Baldwin Spencer (a professor of biology) and Francis Gillen (the station master) sat watching aboriginal totemic rites, I decided to revisit an old theory in sociology. In 1912 Durkheim published *The Elementary Forms of Religious Life: The Australian System of Totemism*, which drew upon Spencer's and Gillen's observations and conclusions. While praised as brilliant, creative, and original, it was otherwise picked apart for its flawed reasoning, sloppy concepts, excessive emphasis on the social, and reliance on one ethnography to reach dead wrong conclusions.[1] As Wilhelm Schmidt ([1931]1972: 115) expressed it, "of all recent works dealing with ethnology and the history of religion, there is none which has reaped such a harvest of praise for its details, combined with such general rejection of its main thesis." Yet, despite this bumpy reception, Durkheim's book still has the unflagging capacity to engage generation after generation of readers. Why does this work stand the test of time while others sit collecting dust on library shelves?

One reason is surely the books rich pile of propositions or what Alexander Goldenweiser (1915: 719–720) dubbed a theory of everything, "a theory of religion, a theory of totemism, a theory of social control, a theory of ritual and a theory of thought." Another is that, despite predictions to the contrary, religion has not faded away in a world of secularism, nor do we have answers to the questions Durkheim addressed. Or, perhaps, despite the spate of articles, monographs, and books linked

---

1 See for example, Imogen Seger's excellent monograph, *Durkheim and his Critics on the Sociology of Religion* 1957. Also see Malinowski 1913; Goldenweiser 1917; Lewis 1917; and Weatherly 1917.

to *Elementary Forms* over the last hundred years, so little has been done with Durkheim's core thesis on religion that it simply remains adrift as a captivating work that generates its own effervescence. Whatever the answer, what Harry Alpert called, the "Durkhemian mystique" is still very much alive in academic circles.

I decided to pursue the logic behind Durkheim's writing of *Elementary Forms* after my visit to the old Alice Springs Repeater Station built in 1871 on the ceremonial grounds of the local Arrernte people (formerly Arunta).[2] But, in truth, I had already become incurably curious over why the core premises underlying Durkheim's theory of religion and society now tally with recent findings in neurosociology, the fossil and archaeological data, and my own research on great ape societies. In particular, I wanted to revisit Durkheim's origin thesis and his totemic principle, which is laced with historical significance but generally dismissed as a pretty wild tale on the genesis of religion. For Durkheim, a religion was not a bag of imaginary beliefs, illusions, or lies but a practical and ongoing reality with roots in the nature of things. And while the faithful justify their religious beliefs on various grounds, the true reasons underlying religion, he said, never change and never cease to exist—thus making it "the duty of science to discover them." Durkheim was also adamant that religion—indeed human society itself—was born in totemism. Indeed, he became so captivated by totems that they became *the* pivotal force not only for his theory of religion, but also for his ideas on the origin of society, kinship, and the family. But, above all, Durkheim sought an understanding of religion itself, remarking "I have made a very archaic religion the subject of my research because it seems better suited than any other to help us comprehend the religious nature of man, that is, to reveal a fundamental and permanent aspect of humanity" (Durkheim [1912]1995: 1).

In this pursuit, Durkheim believed it essential to go back as far as possible to a proto-religious time when humans lived in "promiscious hordes." While nobody had ever seen a real-life horde, Durkheim had hoped that this primal state of humanity would materialize, perhaps in the

---

2 The Alice Springs repeater station opened up communication channels in Central Australia as the Overland telegraph line ran from Adelaide to Darwin. It sits in such arid and rugged terrain that only camel trains delivered mail to Alice Springs until 1926. The site was chosen because it had a permanent waterhole with the repeater station positioned alongside a sacred Arrernte riverbank with major totemic significance (called in native tongue Thereyurre). It is not surprising then that Durkheim thought of Central Australia as *the* place "to study the simplest and most primitive religion that is known at present ..." (Durkheim [1912]1995: 1; Brooks 1991).

remotest reaches of the aboriginal world. But as time passed and with no hordes in sight, Durkheim had little choice but to underpin his totemic theory with Spencer's and Gillen's ethnography, *The Native Tribes of Central Australia* ([1899]1969), despite his conviction that "The Arunta are . . . a long way from . . . the 'perfect type' of primitive civilization" (Durkheim [1902]1985: 107, original emphasis[3]). Moreover, by erecting his thesis on the footings of Central Australian totemism, Durkheim faced the daunting task of dismantling what he considered Spencer's and Gillen's and Sir James Frazer's misguided interpretation of Arunta (Arrernte) totemism and convincing readers of *Elementary Forms* that *his* theory of totemism was right, and theirs was wrong. But outside of Australian totemism, nothing but fragments of broken down totemic systems remained, even among American Indians where the name "totemism" originated. By comparison, the Arrernte system was still relatively intact; and they were, Durkheim felt, at least in the lowest *observed* stage of the totemic cycle.

While the Arrernte ethnography served well enough for his general theory of religion, Durkheim was forced to rely upon assorted aboriginal customs and outright conjecture to connect the genesis of religion with primitive hordes. To cast this event, he began by describing the hunting and gathering lifestyle of the Central Australians, slowly taking the reader back to the lesser known, and, then, to the unknown in an unfolding narrative of a mystical time in prehistory when nomadic hordes roamed about gathering wild fruits and vegetables. Long convinced that religion was not a product of individual consciousness but a collective phenomena with energy drawn from social activity, Durkheim reasoned that the awakening of proto-religious sentiments must reside in the "fission and fusion" cycles of wandering food collectors who when meeting up occasionally experienced an emotional "effervescence" that appeared to come from an external force, or *mana*. In time this invisible and diffused force came to be embodied in totems and totemic emblems, which symbolized in a concrete way these collective representations. Yet, to sustain solidarity, community members had to periodically assemble, which is why Durkheim saw the germinal source of religion residing in the actions of social life itself.

---

3 For Durkheim, Arrernte society had already undergone "grave and profound rearrangements . . ." And contrary to what many social scientists believe, Durkheim believed it was wrong "to see in the Arunta the late representatives of humanity at its origin; and it would be no less a mistake to misjudge everything that subsists among them as the most primitive social forms that we know" ([1902]1985: 107,117).

Could Durkheim's origin thesis have a basis in reality? After all, religion originated at some point in time. Could the genesis of religion be a by-product of collective emotions generated by effervescent gatherings and represented by sacred totems? Is this the wellspring of the religious sentiment, the god figure or what Durkheim called the *totemic principle?* Who then indeed is god?

After publishing *Elementary Forms*, Durkheim became a lightening rod for criticism, especially by anthropologists who attacked him for confusing a primal religion with a simple religion, for confounding the cause of religion with its function, and for partitioning the sacred and profane into artificial categories with little utility. Disapproval of Durkheim's totemic theory was relentless with critics charging that totems are not universal, that totem complexes are not fixed entities and may even be an illusion, and that totems could not be the earliest religion because a totem need not be religious at all. Some scholars were more favorably impressed but, overall, *Elementary Forms* received but faint praise, leaving it to dangle precariously on a crumbling evolutionary framework of the early twentieth century.

The English-speaking world at large became acquainted with Durkheim when Joseph Swain, a young graduate student working on his own dissertation translated *Elementary Forms* in 1915. W. Lloyd Warner wrote as late as 1935 that "It is unfortunate that all the works of this great French social theorist are not available in English, and that he seems fated to continue being misunderstood by English and American anthropologists" (p. 355).

Yet, once scholars outside of France became familiar with *The Division of Labor* (1893), *Suicide* (1897), and *The Rules of Sociological Method* (1895), Durkheim's stature underwent a transformation. Then, over the next decades, Durkheim became a victim of legend with his writings subject to a variety of interpretations and misunderstandings because of some poor English translations, selective perceptions of "would-be admirers" on what they thought he said or did not say, clashing ideologies, and unbalanced translations of articles, monographs, and books. As Steve Lukes (1973: 3) put it, Durkheim "has been variously called a materialist and an idealist, a positivist and a metraphysican, a rationalist and an irrationalist, a dogmatic atheist and a mystic . . . a 'scholarly forerunner of Fascism,' an agent of 'bourgeois conservation,' a late-nineteenth-century liberal, a conservative and a socialist." Indeed, remarked Byron Turner (1992: xiv), "Durkheim's sociology has been surrounded by a forest of contradictory and often misleading interpretation." A case in point is George Catlin's introduction to the first English translation of *Rules of Sociological Method* ([1938:

1964: xxviii) where he wrote that Durkheim "By his ill-considered and scientifically pretentious psycho-mysticism . . . has contributed to give the color of justification to the new religion of the altar of *divus Augustus* and to the neopagan philosophy of Caesar-worship." (For more on this issue also see Giddens 1979; Pickering and Martins 1994; and Gephart 1998).

Fortunately, what Terry Clark (1979) characterized as "an enormous revival of interest in Durkheim and the Durkheim school" also resulted in new translations of his classic works, translations of his little known writings, excellent biographies (e.g. Lukes 1972; Pickering 1984; Fournier 2013), and scores of timely articles, books, and monographs devoted to interpreting and building on his work with regard to the division of labor, morality, social solidarity, rituals, emotions, family life, religion, suicide, education, and the like. But with few exceptions, almost nothing has been done with his core thesis in *Elementary Forms*. Typically, it is conveniently set aside and ignored while his association between god and society following Dominick LaCapra is treated by some scholars "as an erratic or mad peccadillo which may be chalked up to purely personal or historical idiosyncrasies" (quoted in Clark 1979: 130). And so, one can ask: Did Durkheim waste over fifteen years of his academic career seeking the origin of religion in the primitive horde? I asked this question and then decided to find an answer.

My original plan was to confine my research to Durkheim's totemic principle and his origin thesis, but I soon realized that I needed to cast a much wider net if I was to penetrate his underlying logic and the bold assumptions behind his ideas—if only to see if they were worthy of further examination. A deeper understanding would also lessen the chances of misinterpreting his reasoning or missing something important. So I read most of Durkheim's writings, visited the home of his childhood, the schools he attended, the universities where he taught and, of course, to the Montparnasse Cemetery in Paris where he is buried. I also systematically traced his ideas on religion over time, being careful to stick with the facts. To dig a little deeper, I read the key works of individuals known to have influenced him. Focusing on writings that captured Durkheim's thinking at a given point in time proved to be a fruitful approach because he often expressed his ideas initially in a word-for-word lecture format or in articles before they appeared in book form.

As ideas are born and colored in the intellectual atmosphere of a period, this book begins by placing Durkheim in his own social and intellectual world. For added insights I felt it was also important to illuminate his personality, his known strengths and weaknesses, and other distinctive traits. But there is much more. Everyone likes a good detective story, and with most of Durkheim's personal papers lost, the unwritten storyline behind *Elementary Forms* is riddled with unsolved mysteries—from the origin of his ideas and the scholars that influenced him, the curious obsession he had with hordes, clans, and totemic cults to the cryptic journal note he wrote in 1907 telling of a *révélation* he had in 1895, a watershed moment, he said, because it forced him to rethink all his past research to tally with his new understanding of religion. Equally intriguing is the paper trail he left behind with baffling clues into his thought processes that come as close as you can get to a sociological "who-done-it." For Durkheim, though, he was solving the mystery of mysteries—the genesis of religion. What was this serious French scholar thinking when he proposed such a daring undertaking, and, why did he defend totemism as his *raison d'être* for the origin of religion (and society) in the face of fierce and mounting criticism? Durkheim was not known for wild-eyed commentary, nor did he make hasty generalizations; and so, it is essential to understand why he defended so vigorously what many consider a radically unsound thesis.

Durkheim was an impressive intellect in his own time, but I believe he was also ahead of his time. For in tackling the genesis of the religious institution he provided glimpses into humans' ultimate history, a time before institutions existed. Too often, scholars have accused Durkheim of naive and simplistic thinking with regard to his views on totems, clans, kinship, and family life, but my ten years of research revealed just the opposite. For despite some major faulty premises, Durkheim was a well-schooled kinship theorist with a deep understanding of the issues he confronted. What led him astray was his nineteenth-century worldview with its misguided notion of social evolution and erroneous conclusions about aboriginal lifeways. But if we replace Durkheim's developmental model with modern evolutionary theory and update his methodology with social network tools and cladistic analysis, his hypothesis can be turned loose to lead us where it may. And, so in the pages that follow we will visit some very strange and exotic places especially for sociologists and scholars more generally.

I hope that readers will enjoy this book as much as I have enjoyed researching how Durkheim came to develop his theory on the nature and origin of religion. Revisiting Durkheim's ideas on religion can also help to illuminate some of his other novel ideas, such as his view of human sociality. Why did he believe that a group must assemble and recreate itself periodically to sustain solidarity? Why did he view human beings as so emotional and ritualistic? And, why should human collectivism once energized be so fleeting? Is sociality *not* built into the human animal? In Durkheim's time, almost nothing was known about human evolution, but today we can hold up a distant mirror to the past by using data from the fossil, molecular, and archaeological records and from humans' closest hominoid relatives—the great apes. From these vantage points, an analysis of Durkheim's theory of religion and its application leads to the asking of some new questions about religion while offering fresh insights into Durkheim's religious sociology.

Above all else, I wrote this book for Durkheim who died suddenly in 1917 after the devastating loss of his son and many of his graduate students and colleagues during World War I. To make matters worse, he had to endure years of enveloping rounds of scholars attacking totemism along with punishing and widely publicized critiques of his totemic theory. Yet, his thesis is still an open question and, thus, it deserves to be evaluated. This is what Durkheim wanted. This is what he asked us to do. Indeed, his last words in *Elementary Forms* urged us to carry on where he left off: "What must be done is to try out the hypothesis and test it against the facts as methodically as possible" ([1912]1995: 447). The purpose of this book is to start the process of doing just that by bringing new data to bear on an old theory.

Alexandra Maryanski
Santa Barbara, California

1
A Matter of Time

I know originality is impossible; certainly I have never claimed otherwise. I am thoroughly convinced that my ideas find their roots in those of my predecessors. Indeed, it is because they do that I have confidence in their fruitfulness.

Émile Durkheim, 1907,
Revue Néo-scolastique 14: 613

Émile Durkheim's great work, *The Elementary Forms of Religious Life* (1912), has always remained somewhat mystifying, especially to sociologists. True, Durkheim's analysis of ritual and emotional arousal is one of the foundations of present-day sociology of emotions (e.g. Goffman 1967; Collins 2004). The richness and complexity of *Elementary Forms* has also provided fertile ground for scores of Durkheimian scholars in sociology, as well as in the humanities and social sciences in general. Yet, despite its celebrated status, the work remains an enigma for many scholars. As Robert Bellah put it:

> In spite of all the excellent and persuasive reasons Durkheim gave in the introduction to *The Elementary Forms of the Religious Life* for choosing the Australian aborigines as the subject of his greatest book, one must still wonder at this choice. Why did this highly rational, secular, positivistic Frenchman decide sometime after 1895 to devote nearly fifteen of the most productive years of his life to the exotic cults, dancing, and blood-letting of a primitive people?
>
> (1973: xliii)

In turn, Stephen Lukes said that when he read *Elementary Forms*, he had his "mind blown" and "just became totally immersed in Durkheim" (in Clark 1979: 131). Why is this last book by one of sociology's iconic founders both baffling and beguiling?

All of Durkheim's work reflects a fierce determination to legitimate a science of society in the academic world. Yet, to put the nascent discipline on a solid foundation, Durkheim believed he first had to solve the "gravest" problem facing sociology: what holds aggregates together? While his work on the division of labor and suicide has a strong sociological bent, unlocking the secret of social solidarity was a multiplex problem that eventually took him into the strange world of hypothetical hordes, incest taboos, and especially, the curious case of totemism—all for the glory of sociology. *Elementary Forms* thus exposes a wide range of Durkheim's scholarship and, more importantly, a breadth and depth of Durkheim's intellectual engagements in areas of inquiry not normally part of the sociological tradition.

Of course, Durkheim was also heavily influenced by two of sociology's founders, August Comte and Herbert Spencer, who both argued for a view of societies as evolving from simple to more complex forms. Moreover, like Durkheim, both argued that sociology could be a natural science devoted to developing abstract laws and principles explaining the operative dynamics of the social universe. One of Durkheim's overlooked mentors, Alfred Espinas, who arranged for Durkheim's first appointment at the University of Bordeaux and the author of the little-known *Animal Societies* (1878), also emphasized to Durkheim other ideas from Comte and Spencer beyond their evolutionary schemes.[1] Espinas argued for a much broader view of sociology (which Durkheim certainly adopted); and while Durkheim's ideas are drawn from many sources, Espinas also handed Durkheim some early conceptual blocks for the budding science. Durkheim also considered Espinas an important forerunner of sociology, claiming that he was "the first to have studied social facts in order to make a science of them and not in order to secure the symmetry of a grand philosophical system" (quoted in Brooks 1998: 204). As social facts manifest regularities, Espinas said, a science of society is possible. And, perhaps to the surprise of some, Durkheim considered *Animal Societies* "the first chapter of sociology" ([1888]1978: 59).

Perhaps less baffling are Durkheim's references in *Elementary Forms* to independent scholars, now long forgotten, and his active engagement of a wide range of more anthropological scholars' respective analyses of kinship, religion, societal types, and primordial hordes. For sociologists, however, much of this analysis of kinship and religious systems revolving around *naturism, animism,* and *totemism* are often viewed as too "anthropological"

---

[1] Théodule Ribot and Alfred Espinas translated Spencer's *Principles of Psychology* into French in 1874–1875. For Espinas's detailed discussion of both Spencer and Comte see *Des Sociétes Animales* 1877–1878. And, see Geiger 1972, 309ff).

and, hence, easily glossed over. Indeed, what are the details of "primitive" religions doing in a sociological analysis of religion by a sociologist? Why was Durkheim so obsessed with lineages, phraties, moieties, incest taboos, exogamy, systems of cognitive classification and, above all, totems? Moreover, why is so much of *Elementary Forms* taken up with tortuous rebuttals of others who had criticized Durkheim's totemic theory in the late 1890s and early 1900s? And, to argue that the genesis of religion originated from primordial hordes seems especially odd, given that by 1912 evolutionary theorizing in the social sciences was fast becoming passé (because of the perceived racism and ethnocentrism in views of evolution as moving from "primitive" to "advanced" societies with, not surprisingly, the latter being white, European societies that had industrialized).

When Durkheim began to write *Elementary Forms* in the early twentieth century, his work was deeply imbued with a wide range of ideas received from early classical philosophy, early sociology and anthropology, French philosophy, and hard-science views of what the social sciences could become.[2] At the same time, his work on Australian kinship and religion was under attack and seemed to fall down on the wrong side of important intellectual debates. Yet, Durkheim was supremely confident in the validity of his arguments, despite the mounting criticism. Why was he so convinced he was right? One reason was his great faith in his predecessors and in the "proving ground" of facts, especially ones collected by nineteenth-century ethnographers and kinship theorists. In a real sense, Durkheim's aim was not originality, per se, but synthesis of known facts in order to bring truth to light. This trait was probably fostered by his mentor, Émile Boutroux ([1912]1970: 5) who wrote, "A great mind does not seek after novelty or originality; it seeks after truth . . . In reality, they make it their own by the way in which they use it." Where did Durkheim go wrong in his search for the truth? Or did he? To answer this question in a satisfactory way, we need to penetrate the underlying motives and logic behind the complex analysis in *The Elementary Forms of Religious Life*.

---

2 Ernest Wallwork (1972: 6) wrote, "Durkheim was a true conservative (in the best sense of the misused term), desirous of preserving the insights of the past . . . He did not hesitate . . . to go to Plato and Aristotle, Kant and Renouvier Montesquieu and Rousseau for sustenance and support . . . On the other hand, Durkheim was an intellectual radical who invariably rejected traditional formulas in favor of new, and often strkingly (sic) original, ideas." Also see Edward Tiryakian (1965) who places Durkheim in the general tradition of Plato, St. Thomas, De Bonald, and De Maistre in his approach to society as an organic unity.

As will become evident, by 1895 Durkheim had dropped much of the argument in the *Division of Labor in Society* (1893). Gone was the distinction between *mechanical* and *organic* solidarity. Gone was the all powerful *collective conscience* of "swallowed up" minds that was gradually dwindling away in the face of organic solidarity, being largely tempered by the notion of *collective representations*. And, gone was his focus on social evolution from simple to complex, being largely replaced by an increasing concern with the origin of religion and society and with Durkheim's intriguing image of a pre-kinship, promiscuous *horde*. He also dropped *naturism* as the baseline form of religion that he had asserted in his 1893 stage model in *The Division of Labor*, very quietly replacing it with *totemism* in the second edition in 1902 (see Maryanski 2014: 358–359).

Thus, increasingly after 1895, Durkheim drew from many areas of expertise—especially kinship theory and ethnographic portrayals of preliterate societies—that sociologists frequently do not realize were a central part of Durkheim's knowledge base. But, perhaps most important is that Durkheim was fighting for his continued intellectual relevance during the early twentieth century. His ideas about religion, his analysis of Australian marriage rules and descent, and especially his views on totemic beliefs and rites were all under attack by such illustrious scholars as James Frazer and Andrew Lang [who referred to some of Durkheim's premises as "doubly impossible" ([1905a]: 1970: 103). These critics were undermining years of Durkheim's creative work and forcing him to devote considerable energy to defending his views in essays and commentaries, often with his nephew, Marcel Mauss, and ultimately with his very complex analysis in *Elementary Forms*.

This last of Durkheim's great books, then, is so overdrawn and convoluted because he was mounting an offense in one great statement. He was sure, as noted above, that he was right, but he had to convince others of this conviction. Durkheim was thus defending and, in his mind, vindicating himself in this work. For despite Durkheim's otherwise great fame and prestige, he felt that a lot was on the line: his continued relevance in the intellectual world, as well as his intellectual legacy to later generations.

There is, then, an interesting story to tell—indeed a kind of mystery story—about why Durkheim turned to totemism as a critical force, and indeed, why so many other leading scholars were also interested in this force during Durkheim's lifetime. Why did Durkheim begin to sound like an anthropologist more than a sociologist; and why was he examining phenomena such as incest, hordes, the origins of society, exogamy, clans, totems, rituals, innate cognitive categories, and the like. In the short chapters of this book, one of my goals is to tell this story and unravel why the second half of Durkheim's career, was in essence, devoted to making vindicating statements in *The Elementary Forms*.

Part 1 of this book chronicles the path of Durkheim's early years to uncover why he suddenly became fixated on totemism and, then, to reconstruct the reasoning behind his sweeping generalizations on the origin of religion and society. A systematic chronology is especially important because Durkheim rejected or modified some early ideas that are still in circulation today and because of the widely differing views on what Durkheim supposedly said, or did not say. A reassessment of his thesis on the origins of religion also requires that we sort out some mystifying issues in Durkheim's academic history—issues such as his self-described "revelation" igniting his obsession with religion, his quiet removal of *naturism* as primal religion after 1895 (first articulated in *The Division of Labor* see Chapter 5) and replacing it in the second edition of *The Division of Labor* with *totemism* as the origin of religion, his reasons for dropping his famous distinction between "mechanical" and "organic" solidarity and, oddly enough, his reasons in *Elementary Forms* for wanting to avoid even using the name totemism because it grossly misrepresented the social institution he was describing (Durkheim ([1912]1995: 101). If not totemism, what else did he have in mind? Did we miss something important? The answer is yes, and the objective of this book is to (a) fill in some essential gaps in the development of Durkheim's religious sociology and (b), in Part 2 of the book, present data that will cast some new light in support of his ideas on individualism, society, and totemism.

The purpose of this chapter is to provide an essential historical context. For Durkheim's approach to religion, his use of classic evolutionary theory, and his sophisticated application of kinship theory reflect not just late nineteenth-century thought in France but are all contingent on a matrix of ideas adopted from earlier scholars in Europe, Australia, and the Americas. Even his decision to become a sociologist was fostered by historic events before he was born. A natural starting point is sociology's two science-minded founders—Auguste Comte and Herbert Spencer. Some background is also needed on three major nineteenth-century happenings: the great time revolution on the age of the earth, the founding of the English school of anthropology, and the discovery of kinship.

Early Sociology and Durkheim's Sociology

Auguste Comte and the French Collectivist Tradition

After the French Revolution (1789–1797), France was faced with chronic social and political unrest. French philosophers responded with an urgent need to understand the dynamics of social order, a problem that occupied Fourier, Joseph De Maistre, Chateaubriand, and Henri de Saint-Simon amongst others. Out of this call, a revitalization movement began to unfold in French intellectual circles urging the abandonment of libertarian individualism in favor of a collective philosophy to restore a sense of social order in post-revolutionary France. The consensus was that a bold doctrine was needed for the construction of a new social order grounded in morals, religion, and ethics (Nisbet 1966: 3ff; Gunn 1922: 32; Levy-Bruhl 1903). Durkheim is often seen as continuing this tradition because of his first ideas about "the collective conscience" and his later notion of "collective representations," but Durkheim was all too aware of what was lurking beneath the surface of the rosy portrayals of collectivism: *individualism.* Given the egoistic nature of humans, the submission of individuals to the collective must be achieved rather than assumed as "natural" to humans; and thus, *Elementary Forms* represents Durkheim's theory outlining the mechanisms by which commitments to collective representations are generated and sustained, thereby tempering potentially disintegrative effects of human individualism.

When Durkheim began his education, Comte's sociology was subject to ridicule. In fact, it was a banned topic in most French academic circles but, within a short span of years, his ideas were back in vogue. Indeed, the President of France and some of his cabinet of officials attended the dedication of a statue of Comte at the Sorbonne in 1902, thus marking Comte's "rehabilitation." But, despite the decades of obscurity, few French thinkers could avoid being exposed to Comte's ideas; and Alfred Espinas (a pioneering French sociologist) along with others assured that Durkheim would be steeped in Comte's key ideas, especially his ideas about the potential for a science of society. For whatever the merits or demerits attached to Comte's "law of the three stages" and his "hierarchy of the sciences," in which sociology is crowned "queen science," Comte sketched a framework for a truly objective social science, calling it by default *sociology*—as his preferred choice, *social physics*, had already been claimed by a Belgian statistician (Coser 2003: 3; Thompson 1975; and see Pickering, 1993 for an intellectual biography).

Worried that his nascent science would be dismissed as modified philosophy, Comte took the bold step of portraying sociology as *the* sister discipline of biology. What distinguished the two sciences, he said, is the nature of their elements, calling one a "biological organism" and the other a "social organism." Although Comte's use of the organismic analogy led him to elaborate anatomic comparisons between his two "organic" bodies, it helped to solidify sociology's image as the new science of society. Comte's metaphoric imagery is also seen as laying the footings for what became functional theorizing in sociology and even for Durkheim's statements on causes and functions outlined in *The Rules of Sociological Method* as they had been applied in *The Division of Labor in Society*.[3] After 1895, Durkheim's thinking began to change, and perhaps somewhat surprisingly, he was forced to smuggle in some neurology underlying human cognition and actions—an emphasis that is a far cry from his powerful advocacy in *The Rules* for sociologists to study only "social facts" rather than psychological or, heaven forbid, biological facts. And so, Durkheim seemed to be caught in a contradiction with his extreme sociologistic arguments in his early work. But, once we examine Durkheim's work in more detail in reviews, articles, and commentaries in the post 1895 period, it is clear that while he deliberately underplayed reference to human predilections in order to promote sociology as a distinct science in its own right, when it came to his theory on religion and society he was forced to anchor his thesis in the inherent properties of human neurobiology.

Herbert Spencer and the British Utilitarian Tradition

While Comte's positive philosophy was shunned by most French academics during his lifetime, his ideas gained a foothold in England with such luminaries as George Elliot, Henry Lewes, John Stuart Mill, Harriet

---

3 Most scholars regard Comte as less the original thinker and more the brilliant synthesizer who built upon the ideas of Condorcet, Montesquieu, Saint-Simon, and other social philosophers. Saint-Simon (along with Turgot) had already sown the seeds for a science of society to restore social order and stability. Even Comte's *Law of the Three States* rests on footings laid by Saint-Simon (see Hayek 1941 and Gunn 1922). Levy Bruhl (1903: 2) noted that: "Like many of his contemporaries Auguste Comte thought himself singled out for the mission of formulating the principle of social organization." For highly readable accounts of Comte's philosophy in historical perspective see Turner et al. 2012 and Coser 2003. Comte sketched his positive philosophy as early as 1822, in such essays as, "Plan of the Scientific Operations Necessary for Reorganizing Society" (for excerpts of this work see Comte and Lenzer 1998). Harriet Martineau translated Comte's monumental work into English in 1853 under the title, *The Positive Philosophy of Auguste Comte*.

4 For a comprehensive biography of Comte's life see Pickering 1993.

Martineau, and Herbert Spencer.[4] By the 1860s when many disruptive effects of early capitalism gave sway to economic benefits, optimism came to pervade mid-Victorian England, providing a receptive milieu for a doctrine of social progress and the use of science to ensure continued progress.

When Herbert Spencer (1820–1903) took up Comte's call for a science of society, he did so in tune with the British utilitarian tradition by ignoring Comte's collective idealism and moving sociology to a more grounded materialism. He also discarded Comte's singular notion of society (i.e. the great spiritual being) by adopting a plural nomenclature to distinguish among types of *societies*. Yet, he kept the name *sociology* and endorsed Comte's premise that an understanding of society and its natural laws could only be achieved by adopting the empirical methods of science.[5]

Spencer also agreed that social phenomena must be grounded in observation (rather than theory or pure logic), illustrating this principle by anchoring his own grand evolutionary schemes in ethnographic materials gathered from various sources. And his insistence on collecting inventories of empirical facts and cataloguing these facts so that they could be compared was evident in the large and weighty books that he commissioned for publication as *Descriptive Sociology* (1873–1881). These oversized volumes, now mostly forgotten, lent a seriousness to sociology as an empirical discipline.[6] In *The Division of Labor*, Durkheim frequently criticizes Spencer's presumed "utilitarianism" but shows only faint appreciation for Spencer's evolutionary model that forms the basis of his own portrayal of societal evolution from simple to complex forms, an idea reproduced in a less complete form with Durkheim's soon-to-be abandoned distinction between "mechanical" and "organic" solidarity. Durkheim also

---

5 Critics questioned Spencer's decision on keeping the name sociology, calling it a barbarism because it was derived from elements of Greek and Latin. Spencer felt indebted to Comte but made it plain in his "Reasons for Dissenting from the Philosophy of M. Comte" [1864]1968, that he was not Comte's disciple. Comte's speculations had "great value," Spencer emphasized, noting that, "True or untrue, his system as a whole, has doubtless produced important and salutary revolutions of thought in many minds; and will doubtless do so in many more" (p. 24). It is noteworthy that Spencer went to France and paid a visit to Comte before the Frenchmen died.

6 The full title of this fifteen-volume work (commissioned by Spencer) is Descriptive *Sociology, or Groups of Sociological Facts, Classified and Arranged* (1873–1881). Spencer intended these materials to serve as the "raw data" for comparative sociological models on human societies. For a detailed account see Turner and Maryanski 1988; also see Duncan 1908: 156 ff. Segments of Spencer's *Principles of Sociology* were first published as separate issues to individual subscribers or published as journal articles beginning about 1874.

downplayed Spencer's emphasis that this movement from simple to complex societal formations can cause disintegration of societies when new integrative mechanisms of integration do not evolve. Instead, Durkheim sees "abnormal forms" of the division of labor, which might cause temporary episodes of disintegration, as obviated as organic forms of solidarity "naturally" and inevitably take hold. And, surprisingly, Durkheim paid little attention to Spencer's emphasis on power as an integrating force in rapidly differentiating societies. Why should this be so, especially since Durkheim had made positive comments about Spencer's work in a number of publications?

The answer resides in Durkheim's view that culture—first the collective conscience, later collective representations—are more central to societal integration than power, per se, and in many ways, Durkheim's work after 1895 seeks to demonstrate how emotional commitments to culture develop and provide the fundamental basis of integration in all sociocultural formations. And, for Durkheim, the key to understanding how commitments and solidarity evolve is in understanding how the first human societies evolved from proto-societies (often portrayed as "hordes") and how religion is the basis for this evolution of societies. Thus, Spencer's sociology reinforced for Durkheim the importance of scientific theorizing and research employing an evolutionary perspective as well as providing for Durkheim the basic model of societal development. While Spencer also made interesting arguments on the origin and evolution of religion, his psychological "ghost theory" would be rejected by Durkheim in favor of an alternative collectivist approach to religion.

Evolutionary Theory and "The Time" Revolution

A New Sense of Time

An evolutionary interpretation of history dominated the Western world during the entire nineteenth century. Evolutionary reasoning also marked the beginning of modern fieldwork on a wide variety of populations at different "stages" of evolutionary development. Beginning in Classical times, the Greek historian Herodotus and the Roman historian Tacitus, among others, had described "exotic" populations by writing elaborate descriptions of their personalities, traditions, and habits. Over time, as these stories accumulated, gradually eroding time-honored Western notions of a static universe, scholars began to write of a "ladder of evolution" whereby "higher forms had ascended though time, out of a condition represented by present lower forms" (Bock 1956: 61–63; Slotkin 1965).

As ideas of progress and change crystallized into a bold, social evolutionary paradigm, social theorists began piecing together the mountains of documents on exotic peoples gathered over the centuries. To codify these documents, a hierarchical time scale was devised to rank societies from simple to complex in terms of how advanced they were along the road to "civilization." While these stage models varied in scope and grandeur, they all applied the evolutionary logic that complex forms had evolved out of lower, simpler forms. But a looming problem remained over the biblical chronology that the earth was only 6,000 years old.

This problem was met head on by the publication of Charles Lyell's *Principles of Geology* (1830–1833). Lyell's work provided the key evidence allowing all thinkers, if so disposed, to conceptualize evolution over a much longer time frame. Using evidence from deposits of sedimentary rocks, Lyell argued that the observed geological changes on the earth's surface required a vast time frame and, as is well known, Charles Darwin then used Lyell's evidence to buttress his own theory of organic evolution in *The Origin of Species* (1859), a theory that rocked the Western world because it questioned the religious interpretation of the origins of earth, humans, and society.[7]

In the post-Darwinian period, biologists debated the implications of natural selection for understanding human evolution. Social scientists also reacted by casting off the shackles of the past by going into the field to study "the primitive" or by heading to the nearest library to dust off ancient law codes, literary texts, and other archival documents in their zeal to reconstruct the *origins of* law, family, language, religion, and society itself.[8] Durkheim was soon to join these new evolutionary thinkers, released from the time scale imposed by biblical dogma. Over time, more influential on Durkheim than either Comte or Spencer in conceptualizing evolution was a more anthropological figure, Edward Tylor, who founded the British School of Social Anthropology.

Edward Tylor's (1832–1917) English School of Social Anthropology

Edward Tylor was a tall, strikingly handsome English anthropologist who played the leading role in legitimizing mid-nineteenth-century social evolutionary theory. Endowed with a charismatic personality, a keen

---

[7] In 1848, Lyell was knighted for his contribution to science (for a discussion see Gould 2002).

[8] Although Comte's Law of the Three States and other social evolutionary schemes had long preceded Darwin and Wallace's organic theory of evolution, a geological time scale coupled with biological evolution lent a new legitimacy to social evolutionary thinking.

intellect, and strong leadership qualities, Tylor founded comparative ethnology and established anthropology at Oxford University. In his *Researches into the Early History of Mankind* in 1865, followed by his *Primitive Culture* in 1871, Tylor set forth to create a science-driven theory of civilization. A social theorist with an "infinite respect for facts" (Kardiner and Preble 1961: 63 and see Stocking 1968), Tylor institutionalized three empirical methods for reconstructing the stages of human societies: (1) a comparative method to sort and "pigeonhole" societies with similar traits; (2) a reliance on the archeological record to rank and place societies with similar traits in their proper time sequence; and (3) a "doctrine of survivals" to recover the non-material traits of past societies. Survivals for Tylor were quaint cultural leftovers (e.g. customs, opinions, rituals) retained from a past stage of society.[9] Yet, unlike theorists who proposed that every society must pass through each developmental phase, Tylor held that movement was simply progressive from simple to complex forms, a trend already established in archaeology where stone, bronze, and iron tools followed each other in sequence. Under Tylor's tutelage, the cross-cultural method and his "doctrine of survivals" became indispensable for evolutionary theorists because they offered concrete "proof" that contemporary societies had evolved out of more primitive ones.

Tylor also institutionalized a remarkable doctrine, "the psychic unity of mankind," or the belief that all human minds operate in much the same way. Variations in cognitive processes, he said, result *not* from biological differences but from *different environmental conditions* and *different experiences*, resulting in different grades of civilization. In Tylor's words, "when it comes to comparing barbarous hordes with civilized nations, the consideration thrusts itself upon our minds, how far item after item of the life of the lower races passes into analogous proceedings of the higher, in forms not too far changed to be recognized, and sometimes hardly changed at all" ([1871]1970: 6–7). The notion that all humans are similar in cognitive potential under similar conditions was adopted by many social theorists (including Durkheim) in part, because it lent legitimacy to a progressive theory of human cognition and to a belief that societies evolve by following

---

9 In Tylor's words, "When a custom, an art, or an opinion is fairly started in the world ... it may keep its course from generation to generation, as a stream once settled in its bed will flow on for ages ... On the strength of these survivals, it becomes possible to declare that the civilization of the people they are observed among must have been derived from an earlier state, in which the proper home and meaning of these things are to be found; and thus collections of such facts are to be worked as mines of historic knowledge" ([1871]1970: 70–71).

scientific laws. In fact, Durkheim would come to rely heavily on Tylor's doctrine that human cognition is shaped by the environment, that survivals are evidence of leftovers from an earlier stage of society (i.e. the "concept of survivals"), and that all human minds are similar (i.e. the "psychic unity of man").[10] Yet, as a sociologist emphasizing the study of social facts, Durkheim would reject Tylor's type of comparative method because it ripped traits out of context; he would also reject Tylor's approach to religion as originating in animism (i.e. a belief in spirits or souls) because such an approach sought the genesis of religion in psychological phenomena rather than in collective phenomena.

Five Kinship Theorists

As the opening quote at the beginning of this chapter underscores, Durkheim synthesized ideas from a wide variety of scholars. Edward Tylor's work was a critical resource because many of Durkheim's later ideas stem from Tylor's views on evolution. As I have emphasized, at least among sociologists who tend to rely primarily on Durkheim's great books, Durkheim was a broader-based intellectual, even as his early advocacy for sociology as a discipline was highly dogmatic and restrictive. He read widely the works of diverse scholars, and perhaps more than any other founder of sociology, was constantly engaged in debates and dialogues with them, sometimes quietly in his mind and at other times publically in full-blown arguments. His editorship and commentary in the *L'Année Sociologique* clearly reveals the breadth of his readings and scholarship. Indeed, every chapter in Part 1 of this book outlines the extent of this intellectual engagement. For example, many sociologists do not realize that Durkheim was a sophisticated kinship theorist, or that he was actively engaged with the scholarship of a variety of kinship theorists such as Lewis Henry Morgan, Johan Jacob Bachofen, Henry Maine, John Ferguson McLennan, and Fustel de Coulanges—hardly scholars enshrined in the sociological pantheon but, still, very important individuals in molding Durkheim's thinking. As David Maybury-Lewis (1990: 278) emphasized, "Durkheim is not now remembered as a 'kinship' theorist, so it is perhaps surprising to discover how much and . . . how well he wrote in this field [and] some of what he wrote has been undeservedly neglected." And as

---

10 As Paul Radin (1970: xii) emphasized, Tylor belongs to the "tradition of Scotch-English empiricist philosophy and psychology . . . (with) . . . little sympathy for conjectural history and metaphysical entities."

Adam Kuper (1985: 224) related, "Durkheim was preoccupied with the problems of 'primitive kinship' throughout his career." To be sure, the story of how Durkheim came to write *Elementary Forms* begins with the evolutionary ideas received from Comte, Spencer, Darwin, and Tylor, but very early on, Durkheim began to pay attention to early kinship theorists. In fact, many of the essential ideas underlying his religious sociology were extracted from the founders of kinship analysis in anthropology and the social sciences more generally.

The "Discovery" of Kinship

The "discovery" of kinship was probably the most sensational event in the Post-Darwinian period of the 1860s. Once nineteenth-century fieldworkers met the natives face-to-face, they were shocked that aboriginal family life violated the norms of European family life. Until then, the nuclear family consisting of mother, father, and dependent children was simply taken for granted as the fundamental social unit. Why did kinship need to be discovered? As Thomas Trautmann expressed it, "It may seem odd to speak of the discovery of kinship, given that the elements of that entity—family relationships, modes of descent, rules of marriage, gender roles—lie immediately to hand for every human being . . . (Yet) . . . Like the air we breathe, it is all around us and we cannot see it. Kinship had to be discovered . . ." (1987: 3). Once "discovered" and in light of striking differences between aboriginals and Europeans in domestic relations, descent rules, inheritance, and the allocation of rights and obligations, many traditional notions of family life were swept away.

Kinship institutions were also found to organize most social relations in preliterate societies whereas, in contrast, the typical European society confined kinship to a small number of individuals outside other major social institutions. Making sense of these connections mandated the creation of elaborate kinship diagrams and the adoption of a kinship nomenclature with terms such as *gens, lineage, sib, moiety, clan, phratry,* and *tribe* put into service with such newly minted terms as *social father, section system,* and the marriage rules of *endogamy* and *exogamy*.[11] Kinship studies also became fused with legalistic terms such as *corporate group,*

---

11 The basic building block for most human kinship systems is the nuclear family of mother, father and unmarried offspring. Kinship systems vary in the way societies use the marital bond to configure a kinship institution. In a general sense a kinship system is a classification scheme or a network of linkages dictating statuses, roles, affiliations, and types of groupings. Affiliations are built from (a) blood/consanguinity/birth; (b) marriage (or affines);

status, and *contract* because early kinship scholars were often lawyers who sought to uncover ancient laws by tracing survivals in modern law. Discovering kinship also sparked new questions: Why do kinship systems vary so dramatically? What is the relationship between kinship nomenclature and the rules of descent and marriage? Is the nuclear family actually the primal social unit? If not, how were early humans organized?

As noted, many of Durkheim's assumptions on the family, society, and religion were drawn from the writings of five pioneer kinship theorists—Lewis Henry Morgan, Johann Bachofen, Henry Maine, John McLennan, and Fustel de Coulanges (Durkheim's mentor). Given the importance of their ideas in Durkheim's religious sociology, an overview of these eye-opening insights (at least for Durkheim) is essential here at the very beginning to the story that will unfold.

Lewis Henry Morgan

Lewis Henry Morgan (1818–1881) was a highly respected American attorney and politician (who served twice in the New York Legislature), while also the founding father of kinship analysis. More than anyone, it was Morgan's interest in Native American institutions that made kinship a legitimate field of study.[12] Before his time, little was known about

---

or (c) fictive kin by adoption or pseudo-kinship relations (e.g. blood brothers or a totemic "community of the blood."). A *descent rule*, which often regulates recruitment refers to generational lines. In *bilateral or cognatic descent* (e.g. European system), blood lines are traced equally through males and females. In *unilineal descent* (e.g. tribal system), blood lines are traced through one sex only—matrilineal (females) or patrilineal (males). A *lineage* is a direct descent line that traces to a known common ancestor; a *clan* is an indirect line to an ancestor that may be mythical or so remote all descent traces are lost. The terms *sib and gens* are units similar to clans. Clans have a second meaning (used by Durkheim) to refer to a kin-based or non-kin based aggregate or grouping of individuals. A *moiety* is a half of something (e.g. a tribe is split in half with two moieties (each with a number of clans). A *phratry* is a grouping of clans and used when a tribe is divided up into three or more parts (a historial or alliance connection). *Endogamy* is a rule to marry internally or within a social group; *exogamy* is a rule to marry outside a certain social group (often a clan or lineage). A rule of thumb is that in a unilineal kinship system nuclear families make up lineages, lineages make up clans, clans make up moieties, and two moieties make up a tribe (For an engaging and fun to read book on kinship see Fox 1967).

12 Morgan began his fieldwork among the Iroquois Indians of upstate New York, publishing his findings in [1851](1954) under the title, *League of the Ho-De-No SauNee or Iroquois*. This early work contains Morgan's formative ideas on kinship; and while his sweeping generalizations on kinship nomenclature have been reinterpreted, his ethnography remains an excellent description of Iroquois culture.

aboriginal nomenclature (or how native peoples addressed and classified their relatives), except for the familiar Western terms of mother, father, sister, brother, son, daughter, husband, and wife (Tooker 1997: vii). Morgan discovered a more complex system of terminology, but what riveted his attention was that terms reserved exclusively for the Western nuclear family (e.g. father, mother, etc.) were applied to a wider circle of kindred—*outside* the actual nuclear family. Curious to learn if this nomenclature existed elsewhere, Morgan (under the sponsorship of the Smithsonian Institution) put together a questionnaire and mailed it around the world to government agents, missionaries, military personnel, and anyone else who had contact with native populations, asking them to supply whatever information they could on aboriginal patterns of consanguinity and affinity. When completed, "The Tables" (as they were famously called) included information on 139 kinship systems from Europe, Asia, Africa, and the Americas. In 1871, he published these data in *Systems of Consanguinity and Affinity of the Human Family*. Morgan was not alone in finding that native terminologies were dramatically different from Western terminologies, but he was first to give these differences serious consideration.

In his classic work, *Ancient Society* (1877), Morgan used his elaborate kinship tables as evidence for a stage model of the family and society. All humans have similar cognitive abilities, he reasoned; what varied was the *rate* of social advancement with aboriginals still in stages of "savagery and barbarism." Each stage, he maintained, planted the seeds for the next stage, with plenty of time allotted for the unfolding of each distinct sequence.[13] Of great significance (especially for Durkheim) was Morgan's rejection of the nuclear family as a primal and natural social formation, arguing instead that the mother, father, and offspring trinity came much later and, hence, the nuclear family was a purely *invented* creation (Morgan [1877]1985: 384).

In an effort to account for its origins, Morgan proposed that the European family was the end product of a five-stage evolutionary sequence (using his tables of kinship nomenclature as data for his reconstruction). In the first stage, humans lived in a *horde* or undivided aggregate with mostly transient sexual relationships (Morgan [1877]1985: 500). A promiscuous horde was a fanciful conjecture on Morgan's part, but it was the

---

13 It is not surprising that Karl Marx and Friedrich Engels endorsed Morgan's dialectical approach to the origin of the family, kinship, and private property. It lent support to their own evolutionary schemes (See Engels ([1884]1972).

only way he could conceptualize a social formation without marriage ties. In the next stage, family life took root around a group marriage of brothers and sisters (less real siblings but collateral ones who were designated by the terms "brother" or "sister"),[14] followed in the third stage by marriage with relatively stable pairs but where spouses came and went at will. In the fourth stage, patriarchal authority was joined with polygyny or the marriage of one man to several women, a stage Morgan labeled "a special family" type because it was not universal. The fifth stage ushered in an "exclusive cohabitation" with monogamous pairings as described by a Western system of nomenclature. Morgan's stage model thus begins with promiscuous hordes and ends with nuclear families.

For Morgan, the way relatives are classified reflects institutions and social norms, so when relatives are classified together, they are considered identical in some *social* way. He also held that until paternity was certain, blood ties or descent was traced exclusively through *mother's* relatives.[15] Morgan's ideas are far more sophisticated than this overview can convey, and they were so captivating to the educated public that they attracted worldwide attention.[16] In fact, during his lifetime, Morgan was America's leading anthropologist, receiving many honors including membership in the National Academy of Sciences, and was, for a period, president of

---

14 Morgan knew that sibling group marriage was not found anywhere, but he reasoned that the kinship nomenclature of some indigenous peoples were survivals from a time when this type of marriage existed. The nomenclature is correct but Morgan's interpretation is wrong. For example, in the Hawaiian system of terminology, which is concentrated in areas where the Malalyo-Polynesian language is spoken, there are only a handful of kin terms and they merge lineal and collateral relatives. These terms serve to separate a generation of parents from a generation of children—instead of quaint leftovers from Morgan's hypothesized brother-sister marriage. They operate to force Ego to find a marriage partner outside his primary kinship network (see Fox 1967: 256).

15 Western kinship is a subtype of the Eskimo kinship system. It is a bilateral/cognatic descent system and is characterized by small domestic groups, a kindred instead of a single-sided lineage, with "ego" related equally to relatives on both sides of the family. It differs from a unilineal system where "ego" traces his descent typically through one side of the family (see footnote 11).

16 Morgan was mistaken that merging collateral and lineal relatives in aboriginal kinship systems corresponds in *meaning* to the European system. Nevertheless, the idea that kinship terminology is linked with social factors remains factual—only the interpretations have changed. Let me add that when Morgan visited Europe in 1870–1871, he was warmly welcomed by such intellectual giants as Charles Darwin, Thomas Huxley and John Lubbock as well as the kinship theorists, John McLennan and Sir Henry Maine (Morgan 1937).

the American Association for the Advancement of Science. Given his awe-inspiring stature, it is easy to appreciate why Durkheim readily adopted many of Morgan's ideas.[17]

Johan Jacob Bachofen

Bachofen (1815–1887) was a law professor at the University of Basel who took up ancient law to learn about the early history of marriage and the family. Unlike Morgan, who relied upon survey data and personal contacts with American Indians to construct his theories, Bachofen relied upon ancient legal and religious documents, literature, myths, legends, and other archival sources. Described as a "dreamy German Swiss with a round, sensitive face," Bachofen was an armchair scholar of independent means with the leisure time to pursue anything that took his fancy (Hays 1958: 34–35). In 1861, he was thrust into the public spotlight when he proposed a stage of civilization where females reigned supreme. In Bachofen's eyes, the symbolism in classic mythology conforms to regular laws that can "lead us from the known ages of antiquity into earlier periods and from the world . . . that has been so familiar to us . . . into an older milieu, wholly unknown" (Bachofen ([1861]1931: 157).

In 1861, Bachofen published *Das Mutterrecht* (or Mother-Right) where he proposed a three-stage evolutionary model of ancient family life. In the beginning, he said, humans lived in promiscuous roving *hordes* followed by a "gynaecocratic epoch" of matriarchal power when females, in a religious zeal over unregulated sex, take control over all governing and religious institutions. During this phase, females institutionalized kinship and marriage, with secession traced through maternal connections.

Bachofen also held that women invented horticulture, and that the era of gynaecocracy was a universal cultural period when civilization took on a decidedly communal character. This "maternal element" permeated every aspect of civilization and led to the creation of female deities, and to such binary contrasts as preferences for night over day, the dead over the living, the left hand over the right, and the experience of sorrow over joy (Bachofen

---

17 The terms, ethnology and ethnography became popular in the nineteenth century. An ethnologist analyzes and compares the materials of ethnographic research, while an ethnography is a single descriptive field study. The term, ethnology was taken up after M.W.F. Edwards used it in 1839 as the name for the *Société ethnologique de Paris*, after which it was picked up by the "English Ethnological Society" in 1843, who generally fixed the term in the anthropological literature (see Haddon and Quiggin 1910).

[1861]1931: 160–161). By the third stage, males regained their status and power, and kinship shifted from a matriarchal to a patriarchal system. Bachofen's interpretations are more literary than scientific, with leanings toward the mystical, but his provocative theory of mother-right attracted many disciples (see Howard 1904: 39ff for a discussion). Moreover, as the first theorist to systematically explore the idea of a matrilineal stage of organization, Bachofen inspired a generation of evolutionary theorists interested in the origins of marriage and the family.

Sir Henry Maine

Sir Henry Maine (1822–1888) was an imposing nobleman who taught civil law at Cambridge University. To learn more about the roots of English law, he turned to ancient documents, texts, manuscripts, the Classics, and especially Roman law to understand how Western institutions originated and developed. In 1861, he published *Ancient Law: Its Connection with the Early History of Society and its Relation to Modern Ideas*.

In Maine's view, the family of yesterday was very different from today because kinship organized all social relationships with the earliest societies organized around genealogical connections through *males* only (Maine [1861]1905: 116ff). The eldest male headed each independent family with descent lines from father to son. In these patrifocal families, property was held as a collective unit, with individuals dependent upon their kindred and with all power in the hands of the patriarch. During the next stage, the isolated family was folded into an aggregation of patriarchal families creating the *House* or *Gens* (i.e. clan), where families became linked through a common ancestor. The gens (or clan) then led to the progressive development of an aggregation of clans and the formation of the *Tribe*. Finally, the aggregation of tribal units evolved into what Maine called the *Commonwealth*. For Maine, then, patrilineal descent and perceived blood ties (whether real or fictional) served as the primordial cell for early human societies with everything else —from language to law— modified to support a kin-based social order. Maine also emphasized "the absorption of strangers" as a way to expand social networks artificially. Hence, for Maine, the co-occupation of a shared territory was not the facilitator for larger and larger social networks, but, instead, it was feigned descent or "fictive kin" because it preserved in principle the idea of real blood ties (pp. 114–115). Over time, as network relations stretched from the family to the gens, tribe, commonwealth, and finally to the Rise of the State, so did legal rights and obligations shift as well—from strictly family obligations to individual obligations in modern societies. On this shift,

Maine proposed a "relational law of progress" that moves from a dependency on family and *fixed status relations* to the "free agreement" of individual obligations and *fluid contract relations.*

So, for Maine, a male network held the earliest societies together in a common "agnatic" stock. But over time in progressive societies, legal obligations shifted from a fixed family status to an individual one, or as Maine phrased it—from *Status* to *Contract* (p. 151 original emphasis). Maine's patriarchal theory is a simple, unilineal stage model, but it attracted a wide audience, and he became a pivotal figure in the great nineteenth-century public debates over whether human societies were originally organized around male or female lineages.

John Ferguson McLennan

John McLennan (1827–1881) was a tall, rather "gawky" young Scotsman who graduated from the University of Aberdeen, went on to Cambridge, and was later called to the Bar in Edinburgh (Rivière 1970: viiff). In 1857, McLennan became fixated on ancient law, which he saw as the key to unlocking unrecorded history. What struck his fancy was the legal history of marriage customs and especially the mock ritual of "marriage by capture," whereby a bride is abducted by a bridegroom or by his friends before exchanging vows. Discovering that feigned abductions occur worldwide, he reasoned that it must be linked with an early stage of society and, therefore, have sociological significance. It was McLennan's obsession with ritualized "bride-capture" that led him to embark on a bold, lifelong adventure to uncover the origins of society, kinship, and the family. In this quest, McLennan was drawn irresistibly to *totemism.*

In 1865, McLennan published *Primitive Marriage: An Inquiry Into the Origin of the Form of Capture in Marriage Ceremonies.* Taking up the problem of why bride capture should exist either ritually or in symbolic forms around the globe, McLennan expanded his data set to include indigenous populations in the Americas, Asia, Australia, and Africa where traces of this "act of rapine" had been reported. A scholar of remarkable creativity, McLennan concluded that in the past, "It must have been *the system* . . . to capture women—necessarily the women of other tribes—for wives" (McLennan [1865]1970: 20, his emphasis). What universal "social idea" would produce a system where brides were stolen from foreign tribes? It could not arise, he reasoned, when men were free to marry within their own tribe, coining the word *endogamy* or endogamous for this in-group practice. It must have originated, he said, when customs "*prohibited marriage within the tribe,*" coining the term exogamy or exogamous for this out-group practice (pp. 22–23 his emphasis). McLennan's terms were quickly adopted in kinship circles, especially among scholars (such as Durkheim) interested in the incest taboo. McLennan concluded that bride capture resulted from two universal tendencies: (a) the existence of a principle of exogamy (or a marry-out rule) that forced males to seek females outside their own tribes and (b) the existence of chronic warfare among neighboring tribes, which prevented the peaceful exchange of women between tribes. What survived today were just the *symbolic representations* of what had occurred in the primal past.

McLennan then turned to the origins of kinship and society. In McLennan's scheme, early humans were organized into hordes without a formal system of kinship but, instead, were held together with filial affections, a distinctive group name and "the *apparent* bond of fellowship between ... members" who shared a common living area (McLennan [1865]1970: 63, original emphasis). The perception of shared blood ties, he argued, must have "grown" like all other human ideas, but over time a kindred slowly became linked with a "conception of *Stocks*," resulting in a shift from a horde of comrades to a system of blood-based ties where totems—symbolized by plants and animals—were used to distinguish between stocks (McLennan [1865]1970: 63ff—his emphasis; [1869–1870] 1896: 491ff). For McLennan, humans are predisposed to have kindred-like affections based on familiarity. But a kinship system with its perception of unity through blood-ties and "as an institution of customary law" was a slow developmental process (McLennan [1865]1970: 64).

McLennan also maintained that before kinship became institutionalized, societies had to progress through evolutionary stages. The horde stage saw kindred-like affections with unregulated promiscuity. In the next stage, despite "loose and transitory" sexual relations, a conception of "stocks" or descent based on "mother's blood" took root within the horde. Yet, how did bride capture and exogamy arise from promiscuous hordes and female descent? For McLennan, both are linked to a growing hostility between hordes for scarce resources. This conflict placed a high premium on the survival of males over females for warriors and hunters, leading to the killing of females in infancy. Female feticide, in turn, created an imbalance between the sexes, forcing males to steal females from other hordes. A shortage of females then led to a stage of polyandry, whereby several *unrelated* males shared one female for breeding purposes. This kinship system eventually led to stable bonding rules. Then, once female descent and a system of polyandry composed of one female and several *brothers* became institutionalized, group bonds lessened as the conception of stock groups aligned with stock totems became established. Thus, female infanticide was the cause of both bride capture and polyandry whereas the custom of stealing females led to feelings that in-group marriage was indecent, resulting in a rule of exogamy. And once polyandry on the basis of one female and several *brothers* became institutionalized, this system slowly morphed into a kinship system through the male line only. Finally, kinship through agnates or patrilineal kinship (known from Classical times) was replaced by the European kinship system through both sexes, or *bilateral descent*.

McLennan's speculations on bride capture, female infanticide, and a polyandrous stage of human evolution were mostly ignored. But his theory that the first humans lived in sexually unregulated hordes, with kinship later organized around female descent resonated with the ideas of Bachofen and Morgan, who reached the same conclusion using different research methods. Above all else, McLennan was widely recognized for bringing totemism to the attention of the scholarly world. In a remarkable essay, "The Worship of Plants and Animals" ([1869–70]1896), McLennan linked totems with clans, exogamy, female descent, and the earliest stages of religion and human society. In 1881, at the age of 54, McLennan suddenly died while he was working on a comprehensive theory of totemism. Yet, of great consequence for Durkheim is that virtually all McLennan's ideas on totemism and the origins of society were imported into the writings of Robertson Smith, a Scottish theologian that Durkheim named as the central figure responsible for his still enigmatic 1895 *revelation* on the overriding importance of religion in social life.

Fustel de Coulanges

Fustel de Coulanges (1830–1889), a professor of Ancient and Medieval History at the University of Strasburg (and Durkheim's mentor), also sought the origins of kinship and society. In 1864, he published *The Ancient City: A Study on the Religion, Laws, and Institutions of Greece and Rome*, a stylishly elegant text that became a virtual best seller in history (Herrick 1954: 14–15; Jones 1993: 33). Dismissing notions that individuals or Herculean superhumans chart the course of history, Fustel marked historical trends by the changing nature of institutional arrangements, compiled mostly from ancient Greek and Roman documents. By revisiting the "facts of the past" Fustel sought to uncover the ideas behind ancient institutions and, in particular, the relationship between religious ideas and institutional arrangements.

Fustel's picturesque narrative begins with proto-European society before 3500 BCE (before current era) and ends with the beginning of

Christianity. In the earliest stage of Indo-European civilization, all human activity centered on honoring the dead by provisioning them with food and drink and by performing rituals, which led to a belief in ghosts. In time, these rites became "obligatory rules of conduct" as the dead became viewed as sacred beings.

> The "religion of the dead appears to be the oldest that has existed among this race of men ... It seems that the religious sentiment commenced in this way. It was perhaps while looking upon the dead that man first conceived the idea of the supernatural ...".
> (Fustel de Coulanges [1864]1889: 28–29)

Digging deeper into archival documents, Fustel unearthed a connection between two ancient traditions: (1) the worship of dead ancestors and (2) the practice of keeping a hearth-fire burning day and night in each household.[18] These two forces gradually fused together into an ancient religion of ancestor worship and sacred-fire worship. Although this first religion was strictly localized with each household participating in their own distinctive rites, it had a "powerful influence" on all other social institutions and "determined the direction of their progress"(p. 41). Thus, religion was not derived from nature or inspired by a creative individual; it was for Fustel a sociological phenomenon because each household created their own ancestral gods, with ancestor worship so strong a sentiment that it was the foundational religion in nearly all human societies.

In Fustel's model, a domestic household consisted of parents, children, adopted individuals, and slaves (p. 41ff). The ancient family, then, was not organized around blood-ties but something even more powerful—shared rites and practices. The house religion of ancestor/fire worship created marriage and also set the rules for all social relationships in the "kinship" circle (p. 53ff). According to Fustel, "The ancient family was a religious rather than a natural association ... Religion ... did not create the family; but certainly it gave the family its rules ..." (p. 52). Religious customs also dictated an authority structure with succession from father to son. The ancient family then was a patriarchal unit, rooted in the combined worship of dead ancestors and a sacred fire, an association that ushered in laws, morals, duties, and other social institutions.

---

18 Fustel says the Greeks called these sacred altars Bwmos and other names; while the Latins referred to them as ara or focus (de Coulanges [1864]1889).

In the next stage, a new organizational structure evolved, the ancient "gens" or "clan" organized around patrilineal descent, a shared name, mutual aid, a common ancestor, and common religious rites.[19] This unilineal unit was not "an association of families" but a new kinship arrangement that was still isolated from other gens (or clans) in daily life, and with the same domestic religion, but which, in time, grew into a very extensive organization (p. 140 ff). The religious idea and the social system then began to functionally expand together, marked by a sequence of ideas and changing institutions. By the next stage, the gens became integrated parts of a larger kinship network called a "phratry" (in ancient Greek, "phratria" and in Latin "curia"). This alliance, Fustel maintained, "conceived the idea of a divinity superior ... one who was common to all, and who watched over the entire group. They raised an altar to him, lighted a sacred fire, and founded a worship" (p. 155ff). Gradually, as human consciousness expanded, relationships also expanded from the phratry to the next level of association—the tribe. In tandem, then, the "religious ideas" and "human society" cascaded into even larger associations, with a procession of new polytheistic deities based in physical nature coming into existence, seemingly, by growing up "in different minds by an effort of their natural powers" (p. 162). These multiple, nature gods (or *naturism*) eventually replaced earlier religions as they progressed with the social conditions of the time, allowing for the broadening and development of the general consciousness. As the new religions developed, the tribal associations eventually came together to adopt the same religious ideas resulting in a new organizational structure, the city (p. 167). As Fustel put it, "When men begin to perceive that there are common divinities for them, they unite in larger groups" (p. 175). Thus, Fustel viewed societies as social systems, with stable institutions all working in functional harmony with each other.

Finally, the religious sentiment shifted to the Christian form, marking the end of ancient society (p. 519). Thus, for Fustel, powerful sentiments centered on dead ancestors created the first religion. Religion then organized the kinship ties of the ancient family and all other basic social institutions. But above all, "The religious idea was ... the inspiring breath and organizer of society" (p. 175). For what else might serve to integrate society?

---

19 Fustel tells us that the ancient Romans called this organizational arrangement "gens," and the Greeks "yevos."

> The social tie was not easy to establish between . . . human beings who were so diverse, so free, so inconstant. To bring them under the rules of a community . . . there certainly was something necessary, stronger than material force . . . something that should dwell equally in all hearts, and should be all-powerful there. This power was a belief . . . A belief is the work of our mind . . . It is our own creation, but we do not know it. It is human, and we believe it a god.
>
> (p. 174)

Fustel de Coulanges was an unusual historian who asked sociological questions, viewed historical change as a collective process, and took a scientific attitude towards studying history. He stressed that the best way to ascertain truth in history was to get evidence from texts and documents. (For a comprehensive discussion of his method, see Herrick 1954). In 1870, Fustel left the University of Strasburg for an appointment at the Ecole Normale Superièure before taking a senior appointment at the University of Paris in 1875. He returned to the Ecole Normale in 1880 as its Director for three years and, as fate would have it, shortly after Émile Durkheim was accepted as a graduate student in 1879.

Commentary

In sociology, but much less so with Durkheim scholars generally, the received view is in his classic works—*The Division of Labor in Society* (1893), *The Rules of Sociological Method* (1895), *Suicide* (1897), and *The Elementary Forms of Religious Life* (1912). Yet, they represent a limited and selective sample of Durkheim's published work. When all his articles in various outlets are totaled, especially the great number of reviews, notes, and commentaries of *L'Année Sociologique,* they represent an enormous proportion of his vita. Only *Elementary Forms* captures some of the intellectual issues that long engaged Durkheim's time and energy. Thus, there are two intellectual universes for Durkheim, one represented by the first three major books, and the one glimpsed, but not fully seen, in *Elementary Forms.*

Therefore, we need to leave sociology proper to understand where *The Elementary Forms* "comes from," and why the book has always seemed a "bit strange" to many sociologists. Indeed, much of the text is often ignored because it is not interesting to sociology or not fully understood because it engages scholars whom sociologists do not normally study, or even know about. And, the work addresses issues that seem rather tangential to sociology. But, such was not the case. Despite his great fame and prestige,

Durkheim was fighting for his intellectual life—at least in his mind. *Suicide* (1897) was to demonstrate the power of his sociology in studying "social facts" but, instead, this now classic book initially received rather lukewarm and often negative reviews in its time. And, the ideas that Durkheim had been developing and publishing on religion and even kinship in non-book forums were under fierce attack. He appeared to be on the wrong side of key debates, as we shall see in later chapters, and he was desperately trying to convert others to his views—with little apparent success.

In this opening chapter, which is longer than most chapters in this book, I have only set the stage for our story. Durkheim was committed to science and, where possible, to developing abstract laws and principles—ideas he received and internalized from Comte, Spencer, and Espinas. More important in a substantive sense of Durkheim's works was his engagement with kinship theorists, where he increasingly came to see the family as a late evolutionary arrival—an idea that goes against contemporary sociological wisdom where the family is viewed as the first institution in human societies. Moreover, Durkheim emphasized that the first kindred system was organized around females rather than males, another idea that was controversial over a hundred years ago and is still controversial today. And, for Durkheim the "horde" was the earliest social formation among humans.

As Durkheim's career proceeds, he became rather obsessed with the force that allowed the first societies to evolve. This force is not kinship but religion—yet another highly controversial idea in Durkheim's time and also today in evolutionary theories emphasizing "kin selection." So, even as Durkheim was writing the great books that social scientists know so well, he was defending his views from the mounting criticisms that he had had to endure for fifteen years. Indeed, throughout his career Durkheim was a lightening rod for criticism. But underlying his divergent activity was one goal: to uncover the fundamental basis by which societies are integrated, and the origins of the "force" behind societal solidarity. All of this seemingly "outside activity" was dedicated to what he considered the foundational problem of all sociology—what holds social aggregates among individualistic humans together? And for Durkheim, this fundamental force allowing for the first societies is religion, and the next chapters will follow the evidence to document how he came to this conclusion. Then, in the second half of this book data from the archaeological, molecular, fossil, and primate record will be used to examine the validity of his theory of religion and society with some surprising findings in support of his thesis.

2
Points of Departure

All human beings are products of time, place, and circumstance. Philosophers and scientists are not exceptions. They, too, must be viewed as active creatures moving within a specifically definable milieu. Durkheim . . . can be understood only as an actor in a human drama the program notes of which read: Place—France; Time–The Early Days of the Third Republic.
     Harry Alpert (1961: 29) in *Emile Durkheim and His Sociology*

Early Years in Épinal

David Émile Durkheim was born on April 15, 1858, at 6 Rue Leopoldbourg in Épinal, a small town on the Mosel River in the northeastern corner of France near the German and Swiss borders. Located in the Vosges, with its superb mountains, lakes, and magnificent countryside, Épinal is centered in an ethnic enclave that was once the fountainhead of French Judaism. This chapter provides an overview of Durkheim's formative years focused on the events and individuals known to have fostered his personality traits and intellectual proclivities.

The founding of the Third Republic in 1870 was a decisive event in Durkheim's background. By the middle of the nineteenth century, France was still recovering from the aftermath of the post-revolutionary period, having endured six political regimes, with all governing bodies short lived and lasting no more than a few decades. In 1852, Napoléon III (1808–1873), the nephew of Napoléon II, overthrew the Second French Republic (which he had governed as President from 1848 to 1852) and established himself as emperor (1852–1870). Napoléon III had a keen interest in the French economy, and in his push for rapid industrialization, French society underwent great social and economic change. So, Durkheim, much like Comte, grew up experiencing the direct effects of an atmosphere charged with social, economic, and political turmoil. In 1870, Napoléon III was disposed and the Third Republic—the eighth regime since 1789 was established on a shaky foundation with crisis after crisis. Yet, with

Presidential elections and new constitutional laws, it survived and became France's first stable Republic lasting until 1940 (see Bellah 1973). Not only is the founding of the Third Republic a high point in French political history, it is also essential to our story because Durkheim's intellectual pursuits and his passionate concern with social solidarity can only be understood in light of the Third Republic. As William Logue (1983: 152–153) underscored:

> Durkheim's whole career was tied to the newly founded Third Republic ... Durkheim felt acutely the need for a better social medicine than liberal philosophy or any of its rivals on the Right or Left had been able to produce. To succeed where they had failed, sociology had to develop a scientific basis for the understanding of present problems.

By all accounts, Durkheim was raised in the nurturing environment of a small Jewish community and in a household that emphasized hard work, moral conduct, and responsible duty (Lukes 1972; Jones 1986; Fournier 2006; 2013). This upbringing, according to his colleague Georges Davy, fostered in Durkheim such noticeable personality traits as "scorn for the inclination to conceal effort, disdain for success unachieved by effort, horror for everything ... not positively grounded ... [and] conduct by its moral regulation" (quoted in Lukes 1972: 40 and see Davy 1919–1920). During Durkheim's childhood, his father Moïse (1805–1896) served as the local rabbi in Épinal while his mother, Mélanie, ran a home-based embroidery workshop to supplement the meager household income. Durkheim was the youngest family member (Mélanie was 38 and Moïse was 53 when he was born); he had one brother, Félix born in 1850 (and who died in 1889), and two sisters, Rosine born in 1848 and Céline in 1851.[1]

As the son of a rabbi, Durkheim underwent religious training in both Hebrew and Jewish doctrines, but whether he was groomed to be a rabbinate is still debated. Durkheim's nephew recounted that his kinsmen had been "rabbis from father to son for eight generations" (H. Durkheim, quoted in Fournier 2006: 13), and so, Durkheim may have felt obligated to honor the family tradition, especially after Felix had chosen a career in commerce.[2] Louis Greenberg (1976: 625, 630) suggested, however, that the

---

[1] Stjepan Meštrović (1988: 23) discovered in the Épinal City Hall records that Durkheim had a second brother, Israël Désiré who was born in January 1845 but died in September 1846.

family tradition might have ended a generation earlier if Moïse Durkheim had been financially able to continue his own education in philosophy and science.[3] Given his unrealized ambitions, Moïse may have decided to let his sons pursue their own inclinations. In this respect, Durkheim not only broke with the family rabbinic lineage, but he also broke from the Jewish faith by becoming an agnostic (Peyre 1960: 8).

Nonetheless, Durkheim remained close to his family and, as an adult, spent the religious holidays in Épinal, although his secular ways led to occasional grumbling from family members. As his sister, Rosine confided to her son, Marcel Mauss, "I must admit to you . . . that I am absolutely determined to do Passover as I have always done it. What upsets me is that I would like Émile to come and I don't know how to reconcile the demands of his stomach with the ritual obligations of Passover. If he wants bread anywhere but in his room, I'll never be able to sit at a table next to bread" (quoted in Fournier 2006: 16). Whether Durkheim truly abandoned his Jewish faith is still in question although Étienne Halphen insisted that his grandfather "was always *a*religious with a capital and privative A; [and] anyone wanting to find a whiff of Judaism in his works is on the wrong track" (p. 14). Still, Durkheim's Jewish heritage remained important for his identity, and he retained a deep respect for religion (see Strenski 2006). As Alpert (1961: 15) relates, "The author of *Les Formes élémentaires de la vie religieuse* never forgot his rabbinical background . . . and frequently had occasion to recall to his colleagues . . . that he was, after all, the son of a Rabbi." Pickering (1984: 23) agrees, "A deep concern for matters religious is . . . at the heart of Durkheim's thought."

---

2 Durkheim scholars disagree on whether Durkheim even attended a local Rabbi school in Épinal. Lukes (1972: 39) and Pickering (1984: 5) say he did; Meštrović (1988: 28ff) says not and even questions the existence of a Rabbi school in Épinal during Durkheim's time; Jones (1986: 12) suggests that some of Durkheim's education included time in a rabbinical school; while Fournier (2013: 19) notes that despite the family legend of Durkheim training for but then rejecting the vocation, no rabbinical school existed in his hometown or even close by. Peyre (1960) maintains, on the grounds of tradition, that Durkheim was slated to continue the Rabbi family lineage. Whether Durkheim's father even encouraged his younger son to become a rabbi is also debated.

3 In support of an intellectual affinity between father and son, Greenberg (1976: 625) points to a portion of a letter of recommendation for Moïse written in 1831 to a Jewish community leader in Paris *before* Moïse began his rabbinical training. The letter mentions that the senior Durkheim had a "decided taste" for philosophy and science but needed funds to continue his education. Moïse was clearly ambitious as he later became Chief Rabbi of his region, and remained active in his ministry until shortly before his death in 1896.

COLLÈGE D'ÉPINAL

Figure 2.1 Can you find Durkheim?

Durkheim grew up a local boy and attended Épinal schools. As shown in Figure 2.1, after graduating from primary school (typically when a student is 12 or so), Durkheim enrolled at the Collège d'Épinal, a secondary school or *lycée* where he excelled, winning awards for his brilliant scholarship (Lukes 1972: 41; Fournier 2013: 23). After passing difficult written and oral exams, Durkheim was awarded the *baccauréat èt lettres* in 1874 and the *baccauréat èt sciences* in 1875 at the Collége d' Épinal, qualifying him for many civil and government positions in France.

Durkheim had grander ambitions. His *baccalauréat* was also *laissez-passer* to apply for any facility of higher education in the French University system, and Durkheim was set on moving to Paris and gaining admittance to nothing less than the prestigious and very exclusive *École Normale Supérieure*.[4]

---

4 While *baccalauréat* in the American system of education refers to a college degree, in France during Durkheim's time it referred to the completion of secondary school or a lycée. A French secondary education is extremely robust as its purpose is to prepare students for a demanding set of oral and written examinations that must be passed before a baccalauréat is awarded (for details on the French educational system during Durkheim time see Wendell 1907). Also see Clark (1973) for an overall detailed description of the development of the social sciences in the French universities.

The École Normale Supérieure

Gaining Admittance

The *École Normale Supérieure* (or *École Normale*) was established in Paris in 1794 after the First Republic was proclaimed in 1792. Founded by the French Revolutionary government, it was conceived as a Republican school for primary teachers to carry forth the visionary ideals of the Enlightenment and the Revolution but, paradoxically, it evolved into a select, elite institution for training professors and national leaders alike (Karady 1979; Smith 1982).[5] By Durkheim's time, the *École Normale Supérieure* at 45 rue d' Ulm, Paris was admitting on average less than 50 students a year, and only those with exceptional promise in their respective *lycées*. To become a *normalien*, then, was an arduous task, requiring candidates to pass extraordinarily difficult written and oral exams. But upon entry, you became one of the chosen few—that is, one of France's academic elite by virtue of your association with the grande école (Smith 1982: p.5ff; Karady 1979).

In Fall of 1875, eighteen-year-old Émile Durkheim left home with the objective of attending the *École Normale*. He had meager funds, but enough to board at the Jauffret, a student pension in Paris close to the Louis-le Grand Lycée, a secondary school with a proven track record for preparing candidates for the *École Normale*. At the Louis-le Grand, Durkheim attended special classes—known as *cagne* in student argot—that entailed 11-hour days learning literature and philosophy followed by hours more of evening study at the Jauffret hostel. Durkheim would later write of an utter "feeling of emptiness and isolation familiar to all those who come to complete their studies in Paris" (from Davy, quoted in Lukes 1972: 42). Thus, to compete for admittance into the celebrated *École*, Durkheim was faced with a grinding and sequestered routine, straitened finances, an ambivalent future, and the despondency of a separation from his family at a time when his father was seriously ill (Lukes, p. 42). At one juncture, Durkheim passed the *École's* highly competitive written exams, but his

---

5 The original *École Normale* closed shortly after its inauguration in 1795. It was revived under Napoleon Bonaparte who created a vast government educational network to direct primary and higher education. Its charter was then altered so that graduates mostly became professors in *lycées*, although a few went on to earn doctorates for university instruction. Later, its mission shifted to the training of an elite class. After 1811, the *École Normale* became characterized as a liberal, intellectual institution that enjoyed relative independence and freedom within the University system (for a comprehensive biography, see Smith 1982).

examiners decided he was "too cold and dull" to be a *normalien* (quoted in Greenberg 1976: 633). Yet, Durkheim persevered and after three years of *cagne*, as shown in Figure 2.2, he was admitted into the *École* in 1879 (perhaps by affecting a sunny personality).[6] This time the oral examiners in whimsical arbitrariness wrote that Durkheim was "intelligent and determined" and ranked him 11th among successful candidates (quoted in Greenberg, p. 633).

Day-to-Day Life at the *École*

Once Durkheim enrolled in the *École Normale*, he entered an institution with a student body destined to join France's academic and professional elite.[7] *Normaliens* with modest means were eligible for a *trousseau* or an allowance to buy school uniforms and sundries (Smith 1982). Durkheim qualified for a *trousseau*, which took the financial burden off his shoulders, but he still faced personal obstacles. As shown in Figure 2.2, Durkheim at 21 was a relatively tall young man, with a muscular frame and long slender limbs. He had a keen, serious face with a prominent nose, and intense, deeply set eyes highlighted by a mustache and a full, bushy beard. Bellah (1973: xii) imparts that Durkheim was young but not youthful and, when he arrived at the *École*, he was seen as "a strangely sober boy from the provinces, a boy who seemed older than his years . . ." We can only suppose that coming from a family with very modest means and having been educated in the French countryside, Durkheim felt socially uncomfortable and compensated for it by acting overly serious, distant, and morally superior. Some classmates certainly had that impression; according to Coser (2003: 144), Durkheim's "earnestness and dedication made him

---

6 Robert Smith (1982: 19ff) researched the *École* social and political history, and the memoirs of its alumni and said that three years of *cagne* was to be expected before acceptance (although a few students were admitted sooner). Students such as Durkheim from provincial *lycées* usually attended a Paris *cagne* for the first year without taking École exams. The second year was a kind of practice, and not until the third year was a "serious attempt" made. Smith (p. 25) noted that academic excellence and merit were not enough; being accepted required "certain qualities of character." The orals committee was composed of professors teaching at the École during Durkheim's time.

7 *Normaliens* in Durkheim's generation included such eminent figures as Henri Bergson, Gustave Belot, Pierre Janet, Flix Rauh, Maurice Blondel, Ferdinand Brunot, Henri Berr, and Jean Jaurês. By the Third Republic, *École* alumni were considered "the aristocracy of a corps of public secondary school teachers." *Normaliens* also became distinguished politicians, writers, and administrators (see Smith 1982: 17, 104ff).

Phot Pierre Petit ÉCOLE NORMALE, PROMOTION DE 1879 M. Durkheim

Figure 2.2 *École Normale*, Promotion of 1879

in the eyes of the other students an aloof and remote figure, perhaps even somewhat of a prig." These sentiments earned him the nickname, "the metaphysician" by students and professors alike. Throughout his lifetime Durkheim was perceived as "a man extraordinarily serious, extraordinarily dedicated, extraordinarily sincere" (Bellah 1973: xi).

Durkheim was not happy at the *École*, being made to spend three years largely shut away in a bleak and confining institutional setting with sparse, poorly-lit rooms with little ventilation (Lukes 1972: 45–46). As one *normalien* described the experience:

> Extreme claustration: one could go out only on Thursday afternoon and Sunday; Those who took a course at the Sorbonne had to go there in a body along a prescribed route. Forbidden to talk in the study rooms . . . or else-where, for 'all movements are carried out in order and silence;' forbidden to smoke, forbidden to read newspapers.
> (quoted in Smith 1982: 82)

Yet, another *normalien* maintained that such grueling hardships were offset by an intoxicating atmosphere of effervescent ideas. This may explain why Durkheim, despite his unhappiness, eventually adapted to this "privileged" lifestyle and began to freely indulge in the *École's* intellectual life by vigorously throwing himself into its many political and philosophical debates (Lukes 1972: 48), And, surprisingly, despite his quiet demeanor, Durkheim showed himself to be an astonishingly good public speaker. An early glimpse into his lifelong attraction to morality and religion is his engagement in spirited and impassioned debates over the policies of Jules François Ferry (1832–1893), a distinguished Third Republic politician who supported a new collective morality grounded in secular values. What later became the "Ferry laws" called for nothing less than a secular public educational system—that is, schooling completely free from religious instruction.[8] As Maurice Holleaux, Durkheim's classmate wrote:

> [Durkheim] was at the *École* at the time of the ascendancy of Gambetta and the great reforms of Jules Ferry. At the *École* these were the subject of incessant discussions. Durkheim sought out these discussions, often starting them and throwing himself into them with true passion ... I heard him discuss for hours with a logical fervour which was the marvel of his hearers—he could not have been more strained, more nervous, more eloquent. Yet he always remained on the summits and only debated principles.
> (quoted in Lukes 1972: 47)

We cannot know how Durkheim was affected by these debates, but Roger Geiger (1972: 134) suggests that when Durkheim graduated from the *École* he was already committed to the ideals of the Third Republic. It would seem, Geiger added, that Durkheim was "strongly attracted to and quite familiar with the problem of the moral foundation of the secular society–the very problem which was to be the central focus of his life's work."

The *École* also nurtured Durkheim's talent as a gifted lecturer. Maurice Holleaux recounts that in Durkheim's first year he showed "what he was and would be. He was at once the teacher and the orator ... He spoke volubly, virtually without notes, with a passionate ardour and an imperious decisiveness. Those who had once heard him could not doubt his superiority" (quoted in Lukes 1972: 52). However, Henry Bergson, another classmate, remembers Durkheim in less glorified tones:

> His conversation was already nothing but polysyllogisms and sorites ... On the steps of the staircase and even at lunch-time, he would

---

8 The Ferry laws to reform education so passionately debated by Durkheim and classmates, were passed beginning in 1881.

immobilize us with four-forked dilemmas . . . I have always thought . . . that he would be an abstraction-monger . . . I was not so mistaken. With him, one never encountered a fact. When we told him that the facts were in contradiction with his theories, he would reply: The facts are wrong.

(p. 52)

Though Durkheim's cold, outward bearing kept many classmates at bay, he enjoyed a few particular friends, including Maurice Holleaux, Jean Jaures, Lucien Picard and, especially, Victor Hommay. Alpert (1961: 21) writes that Durkheim considered friendship a "sacred trust," and that anyone fortunate enough to earn his regard was rewarded with a "devotion, loyalty, and attachment that were profoundly rooted." Holleaux notes "[f]ew people truly knew him. Few realized what an almost feminine sensibility was concealed by his severity and what treasures of tender goodness were hidden by that heart, hostile to easy outpourings" (quoted in Lukes 1972: 48). A measure of Durkheim's emotional side was certainly revealed when his classmate, Victor Hommay died tragically in 1886 by committing suicide. At that time, Durkheim wrote:

I no longer know . . . how we came to be linked. One can only suppose that it happened by itself, little by little, for I cannot recall any particular circumstance giving birth to a friendship which soon became for me the sweetest intimacy. Throughout our three years at the *École*, we truly lived the same life; we worked in the same room, we pursued the same studies; we even spent together almost all our days of freedom. In the course of those long conversations, what plans did we not make for each other! I can now no longer recall them without sadness and bitterness.

(quoted in Lukes 1972: 49)

Durkheim would remember the *École* as having an uncongenial atmosphere. Holleaux recalled Durkheim's eagerness for vacation time, so that he could take up life again with "good simple people" [Durkheim's expression]. Holleaux also depicted Durkheim as deeply serious and hating all affectation with little tolerance for arrogant, frivolous, and pretentious individuals (p. 48). Nonetheless, Alpert (1961: 21) relates that his educational experience and his friends and professors profoundly affected Durkheim. Over time, his attitude toward his alma mater would soften, becoming bittersweet as he took on the duel role of the serious critic on the one hand and the nostalgic *normalien* on the other [9] (Lukes 1972; Coser 2003). Indeed, as will become evident, his elite credentials would serve him well as a "rite of passage" into circles far beyond what he ever imagined during his three years at the *École Normale Supérieure*.

Durkheim's Two École Mentors

As one of France's premier institutions, the *École Normale* was renowned for its intellectual climate and exceptional academic instruction. It might be supposed that a student with a humble rural background would be reverential and awed by its prestigious Parisian faculty. But not Émile Durkheim who was singularly unimpressed with his *École* instructors, characterizing some of them as "shallow," "superficial," "lacking in intellectual vigor," and preoccupied with "elegant rhetoric and surface polish" (Peyre 1960: 9–10). He was particularly irritated over having to soak himself in Classic Greek and Latin literature during his first year. As Holleaux recounted:

> It was not only the rhetoric, which ... was imposed on young men already saturated with rhetoric. They also had to apply themselves to ... Latin verses and Latin or French dissertations on more or less far-fetched witty conceits. Exercises of this sort were odious to Durkheim ... I saw him groan and vent his indignation over Latin verses from which he could not extricate himself.
>
> (quoted in Lukes 1972: 53)

Durkheim did respect some faculty members, and none more than Émile Boutroux and Fustel de Coulanges.[10]

Émile Boutroux (1845–1921)

Boutroux was a celebrated philosopher with an international reputation. Fred Rothwell, who translated several of his books into English and knew him personally, characterized Boutroux as a charming and noble intellectual with a great compassion for others. In his company, Rothwell wrote,

---

9 Durkheim sent his son, André to the *École Normale* in 1911.

10 Durkheim also had a high regard for the historian Gabriel Monod. At the *École Normale*, Monod rigorously trained his pupils in comparative methodology and in a strictly scientific approach to understanding the past (Monod 1876 and Lukes 1972: 58–59).

"one had . . . a strange feeling of upliftment as though one were breathing a purer and more refined atmosphere" (1922: 162).

Boutroux was just 34 years old when Emile Durkheim entered the *École Normale* in 1879, having graduated from the *École* in 1868 followed by studies in Germany from 1869 to 1870. At the University of Heidelberg, the young French philosopher was so impressed with the interdisciplinary comradeship among German scientists (compared to the highly specialized French academics), that he sent a letter to the French educational ministry detailing how the German academicians worked in concert "because truth is one" (quoted in Nye 1979: 109). Inspired by his German experience, Boutroux made productive use of lively interdisciplinary exchanges throughout his career, making his work stand apart from French philosophers embedded in narrow intellectual circles (Nye 1979). After returning to France, Boutroux was hired to teach philosophy at several *lycées*, earning his doctorate in 1874. He was then invited to join the faculty at the *École Normale*. In 1888, he left to take up a prestigious appointment in philosophy at the University of Paris, and he remained at the Sorbonne until a few years before his death in 1921.

Boutroux's work is all highly regarded, but he is best known for his strikingly original dissertation, *The Contingency of the Laws of Nature* published in 1879, a work that brought to fruition a dynamic spiritualist movement in French philosophy.[11] Boutroux wrote his bold thesis, he said, in reaction to an age that was overly enamored with science. It was also set against the tide of two alternative currents in French philosophy, the Eclectic spiritualist school of Victor Cousins (1792–1867), so named because it was a blend of psychologism, metaphysical idealism, and philosophical history (it was *the* dominant French academic philosophy during much of the nineteenth century)[12] and the positive philosophy of Auguste Comte, whose call for a science of society free of metaphysics was slowly gaining momentum outside of Universities and *lycées*.[13] In his

---

11 This movement began with Felix Ravaisson, Charles Renouvier and Jules Lachelier. Boutroux was a disciple of Lachelier, who was a faculty member at the *École Normale* in the 1860s (Crawford 1924).

12 The Eclectic spiritualist philosophy was an apt name as it was eclectic in its mix of selected components from all philosophies, and it was spiritual in its incorporation of psychological motifs of consciousness and mind. It also postulated a scientific-empiricist feature but this claim was mostly rhetoric. The dominance of the Eclectic philosophy ended during the Third Republic.

13 Comte's *Positive Philosophy* was prohibited reading in the French educational system during the Second and early part of the Third Republic. By 1902, however, Comte's

doctoral thesis, Boutroux argued that philosophy cannot rest on common sense notions of truth or vague romantic idealism; instead, it must be grounded on a foundation that *only* the sciences can provide. Yet, by the same token, the scientific method cannot serve as the ultimate source of all knowledge because the laws of the universe and its contents are not necessarily deterministic or absolute but manifest elements of *contingency* or chance.

To correct this deficiency where explanation is purely one of physical processes, science must be integrated with approaches that allow for creativity, spontaneity, human reason, and free will. To rely on an ultra-science based solely on observation and experience is to ignore other existing realities that, when combined with science, will lead to a more fruitful understanding of the laws of the universe and a higher truth. Boutroux's approach to science also included the notion of the "discontinuity of the sciences" where (in common with Comte) he negated the belief that the sciences naturally fold into each other. For Boutroux, each science has its own elements, its own realm of autonomy, and its own laws of reality. As Boutroux ([1879]1920: 151–152) expressed it:

> In the universe, there can be distinguished several worlds, forming, as it were, states superposed on one another ... Each of these worlds appears, at first, to depend strictly on the lower worlds ... and to receive from them its existence and laws ... [yet] ... We cannot deduce the higher forms from the lower by way of analysis, because the higher contain elements that cannot be reduced to those of the lower. The first find in the second only their matter not their form.

Boutroux viewed his Doctrine of Continuity as a necessary correction to the ultra-science approach rather than a new school of thought. Hence, while he strongly endorsed the distinctiveness, clarity, and transparency of science, he thought it necessary to integrate it with other approaches. In Boutroux's eyes, one needs to search for truth wherever you can find it.[14]

In the classroom, Boutroux was renowned for the crystal clarity of his lectures. Andre LaLande (1922: 539), a former student, wrote that

---

positivism was in vogue with his writings included in the official philosophy syllabus (*Programmes*) of required readings for French *lycées* (Brooks 1998: 256 and see Simon 1965 for an engaging discussion of the opposing Eclectic and Positive intellectual traditions).

14 Boutreax's Doctrine of Continuity later became a point of departure for the ideas of his students (e.g. Henri Bergson). For a discussion of Boutroux and his work see Crawford 1924.

Boutroux, "had the art of making clear the most difficult theories, even those most foreign to contemporary notions, always expressing the thought in the most striking manner, while each of his lectures, admirably composed, threaded its way as if through a little drama of philosophical ideas . . ." Boutroux also captivated students with his remarkable skill of situating each philosopher in his own time and then carefully illuminating each doctrine as a complete and integrated system of thought.[15] As Émile Bréhier, another student remarked, "who could recall without emotion his course on Kant and on Pascal?" (quoted in Crawford 1924: 133).

Fustel De Coulanges (1830–1889)

As discussed in Chapter 1, Fustel had achieved fame with *The Ancient City* (1864) with his analysis of Greek and Roman institutions. Unlike most French historians, Fustel held that the past must be studied objectively by using the methods of the natural sciences. And, this required the "document method" or a careful analysis of the recorded facts to verify your sources and to view the relationships among facts. For Fustel, history is not about single individuals but collections of individuals, and so, he typically ignored historical figures and focused instead on the parts of society or its social institutions (Herrick 1954: 19ff). Given his scientific approach to history, Fustel saw little need for Comte's new "science of society." In his judgment, why bother when history and sociology were the same thing (see Herrick 1954 for a biography).

As a *Normalien* (1850–1853), Fustel had reaped the social and academic benefits of belonging to the elite class of *École* scholars. Endowed with an imposing personality and supremely confidant, Fustel decided, after taking over the *École* directorship in 1880 (shortly after Durkheim's arrival), to overhaul some time-honored traditions.[16] Perhaps by virtue of his own

---

15 Boutroux's ([1912]1970: vii) lecture style at the *École Normale* was structured to provide a "a minute analysis" of different philosophical systems. You cannot, he said, simply collect documents and extract their contents in a mechanical way if you wish to understand a philosophical perspective. Boutroux's approach was quite the opposite of Fustel de Coulanges' "documentary method" where individuals are rarely discussed.

16 Fustel's impressive ego and strong personality was evident even during his student days at the *École*. As one schoolmaster wrote in a report on the young Fustel: "Great ardor at work, but more ambition than force and measure. Confused mind, not disciplined, not docile. Despite severe warnings which he has received from the administration, either he has not understood them, or his pride has refused to recognize them, so that this trimester he has recommended studying history, philosophy, and literature from the heights, and to

experience with house rules requiring attendance at church services, Fustel abrogated the chaplain's post and carved up the *École*'s chapel into student study rooms (Smith 1982: 80). Yet, he retained the brutal and inflexible rules keeping students caged like inmates in rigid confinement.

As an educator, Fustel judged students by their etiquette and seriousness. He had a clear preference for hard-working students from humble backgrounds because he felt they could contribute more to the teaching profession than those from more elite backgrounds (Smith 1982: 26–27). While he made heavy demands on his students, he was popular among those who liked his strong personality and ideas, and he, in turn, was attracted to students eager to engage in research (Herrick 1954: 8). Above all, Fustel preached that excellent scholarship depends upon disciplined training in the proper methods with careful attention given to the analysis of vocabulary, documents, and other surviving inscriptions. He would often repeat to his students that history "is not an art, it is a pure science ... It consists, like all science, in ascertaining facts, analysing them, comparing them, and showing the relations between them" (quoted in Lukes 1972: 59). Fustel emphasized his own ideas, but never pushed students towards his academic interests, encouraging them instead to formulate their own research questions and pursue their own inclinations. It was fine to agree with him but not necessary. He would know if a student was following in his footsteps by the methods used. For his openness to ideas and scientific spirit, Fustel's students admired him greatly and remained loyal long after they left the *École Normale* (Herrick 1954: 102ff and see Fournier 2013: 35, 36).

Émile Boutroux and Fustel de Coulanges Legacy to Durkheim

A number of educators influenced Durkheim during his formative years, but he reserved his deepest admiration and appreciation for Émile Boutroux and Fustel de Coulanges. Both men were bold, unconventional thinkers, which may explain why they gave excitement and inspiration to Durkheim. Although with his Continuity Thesis Boutroux wanted to combine science and metaphysics while Durkheim wanted to keep them separate, Boutroux's inspirational teachings made a strong impression on Durkheim. In particular, he credits Boutroux with equipping him with the tools to

---

consider such things as he knows nothing about" (quoted in Smith 1982: 152–153). Fustel would later say that he learned little from his professors and was self-taught in history (Herrick 1954: 6).

conceptually separate sociology from biology and psychology: "[A]t the *Ecole Normale Supérieure*," Durkheim wrote, Monsieur Boutroux "often used to repeat to us that every science must explain 'its own principles,' as Aristotle states: psychology by psychological principles, biology by biological principles. Very much imbued with this idea, I applied it to sociology" ([1907]1982: 259). As a social philosopher, Boutroux also guided Durkheim's intellectual development by highlighting the writings of Kant and Renouvier as well as the writings of Comte and Spencer. In gratitude, Durkheim dedicated his French doctoral thesis, *The Division of Labor in Society* (1892) to Boutroux with these words: "A mon cher maître M. Émile Boutroux: Hommage respectueux et reconnaissant." During his lifetime, Durkheim remained on friendly terms with his mentor (who was only thirteen years his senior) enjoying his company both socially and professionally.

Fustel de Coulanges had both an advisory and "fatherly" influence on Durkheim. Though he was in low spirits during his first year when he was kept busy with compulsory Latin and Greek prose, Durkheim was in high spirits his second year when he was given permission to undertake his own research.[17] Working with Fustel, he surely internalized an institutional approach to history. Recall that in the *The Ancient City*, Fustel had used archival documents and a comparative methodology to trace ancient Indo-European institutions back to an original "mother" society. In the beginning, Fustel said, human societies were composed of isolated households of both kin and non-kin, and that the first religion was a cult of ancestor/fire worship that unified individuals through shared beliefs and practices, with all other social institutions and even society itself an outgrowth of the religious institution. Fustel's stage model of societal development also emphasized how religion and social structure correspond with one another, with religion at each developmental phase serving as the moral foundation for societal integration.

Under Fustel's tutelage, Durkheim internalized the overriding importance of empirical data for reconstructing history. In addition, Durkheim became familiar with an implicit functional perspective with Fustel's depiction of societies as unified wholes and by showing how the parts of society fit and change together. In fact, Radcliffe-Brown (1945: 36) considered Fustel one of the first scholars to address the "social function of religion." As a pioneer kinship theorist, Fustel also acquainted Durkheim

---

17 Students spend much of the third year preparing for the rigorous examinations for graduation.

with stage model theorizing and such kinship formations as the gens (or clans), phratries, and tribes. It is no wonder that scholars have given emphasis to the relationship between the ideas of Fustel and Durkheim (Lukes 1972; Prendergast 1983–1984; Nisbet 1965; and Jones 1986). And, Camille Jullian, a peer of Durkheim who edited Fustel's posthumous monographs, recalls that Durkheim and Fustel were quite fond of each other, and that Durkheim was particularly influenced in *Elementary Forms* by Fustel's methods and by the tone and character of *The Ancient City* (Herrick 1954: 116). Durkheim also embraced Fustel's view of religion as a collective phenomena (which was rare at the time), his emphasis on how religion corresponds with other institutions, and the role religion plays in integrating society. Yet Durkheim would reject Fustel's assertion that religion itself is the cause of society or that the first religion was the worship of dead ancestors (or animism). If fact, no evidence exists that Fustel was the primary influence on Durkheim's decision to make religion a focal point of his career. On this, we have Durkheim's own declaration that it was only in 1895 that he understood the essential role religion played in social life, and here, he credits Robertson Smith rather than Fustel for this insight.

Still, in a real sense Fustel was Durkheim's academic father. Although Fustel died in 1889, soon after Durkheim began his professional career, Durkheim continued to carry on a running dialogue with his mentor by injecting into his published writings such comments as, if only Fustel had realized such and such. Indeed, Durkheim was so fond of his mentor that he dedicated his Latin thesis, *Montesquieu's Contribution to the Rise of Social Science*, to the memory of Fustel de Coulanges.[18]

---

18 According to Camille Jullian, Fustel had been influenced by Montesquieu's ideas on institutional structures (see Herrick 1954: 11). Both Montesquieu and Fustel were also concerned with the integration of religion and social structure.

3
Networks

The essential in all things is not to force a fixed course upon life but simply to encourage it to come forth on its own.

Emile Durkheim 1888

The Young Philosophy Professor

Despite a serious illness during his final year, Durkheim completed his academic requirements at the *École*, graduating in 1882 with a specialization in philosophy. His professors awarded him the Adolphe Garnier prize for exceptional hard work and academic excellence, but otherwise had little affection for him probably because of his preachy manner and overt disapproval of their curriculum and teaching methods. Whether his illness kept him from doing well on the agrégation de philosophie, the extremely competitive examination used to place students for jobs in *lycées*, or whether his iconoclastic attitude made his professors decide it was "payback" time, when school rankings were published, Durkheim was placed near the bottom of successful agrégés (Gross 2004: 1; Jones 1986: 14). Fustel de Coulanges wrote a warm reference, however, highlighting his originality, intellectual acuity, and maturity of mind (see Lukes 1972: 64).

After graduation, Durkheim applied for jobs at *lycées*, and from 1882 to 1887, taught philosophy in cities outside Paris—from a month's stay at the Lycée de Puy to longer teaching assignments at Sens, Saint-Quentin and Troyes. By all accounts, he was an effective, excellent instructor. As one administrator wrote in 1885:

> M. Durkheim has a very serious and somewhat cold appearance. He is conscientious, hard-working, well-informed and very clever, though his mind is perhaps more rigorous than penetrating and more capable of assimilation than invention: none the less, his teaching is very exact, very precise, very concise and perfectly clear, though the clarity is, it is true, of a scientific rather than a popular nature.
>
> (quoted in Lukes 1972: 64–65)

Durkheim was popular with his pupils. André LaLande (1867–1963), then a sixteen-year-old student at the Lycée de Sens, recalled that students so respected and appreciated Durkheim that "even the mediocre ones, had the greatest consideration for him" (quoted in Gross 2004: 2). Some *lycée* students at one secondary school were so devoted to his person that they followed him when he was reassigned to another *lycée*. In demeanor, Durkheim appeared detached, cold, and utterly professional, but students that came to know him, especially ones invited to his home for philosophical discussions, discovered in Durkheim a "warm heart and unusual sensitiveness" (Peyre 1960: 11). This facet of his character is evident in a graduation address he delivered at the Lycée de Sens in 1883. After an idealistic speech on elite men of genius, the greater humanity, the passion for truth, and the good society, Durkheim ([1883]1972: 33) closed with these touching words to his pupils:

> Dear Students, perhaps at this moment you are reproaching me in whispers for having forgotten you a bit too much today. And yet that is not true at all. While I was speaking, it was of you that I was thinking. Especially of you with whom I have just spent all this past year and who are now going to leave us to try your hand at life ... My dear friends, I would be most happy if you would carry away with you from this school two feelings which seem contradictory, but which strong minds know how to reconcile. On the one hand, maintain a very vivid sense of your own dignity. However great a man may be, never abdicate into his hands and in an irremediable fashion your liberty ... But also, do not believe that you will become much greater by never permitting anyone to raise himself above you ... In a word, know how to respect natural superiority without ever losing your self-respect. This is what the future citizens of our democracy must be.

So at twenty-four, we find Durkheim teaching about in *lycées* near Paris. About this time he decided, of all things, to become a sociologist. But how? France had no established sociology, no courses to speak of and, obviously, no degrees or careers in sociology. Comte wrote his *Positive Philosophy* outside academia and even speaking Comte's name in some circles was still taboo. Durkheim knew of Comte from Boutroux's lectures but also from exchanges with his *École* classmates who locked away in a monkish cloister were known to entertain themselves with vigorous debates over such larger-than-life figures as Charles Darwin, Herbert Spencer, and Auguste Comte (Smith 1982: 64). Some French intellectuals saw a need for a science of society, but hardly agreed on much else. Even Fustel had rejected sociology as a discipline since, for him, the study of society was already part of history. Yet, Durkheim, who is said to have greatly feared failure, apparently never looked back on this decision in his young life (Geiger 1972: 7ff; Lukes 1972: 44).[1]

So, how does a young *lycée* instructor of modest means pursue a discipline still on the drawing board in 1882? His starting point was to read scholars also interested in a science of society, with books and articles by Herbert Spencer topping Durkheim's list of borrowed library materials (Fournier 2013: 46). Yet, Spencer was across the English Channel and Comte, who died shortly before Durkheim was born was, at best, a spiritual mentor. He needed accessible French patrons willing to help him launch a career in sociology. Fortunately, Durkheim wore the mantle of the *École Normale Supérieure*, and *normaliens* take care of their own.[2]

And, so it came to be that shortly after his graduation, Durkheim became acquainted with an elite clique of *normaliens* eager to promote social science and, as destiny would have it, among them was a fervent sociology-minded scholar in the person of Alfred Espinas. As John Brooks (1998: 204) put it, "both institutionally and intellectually, Espinas was the closest thing to a model or paradigm Durkheim had available to him as he began his career."

Alfred Espinas

The Normale Clique

Alfred Victor Espinas (1844–1922), like most influential elites of his generation was a graduate of the *École Normale Supérieure*. His classmates included Emile Boutroux (entering year or promotion of 1865) and, as was emphasized, one of Durkheim's mentors; Louis Liard (promotion 1866), the Director of French Higher Education who would play a key role in Durkheim's first sociology appointment; Félix Alcan (promotion 1862) who established a celebrated publishing house where Durkheim would published his journal *L'Année Sociologique* and *all* his books, including

---

[1] There is no consensus on when Durkheim's attraction to sociology crystallized or when he made his decision to become a sociologist but scholars agree that it was during his early years as a *lycée* philosophy instructor.

[2] John Brooks (1998: 70) writes that the *esprit normalien* was evident in this elite École network despite incompatible viewpoints. Normales could count on each other, especially in competition with non-*normaliens*. This solidarity prevailed among professors and students alike even though it sometimes made for some strange bedfellows.

The Elementary Forms; and Théodule Ribot (promotion 1862) who founded the *Revue philosophique*; the journal where Durkheim would publish many of his articles (Geiger 1972: 68 ff). The *Revue* played a crucial role in legitimating the new "science of society" as it was the first professional journal in France to accept sociology articles (Geiger 1972: 68ff; Brooks 1998: 67 ff).

Espinas graduated from the *École Normale* in 1867 but viewed his training in social philosophy as mentally stultifying. Firing a shot across the academic bow, Espinas rejected the eclecticism (or spiritual philosophy) that dominated the French educational system and sought philosophers outside academia and outside France, notably Auguste Comte and Herbert Spencer. Few social scientists realize the extent of Espinas's intellectual comradeship with both Comte and Spencer, his formidable influence on Durkheim, and his many contributions to the actual development of sociology.[3] Roger Geiger (1972: 94) and John Brooks (1998: 194, 204), for example, concluded that Durkheim's debt to Espinas was huge. For Espinas was the crucial interface between Comte and Durkheim in the latter's efforts to jumpstart a discipline that barely existed and in his need to understand the basis of a moral society for the national resurgence of France. Moreover, according to Davy (1923), Espinas came very close to taking up the role that Durkheim would later play in the formal creation of French Sociology. In fact, when a Chair at the Sorbonne was created for Espinas in social economy in 1893, it was considered "the first official position in sociology in Paris" (Brooks 1998: 23). Espinas also began his academic career as a *lycée* philosophy instructor and then decided to become a sociologist. Taking up this challenge, Espinas devoted his primary doctoral thesis to a topic so esoteric it appeared to doom his academic career but became in the words of Geiger (1972: 68) "a minor classic of early sociology"—one that is not on the radar of most contemporary sociologists.

Animal Societies

It is hard to imagine anyone writing a philosophy thesis in the 1870s so out of line with the prevailing spiritualist trend in French academia.

---

3 John Brooks (1998: 14) relates that Durkheim is often linked with Comte and Montesquieu and Espinas is typically ignored. Durkheim, for example, praised Espinas as "the first to have studied social facts in order to make a science of them . . ." (quoted in Brooks: 204). One reason English speakers are unaware of Espinas's contributions to sociology is that his work has never been translated into English.

Yet, Espinas did just that by training himself in natural history and writing a dissertation on the origin, nature, and development of *animal* societies. His stated reason for such an unorthodox work in *philosophy* was, strangely enough, to put *sociology* on a solid footing by isolating out characteristic traits found in all types of social formations and to explore the relationship between the individual and society. As Espinas expressed it, "*No living being is alone*"—all form some type of association. "From the lowest degree of rank to the most elevated, all animals find themselves at some moment of their existence engaged in some society; the social milieu is the necessary condition for the conservation and the renewal of life" ([1878]1977: 8–9 added emphasis).

Des Sociétes Animales (1878) opens with 150 pages of various approaches starting with the Greeks that dealt in some way with the nature of society. Only human societies are discussed in the introductory review (because so little was known about animal societies), but Espinas's objective is to underscore that all societies are natural phenomena and they are worthy of a field of scientific study. Espinas then identifies two theoretical camps: those who view society as constructed artificial phenomena and those who view society as a concrete phenomenom rooted in nature. Aligning himself with the naturalist camp, Espinas credits Comte and Spencer for establishing sociology as a field of scientific study by using the organismic analogy to compare societies to biological organisms. Comte is praised for his "spiritualism" (i.e. his new religion), notions of a collective solidarity, and for his vision of a sociology that applies scientific methods to construct abstract theories. Espinas also finds in Comte's writings a remarkable "noble" linkage of positivism with a sense of morality, a connection missing in traditional philosophical systems (pp. 113, 116). Spencer is praised for how he applied Comtian sociology for his articulation of evolutionary principles of differentiation and integration, and for his insights on organic continuity (i.e. Spencer's law of evolution of the movement from a small homogeneous to larger, differentiated mass). Espinas concludes by emphasizing that societies are concrete, natural realities, and hence, a kind of organism that must be studied using scientific methods (pp. 140–141).

The rest of *Animal Societies* is devoted to how animals associate with an analysis of the types, continuity, and organic connections among different types of societies. Adopting Spencer's assumption that societies originate as undifferentiated masses, Espinas starts by isolating out types of primal societal functions such as purely "Nutritive Societies," a stage of interdependence where groupings of cells and organisms are born by such processes as segmentation, remaining attached to others in a lifelong functional connection to ingest and assimilate nutrients (e.g. invertebrates such as jellyfishes, worms, corals).[4] In time, these primitive associations take on more complex characteristics, but the tiny organisms remain largely undifferentiated with little social unity or individuality.

In the next stage, "Reproductive Societies" arise where associations are still rooted in survival needs, but the once connected, undifferentiated mass starts to form individualized units. This formation corresponds to the evolution of sexual organs, the act of mating, the introduction of a psychological element, and the beginnings of functional co-operation with a division of labor. Over time, the sexual union for reproductive purposes becomes more complex and leads to "Relational Societies," where nutritional and reproductive agents still operate, but greater reliance is placed upon "mental relations" and "psychological bonds." In addition, Darwinian sexual selection gradually leads to expressive rituals, social grooming, and other emotions between males and females. In the next evolutionary stage, the sexual pairings usher in the origin of family life comprised of females and offspring, whereby Espinas proposes that maternal love is an outgrowth of a mother's extended love of self. Finally, building on animal sociality, human sociality emerges—the pinnacle of the evolutionary process.

Social life for Espinas thus starts as an undifferentiated mass where individuality is not a component. Then, in stair-step fashion, each subsequent societal type is built on the innards of previous societies. For example, the need for nutrients that underlies the basis of "Nutritional Societies," remains a component of even the highest societies as both "Reproductive" and "Relational" societies are still rooted in the functional needs of the organism to survive. He then shows how societies with purely physiological relations to meet physical needs gradually evolve with selection pressures to grow ever more complex into relations resting primarily on cognitive relations (although this is mediated through the ultimate needs for survival and reproductive success).

Espinas also proposed an evolutionary continuity from lower organic forms to higher forms in the moral codes that govern social conduct. For Espinas, morality involves any social action that is altruistic with its roots in sympathy. Conspecific morality, he argued, is an "intrinsic sympathy"

---

4 Espinas's stage model is built on the Darwinian platform that there is an evolutionary continuity among all life forms. It also incorporates both Lamarckian notions of adaptation and Darwinian principles of natural and sexual selection.

that members share by identifying with each other.[5] Espinas goes on to argue that the degree of morality is dependent upon an organism's complexity, but that morality exists in all social animals (contra Descartes, see p. 540) because it is an essential condition for the survival of any society. Given that societies rest on such biological parameters, they cannot be artificial constructs but natural, concrete realities that need to be studied using the tools of the natural sciences. In addition, the organic development of society is itself fostered by the growth of a collective sense over pure individualism. This collective sense, or "conscience (consciousness)" is not only real but also constitutes "reality" from collective consensus over representations about the world (pp. 537–538). As Espinas expressed it:

> ... We will say that a society is, it is true, a living being/entity, but what distinguishes it from others is that it is above all constituted by a consciousness (or conscience). A society is a living consciousness (or conscience), or a organism of ideas.
>
> (p. 530)

Espinas also proposed that self-reliance and autonomy evolved with higher relational societies, such as those produced by humans. Yet, individuality is not the cause but an effect or the product of complex, cognitive relations, with a distinctive collective conscience that is different in nature than individual members of society. This idea was of utmost importance for Espinas as he could not contemplate a science of society in any other way. Reality, then, is not determined by individuals *per se* but by a consensus of individuals or a collective conscience on what reality is. However, in contrast to Comte who largely ignored the individual, Espinas proposed that a crucial interplay always exists between the individual and society. For Espinas, the social whole exists as much for its parts as its parts do for the whole (Logue 1983: 100ff and see Geiger 1972: 68ff).

When Espinas submitted his "philosophy" thesis on *des Sociétes animales* to the Faculté des Lettres de Paris at the Sorbonne in 1876, the committee of spiritualist philosophers (i.e. the Cousin's school of eclectic spiritualism) was perplexed by his evolutionary sociology and baffled by his theory of the collective conscience. But what inflamed their senses was Espinas's inclusion of the *infamous* positivists Comte and Spencer, and they demanded that the offending positivists be removed from the text. Espinas

---

5 Only in subsequent editions of *Animal Societies*, did Espinas develop his ideas on animal morality as fully as discussed here.

refused but acquiesced by removing the entire historical introduction (it was returned in the second edition of his book). Then, despite their skepticism (but given French tolerance and appreciation of genius), they awarded Espinas the doctorate in philosophy. The committee in a lighthearted moment then sent the following unabashed note on *Des Sociétés Animales* to the Dean of the Faculty of Letters: "It is a remarkable work, by the novelty of the subject and by the extent of the zoological knowledge it reveals. Until now there had not yet been a complete study of a scientific nature on animal societies" (quoted in Brooks 1998: 273: note 26). Eligible now for a university appointment, Espinas accepted a post at the University of Bordeaux, where in 1881 he became "titular professor of philosophy." In 1893, the call came from Paris to assume the "chair of the Histoire d'économie sociale" at the Sorbonne.

Durkheim's Publishing Debut

For anyone interested in sociology, the *Revue philosophique* was among a handful of French journals publishing articles in sociology.[6] Its founder, Theodule Ribot was a classmate of Espinas at the *École Normale*, and after graduation the close friends worked together (in 1872–1874) to translate Spencer's *Principles of Psychology*. Ribot then asked Espinas to help him launch the *Revue* in 1876 (and Ribot stayed on as director for nearly forty years) because he wanted to provide a forum for secular philosophy and the new empirically grounded disciplines of sociology and psychology.[7] Durkheim read *Animal Societies*, but probably did not meet Espinas until after he paid a visit to Ribot at his editorial office in 1884, grumbling about a recent article written by Espinas (in another journal) on the *agrégation de philosophie*[8] where, in a diatribe against institutional spiritualist

---

6 Roger Geiger (1972: 73) noted that the *Revue* until the 1890's was largely the only outlet for sociological articles. It also served to introduce the educated French public to the works of such foreign luminaries as Herbert Spencer and Wilhelm Wundt.

7 Ribot rejected the traditional "eclectic philosophy," which combined psychology with metaphysics, in favor of a more objective, scientific psychology. As the first professor of experimental psychology in France (at the Sorbonne and later at the Collége de France), Ribot inspired a generation of philosophers to become experimental psychologists (see Brooks 1998: 67ff for a discussion).

8 Espinas's article was published in 1884 in the *Revue internationale de l'enseignement*. The *agrégation de philosophie* referred to is a competative oral and written examination for the certification of instructors who wished to teach philosophy. Focused on the canonical figures in the history of philosophy, Espinas opposed the dominance of the spiritualist philosophy in favor of a more scientific philosophy (see Brooks 1998: 121ff).

philosophy, Espinas referred to young normale philosophers as "neo-Kantian dilettantes." Durkheim was upset that Espinas would attack those who shared his evolutionary views, and he wanted to reassure Ribot that they were staunch "evolutionists." In September of 1884, Ribot informed Espinas of Durkheim's visit, "What is certain," Robot said, "is that Durkheim appears nourished by *Animal Societies*" (Quoted in Brooks 1998: 204).

By 1884, Durkheim was busy working on his primary dissertation, *The Division of Labor in Society*. In this endeavor, he turned to German literature; and in 1885, at the age of 27, he made his professional writing debut in Robot's *Revue philosophique* by reviewing Albert Schaeffle's *Bau und Leben des Sozialen Körpers* (1875) [*Structure and Life of the Social Body*]. This review is significant as Durkheim's first publication, but it is also an embodiment of reoccurring themes in his later writings, which may explain why Durkheim reviewed a book published ten years earlier—a "tardy but timely" exposition, as Durkheim put it, because Schaeffle's ideas, he felt, deserved more attention.

While *Bau und Leben des Sozialen Körpers* is a massive four-volume tome, Durkheim reviewed only the first volume of nearly 900 pages, which he characterized as "a sort of social statics" [1885]1978: 93). Schaeffle is a realist, he wrote, and in line with Comte, Spencer, and Espinas, visualizes society as a "discrete entity" rather than the mere sum of individuals. This entity can be likened to a biological organism but, according to Schaeffle, it is not an organism because there is a break in continuity as the parts of biological organisms are forged by a "material link" while in the social organism the members of society are forged by an "ideal link" (p. 94). Schaeffle, Durkheim notes, is less interested in using the metaphor to draw analogies between physiological relations and sociological relations and more as a visual aid for conceptualizing the scope of sociology (p. 94). In addition, Schaeffle maintains that above all "lucid ideas" make up the "collective consciousness," that while a product of individual minds acts as a force to both constrain and unite societal members. After a detailed discussion along these lines, Durkheim suggests that if Schaeffle is right, sociology (*la science sociale*) is not an extension or the "final chapter of biology" because there is a break in continuity. As Durkheim expressed it:

> Evolution is not a monotonous repetition; continuity is not identity ... [S]ociology has been shown to have a subject matter no less real than that of the life sciences ... Let it be founded and organized and let it outline its program and specify its method. If there is a real affinity between it and biology, these two sciences, by pursuing their

natural development, will surely meet one day. But a premature fusion would be artificial and, consequently, sterile.

(Durkheim [1885]1978: 111)

Durkheim expressed disappointment, however, in Schaeffle's failure to address one of the "gravest questions" sociology must resolve: the relationship between the individual and society. And in particular, how the human proclivity for individualism can be molded for the collective good. For Schaeffle, the reasoning minds of contemporary individuals will naturally unite them into a "sense of solidarity," whereas for Durkheim, "if society is a being which has a goal, then it may find the reasoning minds of individuals too independent and too mobile for the common destiny to be entrusted to them without fear" (p. 112). So, while Durkheim considered Schaffle's work overall a "beautiful analysis," he raised doubt over Schaffle's notion that humans living in complex societies will be naturally aware of the need for social harmony, ending his review with these cautionary words:

> As a last resort against individualism, we are left, it is true, with what Schaeffle calls the sense of solidarity, *Gemeinsinn*. Every man, no doubt, instinctively understands that he does not suffice unto himself ... The heart can be no larger than the mind. If I do not perceive the invisible bonds, which link me to the rest of society, I will think that I am independent of it and I will act accordingly.
>
> (p. 114)

Durkheim's early concern with "social solidarity" and the problem posed by individualism would come to occupy more and more of his time, slowly pulling him into the enigmatic world of primitive hordes, incest taboos, and totemic cults.

In 1885–1886, Durkheim was awarded a government fellowship for independent study and took sabbatical leave. It was customary for doctoral students with excellent promise to compete for this grant, and as a recent graduate of the *École Normale Supérieure*, Durkheim had sterling credentials. Espinas surely lent a hand by bringing Durkheim to the attention of Louis Liard (1846–1917), his *École Normale* classmate who had recently been appointed by Jules Ferry to be director of French Higher Education (Directeur de l'Enseignement Supérieur). Liard, a strong advocate of a scientific approach to society (believing it would help insure the success of the Third Republic) interviewed Durkheim and then helped him secure a fellowship (Alpert (1961: 38; and Lavisse 1918). Durkheim spent his first six months studying in Paris and the rest in Germany traveling to Berlin, Marburg and, particularly, Leipzig with its stellar attraction the famous Leipzig Institute of Experimental Psychology founded in 1879 by Wilhelm Wundt.[9] Durkheim was greatly impressed with Wundt's scientific rigor and especially his evolutionary and empirical approach to morality (Durkheim [1887a: 267ff; and see Geiger 1972: 143ff for a discussion). After returning to France, Durkheim wrote up his findings on German academia in two lengthy articles that were quickly published, establishing his credentials as a promising social scientist (Karady 1975: 267ff; Joas 1993).[10] His German experience also convinced him that the scientific study of the social life (or moral life) modeled on the natural sciences was possible and necessary.[11] He would later write that his engagement with German scholarship was formative in helping him to develop a "sense of social reality, of its complexity and of its organic development" (quoted in Geiger 1972: 140–141).

A year later, Durkheim's sojourn as a *lycée* instructor ended when he was invited to join the Faculté des Lettres as a chargé de cours (lecturer) at the University of Bordeaux. He was still working on his doctorate, but he was chosen to replace Alfred Espinas who had been appointed in 1887 to Dean of the Faculté des lettres at Bordeaux. Espinas and Liard were both instrumental in securing Durkheim's appointment for he was, after all, a *normalien* with a promising intellect but they also saw in his person a promising champion of both the Third Republic and the science of society.

Commentary

This chapter chronicled the key events that led to Durkheim's academic appointment at the University of Bordeaux. Durkheim is now well schooled in contemporary philosophical traditions—from eclectic spiritualism, Boutroux's continuity theory to Comte's positive philosophy and the writings of Spencer, Espinas, and Schaeffle among others. He can now focus on legitimating sociology as the new science of society.

---

9 Until Wundt established his laboratory for collaborative research most psychology experiments were done by individuals working alone.

10 For detailed discussions of Durkheim's visit to Germany, see Lukes 1972: 86–95; Alpert 1961: 38–42; Geiger 1972: 140–145 and Fournier 2013: 70ff).

11 At this time Durkheim had completed a draft of *The Division of Labor in Society* that he introduced as "an attempt to treat the facts of the moral life according to the method of the positive sciences" (Geiger 1972: 145).

In the next chapter, Durkheim takes up this challenge with an all-consuming commitment to the creation of a science of society. I should mention that in his role as a *lycée* instructor, Durkheim had little academic freedom. It was compulsory for instructors to teach a set formula of topics mandated by the state educational system because *lycée* courses were designed to prepare students for exams that were based precisely on the materials outlined in each institutionalized program. Even slight deviations from the rigid syllabus had potential consequences. During his tenure as a *lycée* instructor, Espinas (not surprisingly) broke that rule by lecturing on Charles Darwin and organic evolution. Parents protested to administrators but Espinas was fortunately supported by school officials (Brooks 1998: 17ff, 102).

Judging by recently discovered lecture notes taken by André LaLande in Durkheim's philosophy course at the *Lycée* de Sens (1883–1884, see Gross and Jones 2004), Durkheim adhered to a strict orthodox philosophy course.[12] Durkheim's compliance means that without the call to Bordeaux, it is likely that he would have remained a *lycée* philosophy instructor (or called to a university position as a philosophy professor). The writing of *Elementary Forms* would also be problematical as it can be traced back to a lecture course on religion that he taught in Bordeaux in 1895. But thanks to Espinas and Laird who in the face of heated controversy engineered a university appointment for Durkheim that combined pedagogy and social science, Durkheim could now teach *sociology*. And thus, without the patronage of Espinas and Laird, Durkheimian sociology may never have been written.

In the next chapter, we will follow along as Durkheim begins his university career, focusing on his lectures and early publications. Then, we will turn to his 1895 *révélation*, and at this juncture become acquainted with another set of players essential to our mysterious story about the origins of *The Elementary Forms of Religious Life*.

---

12 These notes were taken by one of Durkheim's 16-year-old pupils, and Durkheim in all likelihood never saw or read them. André LaLande who later became a well-known philosopher possessed the rare talent of memorizing lectures verbatim— without even taking notes. Durkheim's own lecture notes at the *Lycée* de Sens are lost but LaLande very likely captured Durkheim's early lecture style and a faithful rendering of its contents (see Gross and Jones 2004).

4
The Young Sociology Professor

> *Durkheim's courses . . . are the best evidence we have of his sociological interests and developments. They, much better than his published works . . . reveal what his scientific preoccupations were at a given time, in what direction his researches were heading and what his sociological orientation was at any particular period of his life.*
>
> Harry Alpert (1961: 63)

A mystery story involves a cast of characters with a reconstruction of events to uncover what happened, how and why. In Durkheim's case history, there is a long-standing enigma over why he suddenly took up the study of religion and what it was that triggered so passionate an intensity that religion remained central to his research for the rest of his career. Durkheim never disclosed the details of this remarkable transformation, but he did provide some tantalizing clues for solving this mystery.

One piece of evidence is his public disclosure of a *révélation* that he had in 1895 that compelled him to make all his earlier research compatible with his new understanding of the essential role religion played in social life. Indeed, after 1895, Durkheim begins to impute a religious character to all social phenomena and to become preoccupied with such esoteric topics as hordes, exogamy, clans, taboos, and totems. What, then, so radically altered his thinking? In this chapter we will review his early ideas on solidarity, kinship, morality, and society in order to access the full implications of what happened after 1895. Following the clues he left behind will also serve to help us reconstruct the logic that underlies his writing of *Elementary Forms*. Our story opens in 1887 at the University of Bordeaux where Durkheim has just arrived to take up his new teaching post. Then, in Chapter 5, we can turn to the obscure circumstances surrounding Durkheim's self-reported revelation that occurred in the interval between the publication of *The Division of Labor* in 1893, and *The Rules of the Sociological Method* in 1895.

Durkheim's Debut at the University of Bordeaux

At age 29, Durkheim left Troyes (near Paris) and moved to Bordeaux, a beautiful port city in Southwestern France near the Atlantic coast, and one with a rich cultural heritage and opulent vineyards.[1] Now a *chargé de cours* (junior lecturer), Durkheim could support a wife, and on October 17, 1887, he married 21-year-old Louise Julie Dreyfus in a religious ceremony blessed by the Chief Rabbi of Paris. Louise, the daughter of a wealthy Parisian entrepreneur brought to the Durkheim-Dreyfus household a handsome marriage settlement equivalent it is said to twenty years of Durkheim's university salary (Charle 1984: 45; Lamanna 2002, 11ff; Fournier 2013: 93). Madam Durkheim also inherited large sums of money from her parents and uncle in 1903. This prompted Christophe Charle to remark "these economic and social figures considerably alter the image of ascetic rigor we have of the founder of university sociology" (Charle, p. 47).[2]

While Durkheim's good fortune in marriage had monetary benefits, Louise Durkheim also proved to be the ideal partner for an academic workaholic. Marcel Mauss (Durkheim's nephew) spoke of his Aunt Louise with the highest praise, "She always knew how to provide her husband with the most favorable working conditions. She was very well educated and eventually able to collaborate on his work. For many years she copied some of his manuscripts ... [and] corrected all his proofs ..." Georges Davy, Durkheim's colleague, also considered Madam Durkheim an "admirable partner" and one who "devoted her life fully and joyfully to her husband's austere life as a scholar" (quoted in Fournier 2006: 18). The couple had two children, Marie born in 1888 and André in 1892. So in 1887, it is easy to imagine the newlyweds establishing a new home in Bordeaux, enjoying a comfortable lifestyle and settling into a satisfying conjugal relationship that would last until Durkheim's untimely death in 1917.

What is more, Durkheim now had the academic freedom to chart his own agenda at the *Université de Bordeaux*. His position as *Chargé de cours* was housed in the philosophy department and included pedagogy

---

1 For a delightful read on the history of wine and Thomas Jefferson's visit to Bordeaux's vineyards in 1787, I highly recommend Benjamin Wallace's, The *Billionaire's Vinegar: the Mystery of the World's Most Expensive Bottle of Wine*, 2008, New York: Crown Publishers.

2 In a well-researched essay with an extended range of sources, Christophe Charle (1984) reflected on how the stereotype of Durkheim's ascetic lifestyle came about. But the article itself is focused on Durkheim's marriage into a very affluent family despite his modest background, and how it may be related to the ideals of endogamous networks for this ethnic group. Durkheim is likely to have met Louise though a Jewish network circle in Paris.

(originally taught by Espinas), but he was to teach social science—indeed the first French university courses in sociology created especially for him by Louis Laird, the Director of Higher Education in France (for discussions see, Geiger 1972: 148ff; Alpert 1961: 42ff; and Tiryakian 1978). At the school year's opening reception, Espinas, the new Dean of Faculty and Letters, warmly welcomed Durkheim and announced the addition of *sociology* to the university curriculum:

> This is a great event, if one is to judge by the emotion it has caused ... May social science be far from a supererogatory study here ... it is—and one must say so boldly—the common basis of all the studies to which you devote yourselves ... It is probable that sociology—since one must call it by its name—will assume a more and more important place in all our studies.
>
> (quoted in Lukes 1972: 100–101)[3]

Durkheim's First Courses in Sociology

Social Solidarity

Durkheim wrote out his lectures word-for-word and with such care that many served as drafts for his books and articles (see Fournier 2013: 110). Of special interest are two premier sociology lectures published much as he delivered them during his first two years at Bordeaux. They capture Durkheim's masterful lecture style and his frank and easy manner in addressing his pupils (many of whom were preparing for careers as *lycée* philosophy instructors). But more importantly, these lectures offer a rare glimpse into Durkheim's early thoughts, passions, and goals. The first is the opening lecture for his year-long course on "*Social Solidarity*," taught during the 1887–1888 academic year. Uncovering the forces underlying solidarity was so profoundly important to Durkheim that it would dictate his agenda for the next thirty years. Choosing his words carefully, he laid out the task before him:[4]

---

[3] Lukes (1972: 102) notes that opposition to sociology continued into Durkheim's second year of teaching. Espinas was apparently fending off resistance even before Durkheim arrived to take up his post.

[4] Durkheim's opening sociology lecture was published in 1888 as "Cours de science sociale: Leçon d' ouverture," in the *Revue internationale de l'enseignement* 15: 23–48.

Charged with the task of teaching a science born only yesterday ... it would be rash on my part not to be awed by the difficulties of my task ... The only way to demonstrate movement is to take a step. The only way to demonstrate that sociology is possible is to show that it exists and that it lives. That is why I am going to devote this first lecture to setting before you the succession of transformations through which sociology has passed since the beginning of this century ... From this exposition, you will decide for yourselves what service this discipline can render and to what public it must address itself.

([1888]1978a: 43–44)

Since Plato and his *Republic*, Durkheim continued, many thinkers have theorized about the nature of societies, but with the rare exception of Aristotle and a few others, the social world was deemed an artificial entity, a creative human invention. In the eighteenth century, Montesquieu and Condorcet revived Aristotle's notion, with Montesquieu declaring that society rests upon natural laws but he failed to grasp the true significance of his proclamation. Durkheim went on to credit economists as the first to recognize the spontaneous nature of collective life and the reality of economic laws, but they were not equipped then, nor today, to integrate the social sciences with the natural sciences. Only in the nineteenth century did Auguste Comte give sociology a concrete reality by naming the discipline and declaring that "social laws are natural" and that society, like a living organism, was a real entity. Comte, however, was to leave it to Herbert Spencer to integrate sociology into the natural sciences by adding sociology to his analysis of physics, biology, and psychology. In place of Comte's grand "society of humanity," sociology would be the study of *societies* of organisms and super-organisms. Alfred Espinas then carried the idea of societies further in *Animal Societies*, by identifying "classes and species" and articulating some laws governing their operation. Espinas's book, Durkheim declared, "*constitutes the first chapter of sociology*" [1888] 1978: 44–59, emphasis added).

What Espinas achieved using animal societies, the German scholar, Albert Schaeffle undertook for modern human societies with a careful application of the organismic analogy, emphasizing "social facts" and the proper use of the scientific method. His *Bau und Leben des Socialen Körpers*, Durkheim said, is a genuine treatise on positive sociology. A debt is also owed to the German schools of economists and legalists who raised the status of sociology as a specialized science. Thus, sociology is anchored in the past but like all sciences it has undergone a slow but steady development:

"We have seen its birth with the economists, its founding with Comte, its consolidation with Spencer, its orientation with Schaeffle, and its specialization with the German jurists and economists" (pp. 59–62).

Durkheim also sketched his future plans for establishing sociology as a legitimate science. Societies can be visualized, he said, as a "sort of organism" that while integrated to form a whole is composed of different organs or of specialized parts. Yet, a science does not artificially create its own subdivisions; it must establish them naturally. So we cannot propose definitive plans for the nascent science of sociology but we can bring an awareness of its likely natural branches that include social psychology, a science of law, a science of economy, and a science of morality—keeping the door wide open for future acquisitions (pp. 63–64). The charge of social psychology, for example, would be to describe and investigate language, religious traditions, legends, and other collective beliefs.

Of overriding importance for Durkheim was to establish a science of morality. Moral philosophers, he argued, typically view morality (*la morale*) as an abstract and unchanging entity of ethical codes and ideal standards of conduct but this approach precludes any real understanding of morality. He insisted that morality must be approached with scientific objectivity by conceptualizing moral codes as systematic collections of obligatory rules or obligations that transcend individuals and that are historically and culturally tied to the ongoing demands of society. These systems of beliefs or the obligatory constraints found in a society's customs, mores, and laws are natural phenomena or external social facts that are subject to change over time. Once morality is subjected to scientific analysis, Durkheim added, its true nature and causes can then be determined and "[e]xperience will teach us that these causes are social in nature" (pp. 63, 67).

Durkheim also highlighted "social facts" as the unit of analysis and stressed using empirical observation and the comparative method for objective sociological research. He also proposed a division of sociology into two halves—physiology and morphology. In biology, he said, physiology is concerned with the dynamics of how wholes, parts, and functions of the living organism operate, whereas morphology is concerned with the forms and structures of living organisms. Sociology, he felt, should focus first on physiology and the functions of social phenomena. For unless we prefer to see things only superficially, "we must apply ourselves above all to the study of functions" (p. 66).

A focal point of his 1887–1888 course on "Social Solidarity" was his classification of all societies into two grand societal types with each integrated by a distinctive type of solidarity—a *mechanical* type based on a "similarity of consciousnesses" and an *organic* type, based on a "differentiation of functions and the division of labor." He chose organic for the latter solidarity because he considered it a far more stable solidarity that corresponded to the interdependence of the organs of higher mammals, whereas mechanical solidarity resulted simply from a duplication of likenesses and the fusing of minds. Unlocking the secret of social solidarity was for Durkheim, "the initial problem of sociology." To move forward, we need "to know what bonds unite men to one another or, in other words, what determines the formation of social aggregates" (Durkheim [1888a] 1978: 205–207).[5]

Kinship and the Family

Durkheim's second published lecture is an introduction to "The Sociology of the Family," ([1888]1978b), a course he taught during the 1888–1889 school year. He opened by telling students that having covered the nature of social solidarity the previous year, the objective this year was to investigate a type of sociability—family relations, a grouping that Durkheim seemed to have viewed then as the foundation block for all later social formations.[6] His ambitious agenda included the historical development of families, the investigation of domestic morality, and the origins and functions of family life. After introducing his topic, Durkheim explained why a comparative approach to family life was essential rather than a single focus on the modern European family (despite the fascination it naturally held for students). By itself, he said, the contemporary family lacked dimensional depth, limiting investigation to a purely descriptive analysis. To understand domestic life required both a comparison and a classification of family types into different genera and species, making it then possible to sequentially

---

5 Durkheim's classification of societies into two grand types and two types of solidarity was central to his 1887–1888 course although it was not discussed in his premier published lecture. It was discussed in the published opening lecture of a course offered a year later on domestic relations where he recapped the conclusions reached the previous year on "what bonds unite men to one another or . . . what determines the formation of social aggregates" [1888]1978: 205). The second lecture was published in 1888 as Introduction à la sociologie de la famille in *Annales de la faculté de Bordeaux* 10: 257–281.

6 In a philosophy lecture at the *Lycée de Sens* in 1883–1884, Durkheim refers to the family as "the primary and most natural grouping of individuals" and "the seed from which society as a whole is born" (see Gross and Jones 2004: 255–257). Durkheim was required to adhere to a fixed syllabus of topics as noted earlier for *lycée* instruction, but his expressed strong feelings seem a bit over the top and it would seem to ring true that at this early period of his career he believed the family was the original primal unit.

follow the principle types of domestic relations through evolutionary time to the modern European family. As Durkheim told his pupils:

> [The] study of the past will reveal an explanation of the present... For even the oldest forms of domestic life and those most removed from our own mores have not completely ceased to exist. They survive in part in the family of today ... each time that we establish a familial type, we shall try to find out what it has in common with the family of today and what aspect of the latter it explains ... For what could be more interesting than to see the life of the modern family, so simple in appearance, resolved into a multitude of tightly intertwined elements and relationships and to follow through history the slow development in the course of which they were successively formed and combined?
> (pp. 211–212)

Durkheim also advocated the study of domestic morality by using the scientific method of gathering "a large body of facts" (p. 212). He cautioned though that "social facts" could not be collected by hearsay evidence or personal narratives but by extracting "concrete and tangible forms" from legal codes, formal documents, or by descriptive accounts of collective customs and mores drawn from history and the ethnographic record. Once identified and classified according to similarities and differences in family lifeways, it then becomes possible to investigate the causal factors underlying their origins and endurance over time. Only then, he added, will it become possible to uncover the factors that unify the modern European family by penetrating its very nature (pp. 211–214).

Durkheim also sketched with broad strokes a provisional table for filling in the types of domestic relations, the anatomy of each family type, and the means for making useful comparisons. In this typology, he divided domestic life into four parts: (1) "Kin" (e.g. relations of husband with his relatives; relations of children with maternal and paternal kindred); (2) "The Spouses" (e.g. nature of conjugal bonds, number of legal spouses, rights and obligations, marriage settlements, systems of inheritance); (3) "The Children" (e.g. relations with parents, descent through mother or father, inheritance rights); and (4) "The State" (e.g. legal interventions in spousal and child relations, legal obligations). Using this classification, he said, each family type could then be characterized and compared according to the absence or presence of particular attributes. By classifying systems of relations, he held, useful comparisons could then isolate out the core attributes of the family from secondary manifestations or accidental parts (pp. 208–209 and see Lamanna 2002: 83ff).

Overall, Durkheim stressed the overriding importance of objectivity by proceeding with the detached curiosity used in the physical sciences. Domestic life, he emphasized, cannot be ranked as superior or inferior because such distinctions have no scientific meaning:

> For science, organisms are not ranked with some above the others; they are simply different because their environment is different. There is no one way of being or of living which is the best for all . . . The ideal for each of them is to live in harmony with its conditions of existence . . . We shall never let this principle slip from view.
> (p. 219)

On data sources, Durkheim ranked the historians and ethnologists as the "most important" and "worthwhile" sources, mentioning by name Bachofen's *Mutterrecht* (1861), McLennan's *Studies in Ancient History* (1886), De Coulanges's *The Ancient City* (1864), Maine's *Ancient Law* (1861) and, Morgan's *Ancient Society* (1877) [see Chapter 1 on the kinship theorists]. He also included Lorimer Fison and A.W. Howitt's *Kamilaroi and Kurnai* (1880), a ground-breaking work he would frequently cite in the next twenty-five years because it focused on Australian kinship systems. Durkheim's early interest in ethnology underscored his firm commitment to an objective and broad-based comparative approach to kinship and family:

> We cannot construct theories by comparing with each other two or three facts of the same type. In order to account for the Roman family, we must compare it not only with the Greek family but with all families of the same type . . . From this point of view, the lowest species cannot be ignored. In this way, the domestic law of Australian or American tribes helps us better to understand that of the Romans . . . To sociology belongs the task of proceeding with these extensive comparisons, and that is the way in which it will prove useful to history.
> (pp. 223–224)

Commentary

Durkheim's first premier lecture chronicles a theme that would guide his research agenda for the next thirty years—social solidarity. He was determined to find new sources of integration that would emerge as traditional social bonds were breaking down and could no longer hold society together. And the best way to achieve this goal was to establish a science of society to study solidarity from a scientific perspective.

Another abiding interest is domestic organization. Although Durkheim assigned Fustel's *Ancient City* in his first family course, he had already distanced himself from Fustel's truncated approach to kinship by restricting the history of the family to Western societies. Yet, aside from his many review articles in *L'Année Sociologique* on domestic organization, Durkheim would publish almost nothing on the family. Yet, he so valued his lecture notes on domestic relations that he carried them around with him for years. What happened to disrupt his plans? One likely factor was his shift away from the family as the primal social formation to the primitive *horde*, the term he introduced in *The Division of Labor in Society* (1893). Another is the priority he placed on totemism and religion after 1895. He explained his reasoning for the priority he gave to religion over the family in *Elementary Forms* ([1912]1995: 104):

> ... familial organization cannot be understood in advance of knowing primitive religious ideas, for those ideas serve as principles of the family. This is why it was necessary to study totemism as religion before studying the totemic clan as family grouping.

Yet, Durkheim had in hand a manuscript on the family intended for publication. But he changed his mind on publishing it just before World War 1 and, then, just before he died in 1917, he told Marcel Mauss not to publish the manuscript posthumously.[7] In the next chapter, we will take up the next phrase of Durkheim's career, a time just before he becomes obsessed with totemism and the origin and function of religion.

---

7 Durkheim's publications on domestic relations (outside of his reviews) include his premier family lecture, a fragment of the seventeenth lecture, a final lecture that Durkheim delivered in 1892 on the "Conjugal Family" (which was preserved and published posthumously in 1921); and in 1907, "Divorce by Mutual Consent." Lukes (1972: 179) noted that it was a pity that Mauss did not eventually publish the manuscript, as it was not preserved. We can only speculate on why Durkheim did not want his manuscript published but a good possibility is that his ideas on the family were far-reaching and radical. After 1912, he may have also been rethinking some ideas in light of the crumbling social evolutionary paradigm and the recent findings of a new generation of academically trained ethnographers (e.g. A.R. Radcliffe-Brown and Bronislaw Malinowski) who were seriously questioning nineteenth-century notions of aboriginal life ways.

5
The Révélation[1]

There are no religions which, considered as scientific doctrines, resist critical analysis. From a scientific point of view, most postulate veritable heresies. But we have no right to conclude that they have played or still play today a harmful or evil role in history. For it is quite possible and even infinitely probable that, as inadequate as they may be in their cosmological or sociological explanations, they respond to real and legitimate needs which otherwise would not have been satisfied.

Émile Durkheim, The Principles of 1789 and Sociology
([1890]1973: 36–37)

An Unexpected Disclosure

During the early years in Bordeaux, Durkheim taught pedagogy and sociology with such eye-catching titles for the time as *Social Solidarity* (1887–1888), *The Family* (1888–188; 1890–1891; 1891–1892, *Suicide* (1889–1890), and *Criminal Sociology* (1892–1893; 1893–1894) (Lukes 1972: 617; Fournier 2013: 103; Alpert 1961: 64ff). He was anxious over the success of his sociology classes, which were open to the public and met on Saturdays (Fournier 2013: 103–104). Henri Durkheim recalls that when he lived with his aunt and uncle in Bordeaux, Durkheim spent most days in his office working and most days out of his office working, "Wherever he was, he was working" (quoted in Fournier 2006: 18). From all accounts, Durkheim labored zealously preparing lectures, teaching, working on his Latin and French doctoral theses, and publishing articles and reviews dealing with the family, crime, law, suicide, polity, social organization, religion, socialism, ethics, psychology, democracy, and the economy. When his wife "scolded him" over his excessive working habits, Durkheim would simply say, "one has to do what one has to do"(p. 18). In 1896, his

---

[1] Sections of this chapter are adapted from Maryanski 2014.

hard work was rewarded with a promotion to Professor of Social Science (*chaire magistrale*).

In the early 1890s, Durkheim began preparations for a lecture course on religious history, in part to encourage his nephew Marcel Mauss (1872–1950) to take up the study of religion. Burly and well built with an attractive face, brown hair, a beard, and "sharp, shining eyes," Mauss was then a graduate student at the University of Bordeaux studying under Espinas (who had been called to the Sorbonne in 1892), Octave Hamelin (Durkheim's close colleague in Bordeaux see Strenski 1989: 141–142) and Durkheim. In recounting this experience, Mauss wrote that the religious course was put together for their mutual benefit:

> ... [W]e were looking for the best way to concentrate my energies in order to assist the nascent science to the best effect and to fill in its most serious gaps. We both felt that the study of institutions, the family and law, were sufficiently developed, and the study of ritual also seemed to us quite advanced except in one area. At that time, we were contented with the work of Frazer and, above all, Robertson Smith. Only oral ritual and religious cognition appeared unexplored, so to speak.
>
> (Mauss [1930]1983: 145)[2]

Mauss[3] went on to specialize in religion with Durkheim serving as his intellectual guardian, saying at one point to him "I'm the one [your mother] asked to train you. I trained you according to my ideals" (Fournier 2006: 20). The two were so close that when Mauss left Bordeaux for extended graduate study in Paris, they wrote each other as often as twice a week, with Durkheim's early letters signed in a very affectionate fatherly way, that later became increasingly professional (see Durkheim 1998). As Fournier put it (2006: 20), "Marcel was Durkheim's student, first disciple,

---

2 This quote comes from a short intellectual autobiography Mauss wrote, probably in the early 1930s, detailing his personal and academic qualifications for a position at the Collège de France. He had not intended it for publication and it only surfaced when the Maison des Sciences de l'Homme acquired the personal papers of George Davy (see "An Intellectual Self-Portrait" and the introduction by Philippe Besnard 1983: 139).

3 Marcel Mauss was a gifted scholar in his own right and a dominant figure in French academia for half a century. His popular works include *The Gift* [1925]2000; *Seasonal Variations of the Eskimo: A Study of Social Morphology* [1904–1905]1979 (with some assistance

and closest collaborator." Indeed, Durkheim spoke of his nephew as "almost my alter ego" (p. 20). During the 1894–1895 school year, Durkheim taught his lecture course on religion with Mauss in attendance, but nothing of what transpired is preserved. Durkheim did inform a close friend that his lectures dealt largely with "les formes élémentaires de la religion" (quoted in Pickering 1984: 69). Mauss ([1930]1983: 145) also remembered that it was designed around the "origins of religion," the topic that would profoundly influence his career and his uncle's as well. For despite the overriding importance of religion in Durkheim's later writings, he gave it scant attention during his first eight years at Bordeaux. Durkheim acknowledged as much when he disclosed a *révélation* in 1895 that put religion at the forefront in part because he said he had found a way to study it sociologically. Yet, Durkheim's *révélation* might never have come to light but for the following sequence of events:

In 1907, Durkheim wrote a letter to the editor of the *Revue néo-scolastique* (a Catholic journal) in protest over a recently published essay by a Belgian professor (and former priest). In "The Genesis of Monsieur Durkheim's System," Professor Simon Deploige alleged that Durkheim's had "borrowed" his formative ideas from German scholars—without acknowledgment. In a published response, Durkheim thanked Deploige for taking so personal an interest in the origin of his ideas, but the professor had mistaken his debt to Germany. After reproaching Deploige for implying that he had lifted German ideas without citing his sources, Durkheim said the truth was quite the opposite—that he was actually responsible for introducing the contributions of German scholars to the French public by highlighting their relevance for sociology. In fact, "I rather exaggerated than played down the importance . . ." and Monsieur Deploige knows of my expressed gratitude as well as I do (Durkheim [1907]1982: 258).

In a second letter, Durkheim continued his rebuttal of Deploige's claim that his formative ideas were derived from German scholars or that after his visit to Germany in 1885–1886 he was "utterly transformed" by German sociology. Instead, he attributed his guiding ideas to Comte, Spencer, Espinas, and Boutroux. Then, to settle Deploige's charge that his religious sociology came from Wilhelm Wundt, Durkheim wrote:

---

from Henri Beuchat); and *Primitive Classification* [1903]1963 (with Emile Durkheim). Mauss died in 1950 (see Leacock 1954 for a discussion of Mauss's seminal contributions to both sociology and anthropology. Also see *Oeuvres* (1968) a collection of lectures, reviews, articles etc. by Marcel Mauss that includes a long forward by Victor Karady.

... it is stated that I found in Wundt the idea that religion is the matrix of moral and juridical ideas, etc. I read Wundt in 1887: but it was only in 1895 that I had a clear view of the capital role played by religion in social life. It was in that year that, for the first time, I found a means of tackling sociologically the study of religion. It was a revelation to me. That lecture course of 1895 marks a watershed in my thinking, so much so that all my previous research had to be started all over again so as to be harmonized with these new views. The *Ethik* of Wundt, which I had read eight years previously, played no part in this change of direction. It was due entirely to the studies of religious history which I had just embarked upon, and in particular to the works of Robertson Smith and his school ... [In addition] I certainly have a debt to Germany, but I owe much more to its historians than to its economists and—something which Monsieur Deploige's does not seem to suspect—I owe at least as much to England.

(pp. 259–260)

In 1912, Deploige restated his claim of infringement in his *Le Conflit de la morale et de la sociologie* (*The Conflict Between Ethics and Sociology*). This time Durkheim responded by publishing a scathing review of Deploige's book, calling it "an apologetic pamphlet" to discredit sociology and promote the doctrine of Saint Thomas (i.e. neo-scholasticism vs. modern science). He then reaffirmed that "the science of religion is essentially English and American; it has no trace of anything German ... [And] [I]t is making a systematically truncated 'genesis' of our thinking to neglect everything we owe to Robertson Smith and to the works of the ethnographers of England and America (quoted in Nandan 1980: 160).[4]

What became of the controversy? Nothing really as the charges were groundless, although Deploige's diatribe clearly angered Durkheim and he responded accordingly. The influence of Comte, Spencer, Fustel, Boutreaux, and Espinal would be expected–but Robertson Smith? Why bestow such a noble tribute on a Scottish Old Testament scholar? No one quite knows.

---

4 Whether the dust-up between Deploige and Durkheim was fodder in French academic circles is unknown but few scholars at the time referred to it (Pickering 1984: 61). It had some coin, however, because in 1915 Charles Gehlke (an American Scholar) discussed it in his book, *Emile Durkheim's Contributions to Sociological Theory* ([1915]1968).

Gaston Richard ([1923]1975), one of Durkheim's former colleagues turned critic mentioned it as well in an article in the *Revue d' Histoire et de Philosophie Religieuse* under the title "L'Atheisme dogmatique en sociologie religieuse" ("Dogmatic Atheism in the Sociology of Religion").

As Pickering (1984: 62) noted, "scholars are left guessing ... [because] ... No one knows for sure what elements of Robertson Smith were of such revelatory importance to Durkheim." Robert Jones (1986: 601) concurs, noting in a play mused way that Durkheim's is guilty of a "historiographical discourtesy" by withholding the details of his blazing insight. And, of course, this "discourtesy" opened the academic door to years of debates and speculations. On this, we may quote Jones (1986: 601):

> [A]mong the numerous candidates for the role of pivotal idea ... are Smith's views on the relationship between religion and magic, the "contagiousness" of the sacred, the relations between religious and political institutions, the ritual theory of myth, totemism as the origin of more developed religious systems, his discovery of the primitive origins of Durkheim's childhood faith, and his "revolutionary" theory of sacrifice.

Also open to debate is the degree of Smith's influence. Did Durkheim overstate his debt to Smith? Did others, notably Fustel de Coulanges and Sir James Frazer (to be discussed) also play pivotal roles in Durkheim's turn to religion? Skeptics even question if Durkheim had a revelation in 1895, if ever. Indeed, the mystique over Durkheim's epiphany spans nearly a hundred years.[5] Lukes (1972: 238–239) contends that Smith "deeply impressed" Durkheim and that it must have been a "considerable revelation" given that before then he had published little on religion. Pickering believes that Durkheim's "intellectual change of direction ... has to be located in the work of Robertson Smith." And, that any solution to this mystery must take Durkheim's overwhelming preoccupation with totemism into account (1984: 69–70).

So, taking Durkheim at his word, he experienced a watershed moment in 1895 that opened his eyes to the pivotal role of religion in social life. This led him to discard or revise all his earlier work to mesh with his new insights. Did this overhaul occur? Can we colligate an 1895 revelation with historical facts? What role did Robertson Smith play in this conversion? Durkheim's respect is not easily earned judging from his overt disapproval of most of his École Normale professors (see Chapter 2); and so for

---

5 See for example, Beidelman 1974; Kuper 1985; Douglas 1966; Evans-Pritchard 1965; Stanner 1975; Sumpf 1965; Collins 2005; Alexander 1982; Giddens 1972; Lukes 1972; Richard [1923]1984; Strenski 1998; Rivière 1995; Thompson 2002; Wentworth 1976; LaCapra 1972; Jones 1986; Besnard 1981; and Tiryakian 1979).

Robertson Smith (a stranger to Durkheim personally) to merit such respect is telling. But right now most sociologists might be asking: Who is Robertson Smith? In his time, Smith was a famous academic maverick who shared many character traits with Fustel and Espinas; he was supremely confident, strong willed, dared to challenge authority, and was a strong proponent of science. But before turning to the brilliant Robertson Smith (as he was called), a synopsis of Durkheim's early ideas on religion will be useful in helping us to establish what he found so revolutionary in his 1895 revelation.

Durkheim's Early Publications on Religion

Ecclesiastical Institutions

Durkheim published little on religion before 1895, although in 1886, when he was still teaching philosophy in *lycées* near Paris, he reviewed Herbert Spencer's "Ecclesiastical Institutions," (a division of his *Principles of Sociology V 3* ([1885]1898).[6] In this work, Spencer's objective is to trace religion back to its origins and to predict its future demise. In early human history, Spencer wrote, the "primitive" mind lacks religious sentiments but a "religious consciousness" slowly develops when humans perceive that forces exist beyond the senses. Religion then takes root with the notion of a double self—a tangible daytime self and an intangible nighttime self that leaves the body during dream time (Spencer [1885]1898: 160). After death, only the nighttime self then lives on as an ancestral ghost (p. 160).

In the next phrase as ancestral ghosts slowly transition into permanent patriarchal spirits, ancestor worship is born. So, for Spencer, a cult of spirits or *animism* is the universal starting point of religion, followed by a "cult of nature" or what Albert Réville (1883) called *naturism*. Over time, as smaller societies are compounded into larger ones and as human power relations shift towards greater inequality, the supernatural beings follow along with an agenda that corresponds with powerful elites. Later when social evolution ushers in more warfare, conquest, and the continued integration of developing civilizations, the "great ghosts or gods" are born

---

6 Durkheim's early publications are mostly long book reviews. His customary practice was to first paraphrase a book's main points and conclusions, followed by commentary. Mark Traugott (1978: xi) cautioned that Durkheim had a didactic writing style, making it difficult sometimes to separate his book summaries from his own remarks. Indeed, Durkheim would often augment in his synopsis the issues he planned to later criticize. This has lead to some distorted impressions of Durkheim's ideas and opinions.

along with a pantheon of "secondary ghosts or demi-gods" that are all linked to a religious mythology that again nicely corresponds to a society's organization, especially its political arrangements (pp. 161–163). In lockstep fashion then, as societies develop, culminating in Christianity and other monotheistic religions, the appropriate gods arrive on a timely basis with attributes that respond to the changes in social life and needs of the state (pp. 163–164). The "religious idea" for Spencer then is rooted in the illusion of an invisible double, with later spirits, ghosts, and gods nothing more than an ongoing fiction to legitimate political power and inequalities. Spencer also predicted the replacement of religion by scientific knowledge once individuals realize the "higher sentiments" found in their own creative energy and the deeper causal forces inherent in the universe (p. 171ff).

Durkheim's commentary opens by praising Spencer for his vast knowledge and ingenuity but finds his thesis misdirected and oversimplified. How, Durkheim asks, could a mind start with a "cult of the dead" and then transition to a "cult of nature" or *naturism*? Ancestor worship is far too complex for the first religion. Perhaps *naturism* rose independently, or came first, adding that "according to Réville, the first religious manifestations would have consisted in the worship, pure and simple, of the personification of the great forces of nature" (Durkheim [1886]1975: 17–18).[7] Durkheim also chastised Spencer for his reckless, open-ended sociology:

> Sociology has often been reproached for being a very vague and badly defined science . . . If, indeed, it wishes to study all the phenomena which are to be observed at the heart of societies . . . it is not a science but science itself . . . If, however, religion is reduced to being merely a collection of beliefs and practices relating to a supernatural agent which is conjured up by the imagination, it is difficult to see in it anything more than a fairly complex aggregate of psychological phenomena . . . That is how Spencer's book comes to include a great number of questions which are not relevant to our science. *Sociology and the history of religions are and must remain separate disciplines.*
> (pp. 18–19: emphasis added)

A sociology of religion is possible, Durkheim added, but "the sociologist must apply himself uniquely to the determination of its social role" (p. 19). Religion then looks very different: first, it shifts the idea of God from a

---

7 See Réville's *Les Religions Des Peuples Non-civilisés* (1883).

core component to an ancillary psychological phenomena within a foremost sociological process. Second, it shifts attention away from the "idea of divinity" or how the divine presence is used to symbolize traditional beliefs, customs, and collective needs to what the symbol actually "hides and expresses" (p. 19). Durkheim also questioned Spencer's assumption that the "enquiring mind" accounts for changes in religious sentiments. Change occurs, he said, when collective phenomena no longer function to serve individual and societal needs (p. 20). Finally, he dismissed Spencer's notion of a future without religion. As long as humans live together they will share some common beliefs, but only the future will tell how these beliefs will be symbolized (p. 22).

The Non-Religion of the Future

In 1887, Durkheim reviewed *The Non-Religion of the Future: A Sociological Study* (1887b). In this work Jean Marie Guyau, a young French philosopher, takes up the origin of religion; the breakdown of religion; and the end of religion.[8] Religion is a natural phenomena, Guyau said, arising from superstitions and vague impressions because humans sought explanations for the unknown. Religion then slowly developed by following universal, regular laws. The first religions lacked spirits, souls, and gods, but these secondary products gradually emerged from primal sentiments and evolved into the highly complex religions of today.

For Guyau, religion originates once humans can imagine a more powerful society superimposed above their own (or an extension of their society); one that is universal, more cultural and one possessing greater powers or potency—a "cosmic society." Religions also converge on the belief that social bonds exist between humans and supernaturals, bonds that are physical, social, emotional, and in more complex societies, moral as well. How did religious emotions originate? Guyau places their primary source in the sphere of human sociality, with the religious institution simply an imaginary extension of human relationships. Above all, religion is a rudimentary science to make sense of the world, with all explanations represented either "imaginatively" or "symbolically" by comparisons with

---

8 Jean Marie Guyau (1854–1888) the stepson of the philosopher Alfred Fouillée was the author of nine books as well as a social philosopher and gifted poet. At 34 he died of a terminal illness shortly after writing *The Non-Religion of the Future*. Perhaps to come to terms with his own morality, Guyau wrote near the end of his book that "man's sole superiority in death consists in acceptance" [1887] 1962: 519).

human society. As such, religion functions to regulate the imagination and to bring the unknown into some sense of the known universe (p. 137).

So for Guyau, religion arose to mitigate the human fear of unknown forces and to understand and explain physical events, with the gods simply imaginative creatures (p. 114). Then, as society and religion evolved, they interfaced with other religions (inter-tribal, city) and, at this point, morality unites with religion. Knowing the origin of religion is important, Guyau maintained, because the causes that gave rise to religious sentiments are, in many cases, still maintaining its existence. Yet, religion is slowly dying because science is killing the supernatural. In its place, Guyau predicted a positive "religious anomy" or the emancipation from dogmatic faith, giving humans the freedom to pursue their own speculations or join voluntary associations where the spirit of science will prevail.[9]

In his commentary, Durkheim opens by praising Guyau for his insightful ideas and scientific approach but, most of all, for realizing that the roots of religion are not found in the *conscience individuelle* but are collective phenomena (Durkheim [1887]1975). He advises, however, that substantial corrections to Guyau's thesis are needed. In Guyau's scheme religion originates in (1) the human need to explain the world around them and (2) the social nature of humans. Durkheim proposes instead that sociality and human emotions are primary and the driving forces of the religious sentiment because humans:

> did not start by imagining the gods; that they felt bound to them by social sentiments was not because they visualized the gods in a certain way. They began by attaching themselves to the things they used or suffered from, just as they attached themselves to each other, spontaneously, without thinking, without the least degree of speculation. The theory to explain and make sense of the habits which had been formed in this way came only later to these primitive *consciences*. As these sentiments were moderately similar to those which man observed in his relations with his fellows, he visualized the powers of nature as beings like himself; and at the same time he set them apart from himself and attributed to these exceptional beings distinctive qualities which turned them into gods. Religious ideas, then, result from the interpretation of pre-existing sentiments.
>
> (p. 35)

---

9 See Marco Orru's article, "The Ethics of Anomie: Jean Marie Guyau and Emile Durkheim" (1983) for an illuminating discussion of Guyau's characterization of anomie as a positive future benefit for humankind.

To study a religion, these emotions need to be penetrated by discarding the representations, or the "superficial shell" that symbolizes and expresses them.

All societies, Durkheim said, have two types of social sentiments. The first is personal sentiments or emotions that stem from day-to-day relations associated with honor, respect, fear, and positive affect, whereas the second is communal sentiments that stem from a collective life. Person-to-person sentiments attach individuals to each other but keep individuality mostly intact, whereas communal sentiments attach individuals to the collective whole, giving rise to a sense of obligation beyond narrow self interest. So in place of Guyau's conjecture that person-to-person emotions are the catalyst for religion, Durkheim's sense is that the emotions that attach individuals to the collective whole are what give rise to religious sentiments (p. 36).

Durkheim dismissed Gayau's notion that religion is an illusion by advocating that "each time anyone attempts the study of a collective *représentation*, he can rest assured that a practical and not a theoretical cause has been the determining reason for it" (p. 34). He also rejected the notion that early religions lacked morality and law noting that Gayau had ignored the obligatory nature of religion (p. 34). Finally, he questioned Guyau's claim of a religious anomy (or a liberation from dogmatic faith). Given that faith is grounded in practical causes it will persist as long as such causes exist, no matter what the state or science or philosophy (p. 37).[10]

The Division of Labor

After working for at least eight years on *The Division of Labor in Society: A Study of the Organization of Higher Societies* (1893), Durkheim presented his dissertation to the Paris Faculty of Letters in 1892. This monograph more than anything else reflects his initial all-out effort to understand the nature of social solidarity and the relationship between society and the individual. We need to know, he said, "what bonds unite men to one another or, in other words, what determines the formation of social aggregates" (Durkheim [1888]1978: 205).

---

10 Durkheim's down-to-earth approach is evident in lecture notes taken in 1883–1884 by his student, André LaLande during his time as a lycée instructor (see Gross and Jones 2004: 1ff). Religious-like phenomena are also discussed in his assessment of Thomas Ferneuil's, *The Principles of 1789 and Social Science* (1889). Despite his conviction that most religions "postulate veritable heresies," he is single-minded in the belief that all religions are based on practical and legitimate concerns.

In the *Division of Labor* (*DOL*) Durkheim tackled this problem by committing to the following intellectual preferences: (1) a belief in the theory of social evolution; (2) a passionate determination to use the tools of science; and (3) a commitment to the organismic analogy. "How does it come about," he wrote, "that the individual, whilst becoming more autonomous, [in industrial societies] depends ever more closely upon society? How can he become at the same time more of an individual and yet more linked to society?" This contradiction is resolved, he said, once the *DOL* is seen as both an economic system and a natural adaptation for a new and *superior* form of social solidarity (Durkheim [1893]1984: xxx; 105, 122–123 emphasis added).

As is well known, Durkheim used law as his visible marker of solidarity because binding legal activity underlies a stable organization.[11] So, changes in legal codes should reflect changes in the nature of social cohesion, or solidarity. He then proposed two types of solidarity, symbolized by two kinds of law: (1) repressive or penal law evident in "primitive" or undifferentiated societies and (2) contractual or restitutive law evident in developed societies. In the first type with minimal occupational differentiation, social ties are contingent upon a "collective consciousness" (of shared sentiments and representations)—a *mechanical solidarity*,[12]— whereas in the second type with occupational specialization, social ties are contingent upon an interdependence of functions —an *organic solidarity*. Thus, the main function of task allocation was to provide a superior and more robust form of integration and a new code of ethics, although this transformation to organic solidarity had not yet solidified to fully take effect (p. 24ff).

While Durkheim adhered to the functional logic of Comte and Spencer, he realized that to explain the division of labor solely by its end result or effect is more conjecture than science. So to keep his hypothesis empirically grounded he devised a two-step process: (1) isolate out the parts that integrate the social whole and, (2) isolate out the selection pressures (or the causes) for the existence and variation in the parts. He also realized

---

11 Adhering to his commitment for a "science of society," Durkheim reasoned that as solidarity is an intangible phenomenon that cannot be directly observed or measured (as it constituted a totally moral phenomena), the law best served as a symbolic measure of social cohesion, although in a roundabout way.

12 Durkheim also alleged that not only is everyone tethered to a "collective conscience" of likenesses in mechanical solidarity but everyone is rather alike physically and neurologically. In fact, he was so caught up in his argument, he claimed that human brains develop in a corresponding way (at least for males) when tasks become specialized.

that once the bonds connecting individuals in a *mechanical* solidarity get replaced by bonds connecting individuals in an *organic* solidarity, the *social structure* of a society must also change. This led him to sketch two distinctive types of social formations, segmentary and non-segmentary to correspond to his two types of solidarity. Durkheim then put together a scenario explaining the transition from mechanical to organic solidarity over time (1893[1984]: 126 ff).

In primordial times, he said, humans lived in undivided aggregates or *hordes* that eventually transitioned into clan-based societies held together by an all-powerful regulator—a *collective conscience* with an ecclesiastical character. In a segmented society, religion is *the* unifying force—but it is *not* the cause of this societal type. Instead, it is the organizational arrangements that fuel the power and nature of religious ideas (p. 130). In a mechanical solidarity, stability is anchored by a writ-large "collective personality," which is why a religious character pervades "the entire psychological life of society" (p. 130). Yet, if all minds are fused together in mechanical solidarity, how does individualism, the *sine qua non* for an organic solidarity make any inroads? This transformation occurs slowly, he said, and in a developmental process that supplants the rigid clan structure with an expanding network of interdependent tasks and in direct proportion to the volume and density of a population. Yet, since organic solidarity cannot crystalize until mechanical solidarity largely disappears (as the two cannot coexist), they must move in an inverse relationship—as one regresses, the other progresses (p. 226 ff).

Durkheim now faced a quandary: how do individual consciences break loose from an all-powerful collective entity? If left implicit, the *need* for greater individualism would seem to be the cause leading to that end—an illegitimate teleology. To overcome this stumbling block, Durkheim proposed the existence of a primal individuality, or an inborn part of the human mind independent of all social and environmental conditions. So, in societies with a concrete *collective conscience*, all personal autonomy is simply suspended and deactivated (p. 145).[13] Then, to demonstrate how

---

13 Durkheim proposed that though the personal conscience in clan-based (and in other derived segmentary-based societies) gets submerged in a powerful *collective conscience* "there is a sphere of psychological life which, no matter how developed the collective type may be, varies from one person to another and belongs by right to each individual ... This primal basis of all individuality is inalienable and does not depend upon the social condition." But as individualism increases, "it does not follow that the central area of the common consciousness has grown in size. No new elements have been brought into play,

a shift to more autonomy gets underway, Durkheim concocted a colorful narrative explaining how *personal consciences* slowly gets liberated from the *collective conscience*. And, it is here that we get a long-buried clue into his early thinking on the genesis and evolution of religion.

Durkheim's scenario begins with a small society where members have identical relations with identical things (i.e. this *single* tree, this single bird, etc.) resulting in an all-embracing collective conscience. But once the volume and density of a society increases, so must the collective entity increase its boundaries outside its original circle. To embellish how the ecclesiastical entity weakens as the spirit of individuality strengthens, Durkheim employed its "god-like" property or the transcending force of "divinity" by assembling a stage model of religious evolution with *naturism* as his root religion as shown in the text on the left side of Table 5.1 (1893: 319–320).

A surprise perhaps for readers acquainted with the *Division of Labor* is that the middle paragraph on the left side of the table from the original 1893 edition deviates from the one on the right side from the 1902 edition (or see the French version in the appendix). In the second edition, Durkheim modified the Preface by deleting some materials and adding a new section on occupational groups but he said he refrained from modifying the text material. It was best, he added, to let the book remain as written. And, it mostly did. Nonetheless, as Table 5.1 confirms, he did alter his 1893 religious stage model by removing *naturism* as root religion and replacing it in 1902 with "*totem of the clan*" (1902: 273). And, this small change is actually a big new clue into his early thinking on religion because contrary to long established belief, Durkheim had originally embraced *naturism* rather than *totemism* as his baseline religion, and this means, of course, that his shift to totemism was later and, most importantly occurred *after* 1893.

Now if we compare the 1893 version with the 1902 version, the original text has a consistency that the second one lacks. The original text logically corresponds, for example, to Durkheim's depiction of how a concrete *collective conscience* transitions into more abstract forms. In the first edition, as noted above, community members have exact relations with *exactly* the same objects—"*this* tree *this* bird, *this* plant, *this* natural force, etc." (1893: 318ff, added emphasis). This portrayal of likenesses was surely meant to

---

since this sentiment has existed from earliest times and has always been of sufficient strength not to suffer being harmed in any way. The only change that has occurred is that a primitive element has attained greater intensity" (Durkheim [1893]1984: 145,117).

TABLE 5.1 Durkheim's Stage Models from *The Division of Labor*

Text from 1893 Edition	Text from 1902 Edition
The fact that perhaps best reveals this growing tendency of the common consciousness is the parallel transcendence of its most essential of elements; I refer to the notion of divinity. Originally, the gods are not distinct/separate from the universe . . .	[No change from 1893 edition]
. . . but all natural beings who are susceptible of influencing social life, of awakening the fears and hopes of the community [*lit. trans.* "collective fears and hopes"], are deified. This character is not communicated to them from the outside, but is intrinsic to them. They are not divine because god lives in them; they are the gods themselves. It is at this stage of religious evolution that the name *naturism* was begotten/ given. But little by little, the gods become detached from the things with which they were confounded. They become *spirits* who, if they prefer residing here or there, nonetheless exist outside of the concrete forms under which they are incarnated; this is the reign of *animism*.* Regardless of whether they are multiple or, as with the Jews, brought back to unity; in one case like in the other, the degree of immanence is the same (319–320, emphasis in original).	. . . or rather, there are no gods, only sacred beings, but the sacred character with which they are invested is not related to an exterior entity as its source. The animals or plants of the species that serve as the clan's totem [or "totem of the clan"] are the objects of worship; but this is not because of a principle *sui generis* that communicates their divine nature from the outside. This nature is intrinsic ["within/to them"]; they are divine in themselves. But little by little, the religious forces are detached from the things of which they were at first only the attributes, and are reified. This is how the notion of spirits or gods is formed who, while preferably residing here or there, nonetheless exist outside the particular objects to which they are more specifically attached.* In this sense, they have something that is less concrete/they are somehow less concrete. However, whether they are multiple or have been brought back to a certain unity, they are still immanent to the world (273–274, emphasis in original).
If they are in part separated from things, they are still in space. So, they remain very close to us, constantly mingling with our lives. Greco-Latin polytheism, which is a more elevated and more organized form than animism, is a progressive step towards transcendence. The residence of the gods becomes more neatly distinct from that of humans/men. Retired/regrouped atop the mysterious mountains/heights of Olympus or in the depths of the earth, they personally intervene in human affairs only intermittently. But it is solely with [the advent of] Christianity that God definitely leaves space; his kingdom is no more of this world; the dissociation between nature and the divine is so complete that it degenerates into antagonism. At the same time, the notion of divinity becomes more general and more abstract, because it is shaped not by sensations, as in principle, but by ideas. The human god is necessarily less understanding/comprehension than the gods of cities or clans.	[Virtually the same as 1893 edition] *V. Réville, *Religions des peuples non civilizés*, I, 67 et suiv.; II, 230 et suiv.

correspond with *naturism* where according to Durkheim, "all natural beings who are susceptible of influencing social life ... are deified." In comparison, although the text in the 1902 edition shares the lead-in narrative (i.e. *this* tree *this* bird), the altered stage-model jumps from *this* single animal to *this species*. So, in the later edited version, community members no longer have identical relationships with single, precise natural beings but with *all* "animals or plants of the *species* that serve as the *clan's totem* ..." (1902: 272–273, emphasis added).

Durkheim's 1893 stage model connects him to Albert Réville whose ideas he had entertained in his 1886 review of Spencer's ghost theory. Réville proposed that religion began with "a cult of nature" and he coined the term *naturism*. He also considered *naturism* to be "a religion which has for direct object phenomena, bodies, or forces of nature held as animated and conscious" (1883:vl : 67). Réville also set the boundaries of *animism* by calling it a religion that *evolved out of naturism*, noting that the animistic stage "is only possible when the revered spirits are conceived independently from natural objects, living in no necessary relation with them." He denoted, however, that during the animistic phrase spirits do tend to "meddle with events that relate to the fate of humans" (pp. 67, 228). Indeed, Réville's contribution to Durkheim's 1893 stage model is unmistakable—from Durkheim's adoption of *naturism* as root religion to his second stage or the "reign of *animism*" where the revered spirits are "constantly mingling with our lives."[14]

Why bother substituting the "cult of nature" with the "cult of totemism?" And, why keep the substance of the corresponding text given that it was now at odds with his revised stage model? One explanation is that Durkheim faced a Catch-22 situation: on the one hand, by 1897 he had already embraced totemism as root religion in his publications so he probably felt compelled to include it in the 1902 second edition. On the other hand, he

---

14 In my research, I found that only W. Watts Miller (2013: 234) realized (and certainly before I did) that Durkheim had replaced *naturism* in the first edition of *The Division of Labor* with *totemism* as foundational religion in the second edition. To my knowledge, all later editions whether in French, English, Danish etc. relied on the 1902 edition because the 1893 edition had a limited run; Durkheim said he had not altered the original text; and because the second edition included his famous Preface on occupational groups. I should add that although Durkheim endorsed Réville's origin thesis on the deification of nature and its transition to animism, and adopted Réville's definitions for each one, he did not follow him on the content of religion. For example, Réville like most religious scholars, argued that "non-civilized" peoples are not concerned with mortality (p. 251). Durkheim, of course, claimed from the start that all religions have a moral component.

wanted to keep his word that he had not altered the original 1893 text version. So he deleted naturism, penciled in totemism and otherwise minimized textual changes. The point here is that before his 1895 revelation, Durkheim had endorsed naturism (and not totemism) as the elementary religion. And, this gives us license to reset the timeline for his adoption of totemism, with significant implications, as we will see in the next chapter.

Commentary: Durkheim's Pre-1895 Views On Religion

Durkheim's early reviews offer crucial insights into his early thoughts on religion. From the outset, he rejected the reigning nineteenth-century theory that religion originated in dreams, notions of double-selves, the human imagination, or any facet of psychological phenomena. He welcomed Guyau's collective approach to religion but faulted him for ignoring the obligatory nature of religion and for not recognizing that all religions rest on moral premises. He agreed with Guyau that religion is the product of a social matrix of some sort but played down the importance of beliefs by proposing instead that "habits" and "pre-existing sentiments" are at the vanguard of religion. He dismissed Spencer and Guyau's notion of a future without religion and placed a priority on penetrating the collective *représentation*s of religion to unmask its hidden reality.

In *The Division of Labor* (1893) Durkheim seemed confident that with the crystalization of organic solidarity, the problem of how integration could be sustained in industrial societies would slowly resolve itself. To illustrate how this transformation occurs, he started with an amorphous horde (or single clan) and its transformation into a clan-based society (two or more hordes) where all facets of social phenomena are infused with a religious character. But with increases in volume and "dynamic density," Darwinian-like forces are set into play for a proliferating division of labor (a kind of social speciation). He also demonstrated how the personal conscience slowly gets emancipated from the common conscience by way of ecclesiastical changes in the conception of divinity, using *naturism* as its elementary form.

Why *naturism*? Based on Durkheim's early publications on religion, Réville's *naturism* was his early favorite over Spencer's ghost theory of *animism* (see Jones 2005 for a discussion). A possible reason for this early preference is that nature cults are at least derived from tangible, sensory-derived objects—unlike the illusionary and ephemeral spirit world of ancestor worship. As the primal religion, it is also consistent with his original rendition of a collective conscience so concrete that everyone has identical impressions of the same phenomena. And, it fits nicely with his portrayal of a transitioning god-head when selection pressures favored the restoration of individualism in a society.[15]

Did the origin of religion always interest Durkheim? It is relevant that his early reviews deal with this topic although in Spencer's review he wanted to limit the study of religion to social and regularity functions. By Guyau's review, he had softened this hardline position by speculating that sociality is the catalyst for religion, that practices (or habits) are subsequent to beliefs, that "pre-existing sentiments" or emotions are a causal factor for religious beliefs, and in the *Division of Labor* that Réville's *naturism* is the first religion. He even argued how important it was to discard the "superficial shell" cloaking religion so as to penetrate the underlying emotions, but shows no interest in tackling the problem himself. Yet, Durkheim does convey an air of attentiveness to matters religious. So scholars including Alexander (1982), Pickering (1984), Bellah (1959), and Thompson (2002) who insisted upon Durkheim's early interest in religion were not mistaken as the following underscores:

- Religion is always a collective enterprise rather than a psychological enterprise (1886).
- Religion is derived from human association in a social environment with sociability as its primary cause (1886, 1888).
- Religion is always embedded in the practical reality of collective concerns (1887).
- Religion is always connected with a moral ideal of obligatory constraints, rights and duties (1887).
- Religion is strongly rooted in a moral life of habits, rites, and a shared ideology (1887).
- The social structure of a society is the source of the power and influence of religious beliefs and not the reverse (1893).
- *Naturism* is the primal religion (1893).

I will venture two reasons for Durkheim's early reluctance to study religion. First, he had needed to make sense of religion; it baffled him, writing in *The Division of Labor* ([1893]1984: 118) of a lack of "any scientific conception of what religion is" or why humans would yield to an authority

---

15 Durkheim knew of totems, however, as he used totemism as an example in his 1893 "Preface" (removed in the second edition), of how moral rules vary depending on societal types (Durkheim [1893]1933: 432). Totemism is also discussed in his cited references, notably in the works of Lorimer Fison and A.W. Howitt ([1880]1991); Robertson Smith (1885) and Herbert Spencer's *Principles of Sociology* ([1876]1898: 329ff and see page 353).

that is "a figment of their imagination." Where does the force get its power, he asked? Second, he had published a letter stating "it was only in 1895 that I had a *clear view* of the capital role played by religion in social life. It was in that year that, *for the first time I found a means of tackling sociologically the study of religion* ([1907]1982: 259 emphasis added). If we assume that Robertson Smith played the pivotal role in Durkheim's *révélation*, what prophetic insights did he convey into the birth of the gods?

Appendix

French Text from the 1893 Edition of *The Division of Labor in Society*

Le fait qui, peut-être, manifeste le mieux cette tendance croissante de la conscience commune, c'est la transcendance parallèle du plus essentiel de ses éléments, je veux parler de la notion de la divinité. A l'origine, les dieux ne sont pas distincts de l'univers; mais tout les êtres naturels qui sont susceptibles d'avoir quelque influence sur la vie sociale, d'éveiller les craintes ou les espérances collectives, sont divinisés. Ce caractère ne leur est d'ailleurs pas communiqué du dehors, il leur est intrinsèque. Ils ne sont pas divins parce qu'un dieu habite en eux; ils sont eux-mêmes les dieux. C'est à ce stade de l'évolution religieuse que l'on a donné le nom de *naturisme*. Mais peu à peu les dieux se détachent des choses avec lesquelles ils se confondaient. Ils deviennent des *esprits* qui, s'ils résident ici ou là de préférence, existent cependant en dehors des formes concrètes sous lesquelles ils s'incarnent; c'est le règne de l'*animisme*.* Peu importe qu'ils soient multiples ou qu'ils aient été, comme chez les Juifs, ramenés à l'unité; dans un cas comme dans l'autre, le degré d'immanence est le même. S'ils sont en partie séparés des choses, ils sont toujours dans l'espace. Ils restent donc tout près de nous, constamment mêlés à notre vie. Le polythéisme greco-latin, qui est une forme plus élevée et mieux organisée de l'animisme, marque un progrès nouveau dans le sens de la transcendance. La résidence des dieux devient plus nettement distincte de celle des hommes. Retirés sur les hauteurs mystérieuses de l'Olympe ou dans les profondeurs de la terre, ils n'interviennent plus personnellement dans les affaires humaines que d'une manière assez intermittente. Enfin, avec le christianisme, Dieu sort définitivement de l'espace; son royaume n'est plus de ce monde; la dissociation entre la nature et le divin est même si complète qu'elle dégénère en antagonisme. En même temps, la notion de la divinité devient plus générale et plus abstraite, car elle est formée non de sensations, comme

---

*V. Réville, *Religions des peuples non civilisés*, I, 67 et suiv.; II, 230 et suiv.

dans le principe, mais d'idées. Le Dieu de l'humanité a nécessairement moins de compréhension que ceux de la cité ou du clan.

French Text from the 1902 Edition of the Division of Labor

Le fait qui, peut-être, manifeste le mieux cette tendance croissante de la conscience commune, c'est la transcendance parallèle du plus essentiel de ses éléments, je veux parler de la notion de la divinité. A l'origine, les dieux ne sont pas distincts de l'univers, ou plutôt il n'y a pas de dieux, mais seulement des êtres sacrés, sans que le caractère sacré dont ils sont revêtus soit rapporté à quelque entité extérieure, comme à sa source. Les animaux ou les végétaux de l'espèce qui sert de totem au clan sont l'objet du culte; mais ce n'est pas qu'un principe *sui generis* vienne leur communiquer du dehors leur nature divine. Cette nature leur est intrinsèque; ils sont divins par eux-mêmes. Mais peu à peu, les forces religieuses se détachent des choses dont elles n'étaient d'abord que des attributs, et elles s'hypostasient. Ainsi se forme la notion d'esprits ou de dieux qui, tout en résidant de préférence ici ou là, existent cependant en dehors des objets particuliers auxquels ils sont plus spécialement rattaché.* Par cela même, ils ont quelque chose de moins concret. Toutefois, qu'ils soient multiples ou qu'ils aient été ramenés à une certaine unité, ils sont encore immanents au monde. Séparés, en partie, des choses, ils sont toujours dans l'espace. Ils restent donc tout près de nous, constamment mêlés à notre vie. Le polythéisme gréco-latin, qui est une forme plus élevée et mieux organisée de l'animisme, marque un progrès nouveau dans le sens de la transcendance. La résidence des dieux devient plus nettement distincte de celle des hommes. Retirés sur les hauteurs mystérieuses de l'Olympe ou dans les profondeurs de la terre, ils n'interviennent plus personnellement dans les affaires humaines que d'une manière assez intermittente. Mais c'est seulement avec le christianisme que Dieu sort définitivement de l'espace; son royaume n'est plus de ce monde; la dissociation entre la nature et le divin est même si complète qu'elle dégénère en antagonisme. En même temps, la notion de la divinité devient plus générale et plus abstraite, car elle est formée non de sensations, comme dans le principe, mais d'idées. Le Dieu de l'humanité a nécessairement moins de compréhension que ceux de la cité ou du clan.

---

*V. Réville, *Religions des peuples non civilizés*, I, 67 et suiv.; II, 230 et suiv.

6
W. Robertson Smith and the Scottish School of Totemism[1]

> So long as Christianity is looked upon as a purely individual thing, a converse of me by myself, and of you by yourself . . . it is really not possible to make out for theology a sphere of genuine practical importance . . . But the moment we begin to contemplate Christianity as a social thing, as organized into a Church . . .
>
> Robertson Smith ([1875]1912: 325)

When Robertson Smith died in 1894, the editor of *Nature* (1894: 557) characterized Smith as someone "with remarkable powers . . . who possessed not only one of the most learned but also one of the most brilliant and striking minds . . . an almost unique personality." Smith edited the famous ninth edition of the *Encyclopaedia Britannica;* Harvard offered him the Chair of Hebrew—twice; he held the Chair of Arabic at Cambridge and Sir James Frazer dedicated *The Golden Bough* to Smith (1890) calling him "the greatest man he had ever known." What qualities made Robertson Smith so special during his lifetime? William Wentworth (1976: 103) offered this explanation:

> There is a species of man whose writings ignite a spark or flame in others. Usually such persons have somehow managed to loosen only a few traditional restraints from their thinking, but, by so doing, they . . . combine elements from the familiar world in some unexpected fashion. Such writing confronts us with a simultaneously shattering and integrative image, freshly constituted by a disciplined imagination. These are the people marked by the history of ideas as having said what needed saying next. In his time and place, William Robertson Smith (1846–1894) was such a person.

---

1 This chapter contains sections adapted from Maryanski, 2014.

What did Smith do to ignite Durkheim's passion for religion? To get a sense for the gravitas of Robertson Smith, let me provide some background on his early life and especially his close relations with John McLennan and James Frazer.

The Great Heresy Hunt[2]

Robertson Smith was born in Aberdeenshire, Scotland in 1846, the oldest son and second of seven children. The Smith children were home schooled and reared in accordance with the conservative doctrine of the Free Church of Scotland but their well educated parents also provided daily instruction in the arts, classic languages (Smith was reading Hebrew at age 6), history and the sciences with unbridled freedom to take up any intellectual idea, belief, or interest that caught their fancy. This marriage of conservative religion and a rich intellectual environment equipped Smith with high principles, supreme self-confidence, a love of learning, rugged individualism, a scientific spirit, and a "cast your fate to the wind" approach to life. So, when Smith left home in 1861 to attend Aberdeen University, he carried along the unshakable belief that the search for truth was *the* ultimate objective in life, and that all ideas, whether secular or religious, were open to examination—sentiments that would land him in serious trouble with the Free Church of Scotland (Black and Chrystal 1912a: 1–8 and Beidelman 1974, 3ff).

Robertson Smith was short at 5' 4 with rounded shoulders and a graceful, well-proportioned body. He was rather handsome with an oval-shaped face, high forehead, fine brown eyes, brown hair and a short well-trimmed beard. He spoke with a refined, thick Scottish accent. At Aberdeen University, Smith was a brilliant undergraduate with natural abilities in languages, mathematics, and the sciences. Inspired by a Hebrew professor who advocated that the Bible should be open to free inquiry, Smith traveled to Europe to master "biblical criticism," a method that made it possible to study the Scriptures from a scientific viewpoint. In 1869–1870, Smith was ordained a minister and appointed Chair of Hebrew and Old Testament at the Free Church Divinity College at the University of Aberdeen. Given his gregarious nature and open academic style, Smith was a popular lecturer and spent the next five years speaking to private and public audiences on the need for a more accurate interpretation of biblical literature (Beidelman

---

2 This section on Robertson Smith's background is drawn from Smith's biographers Black and Chrystal 1912a; 1912b; Beidelman 1974; Jones 2002; Maier 2009.

1974: 7). He also began publishing at a fast and furious pace, becoming widely known in England, America, and continental Europe for his expertise on biblical and Semitic Literature. In 1875, he was invited to serve on a committee to revise the authorized Bible, a great honor for a 29-year-old Professor of Theology (Beidelman 1974: 13).

His troubles began to mount, however, when his "radical" views raised the eyebrows of Church conservatives who accused him of making sacrilegious statements that the Old Testament had discrepant narratives, inconsistent dates, used "dummy" names to fill in lineages and, more generally, that biblical writers took liberties by using bogus entries that conflicted with known historical facts. Smith responded that the Bible was written by human hands, not God's hands, and his intent was simply to examine the Scriptures in the context of the times and human experiences.

While Smith was supported by progressive biblical scholars, traditionalists considered him a threatening mischief-maker and had him suspended in 1877 from his college (Beidelman 1974: 3ff).[3] Years passed and as Smith waited, he continued to deliver his "radical" lectures to large and enthusiastic public audiences. He also traveled widely, especially to the Arabian Peninsula where he embraced the local cultures by adopting their dress codes and lifeway by traveling about on a camel.[4] In a conciliatory gesture, his church offered him an olive branch if he simply retracted his damaging Biblical articles, but Smith said no, sealing his fate. In what is called the "great heresy case," formal charges were filed in the ecclesiastical courts, Smith went to trial, found guilty as charged, and was formally removed from his Professorship at Aberdeen College in May of 1881. Though unemployed and with little money, Smith was now a celebrated figure both nationally and internationally (helped along by press coverage of his heresy trial), and in a short time was offered an editorial post in Edinburgh with the *Encyclopaedia Britannica*. In 1883, he was invited to Cambridge University

---

3 Smith's progressive biblical criticism closely followed the work of two-well known champions of the higher criticism, Julius Wellhausen (in Germany) and Abraham Kuenen (in Holland).

4 Robertson Smith was talented in many respects. As Beidelman (1974: 7) wrote, Smith had an "outstanding intelligence, amazing powers of memory, a highly orderly set of working habits, and a deep, driving sense of obligation to realize his full potentiality. This last was not out of any mere sense of self-advancement but out of a belief that this was both an obligation to his parents, who held such high hopes for him, and his obligation to God to develop whatever gifts he had been given . . ." He was also a language polyglot, as he easily mastered Hebrew, French, Dutch, German and Arabic.

and was later appointed Lord Almoner Reader in Arabic and assumed the Chair of Arabic in 1889. From then on, he lived comfortably in his rooms at Christ's College until his early death in 1894 at the age of 48.[5]

Whether Durkheim knew of Smith's heresy trial is doubtful as he was then closeted away in the *École Normale*, but he surely knew of it later as it was the last successful "heresy hunt" in the British Isles. Smith was greatly saddened by his dismissal although his nearly five years of suspension (with pay) gave him the leisure time to explore an ever-widening range of interests. One wonders where his career would have gone *without* the infamous libel suit. Smith's celebrated writings on the Old Testament are impressive, but it was his groundbreaking study of ancient Semite religion that would fire the imagination of a generation of social scientists, including Emile Durkheim.

John Mclennan's Legacy to Robertson Smith

A major figure in Smith's life was John McLennan, one of the pioneer kinship theorists. McLennan (1827–1881) was passionate about uncovering sociological laws and in 1865 wrote *Primitive Marriage*, a work that dealt with the origin of society, primitive hordes, female descent, and the rules of endogamy and exogamy (see Chapter 1). In 1869–1870, McLennan published "The Worship of Plants and Animals" in *The Fortnightly Review*, a provocative essay that first brought totemism into the public eye, touching off decades of wild speculations over totem beliefs and rituals. After gathering evidence around the globe, McLennan concluded that totemism may be a human universal and that even the classical nations of antiquity likely passed through a totemic stage.

In 1869, Smith met McLennan when a small circle of Edinburgh intellectuals created a "talking club," or what became known as The *Edinburgh Evening Club*. The two Scotsmen became close friends, and by 1880 Smith was so captivated by McLennan's totem hypothesis that he wrote "Animal Worship and Animal Tribes Among the Arabs and in the Old Testament," claiming that his own research was "remarkably confirmatory" of McLennan's theories (1880: 78). When McLennan died suddenly in 1881 at age 54 (and around the time Smith was fired from his Professorship in Aberdeen), Smith was devastated both personally and professionally. Determined to keep his friend's ideas in the public eye (for

---

5 Smith was formally charged on his biblical articles published in the *Encyclopaedia Britannica*.

McLennan never held an academic post), Smith imported McLennan's theories into his own new research on ancient Semitic society, bringing together a synthesis of anthropology, theology, and sociology. His career then gained momentum but in another direction. Thus, when Durkheim read *Kinship and Marriage in Early Arabia* (1885) and *Lectures on the Religion of the Semites* (1889), they were not about prophets, ancient Israel or the writings of the Old Testament but on pagan beliefs, practices, and the primal institutions of the ancient Semites.

Robertson Smith's Legacy to Sir James Frazer[6]

After moving to Cambridge in 1883, Smith met James Frazer (1854–1941) a young Scotsman who Smith called "one of the Scotch contingent" (Ackerman 1987: 60). Frazer was of medium height, with striking sapphire eyes and a neatly trimmed beard. His early academic training was at Glasgow University; he was then invited to Trinity College in 1873 and given a fellowship that was eventually awarded to him for life. After reading Edward Tylor's *Primitive Culture* (see Chapter 1), Frazer became fascinated with folklore and religion. Proficient in ancient Greek, Latin, German, Spanish, Italian, French, and Dutch and with a permanent research grant that allowed him to forgo teaching, Frazer became a library workaholic, spending twelve to fifteen hours a day on his research and writing. With wide-ranging interests, Frazer published a massive amount, becoming a world-renowned scholar and receiving many honors including a knighthood in 1914. He is best known for *The Golden Bough*,[7] a classic anthropological opus devoted to aboriginal beliefs and practices. If not for Smith, Frazer said, "my interest in the subject [anthropology] might have remained purely passive and inert" (quoted in Kardiner and Preble 1961: 82).

The two Scotsmen became acquainted when Smith simply sat down next to Frazer at Trinity College and began talking to him. Frazer recalled that

> one subject of our talk that evening was the Arabs in Spain and that, though I knew next to nothing about the subject, I attempted some sort of argument with him, but was immediately beaten down, in the kindest and gentlest way, by his learning, and yielded myself captive

---

6 Frazer's biography here is drawn from Ackerman 1987 and Kardiner and Preble 1961.

7 *The Golden Bough* was published in two volumes (800 pages) in 1890; a second edition of three volumes was published in 1900; and a third edition of twelve volumes was published between 1911–1915, along with a supplemental thirteenth volume in 1937.

at once. I never afterwards ... attempted to dispute the mastership which he thenceforward exercised over me by his extraordinary union of genius and learning.

(quoted in Ackerman 1987: 60)

Smith was then editor of the ninth edition of the *Encyclopaedia Britannica* and learning of Frazer's interest in anthropology and religion invited him to write two articles for the *Encyclopaedia*—one on "Taboo" and the other on "Totemism." Frazer accepted, and in 1887 sent out a worldwide questionnaire asking missionaries, traders, fieldworkers, administrators, in fact anyone acquainted with native populations to provide whatever knowledge they had of aboriginal totems and taboos. After completing his survey, Frazer concluded that totemism was common in Australia and the Americas with evidence in Africa, Ancient Egypt, Siberia, Polynesia, Samoa, Melanesia, Fiji, the Solomon Islands, and China. And, he thought it likely that it had once existed among the Greeks, Romans, and Semites. Based on his questionnaire, Frazer wrote an abridged version of "Totemism" for the *Encyclopaedia* in 1885 (with Robertson Smith looking over his shoulder), and an unabridged version in 1887 that was published as a small book.[8]

In *Totemism* (1887) Frazer began by defining a totem and then described all its known characteristics:

A TOTEM is a class of material objects which a savage regards with superstitious respect, believing that their exists between him and every member of the class an intimate and altogether special relation.

(1887: 1)

- Totems are always a class of objects, usually an animal or plant species
- There are three kinds of totems, a clan totem (for the entire clan), a sex totem (for each sex), and an individual totem

---

[8] Smith's enthusiasm for totemism is evident in his note to the publishers of the *Encyclopaedia*: "I hope that Messrs. Black clearly understand that Totemism is a subject of growing importance, daily mentioned in magazines and papers, but of which there is no good account anywhere—precisely one of those cases where we have an opportunity of being ahead of everyone and getting some reputation. There is no article in the volume for which I am more solicitous. I have taken much personal pains with it, guiding Frazer carefully in his treatment ...We must make room for it, whatever else goes" (cited in Beidelman 1974: 24). Smith also encouraged his publishers to take Frazer's unabridged monograph on *Totemism*.

- The clan totem is paramount because it is shared by those who believe it signifies an ancestor or something else held in common
- Totems in the earliest societies are fused into a religious system and a social system. Over time, the religious and the social side split apart with either system preserved while the other disappears. How the two originally came to be associated is unknown
- Totems are often regarded as sacred
- Eating your totem is usually taboo, with examples from all over the world
- Totem bonds are stronger than the bond of family or blood. Pure totemism is composed of a fraternity of members with an egalitarian ethic
- Totem members practice a rule of exogamy
- Most totemic tribes in Australia and North America are biased towards female descent with changes from female descent to male descent and never the reverse.

Frazer also proposed that a clan totem is likely to subdivide when it reaches a maximal number, morphing into a number of related clans or into a totem phratry (a grouping of clans). As a social system, totemism then undergoes a slow decay and gradually gets replaced by local groups with names taken from districts or important individuals. As a religious system, totemism is also likely to progress from a worship of animal gods to a more anthropomorphic form with animal characteristics, and finally to superior deities with a human form and a higher form of faith. Frazer speculated that all totems are likely to have originated in the same way (i.e. Tylor's psychic unity principle (see Chapter 1); so if you uncover its origins in one locality you are able to generalize its origins to other localities.

Frazer's *Encyclopaedia* entry and small book on *Totemism* met with rave reviews, influencing a generation of totem-minded scholars. But Frazer would later reject his early account of totemism, changing his views repeatedly over the next twenty years on what totemism meant and is. Indeed, to Durkheim's chagrin, Frazer would publish three different theories of totemism, creating a vexatious problem for Durkheim who needed Frazer original account of totemism to support his totemic theory. I should note that Frazer was a quiet, well-meaning, affable scholar and an improbable candidate to play the role of Durkheim's adversary (see Ackerman 1987), but once their clashing views became a bone of contention, Frazer would become Durkheim's *nemesis*. But, before this impeding drama is played out in the chapters to follow, we need to turn to Robertson Smith's role in shaping Émile Durkheim's religious sociology.

Totems and Semites

As an Old Testament scholar, Robertson Smith focused on Hebrew language, culture, and the Scriptures. But, unlike fundamentalists who saw the Bible as an infallible sacred book, or apologetics who tried to explain away incongruities, Smith sought a true historical interpretation by collecting and synthesizing facts, anchoring them in a scientific domain, and, otherwise, treating the Hebraic Scriptures like any other ancient manuscript or document.[9] To this end, he used the comparative method of textual criticism by collating and comparing versions of the same or alternative Biblical manuscripts, noting revisions, inconsistencies, and stylistic traits in an effort to reconstruct linkages and determine ancestor to descendent relationships. To effectively use this methodology for the Hebrew Scriptures, which are a bounded collection of narratives, stories, poetry, drama, prophetic oracles and the like, Smith mastered Hebrew and Aramaic so he could decipher what the words meant originally; he also relied upon ancient secular documents, archaeological records, and other sources to place the Scriptures in their social and cultural milieu (as they were written over nearly a millennium) to glean insights into the background and personality of their many authors. By treating the Old Testament as a unified whole, Smith sought to uncover underlying themes and hidden messages, the historical accuracy of chronicles, myths and stories, and even the logic and motives of its many authors. He also provisionally compared the Old Testament religion with ancient neighboring religions by isolating out shared traits from characteristics that he initially believed were unique to the Hebrew Prophets. It became evident to Smith that the Old Testament had a strong concurrence with other Semitic religions: as Smith ([1882]2002: 57–58) concluded:

> In every way ... the attempt to reduce the difference between the early religion of the Hebrews and that of other nations to broad

---

[9] Smith was a prodigious scholar who published on all aspects of the Old Testament, including the beauty of Hebrew poetry. He also wrote articles and essays dealing with math, philosophy, electricity, calculus and even the human personality (See Smith 1912a, 1912b, 1912c, 1912d). His scholarship is still appreciated as evidenced by a special interdisciplinary conference held in 1994 at the University of Aberdeen to honor the legacy of the brilliant Robertson Smith (see Johnstone 1995; Riviére 1995; and Bediako 1995, 1999). Let me add that even the nineteenth-century educated public found his ideas exciting, in part because as Smith put it, "historical research can always be made intelligible to thinking people, when it is set forth with orderly method and in plain language" (1889: vii).

tangible peculiarities that can be grasped with the hand breaks down. It was Jehovah Himself who was different from Chemosh, Moloch, or Melkarth; and to those who did not *know Jehov*a*h*, to use the expressive prophetic phrase, there was no insurmountable barrier between His worship and heathenism . . . [N]othing is more certain that neither Moses nor Samuel gave Israel any new system of metaphysical theology. In matters of thought as well as of practice, the new revelation of Jehovah's power and love . . . involved no sudden and absolute break with the past, or with the traditions of the past common to Israel with kindred nations (emphasis in original).[10]

If Hebrew traits resembled other Semitic nations, he reasoned, they were likely derived from the same source. So, armed with strong scientific principles, an unshakable belief in seeking the truth no matter the consequences, and equipped with McLennan's theories, Robertson Smith took the adventurous leap of tracing the Hebrew religion back to its ancient heathen roots.

Kinship and Totems in Early Arabia

Smith embarked on his gallant adventure by starting with Arab prehistory because they had remained a tribal people much longer than other Semitic nations. His plan was to initially build a "self-contained" argument distilled from the wealth of Arabian ancient books and documents and his own visits to Arab sites. After completing his analysis, he wrote *Kinship and Marriage in Early Arabia* ([1885]1907) where he proposed that Arabian families were originally organized around matrilineal descent, challenging the longstanding belief that they were always organized around patrilineal descent. And, this shift in descent systems altered the course of Arab history, especially the genesis of Islam (Durkheim later used a similar logic to explain deviations in Central Australian totemism).[11] It was time, he said, to reject the notion that Arab society was always patrilineal because it was simply a fabrication invented by early genealogists.

---

10 *The Prophets of Israel* (1882) laid the groundwork for Smith's *Religion of the Semites*. Durkheim's 1895 religious course supposedly included the history of religion, so it may well have included this text.

11 Smith acknowledged his deep gratitude to John McLennan in the Preface to *Kinship and Marriage* (1885). He wanted readers to know and appreciate the extent to which he

Smith also devoted a chapter to the *social* side of totemism. Finding traces of totemic survivals in early Arabian society (e.g. linguistic evidence, and inferred totem markings), he connected female kinship and exogamy to totemism (Durkheim proposed a similar association in his 1898 essay, "La Prohibition de L'inceste et ses origines"). Then, guided by McLennan's logic, Smith claimed that ancient Arab groups had once been divided into a number of stock groups, each with a totem named after a plant or animal species. The mixing of totems resulted from wives joining their husbands' local group (given that exogamy forced males to marry out of their local group) and wives kept their own totemic affiliation. So, during the reign of female descent, children inherited their mother's totem. This meant that totem members could live either in propinquity—"a local unity" or scattered but linked by a common totemic identity. Smith argued that totemism also had a *religious* side, with the totem possessing a sacred character that equates to the notion of a god (p.218). In *Kinship and Marriage*, Smith extolled the virtues of McLennan's totem hypothesis because "it does justice to the intimate relation between religion and the fundamental structure of society . . ." (pp. 258–259).

Semitic Religion and Totemism

Subject and Purpose of Study

In 1887, Professor Roberson Smith *now* of Cambridge was invited to deliver a series of public lectures at Aberdeen University. He gladly accepted because, after all, it was his Old University (the very one that fired him in 1881 from his professorship). Speaking to a mostly Christian audience, Smith stressed how important the Hebrew Bible was for understanding Christianity, adding that the Scriptures cannot be understood unless they are *compared* with religions of other ancient nations that lived near the Israelites or Hebrews. He also extolled how the scientific procedures of Biblical criticism had confirmed or refuted the accuracy of dates and chronologies in the Scriptures so the time had come to follow the "growth of the Old Testament religion."[12] Smith delivered his lectures in December

---

had relied on McLennan's theories of kinship, exogamy, society, and totemism in his analysis (see McLennan's *Primitive Marriage: An Inquiry Into the Origins of the Form of Capture in Marriage Ceremonies* ([1865]1970).

12 Smith saw himself as following John Spencer, a seventeenth-century Cambridge theologian who tried to trace connections between the ancient Hebrews and other Semite populations. Spencer lacked source materials but Smith, who always went out of his way

of 1888 and in March of 1889; he published the first series (after adding two chapters) in 1889 under the title: *Lectures on the Religion of the Semites: First Series, The Fundamental Institutions*.[13]

Durkheim cited *Religion of the Semites* frequently in *Elementary Forms*. What did he find so extraordinary about ancient Semitic religion? The book captures Smith's ingenious talent for imparting complex ideas in an informal way as the text is composed of eleven engaging lectures on the ancient Semites, a large Middle Eastern population of pastoral nomads who once lived in parts of Africa and the Arabian Peninsula. Though the Arabs and Jews are widely known for sharing a Semitic heritage, they also shared an ancestral legacy with the Phoenicians, the Babylonians, Aramaeans, and the Assyrians. Ancient Semites are important to religious scholars because all three great Western faiths—Judaism, Christianity and Islam—originated in ancient Semitic culture; and all three religions, of course, recognize the Old Testament as a sacred text.

Smith labeled Judaism, Christianity, and Islam "positive religions." He meant that unlike heathen religions that slowly develop by unknown forces, positive religions can be traced to known religious figures. Yet, their connection to heathen religions was never fully severed. As Smith (1889: 1–2) related:

> Behind these positive religions lies the old . . . religious tradition . . . The positive Semitic religions had to establish themselves on ground already occupied by these older beliefs and usages . . . they had at every point to reckon with them and take up a definite attitude towards them. No positive religion that has moved men has been able to start with a *tabula rasa*, and express itself as if religion were beginning for the first time; in form, if not in substance, the new system must be in contact all along the line with the older ideas and practices . . .

---

to acknowledge his sources, credits Spencer with laying down the building blocks for comparative religion. See John Spencer's *De Legibus Hebraeorum, Ritualibus et earum Rationibus libri tres* (*Three Books on the Laws of the Hebrews, Their Rituals and Doctrines*) Cambridge 1685. Smith also acknowledged Abraham Kuenen and Julius Wellhausen who, he said, carried out "this inquiry to a point where nothing of vital importance for the historical study of the Old Testament religion still remains uncertain . . ."(1889:vii.). He refers here to the historical order of the Old Testament documents and especially the Pentateuch documents.

13 Smith's second and third series of lectures were discovered in handwritten form in the Cambridge University library by John Day in 1991. Smith delivered these lectures but died shortly afterward (see Smith 1995).

Method of Inquiry

How do you reconstruct a religion lost in antiquity? In the late nineteenth century, social theorists recreated prehistoric forms by relying on cross-cultural correlations, a comparative method that often lead to spurious correlations by ripping traits out of context (and meaning) or to faulty reconstructions by arbitrarily generalizing traits from "primitive" to contemporary societies.[14] Robertson Smith by contrast had always relied on biblical writings or ancient secular documents. How did he plan to recreate a religion without a written record? One would assume he would adopt the popular cross-cultural correlational method discussed above, and he did for a few traits, but, otherwise, he did a revolutionary thing: he used the tried-and-true tools of a biblical critic to reconstruct ancient Semitic life ways.

Let me outline his procedure (as Durkheim certainly took note). Smith used a methodology common to historical linguistics, and textual criticism. Like any comparative method, it searches for resemblances—but not by *analogy*. Instead, this procedure is designed to isolate out entities *only* on the basis of ancestor-descendant relationships or by *homology*. In textual criticism, for example, alternate forms of handwritten manuscripts (e.g. the Scriptures) are compared and used to recreate patterns or to reconstruct the earliest or original manuscript from which all others were derived. In historical linguistics, it is used to assemble the shared cognates of known language groups to recreate the original mother tongue. So, this methodology can recreate any entity of any sort not by analogy but by identifying cognates among *homologous* entities.[15]

So, Smith began by isolating out Semite populations that shared an ancestral culture, identifying them by known homelands and such jointly held traits as language cognates and cultural features. He also relied on sources such as archaeological sites, ethnographies, historical chronicles, monuments, inscriptions, ancient secular documents, and, of course, the Scriptures to recreate *the heathen religion that stood behind the Hebrew Bible*. He planned to start with totemism as elementary religion and then chart its evolutionary transformations over time.

---

14 Today, no one questions the existence of socio-cultural development and change over time. At issue are the sequences and mechanisms for change (See Edward Tylor in Chapter 1). And, the correlational comparative method is still used today but far, far, more cautiously.

15 The procedures of textual criticism reach back to the sixteenth century, but as a defined scientific method it is usually associated with the father of modern textual criticism, Karl Lachmann who laid down the rules and applied them in 1850. See Platnick and Cameron 1977 for a discussion, and Maas 1958.

The Reconstruction of Ancient Semitic Society

Robertson Smith knew his reconstruction was problematic because aside from his plentiful Arabic materials, only fragmentary materials existed for other ancient Semitics. He also had to bridge a huge time gap between the early heathen religions and the Scriptures. Yet, the plucky Smith went forward anyway, telling his audience that despite his fragmentary sources, they were at least sufficient enough "to furnish a tolerably accurate view" of features common to the Semitic field (1889: 16). Indeed, who could resist this welcoming invitation:

> ... I invite you to take an interest in the ancient religion of the Semitic peoples; the matter is not one of mere antiquarian curiosity, but has a direct and important bearing on the great problem of the origins of the spiritual religion of the Bible ... Nations sprung from a common stock will have a common inheritance of traditional belief and usage in things sacred as well as profane, and thus the evidence that the Hebrews and their neighbours had a large common stock of religious tradition falls in with the evidence which we have from other sources ...
>
> (Smith 1889: 2, 5)

Smith went on to impart this narrative. The ancient Semitic people were nomadic food collectors wandering about within a regional homeland. They had relations with supernaturals but these entities were not single gods but natural agents that were all connected to a system of totemism. Who were these agents? "In the totem stage of society [he said] each kinship or stock of savages believes itself to be physically akin to some natural kind of animate or inanimate things, most generally to some kind of animal" (1889: 117–119). Smith couldn't say whether later nature-gods (or naturism) evolved directly out of totemism but, "there can be no reasonable doubt that it is evolved out of ideas or usages which also find their expression in totemism, and therefore must go back to the most primitive stage of savage society" (p. 118).

An essential feature of ancient Semitic religion was a set of fixed rites and practices. Only later did beliefs and creeds evolve to explain these visible acts. Moreover, solidarity did not rest on the attributes of things "but only the relations of things to one another, and the stated forms of intercourse between the gods and men to which these relations gave rise." Single entities were not characteristic of early supernaturals, Smith said, and it was only in later stages of religions that explicit ideas about divine beings arose—and as purely secondary phenomena. What was essential in ancient Semitic religion were fixed and "sacred institutions" (p. 88).

The cardinal rite (or fixed practice) for Smith was sacrifice. Rejecting the popular theory that sacrifice (of animals) functioned to appease the gods, Smith argued that sacrifice functioned to create solidarity between a community and a sacred being by sharing a communal meal. In Smith's eyes, the sacred rites of sacrifice originated in the formative totemic stages when female descent linked a religious community with a supernatural being. He also insisted that even in early totemism "religion was a moral force ... [as] ... the laws of society ... were also the laws of morality" (p. 53). Thus, the performance of fixed religious rites was obligatory and essential for social solidarity:

> Religion did not exist for the saving of souls but for the preservation and welfare of society, and in all that was necessary to this end every man had to take his prescribed part, or break with the domestic and political community to which he belonged.
>
> (p. 30)

The Origin of the Sacred in Taboo

Smith made a clear distinction between magic and religion. The magic/sorcery domain dealt with vague supernatural forces and often involved unrestrained, antisocial, and often illicit exercise by individuals calling on the forces of nature. The religious domain, in contrast, does not involve an arbitrary relation between individuals and supernatural forces but a stable, friendly relation between superhuman forces and a community of worshippers, a relation with "a power that has the good of the community at heart, and protects its law and moral order" (Smith 1894: 55).

Yet, why are supernaturals associated with magic perceived as arbitrary and unrestrained while supernaturals associated with religion perceived as obligatory with stability, regulation, and authority? This separation was paramount for Smith because he was certain that the "*element of order and statedness, which makes fixed institutions possible, was in fact that which made religion, as distinct from mere superstition, possible*" (Smith 1889: 88; my emphasis).

How did the separation between magic and religion originate? Smith explained that an ancient institution existed that was organized around forbidden things—or the idea of "*taboo.*" All ancient taboos are rooted in an awe of supernatural forces, but there are two types: one type corresponds to obeying rules because they are associated with threat, fear, or punishment by a capricious supernatural, whereas the second corresponds to obeying rules because they are associated with deities, ceremonial worship, and the like. In the earliest societies the boundaries were vague between each sphere of taboo, but the underlying motivations for complying were always radically different. Obeying a capricious supernatural was usually a fear of retaliation or a dread of mysterious or hostile powers, whereas the motive for obeying a consistent and compatible supernatural was an inner sense of reverence and respect (Smith 1889: 143):

> The former belong to magical superstition . . . which, being founded only on fear, acts merely as a bar to progress and an impediment to the free use of nature by human energy and industry. But the restrictions on individual licence which are due to respect for a known and friendly power allied to man . . . contain within them germinant principles of social progress and moral order . . . above all, the very association of the idea of holiness with a beneficent deity . . .
> (Smith 1889: 144)

So, for Robertson Smith (1889: 431), the idea of the holy originally arose from taboos. Yet, if all things tabooed once shared a cognitive domain how does the mind eventually set them apart? This occurs, he said, once friendly supernatural forces are linked with dwelling places that influence their actions. For once a supernatural occupies a fixed local locality, relations between this entity and the community can stabilize and strengthen (as a supernatural is in regular contact with the faithful). In turn, this physical space gradually becomes a ceremonial ground for the rites performed by the community. There are degrees of holiness and it gets extended in new ways by physical contagion and not just to holy beings but to holy ground, holy trees, holy caves, holy stones, holy times, holy plants or any object in contact with a supernatural (pp.132ff, 142–150). And for Smith, "Holy places and things are not so much reserved for the use of the god as surrounded by a network of restrictions and disabilities which forbid them to be used by men except in particular ways, and in certain cases forbid them to be used at all" (1889: 139).

In Robertson Smith's judgment, then, "The distinction between what is *holy* and what is *common* is one of the most important things in ancient religion . . ."(1889: 132 original emphasis). And, "sacred institutions" are paramount and arose with religion itself, with far-reaching consequences (p. 88). For as religion evolves, the separation of the profane from the sacred continues as ritual acts are performed at a sacred locality as an act of faith. Over time, new local sanctuaries, altars and, later, temples are constructed on holy ground for the divine presence, as well as for new gods with each generation learning to respect the supernaturals by observing the rules of holiness. Finally, Smith highlighted how religion functions to shape human cognition:

> The power of religion over life is twofold, lying partly in its association with particular precepts of conduct, to which it supplies a supernatural sanction, but mainly in its influence on the general tone and temper of men's minds, which it elevates to higher courage and purpose, and raises above a mere brutal servitude to the physical wants of the moment, by teaching men that their lives and happiness are not the mere sport of the blind forces of nature, but are watched over and cared for by a higher power.
>
> (Smith 1889: 248)

Robertson Smith had only started his Semitic project before he died at age 48, but he believed he had provided a credible reconstruction of ancient Semitic institutions. And, although he never formulated a general theory of religion, he was certain he had uncovered its first principles that totemism was the first religion, ritual preceded belief in ancient religion, that the function of sacrifice was to bring community members and supernaturals into a natural solidarity, that the holy originated in taboos, and that the separation of the sacred and profane were pivotal in the makings of a religious institution. He was also confident that the characteristics he outlined were human universals. What held for Semitic people "holds good," he felt, for all humanity in the earliest stages of religious history.

Robertson Smith's Legacy to Émile Durkheim

The School of Totemism

By the mid nineteenth century, two schools of comparative religion dominated—the anthropology school of *animism* (i.e. beliefs in souls or spirits) and the nature-myth school of *naturism* ("gods" inherent in natural forces), with both centered on the origin and laws of religious evolution. Robertson Smith belonged to neither school but a case can be made that he belonged to the Scottish School of Totemism, in company with his close friends, John McLennan (1827–1881) and Sir James Frazer (1854–1941). All three Scotsmen were instrumental in establishing totemism on a par with both the animistic and nature-myth schools of comparative religion.

Did Durkheim's 1895 *Révélation* also include McLennan or Frazer? Indirectly yes, because the bones of Smith's framework—that female descent was the first blood kinship, that exogamy and totemism were associated, and that totemism was the first religion—were all derived from Smith's adoption of McLennan's sociological theories. Smith also reaped the benefits of Frazer's *Totemism* and his research on "primitive" religions in the *Golden Bough*, adding credibility to his analysis and bridging some gaps in his reconstruction of ancient Semitic religion.

Yet, Durkheim was already familiar with McLennan's *Primitive Marriage* (1865) citing it in his published lecture on kinship and the family ([1888]1978: 216); he was also familiar with Frazer's *Totemism* (1887) long before 1895 (see Pickering, 1984: 68).[16] Durkheim also named Smith; he singled him out twice and the evidence to follow points to Smith. Still, when Durkheim paid homage to Smith and "*his school*," I believe he was alluding to *all three members* of the Scottish School of Totemism in the 1890s (Durkheim [1907]1982: 259–260, added emphasis). Now, if Durkheim's revelation came from Smith, what did he find so extraordinary in *The Religion of the Semites?*

The Template for Durkheim's Revelation

Smith knew that reconstructing early Semitic society was an uphill challenge. Yet, he had McLennan's evolutionary framework, Frazer's *Totemism* and the galley proofs of the *Golden Bough* (1889: ix). He also had the "tried and true" method of a biblical critic to isolate out the shared features of ancient Semitic nations. So, he assembled his materials and then looped all the connections together—from the relations of individuals to gods, gods to particular sites to totemic cults with animals and plants. Then, utilizing McLennan's theories, Smith connected early Semitic nations with female descent, exogamy, totemic clans, and even the incest taboo. Despite the fragmentary evidence Smith was confident that he had created a workable account of ancient Semitic society.

---

16 Robert Jones (1986, 2005) also emphasized the importance of Frazer's *Totemism* (1887) and his *Golden Bough* (1890) for Durkheim after 1895. Further, he proposed that Durkheim's revelation might have more to do with the early Frazer than Smith (1986, 2005). While I agree with Jones that Frazer played an essential role (as did McLennan), I think that Durkheim's *Révélation* stems from Smith. Frazer had no early theory of totemism and his early publications were mostly descriptive. He also approached religion with more a psychological bent with his interest in the "primitive mind" and mythology. As Ackerman, his biographer, put it, Frazer had a "penchant for psychological explanations" (see Ackerman 1987: 82 and 63ff). Frazer also had little concern for the social and moral functions of a phenomena. As Marvin Harris (1968: 205) once put it: "Frazer's scheme... remains wholly alien to a science of society." But Jones is right on the mark that Durkheim greatly benefited from Frazer's early writings.

Now, if we imagine Durkheim's reaction after reading *The Religion of the Semites*, he was surely pleased that the text reflected many of his premises. For at the time, Durkheim was nearly alone in his belief that *all* religions had moral and obligatory facets, that gods-heads were secondary phenomena, that religions were collective in nature and, that religion was grounded in real and practical things. Yet, all Durkheim had in hand was a laundry list of religious traits. And, was *naturism* the answer? He surely realized that the force in *naturism* was still illusionary despite a grounding in nature.[17]

In contrast, Robertson Smith's structural-functional approach to religion embodied a novel theory and a fresh, innovative methodology. And rather than theorizing about religion in a vacuous free-floating environment, Smith grounded his theory in a single cultural tradition and an ancestral homeland where he could reconstruct an elementary religion and then logically trace its developmental phases. Durkheim's reaction to Smith's totem hypothesis cannot be known but his interface of religion as part of an institutional matrix would please any sociologist, setting Smith apart from all other religious scholars of his time.[18]

Now if we turn to Durkheim's writings on religion right after publishing *The Division of Labor*, there is little to read. In 1894, he published "Les Règles De La Méthode Sociologique" in the *Revue philosophique* (and later as a small book in 1895). In this work his objective is to show that an understanding of social life is to be sought not in psychology but in the nature of society (see Thompson 2002: 92ff for an excellent detailed analysis). Religion is mentioned a few times but it is to address this edict and to illustrate some of the rules that he mandates. For example, social facts (*faits sociaux*) may change so much over time that they no longer correspond to the initial causes bringing them into existence. In regard to certain religious practices, he explains that "Christian religious dogma have not changed for centuries; but the role they play in our modern societies is not the same as in the Middle Ages" (p. 16).

The Rules, of course, is essentially a manual on how to carry out sociological research in an objective and methodical way. What is relevant for our purposes is that his little book mandates a scientific approach to

---

17 Durkheim wrote in *Elementary Forms* ([1912]1995: 78) that "naturism reduces religion to nothing more than an immense metaphor without objective foundation, it ... makes religion out to be a system of hallucinatory images."

18 As the son of a Rabbi, I bet that Durkheim was also curious about Smith's depiction of ancient Semitic religion.

religion. This argues that his 1895 revelation included (as he said it did) a means to study religion empirically.

Is Robertson Smith largely responsible for this new awareness? And, if so, what was in the *revelation*? First, I believe (along with many scholars) that Smith gave Durkheim the template for a religious sociology (see Kuper 1988: 117). As Jeffrey Alexander (2005: 147) expressed it, "Smith's work was revolutionary because it linked the theological ideas of the great religions to religious practice and ritual association, and it argued that this interaction is what gave to symbols their sacred power. Knowledge of Smith's work was evidently crucial for Durkheim . . ." Moreover, while Durkheim always believed that religion was a collective affair, Smith in his lucid way outlined the intimate link between religion and social structure and just how it kindled communal relations. Smith also separated magic from religion, proposed a cognitive polarity between the "sacred" and "profane" and he highlighted the essential property of *taboo* to restrict or prohibit things. He also endorsed Durkheim's assumption that the social environment originally played a paramount role in the origin, structure, and content of religion. In fact, Smith even proposed that human cognition is fundamentally shaped by religious forces.

If we follow the timeline and the evidence, Durkheim's new understanding of religion begins by giving a broader value to totemism. An early clue is found in his 1895 critique of Edward Westermarck's *The History of Human Marriage* (1891). In his commentary, Durkheim attacked Westermark's reliance on psychology to explain the social, which would be an expected response. What is rather jaw dropping is his reaction to Westermark's claim that youngsters raised together develop a *natural* sexual apathy toward their grown-up playmates so that they marry outside the household. In response, he wrote (1895b: 621)

> Westermarck is wrong about the causes of éxogamy, which are all religious and are closely linked to totemic institutions, and on the origins of the successive forms of conjugal society and their evolution . . .

Such a surprising (and out of the blue) linkage of exogamy with totemism appears (in our new timeline) to be a sudden conversion of some sort. In the next chapter we will follow along as Durkheim pursues his agenda for a scientific sociology. And, we will assess just how his research agenda changed in light of his revelation while coming to grips with his new insights into religion and society.

7
A Turn To Religion

The "revelation" of 1895 acted as a spur in intensifying Durkheim's search for religion in heretofore unrecognized places. It seemed as if he had discovered that religion was the missing key to open most, if not all, sociological doors . . . It was not that religion was explained through a study of religion, but society now had its mysteries revealed by the mystery of religion and religion itself was to be understood by its relation to society.

W.S.F. Pickering (1984: 74) in his
Durkheim's Sociology of Religion

When Durkheim disclosed his revelation in 1907, he said it forced him to reexamine all his past research, and if so, signs of this watershed moment should be reflected in his writings and personal letters after 1895. The objective in this chapter is to substantiate this statement by perusing his relevant correspondence and assessing if and how Durkheim reconfigured his research program to make it compatible with his new insights.

In 1894–1895, Durkheim taught his religious course, although his mind was also on other issues relevant to a science of society as well. Intent on bringing the French educational system into the modern era, Durkheim published a pedagogical article, "L'Enseignement philosophique et L'agrégation de philosophie" (Teaching Philosophy and the Philosophy Exam) in 1895.

> . . . [W]hat matters above all [he wrote] is to have professors who know what science is, who are current with its procedures and methodologies, not in a general and vague sense, but practical experience as direct as possible . . . education that doesn't have and doesn't give sufficient feeling to what science is can't bring anything but trouble and confusion to the mind.
>
> (1895: 142, 146)

Durkheim was also busy collaborating with his sister, Rosine Mauss over how to get Marcel, now living in Paris, to diligently prepare for his oral exams (*agrégation*)[1] "I won't talk about your *agrégation*." Mauss's Jewish mother said writing from Épinal, "It's like revenge: Think about it constantly, never talk about it." My advice is to "Work regularly but not excessively." "Go to bed at ten, get up at seven, and plan your day well . . . Stay away from your friends." Writing from Bordeaux, Durkheim advised Mauss to adopt a subdued yet self-assured demeanor during his oral exam, "Say everything you have to say, but take your time and show the necessary courtesy. Don't be aggressive. It's possible to say everything you want without offending anyone . . . One must be moderate in form without yielding anything in terms of content . . . Best of luck" (Quoted in Fournier 2006: 30–31).[2]

The orals committee met in May 1895, and during a round of philosophy asked Mauss: "On probability. Is probabilism necessarily indistinguishable from skepticism?" In answering (and perhaps with Durkheim's religious course in his mind), Mauss invoked the notion of belief as a force: "Th[ings] are probable insofar as they are believed, insofar as we act in relation to them . . . Hence the most erroneous, the most unreasonable ideas were objects of belief, were things for those who acted on them." As an example, he used an Australian aboriginal belief: "If a snake kills a man, it is not the snake who is blamed but the man. He is considered unclean within the clan" (p. 31). The committee viewed Mauss's performance as immensely positive, placing him third (of eight candidates) for the agrégé de philosophie. Mauss now had the credentials to take on the role of Durkheim's collaborator and as Durkheim put it, my "alter-ego."

In 1896, Durkheim was awarded a full professorship in *Social Science*, the first one in France but instead of a celebratory year, it was a heartbreaking one of deep sorrow as Durkheim (age 38) and Mauss (age 24) dealt with the deaths of Durkheim's father, Moïse in February (at the age of 91) and Marcel's father, Gerson (at age 62) in early summer. Durkheim was now head of his family (Fournier 2013: 218).

Despite it all, Durkheim kept an unwavering watch on developments in sociology. In March of 1896, he wrote his young colleague Cèlestin Bouglè

---

[1] A very competitive national exam given yearly for both scientific and literary teaching positions.

[2] Durkheim's affection for his nephew is reflected in the many letters he wrote to Mauss when they were separated. In Mauss's personal archives at the Collège de France more than 500 letters written by Durkheim have been preserved (see Fournier 2006: 352).

(1870–1940) over his growing concern for the future of sociology and for safeguarding the new science from the "charlatans" who were threatening its future:[3]

> Sociology has been compromised lately by charlatans who have exploited its premature fashionableness. It will result in sociology falling into disfavour which will benefit those who are disturbed by it. And it disturbs the little churches which have their faith, their priests and their congregation. It is important to separate ourselves from those who are a discredit to sociology, so as to shield it from well-founded arguments in the attacks it will undergo.
> (quoted in Besnard 1983: 42)

In a second letter to Bouglè in May 1896 Durkheim is more upbeat, thanking him for personally defending both him and sociology. He also wrote of his new book now nearing completion:

> I have cancelled my lectures since the end of April so as to be able to devote myself wholeheartedly to the book I am preparing on *Suicide*. I hope that when it appears, the *reality* of the social fact, about which my view is contested, will be better understood; for what I study . . . is the social current of suicide, the tendency of social groups towards suicide, isolated from its individual manifestations (by abstraction, of course, but no science isolates its object in any other way).
> (quoted in Besnard 1983: 43)

Suicide

Social Causes and Social Types

Suicide: A Study in Sociology (1897) is an innovative work in its approach and application of statistical methods for sociological research. As is well known, Durkheim's objective was to show that suicide is not an individual phenomenon (although the act itself is), but a social phenomena with a clear statistical regularity that can be linked to differential attachments to society. After dividing suicide up into three general types—egoistic, altruistic and anomic, Durkheim linked the suicide rate from different

---

3 After graduating from the École Normale Supériere (entering class of 1890), Bouglé joined the group of agrégés who were forming around Durkheim. Bouglé played an essential role on the *Année sociologique*'s team (Besnard 1983: 12).

European countries with each type of suicide.[4] On the religious life, he found differential rates of suicide between Catholic and Protestant countries with rates lower among Catholics because of their greater dependence and collective involvement; and higher among Protestants because of less reliance on dogmas and practices and higher states of individualism. Judaism, he said, was lowest of all in preventing suicide because it still clung to traditions of an earlier age (p. 376ff).

While religion inhibits suicide because of the powerful control it exercises over thought and conduct, once humans break free from the yoke of religion, he said, by viewing it merely as a "symbolic idealism," it loses the protective role it has played in traditional societies. Nor can the modern nuclear family offer security against suicide because extended kinship networks no longer prevail. In fact, Durkheim worried that since suicide typically varies with the rate of integration (with anomie and egoistic suicide linked to a deficiency in individual attachments to society), the rapid rise of suicide in industrial societies signaled a breakdown in solidarity. To circumvent this looming crisis, Durkheim proposed occupational groups as replacements for the traditional "society of faith, of family and of politics"—a theme repeated in the 1902 edition of the *Division of Labor* (p. 378).[5]

Yet, despite the loss of traditional religion as a barrier to suicide, Durkheim rather welcomed its demise, seeing it as a necessary consequence of an evolutionary process. Individuals, he said, may feel adrift for a while, but religion will never again have the authority "to wring such a sacrifice from us"—that is, the "right of free examination" (p. 376). Besides, he added, new religions will come along, but the only ones that will prevail are those that respect individual initiative and free inquiry (p. 375).

A New Religious Blueprint

Apart from its singular topic, *Suicide* offers the first substantial evidence that Durkheim is abandoning, modifying, or rejuvenating some earlier suppositions. For one, he breathes new life into the "collective conscience,"

---

4 In egoistic suicide, an individual takes his/her life because of extreme individualism and the inability to engage in true collective pursuits; in altruistic suicide an individual is too well integrated into society—a compulsive conformist; whereas in anomic suicide an individual is functionally adrift because of a weakening of societal regulations and the loss of a normative compass.

5 Durkheim felt that occupational groups might be a substitute because they were "omnipresent, ubiquitous and that its control extends to the greatest part of life" [1897]1951: 379).

a concept he entwined with *mechanical solidarity* and portrayed in the *Division of Labor* as withering away to make room for *organic solidarity*. In *Suicide* it undergoes a striking metamorphosis as Durkheim shifts its character from a weakening and inferior form of solidarity built from robotic likenesses to a vital and ubiquitous component in every society, with social life now built from "collective representations" and with the common conscience itself varying only by degree with the nature of social forms (p. 312 and see Pickering 2000).[6]

Suicide also conveys Durkheim's spirited enthusiasm over solving a problem he first expressed in *The Division of Labor:* Why do humans yield to an authority that is a figment of their imagination? In *Religion of the Semites*, Robertson Smith had hinted at who the heathen gods really were, but wanted to wait until he had completed his analysis. Unmasking "heathen" gods was really not on Smith's agenda for, as a devoted Christian, his objective in laying out the first principles of Semitic worship was to acquire a deeper understanding of Judaism and Christianity. Yet, in Smith's lucid depiction of the many relationships embedded in ancient Semitic religion, Durkheim had seemingly worked out the answer to his problem: What is the enigmatic force behind religious phenomena? Why accept the authority of revered illusive beings? He now knew who was behind the curtain. In *Suicide* (1897: 352–353) he proclaimed, "The power ... is society, of which the gods are its reified form." And, in a more far-reaching statement:

> Religion is, in the end, the system of symbols through which society becomes aware of itself; it is the way of thinking proper *to the collective being*. Hence, here is a vast collection of mental states that would not have produced themselves if the individual consciousnesses had not united, that are the result of this union and juxtaposed themselves to those derived from individual natures.
>
> We can analyze these latter as minutely as possible, never will we discover anything that can explain how these singular/uncommon beliefs and practices began and developed, *where totemism is born, how naturism emerged from it*, how naturism itself became here the abstract religion of Yahweh, there the polytheism of the Greeks and the Romans, etc.
>
> (p. 353 emphasis added, translated from the French edition)

---

6 In the *Division of Labor*, Durkheim wrote "that the collective consciousness weakened and became vaguer as the division of labour developed ... [and] that the division of labour becomes the main cause of solidarity" ([1893]1984: 226).

In May of 1897, Paul Lapie wrote to Bouglé of Durkheim's new fixation with religion[7]

... My visit to Durkheim was long and rather confused ...

Basically,

he explains everything, *at this moment*, by religion; the prohibition of marriage between relatives is a religious matter; punishment is a phenomenon of religious origin; everything is religious. I protested but gently against a certain number of assertions that appeared doubtful to me; but I do not have the requisite competence to dispute a gentlemen who is so well informed and so sure of his *current* assertions. Apart from that, he is charming ...
(original emphasis: quoted in Besnard 1983: 64)

Durkheim's fixation takes on a passionate intensity. In 1897, he writes a scathing review of Antonio Labriola's, "Essais sur la conception matérialiste de l'histoire" ([1897: 1978), a work that sought to clarify the Marxist doctrine that economic forces are the prime movers in history, with social life a product of the ways humans are organized into groups. Durkheim's first criticism is that the Marxist doctrine ignores the genesis of social phenomena by leaving it to unspecified causes. Then, after agreeing in principle that social life is to be explained by human association, the postulate itself, Durkheim asserts, is "self-evident" and a "logical extension" of both history and psychology over the last fifty years and, thus, independent of the socialist movement. He then attacks the Marxian doctrine that progress stems from economic forces. Economic materialism, he states, does not only rest on proofs but on "disjointed facts" and simply "pretends to be the key to history!" (p. 128). Finally, to press home his opposition to Marx and his disciples, Durkheim wrote how useless their doctrine is because reality is quite different:

Not only is the Marxist hypothesis unproved, but it is contrary to facts which seem well established. Sociologists and historians tend more and more to meet in the confirmation that religion is the most primitive of all social phenomena. From it, by successive transformations, have come all the other manifestations of collective

---

[7] Paul Lapie would join Durkheim's inner circle as a member of the Année Sociologique group.

activity: law, ethics, art, science, political forms, and so on. Everything is religious in principle. We know of no way to reduce religion to economics, nor of any attempt to accomplish this reduction. No one has yet shown under what economic influences naturism arose out of totemism . . . is it not probable, on the contrary, that the economy depends on religion much more than the second on the first.

(pp. 129–130 emphasis added)

So, by 1897, Durkheim is viewing the social world through a religious lens. As Lapie conveyed to Bouglé, for Durkheim "everything is religious." It is (a) the primal social phenomena; (b) the source of all other collective activity; (c) the cognition of the collective being; (d) the means by which a society becomes aware of itself. Indeed, as Fournier (2013: 202) expressed it, "there is something surprising, even astonishing, about Durkheim's 'revelation.'"

During this transitional phase, Durkheim also abandoned naturism as foundational religion but with major consequences because switching to totemism placed him at odds with his earlier portrayal of the primitive *horde* and his distinction between *mechanical and organic solidarity*. In depicting this earliest formation, both Durkheim and Smith started with the notion of the primeval horde. They also agreed that the stabilization of such a loose-knit aggregation in the absence of blood-based ties required some sort of shared, fixed orientation. So, their initial premises were the same. Yet, stabilization in Durkheim's scheme in the *Division of Labor* required that all personal consciences be *fused* into a concrete *collective conscience*—his fixed placement. Stabilization in Smith's scheme required the opposite—the *emancipation* of personal consciences from dreadful natural forces by a "kinship" alliance with an animal or plant species symbolized by a shared totem—his fixed placement (1889: 117–118). Both orientations resulted in a "unity of minds." Yet, in Durkheim's scheme, all individuality had to be purged by keeping *horde* members tethered to an overpowering collective conscience, which is why, of course, he called this type of solidarity—*mechanical* (Durkheim [1888]1978: 206).

Durkheim saw mechanical solidarity as fragile because of the inferior "mechanical" grip it had on its members compared to the enduring interdependency of organic solidarity as the collective conscience faltered in the face of a rising division of labor. This problem was exacerbated by their clashing regimes, which prevented organic solidarity from taking hold until mechanical solidarity had broken down. Durkheim acknowledged this problem, noting that during the changeover a period of instability might ensue until the superior form of solidarity could crystallize—hence his inclusion of "abnormal forms" in the *Division of Labor* (pp. 120ff, 226ff).

In contrast, *horde* members in Smith's scheme only had to take up a relationship with a concrete animal or plant totem. Then, in lieu of blood ties, totem mates simply had to engage in visible, obligatory, and repeated fixed rituals and practices that, over time, would lay the building blocks for the first working institutions. Thus, Durkheim was not only enamored by the prospect that totemism opened the door to social change without disruption but totemism was far more than a source of solidarity—it embodied a multiplex of emergent properties. For once a totem formation was configured it gave rise to rituals and practices and, later, corresponding beliefs. As the anchor for the birth of the religious institution it also actualized society. In addition, by providing a sense of solidarity over collectively held moral codes, totemism also laid the bedrock for other institutional domains as well as assuring intergenerational continuity over time.

Durkheim's rejection of *naturism* and his adoption of totemism are why "mechanical" and "organic" solidarity, which are still classically identified with his analysis of societal evolution never appear in his writings again except in *The Division of Labor* (and see Némedi 2000). Durkheim also recognized that the solidarity underlying both totemism and organic solidarity are rather similar because both preserve a degree of individualism in a non-kinship matrix of structural interdependences. In clan-based societies (where "kinship" networks are more fictive than real), the social whole fostered by these interdependences could be integrated by totems that signify moral codes to which individuals could develop collective attachments through emotion-arousing rituals—a mechanism of cultural integration that, he believed, unified the earliest societies. Having dropped his former two kinds of solidarity, Durkheim then resurrected the collective conscience, although he tinkered with its meaning to make it compatible with his now favored *collective representations*. So by way of Robertson Smith, Durkheim came to appreciate a social force where unity could stabilize around an object without fusing minds or tracing blood-lines. As Smith (1889: 255) reminds us:

> The idea that kinship is not purely an affair of birth . . . has quite fallen out of our circle of ideas; but so, for that matter, has the primitive conception of kindred itself . . . To know that a man's life was sacred to me . . . it was not necessary for me to count cousinship with him by reckoning up to our common ancestor; it was enough that we belonged to the same clan and bore the same clan-name.

From there it was only a short step for Durkheim to envision totemism as the means for a sense *of* society itself . . . for him it anchored everything! For what Smith and Durkheim brought to light in their writings, as will become evident in later chapters, travels far beyond the simple confines of totemism because the rules that govern totem formations are not "primitive" but simply rely on a cognitive "sense of belonging" as the criterion for membership. But, with totemism, Durkheim now had a thesis to explain solidarity in both small and larger sociocultural formations. By 1897, Henri Peyre (1960: 12) wrote that Durkheim's ideas had crystallized, and from then on he devoted his energies to the expansion and elaboration of his own ideas, culminating in *Les formes élémentaires de la vie religieuse* (1912). Alexander (1982: 238) also contends that "in its essentials, Durkheim's sociology of religion never changed after 1898." And, Pickering (1998: 2) concludes that after his 1895 revelation, Durkheim's masterful work was "in fact the culmination of that revelation." In the next chapter, we will follow along as Durkheim starts to seek outlets for his ideas beginning with his launching of *L'Année sociologique*, the first French sociology journal.

8
A Blueprint for Religion

> *In the same year that Suicide was published, Durkheim helped to found the famous review journal, L'Année Sociologique... the journal, with its core group of collaborators, did more than anything to concretize Durkheim's sociology as a recognized 'school' of thought.*
>
> Anthony Giddens (1981: 18)

La Belle Époque (or the beautiful time) was an epoch in Europe between the late nineteenth century and World War I, characterized by political stability, comfortable life styles, striking changes in literature and theatre (e.g. the Moulin Rouge), new art forms (e.g. Impressionism and Expressionism), and major breakthroughs in medicine, science, and technology (e.g. the telephone and mass transportation).[1] In France, La Belle Époque ushered in an ethos of optimism as the machine age took hold, tripling France's industrial output, that, in turn, lead to better working conditions, rising wages, and new consumer goods, all of which had a major stimulating effect on the French public. The same animating forces took hold in the social sciences, resulting in a more disciplined professionalism, new educational initiatives, the proliferation of academic journals, and the adoption of new scientific theories. Durkheim was to ride this surging academic wave by launching the first officially recognized sociology journal in France.

The Launching of L'Année Sociologique

Purpose of the Journal

Durkheim's high hopes for *Suicide* were dashed when word came of its lukewarm reception. Emotionally bruised by some harsh critics, he wrote to Marcel Mauss:

---

[1] In the United States, this time is called the "Gilded Age."

I thought that my *Suicide* would clear up the ambiguities and determine an agreement. I now see that that will not be the case ... This one challenges one thing, and that one challenges another. I am beginning to see that I am powerless against prevailing opinion ... My only ambition is to see to it that my work is not sterile. I do not want to be praised for my talent or my style, but I do want to feel that all the trouble I have taken has served some purpose.

(quoted in Fournier 2013: 270)

Another ploy to jumpstart sociology and keep his ideas in the forefront was to launch a journal—*L'Année Sociologique* (*The Sociological Year*). While the idea for a journal came from a number of sources, it was Célestin Bouglé (his future collaborator) who convinced Durkheim that it was a good time to start a sociology journal when they met in Paris in April 1896 (Besnard 1983: 12; Fournier 2013: 261).[2] Durkheim was probably also inspired by thinking back to his 1885 visit to Wilhelm Wundt's laboratory in Germany where he was greatly impressed by Wundt's collaborative research model. Indeed, Durkheim followed the German template of close collaboration by recruiting the Année personnel very carefully—everyone had an academic background and, not surprisingly, more than half the team had attended the École Normale Supérieure (Clark 1968). Even Félix Alcan, the publisher was a *normalien*.

The format of *L'Année Sociologique* was truly novel. Durkheim was senior editor but the journal was partitioned into six major sections, each headed by an assistant editor. Like conventional journals it published "avant-garde" articles or *Mémories originaux*—but only occasionally. Instead, it was a journal full of reviews drawn from many academic fields— general sociology, anthropology, archaeology, ethnology, ethnography, criminal sociology, social theories, social psychology, family and kinship, law, morals, religion, and the like. Some write-ups were short biographic references or crisp notes; others were long, detailed commentaries on articles and books that in some way reflected well/or badly on a scientific sociology. To obtain materials for review, the journal contracted with libraries and periodicals (e.g. *American Journal of Sociology, Folklore*) with a concentration on articles and books from the previous year; the first

---

2 Besnard (1983: 12) noted that Bouglé appears to have played a major role in setting up the journal. This is confirmed by Durkheim who wrote to Bouglé in March 1898 after the first volume was published, "I reciprocate your congratulations about the Année since, on that point again, you are the one who spurred me on" (p. 12).

premier volume in 1898, for example, drew from materials published in 1896–1897. Durkheim's friend Lucien Herr, the legendary librarian at the École Normale Supérieure, was especially valuable as a resource for keeping the Année team abreast of recently publications.[3] Under Durkheim's stewardship from 1898 to 1913, twelve thick volumes were published, comprising 8,866 notes, notices, bibliographic references, and reviews (Nandan 1977: xxxvi; xxvff; Nandan 1980: 1ff; Besnard 1983: 11).[4]

Religious sociology under Mauss's editorship was given special status along with family and domestic organization under Durkheim's editorship. In fact, Durkheim and his associates took pains to point out that in the *Année* classification scheme, religious sociology had priority over other social science branches (Nandan 1980: xvi). Because the journal was not only for sociologists but for anyone interested in such wide-ranging fields as archaeology, anthropology, aesthetics, Egyptology, even pedagogy, it became well known in Europe in both the social sciences and humanities. And, due in large part to the team effort of the *Année* personnel, the journal became a well-established institution.[5] As Randy Collins (2005: 102) noted, "The purpose of the *L'Année Sociologique* was to display what the world of scholarship had to offer collectively that could be shaped into a new science; the Durkheimians saw themselves as the inner circle of a wide ring of proto-sociologists, whose contributions they would collaboratively theorize into clear and general principles of the new sociological science."

To what extent did Durkheim launch the *Année* because of his new involvement with religion? In December 1897, he sent Mauss a revealing note:

> ... [I]f I ask of you the sacrifice of a large part of your time for the forthcoming *L'Année*, it is because I truly believe that it is worth all the trouble. Outside of its documentary interest *L'Année Sociologique*

---

3 Lucien Herr was a normale whose fondest wish was to become the librarian at the École Normale Supererieure. As Herr wrote in his application, "My whole dream, my whole ambition, is the library of the Ecole." His wish was granted and he became a legendary figure, serving as the École's librarian from 1888 until 1926 when he died (see Smith 1982: 66–68).

4 The last two volumes (11 and 12) covered a three-year period (1906–1909 and 1909–1912).

5 According to Yash Nandan (1980: xvi-xvii): "L'Année earned its universal reputation as the most unique publication in the entire history of sociology for having been a repository of books in the major Western languages, and for devising a classification system of sociology which made a permanent impression and guided the activities of those who collaborated with Durkheim." Also see Giddens 1970, 1979, 1981.

must represent an orientation. Basically, the sociological importance of religious phenomena is the crowning success of all that I have done; and that [the *Année*] has the advantage of summarizing our total orientation in a concrete manner, more concrete than the formulas that I have employed up until now. The more that I reflect upon it, the more I believe that it is necessary to serialize our articles in a way that will represent a movement forward in a definitive sense. Now, the suitable direction is that one.

(Durkheim [1897]1998: 91)

In 1897, Durkheim's writings on religion are still thin (aside from *Suicide*). Yet, his note, when taken at face value, is imparting to Mauss that his new understanding of religion is so revolutionary—"the crowning success"—that it eclipses all the research and writing he had *actually* done through pluck and effort.

L'Année Sociologique: 1898 Opening Comments

Durkheim portrayed the *L'Année Sociologique* as an interdisciplinary periodical and not a sociology journal (as there was not enough sociology written yet), with materials relevant for a science of society. He also stressed the cooperative ties between history and sociology, even though most historians, he said, consider sociology of little value or importance:

... history can be a science only to the extent that it explains, and explanation cannot proceed except through comparison ... one cannot adequately describe a unique fact, or a fact of which one has only rare instances, *because one does not see it adequately*.

It is for this reason that Fustel de Coulanges, in spite of his profound insight into historical matters, came to erroneous conclusions regarding the nature of the *gens*, in which he saw nothing but a large agnatic family: he was not acquainted with ethnographical analogies to this type of family. The true character of the Roman *sacer* is very difficult to grasp and, above all, to understand, if one does not see it in relation to the Polynesian *taboo*.

(Durkheim [1898]1960: 342, emphasis in original)

Durkheim also highlighted the inclusion of two *Mémoires originaux* in the premier issue of the journal and, thereafter, on occasion. One essay was on the stability of social forms by George Simmel and the other was on the origin of the incest taboo by Emile Durkheim.[6] Not surprisingly, his incest paper was of such great import (at least to him) that it appeared on page one of the journal. It is, however, also essential to our story because it represents Durkheim's first attempt to advance his religious agenda. W.E. Stanner ([1967]1975: 276) also refers to Durkheim's incest paper "as a first cast, rough but nevertheless recognizable, of the foundations of *The Elementary Forms*."

Incest: The Nature and Origin of the Taboo[7]

In "La prohibition de l'inceste et ses origines" ([1898]1962), Durkheim opens with two questions: Why do most societies prohibit incest? And why has no one yet answered this question? On the latter question the likely cause, he said, is flawed assumptions and methods because it is wrongly assumed that a horror of incest comes from human's evolved nature (e.g. Westermarck's hypothesis), degeneration of offspring (Henry Morgan's hypothesis), or present-day social or individual circumstances.[8] On why most societies prohibit incest, Durkheim advises a return to the past:

> In order to understand a practice or an institution, a judicial or moral rule, it is necessary to trace it as nearly as possible to its origin; for between the form it now takes and what it has been, there is a rigorous relationship... There are social phenomena, just as there are organic phenomena, and although the manner in which they must develop is not fatally predetermined by the properties which characterize them at their birth, these properties do not cease to have a profound influence on the entire course of their history.
> (Durkheim [1898]1963: 13)

---

6 The title of Simmel's article is "Comment Les Formes Sociales Se Maintiennent" (How Social Forms are Maintained).

7 The English translation of this essay is considered a poor rendition, in part because Durkheim's long paragraphs are so broken up that his prose appears fragmented, along with other issues (see Needam 1966).To offset these problems and to capture the spirit of Durkheim's intent, both English and French versions were used for this synopsis.

8 Durkheim dismissed both Morgan's theory ([1877]1985) that incestuous relations cause deleterious offspring, and Edward Westermarck's thesis in *The History of Human Marriage* (1891) that children growing up together in the same household are unlikely to mate or marry each other because they develop a sexual aversion to familiar playmates.

Durkheim's logic here is reminiscent of Robertson Smith where in *Religion of the Semites* he traces the Hebrew Scriptures back to an ancient Semitic religion: "The record of the religious thought of mankind, as it is embodied in religious institutions, resembles the geological record of the history of the earth's crust: the new and the old are preserved . . . layer upon layer" (Smith 1889: 26).

Although Durkheim is ostensibly concerned with forbidden sexual unions, his actual intent is to establish a causal relationship among *three* variables: the incest taboo, exogamy, and totemism. So, in this first *Mémoire*, Durkheim will connect the incest taboo with the earliest rule of exogamy. He will then trace the incest taboo and exogamy back to a primordial totemism. This essay illustrates Durkheim's dramatic swing to religion, his *new* emphasis on tracing present-day social phenomena back to their primal roots (see his critical review of Spencer's historical approach in 1886) and it embodies his formative assumptions on religion, family, and society itself.

Durkheim's narrative unfolds in storyline fashion. In the beginning, humans were organized into roaming hordes where incest was *not* forbidden. But in time cooperative unions between hordes emerged (morphing into clans) and this transformation lead to the first incest taboo: " . . . it was the clan . . . that, in all likelihood, gave birth to the first repressive rules of incest" (Durkheim [1898:1963: 27–28). As incest rules require acknowledged relationships organized by society, they originated in clan-based societies because it is the prototypical social organization. For Durkheim, the *earliest* clans were domestic groupings who believed themselves related to each other on the basis of some compelling object, or *totem*:

> We shall call a *clan* a group of individuals who consider themselves related to each other, but who recognize this relationship in only one manner; namely, by the very specific sign that they are bearers of the same totem. The totem . . . serves the members as both an emblem and a collective name.
>
> (p. 15, original emphasis)

Though Durkheim's objective is to connect totemic cults with clans, he did not assume (as some have accused him) that all clans by definition have totemic affinities . . . just ancient primeval clans.[9] In the *earliest* societies, then, clan members are linked solely by totems because relational bonds

---

9 This is evident in a letter Durkheim wrote to Bougle to clarify what he meant, "No, one must not define the clan by the totem. I did it in my Mémoire, because this narrow

are forged solely by the sharing of some heraldic device or natural object. When kinship defined by blood ties or marriage arose, however, the primordial clans were all matri-clans where totemic membership passed exclusively through the female line:

> We believe it indisputable that the totem, at the outset was transmitted exclusively by the uterine line; and that the clan, as a result, was composed only of matrilineal descendants... The more rudimentary societies are in their development, the more frequently is the maternal clan found... Never has one seen a paternal clan change into a uterine clan; one cannot cite a single case where such metamorphosis was directly observed.
>
> (p. 45)

Where clans still exist (e.g. American Indians and Australian aboriginals), a rule of exogamy also exists to marry out of your clan. Durkheim then proposes that exogamy preceded and is the initial stimulus for the later birth of the incest taboo: "Exogamy, then, is the most primitive form that the system of matrimonial prohibitions, for reasons of incest, has assumed. All these prohibitions observed in the lower societies are derived from it" (p. 53).

Given that exogamy *preceded* the incest taboo, what is the origin of exogamy? Durkheim reasoned that since the incest taboo did not appear before the first clan grouping (as a horde is a stand alone promiscuous mass), he attributed exogamy to the unity of a clan generated by collective sentiments of a religious nature. And, since early matri-clans were totemic, the answer must lie there:

> Since the totem is a god and totemism a cult, is it not rather in the religious beliefs of lower societies that one must go to look for the causes of exogamy? And ... we are going to show that it is only one specific case of a much more general religious institution found at the basis of all primitive religions and even, in a sense, of all religions. That is *taboo*.
>
> (pp. 69–70)

---

definition facilitated the argument. But if one were to stick with it, one would be obliged to refuse the name of clan to all the vestiges and forms derived from it, such as the people ...One calls a clan a group of individuals who consider themselves like each others parents (i.e. originating from the same origin) and who recognize this kinship by this sign and only by this sign do they all share the same name, that is the name of the group... (Durkheim ([1900a]1976: 170).

Every society, Durkheim said, has social customs where items are restricted or prohibited, because the objective is to prevent or limit certain types of contact among specific members of a society. Such *taboos* are often placed on things or categories of things in which a supernatural principle of some sort exists. Now an important thing creating clan unity is the sense that its members are made from the same substance as their totem emblem, a substance symbolized by blood. The "community of blood" is the foundation of the shared principle for its members' identity. "For the chief functions that the blood fulfills in the organism designate it for such a role. Life ends when it spills out; therefore, it must be the vehicle of life" (pp. 88–89).

So, the life of a clan is dependent upon sharing its common blood and the official symbol of the clan is a totem represented by an animal or plant species. In fact, the "totemic being is immanent to the clan ... It is the very blood itself." Individuals believe that they are related by virtue of sharing the same totem, which is, at one and the same time, their ancestor, their god, and their protector. Thus, the center of a religion is born of the totemic cult for "... it is in the blood that this god resides; from which it follows that the blood is a divine thing, [and] when it runs out, the god is spilling over" (p. 89). As a taboo is placed on all things considered to be divine, and since blood is divine, it therefore must be tabooed and whoever is connected with blood must equally be tabooed:

> ... taboo is the mark placed on all that is divine; it is therefore natural that the blood and whoever it concerns should be equally tabooed, that is to say, retired from vulgar commerce and from circulation ... Since the blood sustains the strictest relationship with the totem, it is not surprising that it should also be the subject of the same prohibitions.
>
> (pp. 89–90)

In the earliest societies, Durkheim argued, blood relationships are traced through females who are directly connected to the blood. Women also bleed each month, so, they are directly in contact with blood. All males must then sexually avoid females of their clan because they are intimately connected to the supernatural totem. From that time on, women were *taboo* to clan-mates and, therefore, off limits whether to mate or marry. Females, however, from other clans are sexually permissible. Herein, then, lies the origin of *exogamy*—a female-biased rule of reciprocal exchange. Over time, the rule of exogamy slowly became institutionalized such that even after clans evolved into other organizational types, sexual avoidance continued and eventually evolved into the incest taboo:

Once this prohibition had entered into the mores, it remained and survived for its own reasons. When the totemic beliefs which had given birth to exogamy were extinguished, the mental states that they had incited still subsisted . . . In making this hypothesis, we do not mean to say that exogamy has been a contingent accident. It is too closely linked with totemism and to the clan, which are universal phenomena, for one to stop at such a supposition. One should rather see in our formula only a process of exposition, aimed at isolating the variable of each factor.

(pp. 110, 112)

What of the incest taboo? It is nothing more, Durkheim said, than a derivative of the rule of exogamy, an eminent social thing to be explained by social causes. And, the law of exogamy is just a specific case of a more general religious emotion–that of taboo. As societies developed over time, clan organization was overtaken by more complex social forms (e.g. village, state, etc.), and clans gradually disappeared. The rule of exogamy and the incest taboo, however, became a fundamental part of the kinship institution, although incest and exogamy rules apply in contemporary societies only to relatives in extended or nuclear families.

Durkheim also provided a sophisticated account of why totems disappear and clans still remain intact. The first clans were matrilineal with female exogamy. So a bride moved from her natal clan to join the groom's clan but she kept her totem identity and passed it on to her offspring. In turn, children of the marriage would then inherit their mother's totem identity but grow up and live in their father's territorial residence. Thus, once females leave their natal homeland, members of a clan would soon be scattered about in different clans rather than living together in a shared totemic community. In time, the totem identity of future generations would weaken because they would no longer participate in day-to-day activities. In contrast, as children grow up in their father's territorial group, their ties to the fatherland would strengthen. Although individuals could still retain membership in the "community of the totem," this force, in Durkheim's view, would gradually lose its integrating power. In its place, a territory or a "community of the land" (in lieu of a totem) would serve as the new integrating force: As Durkheim explained:

[A] common adherence to the totem has as its sole function that it is a symbol of the community of existence . . . By that we do not mean that the totem is only a word, a verbal sign; it is the symbol of an entire ensemble of traditions, of beliefs, of religious and other practices. But when the different parts of the same clan no longer live one life together, the totem no longer has its original significance, although it retains its prestige for a long time because of habit.

(p. 40)

So while members can always identify with a motherland totemic community, a collective emblem is no match for the powerful pull of a fatherland. The combination of totemic matriliny coupled with a female-biased pattern of exogamy always gives rise to a dual identity: a "community of the totem" and "a community of the father-land." And, once a totem-based community is undermined by inaction, the unity and authority of the totemic force lessens and gradually withers away.

The Anatomy of a Religion

In 1899, a second volume of *L'Année Sociologique* was published. In the opening introduction, Durkheim expressed pleasure over the very positive reception of the first volume because it meant that the program laid out had been understood, although a few points needed to be added. One is for sociology to begin establishing classifications and relationships among social phenomena. At present, he said, each social science isolates phenomena, but too often this results in mere descriptions of distinctive, independent units rather than the development of more generic categories of phenomena and their laws of operation. Jurists, for example, need to be familiar with the science of religion and the economists with culture and social customs because what the social sciences study are but varied manifestations of the same reality—a social reality. The social sciences also need to adopt the same scientific procedures by studying phenomena as social facts that can be described, explained, and associated in order to isolate their determining causes (Durkheim [1899] 1960: 347–52).

Yet, most social sciences are closed to this approach. The science of religion, for example, is concerned with beliefs and rites in only the most general sense, and independent of any particular social system and the same disconnect exists in political economy where social facts are viewed as free-floating units in time and space. The challenge, then, is to close this discrepancy by making "all these special sciences as many branches of sociology" (p. 349). We can then investigate social facts not just in a summary view suggestive of philosophical conjecture but, instead, for themselves. Efforts can be made to understand them, to convert them into types and laws, and to do so in a sociological spirit.

Durkheim also defended the historical method of taking social phenomena back to its earliest beginnings. Why should sociologists bother to go back to remote periods of time? It is essential, he argued, because "One does not know social reality if one has seen it only from the outside and has ignored its foundations . . . In order to be able to say . . . what will be, or what the society of tomorrow will be like, it is indispensable that one study the social forms of the most distant past" (pp. 351–352).

Durkheim also recounted the astonishment of readers who questioned why religion was given first rank in the journal. This emphasis on religion is appropriate, he emphasized, because religion is the seed for *all other social phenomena*:

> Religion contains in itself from the very beginning . . . all the elements which in dissociating themselves from it, articulating themselves, and combining with one another in a thousand ways, have given rise to the various manifestations of collective life . . . One cannot understand our perception of the world . . . of life, if one does not know the religious beliefs which are their primordial forms.
>
> (pp. 350–351)

Yet, the impact of religion on contemporary societies will likely diminish, he said, musing on, losing ground to the social forms it has generated. But we cannot understand these new structures unless they are linked with their primeval religious origins, even though these new forms are no longer religious phenomena, properly (p. 352). After this short introduction, Durkheim's second *Mémoires originaus* followed, "Concerning the Definition of Religious Phenomena."[10]

The Components of Religion

Once again, Durkheim's *Mémoire* appears on the front pages of *Année*, a testimony to its importance (for Durkheim). The purpose of this essay, Durkheim wrote, is to come to grips with what religion is, and what it is

---

10 Volume 2 included a second *Mémoires originaus* on religion, *Essai sur la nature et al fonction du sacrifice* (The Nature of Sacrifice) by Henri Hubert and Marcel Mauss. Publishing back-to-back essays on religion was not a "fortuitous coincidence," Durkheim said, but consciously done to give sociologists a quick look at the wealth of materials on religion and what these insights would generate. Seemingly, he is following through on the research plan he discussed with Mauss on serializing the nature of religious phenomena in his journal.

not. This is essential because a sociology of religion must deal with *religious facts* rather than all encompassing notions of religion.

> If we can find some social facts which have immediately apparent characteristics in common, and if these characteristics have enough affinity with those vaguely denoted by the word religion in everyday language, we shall group them under the same heading. In this way, we shall form a distinct group which will be defined quite naturally by the very characteristics which serve to form it ... *our aim is not simply to state precisely the usual meaning of the word, but to give ourselves a subject for* research which can be tackled by ordinary scientific method.
>
> (p. 75 emphasis added)

To get a working definition, he advises putting aside all personal religious beliefs so the facts can be confronted objectively [1899]1975: 74–75).

A first step is to isolate out some distinctive features that characterize religious phenomena and, then, to search both historically and worldwide for these characteristics in both developed and less developed societies. Once correspondences are found, even crude affinities to traditional notions of religion, boundaries can be demarcated, and the social facts that form these boundaries can illuminate each other, making it possible to tackle our subject matter using the tools of science (p. 75).[11] What is essential, he said, is to treat social facts as external "things," and to avoid vague preconceptions about the nature of individual consciousness or experience that are simply ideological constructions of psychological phenomena. Equally important, any idea of finding *true religion* (p. 76; original emphasis) must be abandoned. For how shall we objectively distinguish a true religion from a false one? The oldest one? The youngest one? Islam is younger than Christianity; is it then the superior religion? Can we identify in Islam a more genuine religiosity? To do so would require a yardstick of established characteristics already in hand. To be objective, it is essential to put aside preconceptions, and let the social facts arrange themselves according to their shared qualities and characteristics ([1899]1975: 74–75).

In addition, Durkheim negated two popular religious characterizations —that all religions imply a belief in mysterious or unknowable forces and/or a belief in a superhuman or god. Neither, he asserted, is a primary characteristic because ideas about mysterious forces are found mostly

---

11 Durkheim refers the reader to the *Rules* (1895) and the section on social facts.

in advanced religions, whereas supernatural beings or gods are not ubiquitous to all religions—even ones in advanced societies (e.g. Jainism and Buddhism). If we equate religion with divine beings we restrict the sphere of religion to a small sample of societies. Moreover, gods are merely secondary components literally created by concentrating a bundle of religious characters into a singular shape or concrete form.

In comparison, if a "god" force is not crystallized into one entity but diffused among an amorphous class of objects or an immense collection of things, we have sacred things without a divine being or god. His case in point is, of course, the cult of totemism:

> [The] totem is not a given member of the animal or vegetable species which acts as a symbol for the group; it is the species as a whole. In a clan which has the wolf as its totem, all wolves are equally venerated, those existing today, along with those which existed yesterday, along with those which will exist tomorrow . . . there is neither god nor gods but a vast category of sacred things.
>
> (p. 85)

If the sacred (*sacré*) can exist independently of a god conception, it means that the idea of divinity was devised later in time once a need arose for greater organization and unification. Durkheim also thought it misguided to focus initially on the contents of religion because religious phenomena can vary enormously both historically and across societal types. At the outset, he said, it was best to concentrate on "the exterior and apparent form of religious phenomena" and let the content of religion be brought to light slowly as scientific knowledge increases (p. 87).

Defining Characters of Religion

Rituals are characteristic of religion. Yet, if religious rituals are observed without connecting them with anything else, they will appear as a habitual series of actions or fixed practices, a definition that applies equally to secular rituals. How, then, do we distinguish between religious rituals and secular rituals? One way is to observe that religious rituals are typically compulsory behaviors, although so are legal and moral codes of conduct. How, then, do you tease these apart? It is reasonable to assume that fixed actions associated with sacred things are religious in nature but the problem then is how to establish and identify sacred things (p. 88).

Beliefs are characteristic of religion. These convictions will vary in importance and degree of sophistication (a simple myth or a formal doctrine), but they will share a distinctive attribute: members of a religious community are compelled to accept them. That is, "*représentations* of a religious kind are in opposition to others in the same way that obligatory opinions are in opposition to freely held opinions" (p. 89). And it is this obligatory facet of faith-based beliefs, Durkheim argued, that can serve to clarify and define beliefs.

So, for Durkheim religion is an irreducible and distinctive set of phenomena. Two of its defining characters are its obligatory beliefs and its obligatory rites. Beliefs compel us to subscribe to particular collective *représentations* and rites compel us to engage in collective practices. Which came first, beliefs or rites? In this chicken/egg conundrum, Durkheim agrees with Robertson Smith that in the very early stages of religion rites or rituals were well developed, beliefs were crude and simple (p. 99: footnote 25).

Science is also a belief system made up of collective *représentations* but it differs, Durkheim noted, from religious *représentations* in that compliance is usually voluntary. Many secular beliefs such as love of country or the national flag also embody a sacred quality and a collective binding force, but secular beliefs differ from religion beliefs by a lack of corresponding, obligatory rituals. Magic and religion are often intertwined, but pure magic by itself while resting on ceremonial rituals, is not associated with gods or sacred things (p. 99: footnote 24). Hence, religious beliefs and practices never stand alone; beliefs are always linked with definite rites, and rites are always linked with definite beliefs for both represent different facets of the same reality. Given this essential constituency between belief (thought) and rites (actions) Durkheim proposes the following definition:

> [P]henomena held to be religious consists in obligatory beliefs, connected with clearly defined practices which are related to given objects of those beliefs. As for religion, it is a more or less organized and systematized whole, composed of phenomena of the kind mentioned.
>
> (p. 93 emphasis in original)

The Source of Religious Authority

Having isolated out obligatory beliefs and rites as religion's two defining characters, Durkheim expresses optimism that a science of religion can move forward and become part of sociological science (p. 93). Religion qualifies as a sociological phenomena and not a psychological one because it is made up of customary beliefs and practices stamped with compelling obligations that the faithful must obey. Given that these duties and commands are placed on individuals by a moral authority, this authority must originate outside the individual. What superior being has the abiding power to give orders and enforce obedience? Who indeed? If we refuse to assign this authority to otherworldly forces (or the laws of nature), only one candidate qualifies for this position—society itself:

> From empirical knowledge, the only thinking being which is greater than man is society. It is infinitely superior to each individual, since it is a synthesis of individuals. The state of perpetual dependence in which we find ourselves in the face of society inspires in us a feeling of religious awe. Thus, society dictates to the believer the dogmas he must uphold and the rites he must observe; if this is so, it is an indication that the rites and dogmas are its own handiwork.
> (p. 93)

If religious phenomena are products of "collective states of mind" (l'esprit collectif), the science of religion cannot seek "religiosity" in individual experience, he emphasized, but in the nature and organizational arrangements of societies. And, this change of direction forces us to now pose questions in sociological terms: How did these collective sentiments originate? Why are they dressed up in so many varieties of material coverings? What social functions are met by particular organizational arrangements? To penetrate this mystery, he said, we need to discover the laws of "collective conceptualization" (p. 95).

The Duality of the Sacred and Profane

Durkheim asks: What is the nature of sacred things? They are phenomena known to exist, crucial to all religions, and are irreducible to anything else. But what do they include and how does the distinction between sacred and profane arise? Is the sacred distinguished by the overpowering and extraordinary energy it releases? Yet, natural forces with a secular character can also harbor powerfully charged energy, whereas some secondary religious rites and objects (e.g. an amulet, holy water) evoke but weak forms of active properties. Addressing this rhetorical question, Durkheim attributes the sacred/profane partitioning to a difference in their natures both by degree such as the emotional anxiety generated by treating a sacred phenomena with irreverence, and by a qualitative distinction in how each type is cognitively perceived and processed in the mind. Sacred phenomena are *représentations* forged by a group or a society, and they include traditional beliefs, collective attitudes towards objects, and collective emotions. In contrast, profane phenomena are personal *représentations* forged by the sensory modalities of each individual. Each is a distinctive type of "intellectual phenomena," as the profane is a product of individual brain activity and the sacred is the product of interacting collective brains:

> Sacred things are those whose *représentation* society itself has fashioned . . . Profane things, conversely, are those which each of us constructs from our own sense data and experience . . . This duality of the temporal and the spiritual is not an invention without reason and without foundation in reality; it expresses in symbolic language the duality of the individual and the social, of psychology proper and sociology.
>
> (pp. 95–96)[12]

Commentary

By 1899, Durkheim's strategy of serializing his ideas on religion and totemism is proceeding along nicely. In Volume 1 of Année, he connects the origin of exogamy and the incest taboo with totemic cults. This appears to be a follow up to his 1895 editorial comment on *The History of Human Marriage* that "Westermarck is wrong about the causes of exogamy, which are all religious and are closely linked to totemic institutions" (see Chapter 6). In addition, in line with Robertson Smith, *taboo* (which Durkheim linked with menstruation and blood) is believed to have given rise to the sacred sentiment. Durkheim has shown (at least in his mind) how

---

[12] In 1898, Durkheim published in the *Revue de Métaphysique et de Morale*, "Individual And Collective Representations," where he clarifies by analogy what distinguishes individual from collective representations. Both personal and collective representations are distinctive in their own right, he said, for both exist on an emergent plane and each has its own creative synthesis. His intent is to show that personal representatations cannot be reduced down to the cerebral neurons and collective representations using the same logic cannot be reduced down to the sum of individuals. As Durkheim expressed it, "If [personal] representations, once they exist, continue to exist in *themselves* without their existence being perpetually dependent upon the disposition of the neural centres, if they have the power to react directly upon each other and to combine according to their own laws, they are then realities which, while maintaining an intimate relation with their substratum, are to a certain extent independent of it . . .When we said elsewhere that social facts are in a sense independent of individuals and exterior to individual minds, we only affirmed of the social world what we have just established for the psychic world" ([1898]1965: 23–24). For a detailed analysis of Durkheim's notion of representations, see Pickering 2000).

totemism, exogamy, and incest taboos are intrinsically related and a function of social causes. Where did Durkheim get such ideas? Where else other than the McLennan-Smith-early Frazer school of Scottish totemism.

In Volume Two of *L'Annee Sociologique*, Durkheim's focus is on isolating out the essential features of all religions. He urges the casting aside of personal ideas on religion and the application of the scientific method. Dismissing notions that aboriginal societies have only rudimentary or inferior religions and that "god" is an essential component of religion, he put forward the cult of totemism as a religion without god or gods, a religion with only a huge category of sacred things. To identify universal religious characters, he advocates applying what is his own version of the historical comparative method by defining religion per se as a system of parts and isolating out the parts shared by all known religions. He concludes that obligatory rites and obligatory beliefs are *the* two universal components of religion.

A third universal is the contrast between sacred things and profane things. Both are representations, he says, but they profoundly differ: profane representations are a product of individual experiences, whereas sacred representations are a product of collective experiences. As these two types of representations enter all human consciousness by different routes, they are perceived as different in nature, with the sense of duality itself an objective expression of how the mind bifurcates each type of representation. Again, Durkheim declares (as in *Suicide*) that society is the infinitely superior and mysterious force behind the obligatory dogmas and practices of religion, reinforcing the idea that religion is an imminently collective phenomena. As the sacred has a social origin it too must be explained in sociological terms. So religion in essence is a trinity of obligatory beliefs, defined rites, and collective representations of a sacred nature.

Yet, Durkheim's effort to promote his new totemic theory will soon be sorely tested in light of a sudden and astonishing event—a newly published ethnographic account of a full-blown totemic system among the aboriginals in Central Australia. This unforeseen event will set off a fireball of controversy over totemism, forcing Durkheim to sharpen his intellectual weapons to defend his ideas in an uphill battle against his critics and, surprisingly, to cross swords again and again with none other than Sir James Frazer.

9
Smashing Totemic Blows

It appears to my uncultured mind to be quite natural and logical that the black fellow should believe that he descended from an Animal (as an evolutionist you will admit that they get nearer the truth than the millions who believe in descent from Adam and Eve) . . . I dont(sic) expect you to agree with me, knowing as I do that you think there is something deeper and vastly more important at the root of the totem question but . . . I feel sure that the totems merely originated in a desire to account for origin and for no other purpose.
F.J. Gillen in a letter to Baldwin Spencer ([1898]2001: 219)

By 1900, *L'Année Sociologique* was hailed as an up and coming success. The yearly journal kept Durkheim and his collaborators busy, for it was labor intensive as the objective was to review all sociologically related books and articles published in the previous year. As Paul Lapie wrote in a correspondence to Célestin Bouglé in 1897, ". . . Durkheim has just thrown three or four fat books at me . . . they are in German and they are long. I had hoped to get by with two or three books, but an avalanche threatens" (quoted in Besnard 1983: 65). Yet, the devoted *Année* team enthusiastically took up this challenge. For as Edward Tiryakian (2009: 2) underscored, "Durkheim did not do sociology as an isolated individual, but rather as team leader . . . providing them with a division of labor that was an empirical manifestation of the justification for his own doctoral dissertation, *The Division of Labor in Society*." And due in large part to this close-knit collaboration, *L'Année Sociologique* acquired a reputation as both a distinctive journal and the visible fountainhead for the new French School of Sociology. By the turn of the twentieth century, Durkheim's goal of legitimating a "science of society" was becoming a reality as the "Durkheimians" under his leadership laid the building blocks for the new discipline (see Clark 1968; Besnard 1983; Giddens 1979 and Nandan 1980).[1]

---

1 Reviewers consisted of a core team and periodic contributors. During the early period 1899–1903 (volumes 2 to 6), the focal group had a "Bordeaux bias;" with several of them

As *Année* was mostly a journal of reviews, with some quite long and comprehensive, this format afforded Durkheim an unbridled license to question any issue using the same assertive style he had perfected since the start of his career. As Giddens (1970: 171) noted, "Durkheim often used reviews as a platform for the elucidation of his own theories, and for rebuttal of the attacks of his critics." Now with his turn to religion, his commentary even on economic issues was often cast in a religious light. For example, in his 1899 review of "Die ökonomischen Grundlagen der Mutterherrshaft" (Economic Bases of Matriarchy), where Heinrich Cunow had proposed that "uterine filiation" came late in human history and originated with garden farming, Durkheim wrote a biting criticism of what he thought was faulty logic:

> Cunow would have been less facile about ending with this explanation if he had not completely misunderstood the importance of the totem and of the totemic group. Far from being a conventional sign only, the totem is the symbol of religious life; and religion knows no bounds when extending its sway. As a result, the transmission of the totem through the female line is of capital importance for the constitution of the primitive family . . . everything combines to prove that it is the primitive factor, that originally the clan was organized exclusively according to the female line of descent.
> (quoted in Nandan 1980: 170)

In step with *Année*'s success, Durkheim's academic stature was also accelerating with the publication of *The Division of Labor*, *The Rules of the Sociological Method*, *Suicide*, and his many articles and reviews. He was now at the forefront of sociology. In 1899, *The Rules* was translated into Russian (the first full translation of one of Durkheim's books), but even his controversial essays on incest, exogamy, and totemism were gaining adherents, adding to a growing international reputation (Fournier 2013: 322). Yet, as Durkheim was busy airing his ideas in the *Année*, news came of a groundbreaking ethnography that would overturn most long-held notions of totemism, including its characteristic link with exogamy.

---

agrégés in philosophy who had studied under Durkheim (including, of course, Marcel Mauss). The "Bordeaux school" was the name used for the Durkheimians at this time. After Durkheim moved to Paris, the focal group of collaborators was *Normales* who had attended the École Normale Supérieure, 1904–1913 (volumes 7 to 12). (See Besnard 1983 and Nandan 1977 for a detailed analysis of the *Année*).

130 • Smashing Totemic Blows

The publication of Baldwin Spencer's and Francis Gillen's, *The Native Tribes of Central Australia* (1899), dropped a bombshell that ignited a decade of lively controversy, with potentially dire consequences for Durkheim's religious sociology. To appreciate the magnitude of the challenge he faced after 1899, a little background is needed on why a single ethnography had such a shattering impact on all that was previously known about totemism. Even the events surrounding this episode were extraordinary; indeed, it would not have occurred at all, if not for the collaboration of three strange bedfellows—Baldwin Spencer (a biology professor), Francis Gillen (a telegraphist), and James Frazer (a Cambridge don). Nor would Durkheim have had to concoct a string of creative explanations to support and defend his totemic theory for the rest of his career and to engage in intellectual combat with an implacable protagonist, Sir James Frazer. This little known story is also needed to comprehend the motives behind his feisty statements and responses, revealing deeply charged emotions that accompanied his writing of *The Elementary Forms*. Of all things, Durkheim's looming crisis took shape in the Australian outback and, oddly enough, because of a single-stranded iron wire supported by 36,000 wooden poles.

Totemic Circles and a Nemesis

The Spencer and Gillen Partnership[2]

In 1862, an exploring party headed by John Stuart left Adelaide and journeyed deep into the Australian interior to map the region. Ten years later, the Overland Telegraph Line transmitted a *Morse Code* message along the route that the Stuart party had taken from Adelaide to Port Darwin, a distance of 1,975 miles (3,178 kilometers). This amazing feat of a land line connected up to an overseas marine cable from East Java to Port Darwin in the Northern Territory ended Australia's extreme isolation by ushering in fast and direct communications with telegraphic networks around the globe (Mulvaney 2000 et al.: 3; Donovan 1988). To keep the traffic moving from Adelaide to Darwin, a series of related telegraph stations were built about 250 kilometers apart across outback Australia, with each one situated near natural water sources because the outback is mostly wind-blown sandy desert or bushlands. These small, far-flung repeater stations soon

---

[2] This narrative was drawn from the following sources: Mulvaney 2000 et al.; Spencer 1896; Blackwell and Lockwood 1965; Heppell and Wigley 1981; O'Byrne n.d.; Brooks 1991, Hartwig 1965, Williams 1997; Stokes 2001; Donovan 1988.

became local administrative centers and the nucleus for the first European/Australian settlements in the Australian Center. Ranchers, miners, and corporate businessmen followed closely behind as the lands surrounding these riverbank sites were found suitable for grazing cattle, goats, and sheep.

Alice Springs, the largest repeater station, was situated on a high bank about 1,000 miles (1,609 kilometers) from the coast and smack in the middle of the Overland Telegraph Line that ran from Adelaide to Darwin. It had a waterhole, police station, telegraph station, post office, and a cluster of residential buildings for linesmen, stockmen, telegraph operators, their families and domestic staff. This heartland outpost was so remote that mail delivery took two months by camel train, although by 1890 service had increased to every two weeks because of mining activity and the large expansion of cattle ranching in the vicinity (O'Byrne, n.d.). Adjacent to the Alice Springs station was Stuart, a township with a white population of less than twenty-five individuals. From its beginnings, Stuart served as a service and supply center for the mining experts, prospectors, missionaries, government surveyors and, especially for the pastoralists who grazed their cattle in the surrounding bushlands (Heppell and Wigley, 1981: 1ff; Blackwell and Lockwood 1965, 47ff).

To the East and West of the Alice Springs region (or Mparntwe) sit the MacDonnell Ranges, rising on the skyline to an elevation of 5,000 feet (1,524 meters) and gloriously configured with steep rocks, gaps, domes, beautiful valleys, caves, water pools, and other wonderous formations. No seas or bays penetrate very far into the Australian landmass so the MacDonnell Ranges by attracting rain clouds is what springs to life the rich flora and fauna in the Alice Springs countryside and these infrequent but large downpours fill the local creeks and rivers and briefly flood the landscape. While the tiny European settlement was nestled between the telegraph station and the Stuart Township (later renamed Alice Springs), the region itself is the ancestral home of the Arrernte (formerly spelled Arunta), a nomadic population of hunter-gatherers who had long used the station site and the MacDonnell Ranges for meetings and sacred ceremonies, with most of its topographical features linked with strong totemic associations. But once the pastoralists usurped their ancestral lands by fencing in the open terrain for cattle ranches with large-scale stockyards the water supply was interrupted. And once the native flora and fauna was disrupted or trampled upon by the grazing of hundreds of thousands of cattle in the surrounding countryside, a mostly sedentary population of Arrernte lured by government rations settled in fringe camps near Alice Springs.

In 1892, Francis James Gillen (1855–1912), an Australian-born Irishman who had worked as an operator for the Overland telegraph line, arrived in

Alice Springs to take up his new post as stationmaster, postmaster, Central Australian magistrate, and sub-protector of aboriginals. In 1894, Professor Baldwin Spencer (1860–1929), a British zoologist who had moved to Australia to establish the biology department at Melbourne University, visited Central Australia as a member of the famous Horn Scientific Expedition sponsored by William Horn, a wealthy pastoralist and mining industrialist. Spencer's official role was to take pictures and collect samples of plants and animals for scientific study and, thus, when the Horn expedition reached Alice Springs, Spencer met Gillen who volunteered his help in collecting specimens. Gillen was the local authority on native lifeways and was so keen on studying their traditions that he learned the native language. His bubbling enthusiasm sparked Spencer's interest so much that after he returned to Melbourne, they corresponded regularly with Gillen, sending boxes of specimens as well as detailed information on native customs and manners, including lots of photographs (as Gillen was an excellent photographer).

In 1896, Spencer returned to Central Australia on sabbatical leave planning to split his time between a visit with Gillen and a field expedition with Ernest Cowle (1863–1922), a local bush policemen whom he met during the Horn Expedition to Alice Springs. Cowle's role as peacemaker was mostly devoted to enforcing the directives of white landowners by arresting aboriginals who encroached on pastoral lands, routinely sending them off by train to the Port August jail (and on this he was uncompromising), but he was well-educated and understood the disruptive effects of European hegemony. But as luck would have it, a severe drought in Cowle's locality forced the cancellation of the Cowle-Spencer expedition; as a result, Spencer spent his leave with Gillen in Alice Springs (Mulvaney et al. 2000).

The Gillen-Spencer partnership thus became a reality, although the initial success of their collaboration depended on Gillen's relations with the native community. As stationmaster, one of Gillen's jobs was to serve as protector of aboriginals; and unlike most constables and government authorities, he had a deep compassion for the loss of their cultural autonomy, recognizing that they had little choice but to settle near missions, telegraph outposts, or pastoral stations for charity handouts, government rations, or to work in the stockyards for food. After Gillen charged a ruthless constable with murdering a local native, banishing him to a remote area, the Arrernte people accorded Gillen great respect and honor because he had stood up for their rights (which few administrators did at the time).

Irresistibly drawn to Arrernte culture, Gillen decided to sponsor a series of native ceremonies to be held in Alice Springs, an amazing feat in itself as the Australian government was now forbidding large assemblies of aboriginals. In this effort, Gillen sent around "the hand-beckoner," a *churinga (tywerrenge)* or sacred stick or stone that served as a formal summons. What is so extraordinary about this planned event is that *no* Westerner had *even* glimpsed these sacred ceremonies. But, given their great respect for Gillen (who they considered a blood brother), the elders gave their permission to witness the sacred ceremonies in their entirety. Gillen ([1896] 2001: 138) wrote to Spencer in August 1896,

> ... I have, after much palaver with the old men here, arranged for an Engwura Ceremony to take place sometime in November, I am to assist them with rations. They have already begun preparations and some of the young men are scouring the Country in search of feathers, etc. It is many years since the last Engwura was performed here and only two or three of the younger generation have been through it.

To include Spencer, a complete stranger, Gillen told the headman that Spencer was his brother. In November of 1896, Spencer wrote to his friend Lorimer Fison, a well-known ethnologist:

> How ever Gillen persuaded them to let me in I can't imagine but the first night I got there the old head man came up to me and of his own accord said "you Bultharra Udnirringeta" which meant that I was a Bultharra man of the Udnirringita or large grub totem the same as himself and then he called me "Wetteey-aitcha" which means my younger brother. After that I went in and out amongst them and they took no more notice of me than if I were one of themselves which in fact I now am. Gillen they call the "Oknirrabata" which means "Great teacher" and they seem really anxious to let us know all about them.
> ([1896] 2001: 144: note 331)

So in the Australian summer of 1896–1897 and despite the tremendous odds, Spencer and Gillen became official members of the Arrernte "brotherhood" with Spencer staying on for months so he would not miss any ceremonies. Indeed, they even joined the natives by occupying a wurley (native hut), enabling them to take night photographs and detailed notes so to assure accurate descriptions of everything they witnessed. The assembly opened at Alice Springs, with two ordinary dancing corroborees (informal gatherings) followed by a surprising number of nearly 200 formal ceremonies, with each ceremony connected with some particular totem and locality in Central Australia. The traditions refer back to a long past time called the "Alcheringa," which means the *dreamtime* when ancestors were designated by the name of some animal or plant species. Each totem group had their special ceremonies, and only totem mates could perform these rituals. In their ethnography, Spencer and Gillen described aboriginal physical features (e.g. height, eye color, skull measurements), the splendor of their artwork (often depicting a dreamtime story) and notably their totemic designs and how they are symbolically carved on weapons, tools and worn on the backs of men undergoing initiation.

They also detailed the totemic system and other social formations with elaborate descriptions of sacred ceremonies, including magic rites, marriage sections or classes, burials, and especially initiation rites—a series called *Engwura*. They discovered that Arrernte marriage rules are not governed by totem membership but by marriage classes, a finding that was to put Durkheim ideas about totemism, religion, and exogamy into a freefall. They also detailed how the natives map out the countryside very carefully with special camping grounds and how totem ancestors are around these camping grounds (with a churinga or sacred stone in hand). They also found that totem members have a ceremony for increasing their totem species and that eating your totem is *not* tabooed as it is in other parts of the world.

Thus, what Spencer and Gillen documented was an amazing number of rites, legends, and myths never before seen or heard of except by Australian aboriginals. Their work involved the local Arrernte people and neighboring bands. Glossed over in a cosmic irony is that their ethnography did not describe an undisturbed or pristine native population but one desperately struggling to survive in a post-colonial environment, despite the loss of autonomy, the decimation of their population, the destruction of their culture, European diseases, malnutrition, and the take-over of their ancestral lands by the cattle industry—a process set in motion soon after the first telegraph lines were strung in 1872. Ernest Cowle, the bush policeman, voiced his skepticism that settled aboriginals provisioned by government rations bore any resemblance to their former food collecting lifeway. In an acerbic quip, Cowle dubbed *The Native Tribes of Central Australia*, "Grimm's Fairy Tales," updated by Spencer and Gillen. And, in jest he told Spencer (who was making plans with Gillen for more research) how much the aboriginals appreciated advance notice of their visits as it gave them time to "invent some habits and customs" (see Mulvancy et al. 2000: 37ff and a discussion of Cowle's role in Central Australia).

The Spencer, Gillen, and Frazer Collaboration

Yet, despite the misleading impression of an undisturbed aboriginal culture, *The Native Tribes of Central Australia* was a remarkably acute ethnography for its time (Morphy 1998).[3] To get it published, however, might be problematic because Spencer was by training a biologist, not an ethnologist, and Gillen was a telegraphist and stationmaster. So Spencer turned to his social scientist friends for assistance and as luck would have it, he was put in touch with none other than James Frazer.

By 1896, Frazer was no longer an unknown Cambridge don as his book on *Totemism* (1887) and his two volumes of the *Golden Bough* (1890) (on aboriginals and ancient religion) now afforded him a worldwide reputation and a distinguished network of international scholars (Ackerman 1987: 148). In early 1897, Frazer received a letter from Lorimer Fison (1832–1907), the Australian ethnologist with an enclosed letter that Spencer had written to Fison about totemism. Soon, Frazer and Spencer were corresponding regularly, with Frazer seeking answers to questions suited to his special interests, such as the relationship between exogamy and totemism. In a short time, Frazer became a virtual partner in the Spencer/Gillen collaboration (Kuper 1988: 101ff). Indeed, as Ackerman (1987: 154), Frazer's biographer expressed it: Spencer "immediately assumed the role of disciple to Frazer the master and put himself and Gillen at Frazer's service. Any questions he was unable to answer himself he would refer to Gillen who remained in the bush and was therefore able to do research on the spot. From Frazer's point of view it could not have been better." In 1897, Frazer offered to read the manuscript proofs and to help them interpret the rituals they observed. In September 1898, Frazer wrote to Spencer with his suggestions on a new theory of totemism:

> In going through the second proofs of your book I have been more than ever struck by your account of the Intichiuma ceremonies. Such ceremonies for the multiplication of the totem plant or animal have

---

3 As Howard Morphy wrote: ". . . Spencer and Gillen spent more time in data collection than any of their predecessors. Their joint fieldwork lasted for nearly a year and a half and for most of that time they lived with Aboriginal people . . . Gillen was able to work in the Aranda language and recent linguistic research has tended to confirm the accuracy of his and Spencer's translations. They were meticulous in cross-checking their data and in seeking clarification of things that they had failed to understand. They pioneered the use of film, photography, and sound recording in the field . . . Their ethnography has stood the test of time and continues to be cited by current researchers to an almost unparalleled extent (1998:18).

not been . . . reported from any other part of the world, and taken in conjunction with other facts that you mention seem to set totemism in an entirely new light, at least so far as the Central Australian tribes are concerned. It almost looks as if among these tribes totemism were a system expressly devised for the purpose of procuring a plentiful supply of everything that the savage regards as desirable—food, water, sunshine, wood etc . . . What do you think of this as an hypothesis to explain totemism as it is among your tribes?

([1898:]2005: 124–125)

Frazer also encouraged Spencer and Gillen to accept speaking engagements and write theoretical papers especially on totemism (as the book is mostly descriptive). To their credit, they took his advice with a series of public presentations along with published articles in prestigious journals. Frazer followed suit with his own articles, although he stripped totemism down to a few plain essentials by divorcing it from its rich body of totemic folklore and touting it as a glorified system of magical performances by a "band of magicians" or a "primitive co-op" to increase the food supply. He also severed the link between exogamy and totemism by portraying each as phenomena that existed independently of each other. In contrast, Spencer and Gillen viewed the Arrernte totemic system as extremely complex and embedded in a sacred ritualized context with strong religious overtones. Yet, they went along with Frazer's magic hypothesis (albeit unhappily), perhaps because they respected his judgment or perhaps in gratitude for all his help (as it had been substantial).

The publication of *The Native Tribes of Central Australia* (1899) was an unexpected bonanza for Frazer as it equipped him with a new data set and, for an armchair scholar, the unabridged freedom to propose all kinds of new interpretations that directly conflicted, of course, with his earlier published accounts of totemism. As Ackerman (1987: 154–155) summed it up:

> The importance of Spencer and Gillen's research and information over the next several years for Frazer's subsequent work cannot be overstated. They enabled Frazer to propose not one but two new theories of the origin of totemism; they gave him the empirical basis for his distinction between magic and religion and for the idea that the former everywhere preceded the latter; and they promoted to center stage the question of exogamy and its possible relation with totemism. These themes would engross Frazer for the first decade of the new century.

In 1900, Frazer revised the *Golden Bough*, which now included the Central Australian materials, raising his stature publically and academically (Ackerman: p. 162). He was now a world-famous scholar, and a formable opponent for Durkheim.

So, in the scheme of things, Baldwin Spencer and Francis Gillen had documented a full-blown totemic system—not simply leftover fragments of former ones. Unfortunately, it was the antithesis of what Durkheim had theorized on religion and totemism. Their ethnography had weakened its sacred qualities by finding that it was okay for members to eat sparingly of their totem and, most importantly, it broke apart the intimate linkage Durkheim had made between exogamy and totemism. And, Frazer's new utilitarian theory of totemism as a primitive economic system to increase the food supply amounted to a simple principle of reciprocity. Instead of a religious cult—and the earliest religion at that—totemism was now reduced to a series of magical rites for increasing the fertility of plants and animals. Durkheim's totemic theory was in serious trouble.

What was Durkheim to do? He had anchored his theory in surveys and data sets around the globe and from the best authorities of the times, including Fison and Howitt (1880), the early Frazer (1887, 1890), Morgan (1871, 1877), McLennan (1865, 1869–1870), Powell (1881), Robertson Smith (1885, 1991) and other Australian, European, American, and Canadian scholars. This body of research still upheld the long-established ideas about totemism. But Spencer and Gillen were the only Westerners who had actually witnessed totemic ceremonies. Even some traditions of the Arrernte tended to support the idea that early ancestors feasted on their totem animals and married within their totem group. And, the totemic ceremonies watched by Spencer and Gillen in such a remote wilderness were unlikely to be the result of diffusion from coastal populations. What, then, accounted for such distinctive totem traits? And, why did the central aboriginals also deviate not just from characteristic totemic traits but also from other tribes with totems in other localities? Did the Arrernte really represent the most primitive form of totemism? Durkheim had a baffling problem to resolve. He could not abandon his totemic theory (as he was convinced he was right) nor could he mount an empirical case for his position. Facts were facts, and so, he could not openly dispute such a well-done ethnography, and there was no way of getting around that stumbling block. What he could question, however, was *their interpretation of what it all meant.*

Durkheim's First Line of Defense

In 1900, Durkheim mounted a campaign to defend his theory of totemism in the third volume of *L'Année Sociologique* by enlisting his nephew's help in drafting three critical reviews in a three-way punch—two on Spencer and Gillen's *Native Tribes of Central Australia* (1899) and one on Frazer's latest articles on totemism. As editor of the religious section Mauss signed the first review. He began with an overwhelmingly positive endorsement of Spencer and Gillen's ground breaking accomplishments, praising them as competent and keen observers who have faithfully documented a large quantity of remarkable, unexpected, and novel facts that now question traditional theories of totemism (Mauss 1900a: 205–206). After a synopsis of the book, the review shifts to a more negative mode, with an assessment of Spencer and Gillen's many shortcomings, including their interpretation of the eating of the totem, their insufficient research and simplistic analysis of the rites associated with the *churinga* (which means sacred), and their gross mistake of placing too much value on the reenactment of rites related to ancient tribal mythology (p. 212). Mauss also found it disappointing that such a lengthy book lacked comprehensive details on mythology and ceremonial chants. Another bone of contention is Spencer and Gillen's view that Arrernte totemism is in a primordial stage of development. Mauss proposes that social changes have been introduced to weaken the social sphere of totemism and strengthen the sacred sphere. And, that Arrernte totemism is actually in a more advanced stage of development.

Durkheim signed the second review as editor of the family and kinship section. His tone is neutral and objective, lacking the traces of emotions evident in Mauss's review. Durkheim starts by praising Spencer and Gillen for their attentive observations of aboriginal organization and religious practices and for their detailed information on exogamy and marriage patterns. After a discussion of aboriginal matrimonial classes, Durkheim relates how Spencer and Gillen have gleaned additional information on Arrernte marriage patterns, especially on how they take place across subdivisions of different classes. These cross-filiations are then used to support their hypotheses but unfortunately, he stresses, Spencer and Gillen are unable to provide coherent explanations for the flexibility of these patterns. As an example, Durkheim notes that the Arrernte have a patrilineal descent system and their neighbors, the Urabbuna, have a matrilineal descent system but both systems can accommodate the two descent systems by establishing some form of class equivalency so the groups can intermarry (Durkheim 1900: 332–333).

On totemism, Durkheim sets aside Spencer and Gillen's interpretation of totem groups and offers his own explanation for why Arrernte totemism does not follow the longstanding pattern, by explaining how the gradual dispersion of matriliny totem members (because of female exogamy) led to a shift of allegiance to patriliny territorial groups, concluding that although the Arrernte social system is still rooted in groups and matrimonial classes, the system itself has evolved and transitioned into a more complex stage of totemism (1900: 334–335).

Mauss signed the third review, turning this time to Frazer's articles on "The Origins of Totemism" and "Observations on Central Australian Totemism" (1899). He starts in a neutral tone but ends in an antithetical tone by calling Frazer's conclusions insufficient and unsatisfactory. In his review he disparages him for his failure to address issues of organizational structure, for his lack of appreciation for the rich complexity of the initiation ceremonies, for his simplistic notion that Australian totemism is a cooperative system of magic and, above all, for his belief that the Arrernte system is a primitive form of totemism (Mauss 1900b).

Commentary

The Spencer and Gillen ethnography is a smashing success. It successfully challenged the two essential canons of totemism that had been established over the previous thirty years that (1) a totem member cannot eat his totem and that (2) a strong association exists between exogamy and totemism. Frazer's hypothesis that totemism is simply a system of magic with spells and enchantments to increase the fertility of totem species only added fuel to the firestorm. On the heels of this crisis, Durkheim had to deal with another upsetting finding—this time from the American ethnographer, Franz Boas, a leading figure in American anthropology. Boas, who worked with the Kawkiutl Indians in the Pacific Northwest, was now questioning the longstanding belief that the first human kinship systems were organized around female descent with male descent a later stage of development. Durkheim had argued that the progressive trend was always from female to male descent with no documented cases favoring the latter. The reverse for Durkheim was impossible. Yet, the impossible materialized among the Kawkiutl Indians of the Pacific Northwest with Boas claiming the adoption of maternal laws by a tribe on the paternal developmental stage (Boas 1897: 334–335).

Durkheim reviewed Boas's "The Social Organization and the Secret Societies of the Kwaikutl Indians" in L'*Année Sociologique* in 1900. In this review, Durkheim adopted a mild-mannered tone, and simply conveyed that he was unconvinced of the author's claim of an intermediary stage between patrilineal and matrilineal descent. He then detailed how recruitment in the clan under consideration is quite peculiar as it is neither matrilineal as in the Northern tribes nor patrilineal as in the Southern tribes. The problem, Durkheim said, as Boas had already noted, is the lack of an established territory for clan members. So the transitory state reported is the result of contract with tribes where matriliny is practiced. And, the result is the conservation of patrilineal descent and the taking up of some laws of matrilineal descent. Then, for emphasis, Durkheim reiterates the hypothesis that there has not been a single observed case of a shift from patrilineal to matrilineal descent.

At this juncture, however, Durkheim's totemic theory is in jeopardy. His assumptions that matrilineal descent is the first kinship system, totemism is the first religion, and that exogamy and incest are linked with totemism and are the earliest taboos are all unraveling. This crisis marks yet another turning point in his career as he pushes forward, getting more and more involved with religious phenomena (Alpert 1961: 54–55). In 1900–1901 Durkheim teaches a course on "The Social Organization of Primitive (Australian) Societies," affording him time to engage in a complete analysis of Spencer and Gillen's data and to reinterpret their argument so that eating one's totem and marrying within one's totem makes sense in light of the old established argument. He would title this ingenious paper "Sur le totemisme," and follow it up later with an essay on the Australian matrimonial class system. He would also go on to connect his theory of religion, with a theory on human classification and cognition. As we will see, much of Durkheim's work leading up to the writing of *The Elementary Forms* was plagued by his creative efforts to beat back the challenges to his theory of religion and society.

10
The Great Totemic March

I have changed my views repeatedly, and I am resolved to change them again with every change of the evidence, for like a chameleon the candid enquirer should shift his colours with the shifting colours of the ground he treads.
James Frazer, ([1910]1968: xiii) in *Totemism and Exogamy, Volume 1*

In June of 1901, Durkheim rushed to Éspinal to be with his mother Mélanie who died shortly after her son arrived: "My poor mother did not suffer [he wrote to a friend] but we all did... We had known for three days that it was all over" (quoted in Fournier 2013: 384). In the same year, Durkheim published a second edition of *The Rules of Sociological Method*, taking the opportunity, he said, to clear up some misconceptions and impressions. He had good reason now to be optimistic about sociology's future with the surprising renaissance of Comtean positivism. Once tabooed in academic circles, it was now in vogue. In 1902, after a white marble bust of Auguste Comte was erected in the Sorbonne Square, the occasion was formally celebrated with the Senate, Parliament, the President of the Republic, international delegates and other luminaries in attendance.

In 1902, Durkheim was called to the University of Paris to take up a new academic appointment—*chargé de cours* (Chair of Education) in the Faculty of Letters. In 1906, he was awarded a Full Professorship, and in 1913 the Chair of Education and Sociology. Though he was appointed to teach pedagogy, he was permitted to teach sociology, although his early years at the Sorbonne kept him fully occupied with administrative duties and pedagogy courses on such wholesome topics as intellectual education, moral education, primary education, morality in schools, and Renaissance Pedagogy (Fournier 2013: 398–405; Fauconnet 1923; Alpert 1961: 61–62).[1]

---

1 Durkheim was forthright on his approach to pedagogy: "Being a sociologist ... I shall discuss education in the capacity of a sociologist" (quoted in Fauconnet 1923: 530). Before he died in 1917, he had completed a manuscript composed of eighteen lectures on moral

In 1902, Durkheim also published a second edition of the *Division of Labor in Society* (1902). In the text he quietly replaced *naturism* with *totemism* in his stage model of religion (see Chapter 5). In the Preface, he deleted about twenty-five pages but added material on occupational groups, making his newly added section prominent by appending a new coda to the book title: *Some Remarks on Professional Groups* (see Watts Miller 2012). Critics grumbled that it advocated a corporate-style morality as a new form of solidarity. Otherwise, Durkheim left the text intact, apparently viewing it as passé and even distancing himself intellectually, confiding to a colleague that the book "is of interest only to beginners, and I am republishing it for beginners" (quoted in Fournier 2013: 378). One wonders if he was alluding here to his own initial effort to study social solidarity.

In 1903, Durkheim wrote a long essay "Sociology and the Social Sciences" (with Paul Fauconnet). As the title suggests, it dealt with the separation of sociology from philosophy and the integration of the social sciences into branches of scientific sociology. Lucien Lévy-Bruhl remarked that Durkheim was surely the successor of Auguste Comte (LaLande 1905). Critics of positivism, however, called Durkheim "a crummy Comte," while his enemies at the Sorbonne mocked him for his disrespect for religion (Azouvi 2007, in Fournier 2013: 547). In 1905, Durkheim fueled this image when he announced at a public lecture his plans to prove that "*God is Society,*" the true Creator and Eternal force of support and mortality (quoted in LaLande 1906: 255ff).

By all accounts *Année* continued a great success, especially among anthropologists. As Sidney Hartland wrote in *Folklore* (1902: 314), "The fifth volume of *L'Année Sociologique* is in nowise inferior to its predecessors in variety or interest . . . causing *L'Année Sociologique* to become indispensable to every student of anthropology . . ." Yet, while the *Année* hummed along with Durkheim writing his crisp reviews, many with a strong religious cast, his own work on religion and totemism was steadily being undermined by the growing skepticism that totemism was not what it had originally seemed to be. As Alfred Haddon writing in *Nature* put the problem in 1902:

> When one surveys the fairly extensive literature of totemism one is struck with the very general insufficiency of the evidence . . . full and

---

education in primary school (*L'Education Morale à l'École Primaire*) and see Fauconnet 1923 and Pickering 1979 on Durkheim's pedagogical writings, studies, and his educational perspective.

precise information is lamentably lacking. The foundations upon which students at home have to build their superstructures of generalization and theory are usually of too slight a character to support these erections with much chance of their permanence.

Durkheim also had to contend with Frazer's latest theory that magic (rather than religion) was linked with totemism. The critical reviews in *Année* that he and Mauss had written had done little to challenge the new discoveries and conclusions. A more compelling argument was needed, and Durkheim provided it in two *Mémoire Originaux*, "Sur le totémisme" in 1902, and "De quelques formes primitives de classification: contribution à l'étude des représentations collectives" (Primitive Classification) in 1903, co-authored with Marcel Mauss.

Totemism

Durkheim's essay "On Totemism" ([1902]1985) is a very sophisticated analysis of the Australian kinship system (despite what sociologists tend to believe about it). It captures his extensive knowledge of Australian literature, his command of kinship theory and nomenclature, and his obsession with totemism as the first religion. This *Mémoire* is nothing less than a masterful response to Spencer and Gillen's discovery that the Arrernte (Arunta) do not follow the traditional principles long associated with totemism. Above all, it represents Durkheim's best effort then to salvage totemism, making it abundantly clear that he is not budging an inch on his belief that totemism is the touchstone for understanding the origin of religion, exogamy, and the incest taboo. Let us briefly explore the main themes in this definitive article and the sentiments expressed "between the lines," given how much he had on the line here.

Durkheim opens by highlighting a longstanding problem: nobody until Spencer and Gillen had ever witnessed "a truly totemic religion" [note the words *totemic religion*] and this has led some scholars to revise their understanding of totemism [but he's not one of them]. Frazer now claims these new findings contradict the fundamental tenets of totemism and "by a remarkable coincidence," Durkheim added [tongue-in-cheek], Frazer, Spencer and Gillen independently reached the same conclusions (Durkheim [1902]1985: 91). But Frazer's reversal is especially telling because he helped to establish the traditional view of totemism and is now proposing that these assumptions should be abandoned. This concordance requires that we look again at totemism because:

Everything that concerns totemism necessarily has repercussions extending into all the domains of sociology, for totemism lies at the root of a multitude of institutions. If this transformation is really necessary, therefore, it cannot fail to require other reforms in the most disparate directions—e.g. all questions relating to the origins of kinship, marriage, sexual morality, indeed even social organization would be posed in new terms, and would have to be subjected to study all over again. For this reason, it seemed worthwhile to ask for ourselves whether the facts observed permit the interpretation proposed, or whether there is not another interpretation which is preferable.

(p. 91)

Durkheim starts by reviewing two canons of totemism: (1) that one cannot kill or eat their totem plant or animal and (2) that totem mates cannot mate or marry each other. Many Australian tribes are still practicing these established restrictions, he said; it is the Arrernte (Arunta) of Central Australia who no longer follow the totemic interdictions in the way formerly understood. Yet, they do divide up into local groups with distinctive plant and animal names, and totem mates do feel a close kinship bond with a totem serving as their collective emblem. At issue here is that totem affinity does not play the customary role of regulating sexual unions and marriage. And, [worst of all] the oral traditions tell of a time when men and women *always* married individuals belonging to the same totem—that is, endogamy rather than exogamy was the traditional practice ([1902] 1985: 92). In addition, the interdiction in practice today against eating your totem symbol is now a "half-taboo"—that is, you can on occasion eat your totem with only special animal parts such as the liver strictly forbidden.

What happened in the past? Was the taboo restricted and now relaxed or the reverse; something was modified but in what direction? Frazer proposes that we should trust the native's recollections that in times past one could freely eat one's totem. And in Frazer's imaginings, Durkheim added, eating one's totem became more restrictive after the Arrernte developed the logical faculties of understanding that a totem and its members belong to the same species and conspecifics do not eat their own kind. If a totemic complex does exist without alimentary interdictions or a rule of exogamy, then what constitutes totemism must be modified.

Having presented these newly discovered facts in his customary agreeable manner, Durkheim's objective now is to dismantle Spencer, Gillen, and Frazer's suppositions by replacing them with his own version of events (p. 93).

If we cannot use our old characterizations, how do we characterize the Arrernte totemic cult? Frazer proposes that the answer lies in the *Intichiuma*, or the yearly ceremony practiced by each totemic group to increase the fertility of the species symbolizing each totem. To achieve this result, according to Frazer, the natives employ sympathetic magic (i.e. "like to like" or the notion that similar things influence each other) by imitating the shape, gestures, and vocalizations, of totem animals. As members of other totems have no taboo against eating the totems of other groups, the result is a writ large cooperation or an economic system of reciprocity. Looked at from this vantage point, Durkheim says, the religious character of totemism is lost as the rites are not addressed to higher moral forces. Instead, as Frazer conceives it, the *Intichiuma* ceremony involves a crude, magical set of practices, a complementary economic enterprise without religious rites. Yet, what stands out in Spencer and Gillen's book:

> ... is that the milieu in which the Aruntas live is deeply marked by religiosity and that this religiosity is of an essentially totemic origin. The territory is completely covered with sacred trees and groves, with mysterious caves where the objects of the cult are piously conserved. These holy places are approached only with a feeling of religious terror ... Moreover, to all of these locations totemic legends are attached, and totemic rites are celebrated there ... [In fact] the rites of the Arunta are comparable at every point to those found in incontestably religious systems; thus they proceed from the same ideas and feelings and, as a consequence, it is arbitrary not to apply to them the same designation.
> (1902: 94–95)[2]

Durkheim then turns to one of Frazer's key assumptions: Are the characteristic traits of alimentary and matrimonial interdictions fundamentally linked to totemic institutions or not?

In his counterattack, Durkheim asks: Did the Arrernte start out with endogamous totems? If so, then we must conclude that exogamy is independent of totemic beliefs. As Durkheim's totemic theory hinges on keeping the intimate link between exogamy and totemic beliefs (see his 1897 essay on the incest taboo), he must restore this association. So he continues to build his counter-offensive.

---

2 Here Durkheim emphasizes more the rites, and not beliefs, viewing the Arrernte of being largely unaware of the religious forces constraining them to act in certain ways.

As exogamy and totemism are known to co-exist in a large number of societies, this association should not be abandoned because one single study appears to run counter to all others. At the very least, he cautioned, a second hypothesis should be seriously entertained: Arrernte totemism is simply a more developed and aberrant form of totemism. Although Frazer dismisses this conclusion given the Arrernte desert location and limited contact with outside societies, the Arrernte are capable of an indigenous social evolution, stemming from changes in their hunter/gatherer lifestyle, interactions with neighboring tribes, environmental changes, and the like (p. 96). Indeed, their strong tribal unity, group leadership, and refined domestic relations all point to a long historical past and a much more developed stage than other Australian populations. And, during these developmental phases, Arrernte institutions lost and gained attributes so that their current lifestyle can only provide a relatively incomplete sketch of their former organizational arrangements (p. 96).

The rest of Durkheim's essay is devoted to his ingenious reinterpretation of many generalizations drawn by Spencer, Gillen, and Frazer. First, Durkheim calls attention to the exogamous groups that do exist in Arrernte society. The entire social structure is divided into two big groupings—each representing one half of the society or two phratries [or moieties].[3] Each phratry in turn, is divided up into two sections or classes. Each of the sections/classes within each phratry has its own distinctive name (e.g. Bulthara) but if the two are merged together to form a compound name—one phratry (or moiety) is called Bulthara-Panunga—and the other is Kumara-Purula. These two sections *within* a phratry are not artificial entities since they naturally gravitate toward each other, and otherwise distinguish themselves from sections or classes of the opposite phratry. With this in mind, an exogamy rule prevails but the taboo is not between sections/classes. Instead, you must marry someone *outside* your phratry. As societies with two phratries are frequently found in both Australia and America, we now have information about the inherent nature of phratries. As Durkheim explains:

---

3 Durkheim uses the term phratry instead of moiety. Both terms are used to conceptualize relationships among a specific grouping of clans so he is not technically wrong. But today the word phratry is generally reserved for a society with three or more large groups within a society. Moiety is the better term when a social system is divided up into two large groups, but we will continue to use Durkheim nomenclature here and in the chapters to follow to avoid confusion (see Chapter 1 p.13 footnote 11 for kinship terms).

What becomes clear from the multiple descriptions we have been given is that . . . [the phratry] . . . is nothing else but the original form of the clan. It is a primary clan which, in the course of its development, has become segmented into a certain number of secondary clans, although the latter have not lost their feeling of common origin and solidarity . . . That it began as a clan—indeed, a clan of this nature— is evident from the fact that it often has a totem, and also that the totems of the different secondary clans are sometimes clearly derived from that totem. Thus, the second is anterior to the first.

(p. 97)

Hence, Durkheim proposes that Arrernte society is a compound of two primary totemic clans or two exogamous groups. This means, he said, there was a time when marriage was taboo for members of a totemic group. It cannot be said, then, that membership in a particular totemic group did not influence marriage or that totemic groups once practiced endogamy. At present, however, members of the same totem are found in both phratries. For example, members of the Kangaroo totem are found in both the Bulthara-Panunga and the Kumara-Purula section/classes that makes marital relations within a totem possible. If each totem was strictly contained in a single phratry, the totemic group would also be exogamous as the two phratries are now. Yet, this mingling is relatively recent, Durkheim argued, because nearly all members of a given totem are confined to one phratry; only a handful is actually found in the complementary one. The source of this unequal ratio points to a time when totemic members were subdivided into totemic clans within a single phratry. Close bonds also exist between a totem, its collection of "religious treasure[s]" such as *churingas* (i.e. sacred engraved wooden or stone objects), and its head representative who must reside in the phratry where the totemic cult is dominant, and the *churingas* must stay in that phratry (p. 98). So each totem cult identifies for the most part with a single phratry.

As to why some totem members drifted to the opposite phratry and why the exogamous rule detached from the clan-totem to become a phratry rule, Durkheim proposes that the social system underwent a social revolution, buttressing his argument with Spencer and Gillen's account of how Arrernte traditions support this hypothesis (p. 99). He also cited evidence from the neighboring Urabunna who are also organized into two phratries but retained the traditional formation of exogamous totems. In contrast, the exogamous rule for the Arrernte shifted from its specialized totemic association to a more generalized phratry association. The cause of this revolution, Durkheim said, was a change in Arrernte filiation. At present, a child follows the father's line of descent within a phratry but in the past the child likely followed the mother's line. To support this assumption, Durkheim emphasized both the higher status of women and the current terms used in kinship nomenclature with the interfacing of the two types of descent—one corresponding to a former matrilineal system. The alleged shift to patriliny also lent credibility to Durkheim's notion that the transition signaled a gradual breaking down of totemism and, in turn, a society in a far more advanced stage of development than that portrayed by Frazer:

> The Arunta are thus a long way from offering us, so to speak, the "perfect type" of primitive civilization. In reality, at the moment they have been observed, they were already very noticeably removed from their initial state; in the very structure of their society, grave and profound rearrangements have been produced. And it is precisely these rearrangements which will enable us to explain this totemic endogamy that has been made the essential characteristic of primitive totemism.
> (p. 107)

In this eloquent essay, Durkheim applied his ingenuity at synthesis and his brilliance as a kinship theorist to demonstrate how a revolutionary change in Arrernte kinship relations set into motion different and sometimes opposing kinship rules that dispersed clan members into two phratries and altered the original social structure. Yet, when looked at through the relational lens of a sociologist, he said, Arrernte totemism is simply an alternation from its original and essential form. And, in his eyes, totemism is a religion closely aligned with clans, where the totem is sacred to those who share the same emblem. As he expressed it:

> It is wrong to see in the Arunta the late representatives of humanity at its origin; and it would be no less a mistake to misjudge everything that subsists among them as the most primitive social forms that we know ... A transformation which, ordinarily, is produced only in a rather late period, came among them to seize totemic institutions at a time when they were still rather strongly organized. But they have survived only after having suffered variations and alterations which indicate to us in what sense and in what way they were destined to evolve; and from this it is possible to see how totemism is linked to the religious systems which have followed it.
> (pp. 117–118)

Durkheim's essay also illustrates his effective application of the concept of survivals. It also demonstrates his method of starting with data that refutes his totemic hypothesis and then shoots it down by showing why his thesis still has validity—in this case the connection between exogamy and totemism. He was also able to account for the Arrernte odd matrimonial rules, food restrictions, and for Frazer's notion that the Arrernte totemic system was nothing more than a primitive economic system. Moreover, while religion itself is but lightly touched upon, he depicted the Arrernte as living in a religious atmosphere in every respect, challenging Frazer's notion that their totemism is rooted in magical beliefs and rites. Last, he argued that because Arrernte totemism was not in a primitive stage but an advanced and transitional stage, it was a gross mistake to reformulate the longstanding canons of totemism.

After publishing his totem essay some scholars applauded his efforts, calling it creative, original, ingenious, and erudite (see Sidney Hartland 1902). Adversaries at the Sorbonne, however, called him a totemist because he reduced everything to totems. One colleague protested, "Too much is too much" and suggested that the *Année* take up "something other than totem and taboo" (Fournier [2006]2013: 435).

Primitive Classification

Durkheim's next *Mémoire*, of all things, is on the human classification process. A class is a set or category of things, Durkheim said, but what is perceived as belonging or assigned to a class of phenomena is not simply by observation. "My work suggests," he wrote to Marcel Mauss, "that there is a question here, that this way of thinking evolved, and that we need to ask how" (quoted in Fournier 2013: 438).

In 1903, when Durkheim was 45 years old (see Figure 10.1) he coauthored with Mauss *Primitive Classification*, a strikingly original *Mémoire* that represents Durkheim's ongoing effort to establish totemism as the bedrock for religion and just about everything else—even the logical cognitive operations used to represent the tangible world. Durkheim and Mauss take it for granted that the mind is equipped by nature with a capacity to perceive, coordinate, and categorize actions that fall under the sphere of economic/practical concerns, or what they call "technological classifications" (p. 80). But other classifications are initially raw, unfocused, vague impressions, especially with regard to the sorting, ranking, and differentiating of abstract ideas and assumptions:

Far, then, from man classifying spontaneously ... humanity in the beginning lacks the most indispensable conditions for the classificatory function ... We may well perceive, more or less vaguely, their resemblances. But the simple fact of these resemblances is not enough to explain how we are led to group things which thus resemble each other ... to classify is not only to form groups; it means arranging these groups according to particular relations.

([1903]1963: 7–8)

If logical classification is not an inherent process, how did the prototype originate and what model was used to assemble these complex constructions so they could be represented in the mind as coordinated relations? To cast light on this problem, they start by isolating out the components of logical classifications found in three societal types—Australian aboriginals, American Indians, and traditional Chinese society. They then sketch with broad strokes an evolutionary account of this general process to document how "primitive" classifications, while rooted in religion are linked developmentally with later scientific classifications without a break in continuity.

Figure 10.1 Émile Durkheim 1903

The Australian System of Classification

Durkheim and Mauss consider the Australian aboriginal system of classification the most elementary known. Bringing together evidence from a broad range of published sources, they start by describing the typical separation of an Australian tribe into two parts, or two phratries [or moieties], and how everything else, whether organic or inorganic, is then divided up between these phratries. A more complex division occurs with the introduction of marriage classes (or sections) that regulate marriage by restricting the classes that an individual can marry in the opposite phratry (or moiety). In this scheme, the universe of things is divided among the different classes/sections. Another significant designation is a taxonomy of totems where individuals are grouped into clans represented by a plant or animal species. The universe of natural things, whether animate or inanimate, is then divided up and ranked, as constituent parts of the totemic social groups (p. 17ff). In support, they cite a number of scholars, including Baldwin Spencer's friend the Australian ethnologist Lorimer Fison ([1880]1991: 167), who wrote,

> The Australian totems have a special value of their own. Some of them divide, not mankind only, but the whole universe, into what may almost be called gentile divisions; and they may help us to a better understanding of totemism, or animal worship.

Australian societies thus reveal a clear division of things into phratries, marriage classes/sections, and totemic clans, although the degree of relatedness of objects belonging to each unit is relatively vague compared to modern classification schemes. This inexactness, they suggest, stems from a logic governed by relations of kinship, totemic animals, and diverse underlying associations and categories that would require a stretch of imagination to understand in "modern" terms. That Australian aboriginals have only a "primitive mass of representations," with a curious asymmetrical collection of things, is a testimony in their judgment to the many obstacles faced in the original establishment of logical classifications (p. 20).

In short, Durkheim and Mauss propose that the main operations and category levels in the organization of Australian aboriginals perform the function of placing members into the assigned ranks of phratries, totem clans, and marriage classes. This taxonomic scheme, in turn, is then copied for the classification of all tangible things (p. 11). Where did native Australians get the organizational plan for these logical combinations? For Durkheim and Mauss the answer is a foregone conclusion:

[T]he ideas are organized on a model which is furnished by society. But once this organization of the collective mind exists, it is capable of reacting against its cause and of contributing to its change.

(p. 32)

The American Zuñi and Omaha Systems of Classification

A more complicated taxonomy is found among the Zuñi, native American farmers of the Southwest who live in widely separated *pueblo* settlements, with each village a tightly-packed social concentration. A distinguishing feature of the Zuñi is the labeling, ordering, and coordination of everything in the universe, whether animate or inanimate, into a series of fixed classes that are distributed in fixed places within an integrated system. The cornerstone principle of the Zuñi system is the division of space into seven sectors: the north, south, west, east, nadir, zenith and the, all important, emblematic center. Every phenomenon in the Zuñi cosmos from humans to animals, plants, social activities and events, to the colors of the rainbow, are allocated to one of these sectors, with the center "the navel of the world, representative of all the regions . . ." (pp. 43–44).

Although the Australian and Zuñi classification systems appear to share little in common, Durkheim and Mauss propose that they are actually closely linked because the Zuni also separate the universe into parts that are *"exactly the same as that of the clans within the pueblo"* (p.44, original emphasis). As noted, a pueblo is a nucleated settlement divided into seven sectors, with each one allocated a portion of space that is related to the north, another to the nadir, to the center, etc., and with each sector identified with specific things and a characteristic color. In turn, residents of each sector (or region) belong to one of three totemic clans (e.g. the frog, rattlesnake, and water clans in the nadir region)—with the exception of the center sector, with its single "macaw" clan. Thus, given the way things are distributed among Zuñi clans, their distinctive groupings, and their characteristic moral unity, Durkheim and Mauss surmise that early in Zuñi history, each sector with its three clans was originally a single clan. At that time, the tribe itself was divided into a total of seven clans (counting the center single "macaw" clan), with each of the original seven clans associated with a totemic animal and a regional locality. So, despite the fact that the Zuñi logically classify their world by dividing up all things into sectors, the Zuni system has much in common with the Australian system because their model was derived from an earlier classification scheme that divided the world by clans. From available evidence and reasoning, Mauss and

Durkheim reconstruct the likely developmental phrases of Zuñi early history, starting from the present back to an inferred history—from seven clans to six clans, to four clans, to the traces of two phratries (or two primary clans), the original structure of the tribe. They conclude that much like Australian society, Zuñi society began with two primary clans or two phratries and two totems, the raven totem (now extinct) and the Macaw totem (the existing single clan in the representative centre), with the myths still recalling this baseline social structure (p. 53). Hence, given that in early Zuñi history their taxonomic scheme was rooted in clans and totems, their society is simply a more complex, developmental expansion of the Australian system (p. 55).

To buttress the hypothesis that Australian and Zuni classifications are derived from corresponding blueprints, Durkheim and Mauss construct a social evolutionary stage model using the Omaha tribal system of the Sioux American Indians as the representative intermediate stage between the Australians and the Zuñi. Among the Omaha, the classification of things by clans is still evident, but the social process of classification by sections (as with the Zuñi) is still in the formative stage (p. 55). An Omaha tribe is divided into two phratries, with each comprised of five residential clans. Although the Omaha are now strictly patrilineal and their totemic cults are slowly breaking down, the clans are successively divided into sub-clans and segments of sub-clans. To illustrate, Durkheim and Mauss focus on the *Chatada* clan, a part of the first phratry and the only remaining complete clan. The Chatada clan consists of four sub-clans, with each sub-clan further divided into a number of segments associated with totems (e.g. black bear, turtle, eagle). Within this entity, the classification and distribution of things is consistent with the classifications of Australian societies. In addition, although still in the formative phases, there are budding forms of a systematic scheme of spatial orientation roughly corresponding to that seen in Zuñi social formations. In other Sioux tribes, they add, systematic patterns of spatial points are even more distinct, and these orientation systems cannot be reducible simply to localized causes (pp. 57–60).

In summary, Durkheim and Mauss argue that the evidence points to *clans and totems as the starting point for all systems of human logical classification*. Once totemic units are superseded by localized groups, however, taxonomic schemes are elaborated by shifting to the next classification phrase by establishing relations organized around more complex spatial orientations (p. 66). Yet, despite the differences in conceptual frameworks, the configuration of these taxonomic schemes reflects a purely social origin.

The Chinese System of Classification

A more formal and elaborate taxonomy, but one the authors contend is congruent with the ones discussed, sits at the basis of Taoism, which is both a philosophy and a religion. While this scheme is found throughout Eastern Asia, Durkheim and Mauss outline its main features by focusing on the ancient Chinese system of divinity as the best way to illustrate how it corresponds with the general principles of both the Australian and American classifications.

The Chinese system is structured around a number of interfacing systems. One foundation block pivots on the division of space into an orientation of four cardinal quarters with each region given both the name and the characteristic color of a presiding animal (e.g. white tiger). Other symbolic creatures reign over the sky and earth. In principle, then, all things must conform to a particular orientation. The space circumscribed around each cardinal point is also divided up, creating eight divisions that align with eight "compass points" linked with "eight powers" and represented by "eight trigrams" occupying the middle point of this divinatory compass (e.g. earth, sky, clouds, sun, thunder, water). A category of fundamental elements are associated with these compass points with collections of things in the universe linked to these components; another typology of five elements also exists to allocate things under particular principles as well (pp. 67–68ff).

As a systematic whole, the traditional philosophy turned upon combinations of infinite elements, complex designs, and carefully crafted details for the purpose of regulating human conduct. By integrating every domain of human cognition including notions of space, activities, seasons, objects in space, and even notions of time itself, it dominated every detail of nature and the human life cycle (pp. 71–73).

Thus, despite the lack of a direct historical link, Durkheim and Mauss propose that in Chinese society and in many other complex societies, traces of primordial systems of classifications rooted in the same organizational principles found in simpler societies can still be found in their current classification system. There are no strict lines of separation. Above all, myths reveal categories that correspond to the logical classifications of the Australian and North American Indians. Moreover, as all mythology is essentially a taxonomy rooted in religious notions rather than scientific notions, myths also provide clues into the essential role religion has played in the genesis of the classificatory system in general. And, these conditions are societal. As Durkheim and Mauss convey:

Highly organized pantheons divide up all nature, just as elsewhere the clans divide the universe ... To attribute certain things in nature to a god amounts to the same thing as to group them under the same generic rubric, or to place them in the same class; and the genealogies and identification relating divinities to each other imply relations of co-ordination or subordination between the classes of things represented by these divinities ... These classifications are such essential elements of developed mythologies that they have played an important part in the evolution of religious thought; they have facilitated the reduction of a multiplicity of gods to one, and consequently they have prepared the way for monotheism.

(p. 78)

The "Inevitable" Conclusions

Durkheim and Mauss thus "conclude" that the logical classifications of aboriginals or traditional peoples are not peculiar or unprecedented but are linked in a developmental sequence without a break in continuity to the first *scientific* classifications. Traditional and scientific classifications vary in content but share the following essential characteristics (p.81).

- Both science and traditional classifications are sophisticated systems of "hierarchized notions" but with different taxonomic designations. Once assigned or considered a member of a category, a thing is then ranked in a hierarchical arrangement of fixed relations and imbued with all kinds of meanings and implications. Taken together, both types of classifications comprise a unified and interconnected system of relationships arranged by rankings, statuses, and authority.
- Both science and traditional classifications are "speculative" systems that exist to "advance understanding" by making the relations that exist among things, coherent, explicit, and unambiguous. The mind has a need to connect essential concepts with other ideas and other things in a taxonomic scheme for the unification of knowledge. As traditional classifications are knowledge-based logical procedures, they are scientific and comprise the "first philosophy of nature."

Durkheim and Mauss also hypothesize that because totems are of cardinal importance to Australian aboriginals with everything else placed in relationship to it, this ancient taxonomic system may have played a role in the awakening of the classificatory mode itself. If so, the model for logical classification is rooted in a totemic social formation. Society, however, did far more; it also served as the master blueprint for logical classifications:

> Society was not simply a model which classificatory thought followed; it was its own divisions which served as divisions for the system of classification. The first logical categories were social categories; the first classes of things were classes of men, into which these things were integrated. It was because men were grouped, and thought of themselves in the form of groups, that in their ideas they grouped other things, and in the beginning the two modes of grouping were merged to the point of being indistinct. [Phraties] were the first genera; clans, the first species. Things were thought to be integral parts of society, and it was their place in society which determined their place in nature.
> (pp. 82–83)

Yet, why do things sometime get assembled in contrast to their nature? Durkheim and Mauss speculate that this tendency is a function of having been originally visualized as social groups that occupy distinct spatial orientations (e.g. the phratry into the tribe; the clan into the phratry) so the relations that link them together are also of a social origin because groups of things are then arranged in a similar way. "Thus logical hierarchy is only another aspect of social hierarchy, and the unity of knowledge is nothing else than the very unity of the collectivity, extended to the universe" (pp. 83–84).

Finally, they propose that the forces that logically divide and link things together are combinations of emotions; in fact the same sentimental elements that underlie domestic and general organizational relations:

> It is thus states of the collective mind (âme) which gave birth to these groupings, and these states moreover are manifestly affective. There are sentimental affinities between things as between individuals, and they are classed according to these affinities... For in order for it to be possible for ideas to be systematically arranged for reasons of sentiment, it is necessary that they should not be pure ideas, but that they should themselves be products of sentiment...
> (p. 85)

So, things and ideas are separated or connected on the basis of their emotional value, with religious sentiments, of course, being the dominant characteristic for logical classification in the earliest societies. Moreover, the first schemes of nature were not that of the individual but, instead, of the collective. But society must first be objectified which is why that even the idea of a logical classification was difficult to formulate, as it requires a taxonomy of concepts. Once formulated, however, the affective bond in logical classification has continually weakened over time, opening the door wider and wider for the entry of scientific classifications and the quiet, reflective thought of individuals (see Schmaus 1998 and Allen 1994 for a thoughtful and engaging analyses of Durkheim's and Mauss's theory of these universal shared categories).

The Great Totemic Debates

In 1901, Spencer and Gillen set off on a twelve-month expedition to study the customs, beliefs, and organizational arrangements of tribes in neighboring northern sectors of the Northern Territory, including coastal regions near the Gulf of Carpentaria, in an effort to corroborate their earlier findings. In 1904, they publish *The Northern Tribes of Central Australia* with 800 pages of massive details, reaching opinions similar to their work on tribes in the Alice Springs locality. In this sequel volume, they claim that the shoreline coastal populations are far more culturally sophisticated than the Alice Springs Arrernte who still harbor the most ancient institutions given their inland location. Durkheim, of course, had reviewed Spencer and Gillen's far-reaching conclusions in *Native Tribes of Central Australia* in 1900, together with spiky reviews of Frazer's corresponding articles. Durkheim's essay "On Totemism" in 1902 had served to mitigate Spencer and Gillen's conclusions (see for example, Hartland, 1902), but their findings had singularly engaged the imagination of the educated public and intellectuals alike. Seizing on this momentum, Spencer and Gillen in their follow-up study had carefully mapped the band localities, added tables, figures and took many photographs, using the new image-making technology to produce vivid, dramatic even tantalizing "real" images of aboriginal lifeways. The "proof" bearing on their earlier findings was a major setback for Durkheim.

While the *Native Tribes of Central Australia* (1899) originally fired up great totemic debates and controversies, the Spencer and Gillen sequel ushered in a barrage of totemic fire-fights especially in England, America, and France, and to a lesser extent in Canada and Germany. The issues turned on the following:

- Is totemism a religious cult, a form of organization or both?
- Totemism lacks an accepted definition. Are personal totems, sex totems, clan totems, moiety totems, and phratry totems all real totems? If not, how do these terms differ and what characterizes real totemism?
- Should totemism be restricted to clan style organization where a totem is inherited and members share a common emblem represented by a species of animal or plant? Did the phratry or moiety style of totemism precede or follow clan totemism?
- What is the relationship between exogamy and totemism? If exogamy is characteristic of totemism, why is it not found everywhere?
- Totemism is found with both male and female descent. Are their traces of an earlier matriliny that was later replaced by patriliny?
- What forces cause the modification or the breakdown of totemism over time?
- What is the origin and function of totemism? What forces bring it into play? Is it individual spirits, a dead ancestor, a deliberate choice, or something else?

In 1904, Crawford Toy, a Harvard Professor proposed that totems and totemism should be restricted to the following definition (146–47):

> [We] ... reserve the designation "totemism" to indicate an exogamous organization in which a clan thinks itself allied by an intimate and sacred bond to a species of animal or plant or to some other natural object, every person male or female of the clan being born into the clan, all the members of the clan refraining from eating of the totem object when this is edible ... Exogamy is commonly assumed as a characteristic of clan totemism ... it is so generally found in communities in which totemism in a strict sense exists that we are warranted in regarding it provisionally as a characteristic of totemism.

A corresponding controversy also erupted over the proper use of such terms in kinship nomenclature as clans, gens, sibs, moieties, phraties, tribes, and totemism. American researchers were accused of using these terms far too loosely, whereas in Europe they were more narrowly defined. Debates also ensued over how far one should go in proclaiming a society to be totemic, or becoming totemic or being non-totemic. J.W. Powell (1902: 75), for example, remarked that what Frazer called totemism was also called shamanism in America. What kinds of flexibility within totemism are possible? Should totemism be restricted to consanguinity or just a grouping of relations? Can we speak of a totemic cult as a kin-based unit without blood ties? Discoveries of totemism in Polynesia and Melanesia also fueled stormy debates over differences between "true," "modified," and "pseudo" totemism. Did all cases of totemism have the same origin? What features are really characteristic of totemism?[4]

As these controversies raged on during the early years of the twentieth century, a number of classical books on totemism were published—Andrew Lang's *The Secret of the Totem* (1905a); A.W. Howitt's, *The Native Tribes of South-East Australia* (1904); Carl Strehlow's *Die Aranda-und Loritjastämme in Zentral-Australien* (1907); Salomon Reinach's *Cultes, Mythes, et Religions* (1905); Northcote Thomas's *Kinship Organisations and Group Marriage in Australia* (1906) and James Frazer's *Totemism and Exogamy* (1910), which generated ever-more salient questions. Yet, few, if any, works had generated as much excitement or widespread interest as Spencer and Gillen's 1899 book, *The Native Tribes of Central Australia*.

In 1905 in response to Spencer and Gillen's latest work, *The Northern Tribes of Central Australia* (1904), Durkheim publishes "Sur l' organisation matrimoniale des Sociétés Australiennes," which is more or less a continuation of "On Totemism" (1902). In this *Mémoire*, Durkheim praises Spencer and Gillen for their latest ethnography but goes to great lengths to contradict their interpretations by offering an extremely dense analysis of aboriginal matrimonial patterns in an effort to account for why some individuals violate the taboo against marrying within their own totem. In this logical counter-demonstration, Durkheim starts by summarizing earlier research on Australian tribes and their division into two phratries, with each phratry further divided into two "classes" (or sections) for a total of four classes within a tribe. Spencer and Gillen reported that among tribes in the Northern region, each phratry is subdivided into four classes instead of two classes for a total of eight classes (p. 122). To account for this expanded formation and to challenge Spencer and Gillen's claim of a distinction between the four-class and eight-class systems, Durkheim compares the cross-lineal marriage patterns of both the northern and central tribes and concludes that the systems are derived from the same origin and are "perfectly identical," and, hence, are simply different solutions to the same problem.

---

4 See for example, Hartland 1901, 1903, 1904, 1905, 1906; Powell 1902; Rivers 1907,1908, 1909; Lang 1902, 1904a, 1904b, 1904c,o 1905b; 1906, 1908, 1909a, 1909b, 1910; Frazer 1908, 1909, 1912; Schmidt 1908; Seiligmann 1908a, 1908b; Thomas 1904a, 1904b, 1904c, 1905a, 1905b; Swanton 1905, 1906a, 1906b; Howitt 1907; Toy 1904; Hill-Tout 1904; Merriam 1908; Mathews 1908; Webster 1911; Lowie 1911; Brown 1912; Long 1912; J.T.S. 1912; Goldenweiser 1912.

The only real distinction, he said, is terminology such that in certain tribes the same name is used to designate classes of different generations, making it only appear that the systems are different (p.127). Spencer and Gillen also proposed that the first kinship systems were organized around patrilineal descent, which is antithetical to Durkheim's theory that kinship originated in matrilineal (and a maternal totem). To keep his theory afloat, Durkheim has to also reinterpret their findings by accounting for the duplication of the four classes into eight classes. In this effort, Durkheim hypothesizes that the eight classes are the result of a marital prohibition that emerged in the shift from matrilineality to patrilineality (pp. 132–136), using some of Spencer and Gillen's older work as well as others to buttress the connection between a patriliny totem and the formation of the eight classes. Durkheim also concludes that Spencer and Gillen's latest findings overwhelmingly show that the Arrernte (Arunta) do not represent the "primitive" original stock of aboriginal customs but, instead, reinforce Durkheim's thesis that Arrernte beliefs and practices are in a far more developed stage of advancement than that proposed by Frazer, Spencer, and Gillen (p. 145).

At this time, Frazer was busy writing a barrage of articles on magic, religion, and totemism. In 1905, he published "The Beginnings of Religion and Totemism Among the Australian Aborigines" and concludes that Central Australian aboriginals have little or no idea of religion. Instead, given that they practice only magic ceremonies and represent the most culturally primitive populations known, it confirmed that magic preceded religion around the globe (]1905]1968: 142). On the origin of totemism, Frazer concludes that since each totemic group has a local center, once a pregnant woman feels the presence of a fetus in her womb, she connects it with a particular totem center and the child belongs to that totem after birth, calling it a "conceptual or local totemism," when kinship and paternity were still unknown. Frazer also argued that totemism preceded exogamy, and that exogamy has no causal association with totemism. He also maintained that if his totemism hypothesis is true, the notion that matrilineal descent always precedes patrilineal descent was wrong because, in fact, either type of descent is possible (p. 160ff).

In 1910, Frazer wrote *Totemism and Exogamy*, a four-volume work that brought together *everything* known about totemism and exogamy. In his literature review, Frazer trivialized Durkheim's essay on "The Origin of the Incest Taboo" (1897). He also dismissed Durkheim's essay "On Totemism" (1902), his association of exogamy with a religious sentiment, his notion that female descent preceded male descent and his theory of religion and totemism, viewing all as greatly flawed and failing to account for the facts.

He even dismissed Durkheim's detailed treatment of the Australian four-class and eight-class matrimonial systems (discussed above) as full of fatal defects and misapprehensions. Then, to add injury to insult, he publically apologized to Durkheim for leading him astray with his own earlier ideas ([1910]1934, 4: 101–103):

> ... Professor Durkheim finds the origin of exogamy in totemism ... such a conception of totemism rests on a fundamental misapprehension ... and I am the more concerned to emphasize the mistake because I formerly committed it myself and have drawn Professor Durkheim after me astray ... Professor Durkheim [also] errs in confusing exogamous classes or phratries with totemic clans ... It is the more incumbent on me to correct this confusion because I fear I am again at least partly responsible for it.[5]

Surprisingly, Durkheim was a minor player in the great totem debates, choosing to keep a rather low profile. He did, however, pay careful attention to how it was playing out in books and journals, as evidenced by his many *Année* reviews on totemism and related topics (see Stanner 1975 for a discussion). For the most part, Durkheim kept himself busy with delivering lectures, reviewing articles and books in his journal, attending conferences, participating in PhD dissertations, and writing articles here and there.

In 1906–1907, Durkheim taught a public lecture course on "The origins of the religious life" and in 1908, he wrote to a friend telling him of the new book he was writing (then titled) "The Elementary Forms of Religious Practice and Thought" (Durkheim ([1907]1975). Durkheim knew that his project was ambitious, and would be controversial. He knew that he had enemies at the Sorbonne and, in general, had long been a favorite target for criticism. He was comfortably wealthy (see Chapter 4 and Christophe Charle 1984), so he was not focused on book royalties, nor was his primary aim to enhance his academic status. Indeed, he had already achieved high status with a permanent Chair at the Sorbonne along with reaping many benefits as editor of the *Année*. Perhaps most of all, he had successfully jumpstarted the new "science of society."

---

5 Frazer had three theories of totemism. He first thought that totemism originated in the idea of an external soul or the notion of putting the souls of living individuals into a plant or animal object. Next, that totemism was a magic system, whereby each totem group took personal care of an animal or plant species so to benefit the community—his economic theory. Finally, totemism originated in a lack of paternity and ideas about a child as a product of a spiritual reincarnation.

What had come to nothing was his religious sociology, which was reflected in the fierceness of the criticism in France and in international circles. Frazer had dismissed his assumptions as dead wrong; Andrew Lang in his *The Secred of the Totem* (1905) had made fun of his totemic theory, calling it in barbed wit, "doubly impossible"; and scholars in America had questioned even the validity of the totemic complex (e.g. Goldenweiser 1910). At this juncture, his totemic theory was in a tailspin and destined to be buried in obscurity in *L'Année Sociologique*. In *The Elementary Forms of Religious life* (1912), he could address his critics by defending his views on both religion and the origin of society itself. What made the book so long was the drawn-out defensiveness of his defense, but if this aspect of the book is edited out, then Durkheim's line of argument suddenly becomes more succinct and clear. In the next chapter, we will follow along with Durkheim as he constructs a satisfactory hypothesis by going on the offensive in true scientific spirit and methodically laying out "the facts" in support of his totemic scheme.

11
Totemism
The Elementary Religion

> *In the world of experience I know of only one entity that possesses a moral reality richer and more complex than that of individuals; it is the community. I am mistaken; there is another who could play the same role: the Divinity. Between God and society, one must choose. I will not examine here the rationales that favor one or the other as both are coherent. I would add only that I am indifferent to this choice as I view the divinity only as society transfigured and symbolically imagined.*
> Émile Durkheim 1906 "Détermination Du Fait Moral"
> *Bulletin de la Société* Française *de Philosophie*

Although Durkheim's theory of religion had long crystallized in his mind, it was not until 1912 that *Elementary Forms of the Religious Life: The Australian System of Totemism* was published. By this time, social evolutionary theory was under fire by a new generation of social theorists turning away from nineteenth-century "armchair" stage models in favor of empirical approaches emphasizing the importance of fieldwork, the distinctiveness of each culture, and the significance of diffused traits on social change. Totemism was also on the chopping block, as it was linked to what many considered flawed evolutionary models. Durkheim was publishing his theory in a growing anti-evolutionary climate, and one where totemism was fast becoming "yesterday's news."

Why had he waited so long?[1] One reason for his reticence was surely a lack of evidence to support his totem theory. Totems had long been documented around the globe, but these reports consisted mostly of fragmented leftovers of totemic institutions. Only in Australia did totemism still prevail in any integrated and meaningful sense but the beliefs and

---

[1] In 1909, he did publish Chapter 1 as an article along with articles on *animism* and *naturism* that became the second and third chapters of *Elementary Forms*. For an abridged text of *Elementary Forms* see Cosman, 2001.

practices of Central Australian aboriginals studied by Spencer and Gillen deviated from most reports of characteristic totemic traits. Durkheim was at an intellectual crossroads. In his *Année* reviews, he and Mauss had criticized, with little success, the assertions of their critics by arguing that the Arrernte were far removed from the earliest stages of totemism. Indeed, if the Spencer/Gillen and Frazer account of totemism was really true, Durkheim's efforts to establish totemism as primal religion was for naught, along with his premises on exogamy, incest taboos, and matriliny as the key elements of the first kinship system. In fact, the entire theoretical edifice he had erected over the past fifteen years would collapse. To make matters worse, Spencer and Gillen's follow-up ethnography on Northern aboriginals, published in 1905, strategically strengthened their initial conclusions and, thus, further eroded Durkheim's thesis.

Durkheim may have also clung to the possible discovery of a more primal society, a single-clan or undivided horde that he had long hypothesized to have existed. Did such a formation still exist in some remote corner of the world? If so, it had yet to materialize, leaving him little choice but to use Spencer and Gillen's ethnography and simply make "the facts" fit his doctrine.

In this chapter, we will start with how Durkheim met this challenge by positioning his thesis in the historical light of American totemism (also see Watts Miller 2013 for historical background on the writing of *Elementary Forms*). We will then turn to *Elementary Forms* and his carefully crafted effort to empirically ground his theory in the Spencer/Gillen ethnography and to then convince his readers that Spencer's and Gillen's interpretation of events was wrong and his account was right.

The History of Totemism

What convinced Durkheim that religion was born in totemism? Robertson Smith played a pivotal role as Durkheim adopted his ideas on totemism and his method but ignored his reconstruction of ancient Semitic society. Durkheim needed more direct sources to anchor his thesis. A clue on his train of thought stems from a proclamation Durkheim published in *L'Année Sociologique* in 1913 in a rebuttal to Simon Deploige's renewed attempt (in a new book) to link the origin of Durkheim's sociology with Germany (1913: 327):

> ... it is well-known that the study of religious phenomena has assumed a leading role in our research. The science of religion, however, is essentially English and American and not at all German

(literally, "nothing to do with German"). We would have to systematically truncate our thinking to create a "genesis" [referring to research on religion] that neglects Robertson Smith and the ethnographic work in England and America.

Durkheim had paid tribute to Smith and the English in 1907, but what had the American ethnographers done to earn his gratitude? In the scheme of things, the American ethnographers were first to identify what came to be called totemism and, as a time-honored source, Durkheim realized he would be able to assign them a place of importance in legitimating his totemic theory (see [1912]1995: 85ff).

What's in a Name?

In *Elementary Forms*, Durkheim's narrative on the history of totemism covered how it was identified, how it was originally seen as an American institution, and why it was historically important. At the same time he expressed his disdain over being forced to use a word so impoverished and crusted with ambiguity:

> Regarding the word 'totem': The Ojibway, an Algonquin tribe, use this word to denote the species of things whose name a clan bears . . . It is not quite right for an institution of such importance to bear a name that is given haphazardly, taken from a strictly local dialect, and in no way reflecting the distinctive traits of the thing it expresses. But today this usage of the word is so universally accepted that it would be an excess of purism to rebel against it . . .
> (Durkheim 1995: 101 and footnote)

To downplay this problem, Karen Fields (1995: 101) related that Durkheim applied "totemic" (*totémique*) to coats of arms, decorations, collective representations, marks, and groups but not to the species serving as a group's totem. His intention, she believed, was to keep reminding the reader that plants and animals are merely surrogates for the totem rather than the totem itself. In contrast, Spencer/Gillen and Frazer had highlighted plant and animal species as the paramount objects with totemic rites a form of magic to increase fertility. We can only guess at the name Durkheim would have wanted—or perhaps invented.

Nonetheless, the upside of keeping totemism was its long history that Durkheim used to his advantage. Playing up this antiquity, he started with the first published account of *totam* by John Long in his *Voyages and Travels of an Indian Interpreter and Trader* ([1791]1904). Coining the term *totamism*, Long wrote that the destiny of American Indians is often attached to their *totam*, and that examples of *totamism* where individuals link their fate with animals can be found around the globe (pp.124–125).[2]

Durkheim also played up the "Americanists," who had early on associated totems with clans. In 1836, Albert Gallatin reported that clans exist among most Indian nations and that: (a) no man could marry into his own clan; (b) that every child belongs either to his father's or mother's clan; and (c) that each clan has a totem name, usually an animal. As the totem is a sacred object, it is considered a crime for a woman to marry a man of the same totem, a violation that resulted in death. Gallatin's account was valuable for Durkheim because it supported a linkage among clans, exogamy, totems, and the sacred.

Henry Rowe Schoolcraft (1793–1864) also figured prominently in *Elementary Forms*. Schoolcraft studied Native Americans, first as an Indian agent for the tribes of Lake Superior and later as Superintendent of Indian Affairs for the state of Michigan. A prolific writer, Schoolcraft published a series of books and hundreds of articles that were read widely by academics and educated laypersons, including Henry W. Longfellow who used Schoolcraft's cultural materials to write his epic poem "Songs of Hiawatha" (see Mason 1962, for a discussion).

Between 1851 and 1857, Schoolcraft published *Historical and Statistical Information Respecting the History, Condition and Prospects of the Indian Tribes of the United States*, a six-volume compendium under the authority of the Bureau of Indian Affairs and an act of Congress. To compile this amazing work, Schoolcraft invited Indian specialists or anyone with first-hand knowledge of Native Americans to contribute to his treatise. Each volume is huge and immensely rich in content with colorful pictographs depicting American Indian technology, customs, traditions, physical traits, etc., along with an encyclopedia of information on Indian social institutions. It must have been a daunting task for Schoolcraft to digest and integrate materials that represented an entire continent of Indian populations, with contributions that ranged from sizable field diaries and notebooks to official documents and brief memorandums to comprehensive ethno-

---

2 Originally Long's book was printed and commercially marketed in 1791. Durkheim's copy was a reissue in 1904 by Reuben Gold Thwaites who edited a series of volumes on what he considered rare and best reprints on the social and economic conditions in early America settlements. The date of this reprint suggests that Durkheim read Long's book sometime after 1904 (although he was probably already aware of Long as Frazer had cited him in his 1887 book, *Totemism*.

graphies. As Schoolcraft's texts originally lacked an index, it took time and effort to mine through six massive volumes (which I can personally testify to).[3] Durkheim found what he sought: totemic symbols were widespread among American Indians and were used as badges, signs, or marks of collective identity. Schoolcraft also detailed what he called existing "totemic systems" where sepulchral symbols such as raised earth mounds resembling such animals as "The Fox, the Bear, the Wolf, and Eagle" are associated with these designated symbols. Calling them "totemic mounds," Schoolcraft considered them "one of the characteristic features of Indian society and institutions . . ." ([1851]1969 v1: 52–53; [1854] 1969 v4: 128). He also described invented representative totem symbols cut, inscribed, or painted on rocks, trees, wooden implements and the like ([1854]1969 v4: 251).[4]

Schoolcraft also connected clans with *totemic ties*, viewing them as a means to create a spirit of fraternity ([1851]1969 v1) emphasis in original). He also maintained that American totemic clans had a long history. North American tribes had "from the earliest time, a tendency to family unions, or large combined families, connected by . . . the *totem* . . ." ([1851]1969: 662 v 4). Some tribes on the "totemic plan" were organized around clans with female descent: "The descent of the chiefs by the female line . . . marked the Iroquois, the Cherokees, the Natchez and other North American tribes." He wondered if this was purely an American aboriginal law (p. 666). Schoolcraft regarded the "totemic plan" as a type of institution, an identity and a device to mark divisions of a tribe into clans, highlighting that

---

3 Durkheim (and likely Mauss) probably looked through all six books as it was not until 1954 that an actual index was compiled for the volumes (see Nichols 1954).

4 Specifically mentioned were the Cherokee, Algonquin, and Iroquois. According to Schoolcraft the Algonquin sign is called "Totem" although it is actually pronounced "dó-daim" ([1851]1969: 52). On a related note, while "totem" is derived from an American Indian dialect, the word itself is *not* an Indian word. What surely occurred is a sound modification. Franz Boas (1889) found that the sounds (or phonemes) that do not exist in one's native language are often psychologically perceived and classified according to their similarity to the sounds of one's native language. Thus, Long (1791) coined the word "tot*a*m" while perhaps not realizing he had modified the sound. Schoolcraft (1851) then modified Long's word by changing it to "tot*e*m" and "tot*e*mic." Schoolcraft thought that the pronunciation of "totem" was derived from *dodaim* (i.e. a village) although no such word exists in any Chippeway or any Algonkin dialect. However, it is derived from an Algonkin word. Following Trumbull (1882: 22), it comes from a root that means "to have, to possess" and "to belong to." It's a contraction of *wuT0HTIMöin*" or what is analogous in Chippeway to the verb *wu*Totem*u*. This lends itself to such corresponding terms as *odèna* (his village) and *od odem an* (his family mark). See Trumbull 1882 for a discussion. Indeed, Schoolcraft noted that even the popular names for Indian nations such as Mohawk, Cherokee, etc. are not what the Indians call themselves (p. 195).

totems are represented not by a single animal but by a well-known species. And, he equated totems with the system of heraldic symbols or "coats of arms" found in developed societies. He also stressed that American Indians never change their totem affiliation, and they must always marry someone from a different totem ([1851]1969:v1: 420).

Given Schoolcraft's expertise, Durkheim surely felt he had placed totems on solid historical grounds. Schoolcraft had documented their antiquity and importance to Native Americans, and he had underscored that aboriginals *did not* worship their totems but, instead, viewed them as representative of their tutelary spirits. Schoolcraft had also expanded the "totem" nomenclature to encompass such terms as totemic bonds, totemic systems, and totemic institutions. He did not, however, equate totems with religious significance. For Schoolcraft, they functioned to promote solidarity for totem members and to build social networks across totem boundaries.[5]

So, Durkheim owed a considerable debt to the early American ethnographers, especially Long, Gaudin, and Schoolcraft. By emphasizing the historical and widespread nature of totemism among American Indians, Durkheim could argue for its antiquity as an early social institution, with wide-ranging implications. These pioneer American ethnographers also cemented the relationship among totems, clans, and exogamy. Indeed, without the Americanists, Durkheim's claim that totemism was a near universal and the starting point of human society itself would be groundless. In particular, Durkheim drew much from the voluminous writings of Schoolcraft who linked totems to a social institution designed to create communal bonds.

Last, the famous kinship theorist Louis Henry Morgan (see Chapter 1) played a sterling role in legitimizing Durkheim's theoretical synthesis. After extensive fieldwork among American Indians, Morgan proposed that human organization began with a promiscuous "horde" and argued for the priority of female descent over male descent for the earliest clans (which he called "gens"). Morgan also documented clan exogamy and the widespread distribution of clans named after animals, noting that these animals had "emblematical signification, which reached beyond the object itself" ([1851]1954: 76ff).

American ethnographers served then as a crucial backdrop for Durkheim's totemic theory. They provided a baseline history of totemism, reinforced the connection of totems with clan exogamy, promoted the notion of totems as symbolic markers to distinguish clans, associated the

---

5 Schoolcraft was clearly fascinated with totems as they are a very common theme in his books and articles.

mother's line with the origin of kinship, and they advanced an institutional approach to totemism. Let's turn now to a compact synopsis of the profound ideas in *Elementary Forms*, keeping in mind the enormous hurdles that Durkheim faced in mounting his totemic theory on an Australian ethnography that not only failed to support his thesis, but actually contradicted nearly every assumption he had made on the origin and nature of totemism.

Subject of the Study: Introductory Remarks[6]

Elementary Forms is a monograph on Australian aboriginals. It is also a synthesis of Durkheim's ideas that can be traced back to his family course in 1888 and his early conception of the *primitive horde* in *The Division of Labor* (1893). To assemble these materials into a systematic configuration, Durkheim relied on his artistry as a lecturer and debater, a masterful reviewer (which the *Année* had fine-tuned), and his genius as a synthesizer. He would need all these talents if he was to convince a skeptical intellectual world that totemism was the first religion and that his thesis on the nature of religion and society was a reality. While doing so, he had to impart a proper deference to Spencer, Gillen, and Frazer without seeming to be on the defensive. To engage the reader he also had to avoid a stiffy laundered tone and, instead, convey a relaxed and affable tone brimming with confidence and to lay out his argument in a logical and straightforward manner. To carry this all off, Durkheim adopted a conversationalist style, used a narrative format (reminiscent of Robertson Smith) and invited the reader in a companionable spirit to join his quest in discovering the genesis and nature of religion.[7]

Durkheim opened by stating that his objective was (1) to describe, and analyze the simplest society known to uncover the origin and foundational religion, and (2) to uncover the foundational categories of human cognition. Given that the book's original title was *Les Formes élémentaires de la vie religieuse: le système totémique en Australie,* Durkheim implicitly

---

6 Durkheim's Preface was first published in 1909 under the title "La sociologie religieuse et théorie de la connaissance."

7 Think back to Robertson Smith's persona in *Religion of the Semites* (1889) . . . I invite you to take an interest in the ancient religion of Semitic peoples; the matter is not one of mere antiquarian curiosity, but has a direct and important bearing on the great problem of the origin of the spiritual religion of the Bible . . . You observe that in this argument I take it for granted that, when we go back to the most ancient religious conceptions . . . (pp. 2–3).

linked Australian totemism with the simplest religion in his opening sentence. His method of inquiry was evolutionary, ethnographic, historical, and explanatory because sociology, he said, was dedicated not just to describing events but understanding and explaining the observable reality of all humankind. The focus, then, was not to be on the idiosyncrasies of "primitive" religions but on the nature of religion itself as an abiding aspect of humankind. Durkheim also clarified why a simple religion and the historical method were essential for this analysis (Durkheim [1912] 1995: 3):

> [W]e cannot arrive at an understanding of the most modern religions without tracing historically the manner in which they have gradually taken shape . . . History alone enables us to break down an institution into its component parts, because it shows those parts to us as they are born in time . . . history [also] puts into our hands the only tools we have for identifying the causes that have brought it into being . . .

It is also essential, he said, to start with an informed idea of what religion is and this understanding requires comparative evidence.

After dismissing dialectical and what he thought to be lofty theoretical approaches that best suit cognitive ideals, Durkheim advocated applying the scientific procedures of the comparative historical method of seeking correspondences by isolating out the components shared by all religions. "Since all religions may be compared, all being species within the same genus, some elements are of necessity common to them all . . . It is these enduring elements that constitute what is eternal and human in religion. They are the whole objective content of the idea that is expressed when *religion* in general is spoken of" ([1912]1995: 4, original emphasis). Yet, despite the fact that these elements rest on the same active forces, it is best to begin, he said, by studying simpler societies to make it easier to distinguish between primary and secondary phenomena and to assemble the facts and relations among them. The more complex religions and their embellishments can then be taken up in future research.

Approaching religion from a scientific point of view also opens the door, he said, to social phenomena closely aligned with religion—namely, a worldview or a cosmology and the place of a religious community within it. And once the nature of reality is perceived through the subjective lens of a religious-based cosmology, these collective experiences become the first organizing schemes for classifying and grouping knowledge and the building blocks for the first *collective representations*. In the same way, the social structure of a group comes to serve as a model for conceptualizing the space in which humans live as composed of "dimensions" such as height, depth, and width, connected by space and time.

In these opening remarks, Durkheim is forthright, setting a tone of certainty without any possibility that he could be wrong. His method of inquiry is to apply the scientific procedures of the historical method, making it clear that his choice of a simple religion is not for its own sake but for best ascertaining the origin, essence, and fundamental components of religion. In concluding, Durkheim alleges that even the fundamental categories of human cognition stem from religion. In the main, he assumes that the processing capacity for thought, reasoning, and the ability to acquire knowledge are human proclivities—that is products of organic selection. But the way humans divide up and organize space, time, number, people, objects, and understand the world are products of *social* selection. These *collective representations* are distinct from *individual representations* because they result from "an immense co-operation" among generations of minds who have unified their knowledge and experience over wide stretches of time and space. For this reason, *collective representations* are "infinitely richer and more complex" than *individual representations* (p. 15).

Humans have a dual nature: a nature characteristic of a single person, and a nature characteristic of a collective enterprise that Durkheim refers to as the "highest reality in the intellectual and moral realm that is knowable through observation"—that is, society itself ([1912]1995: 15):

> Society is a reality *sui generis*; it has its own characteristics that are either not found in the rest of the universe or are not found there in the same form. The representations that express society therefore have an altogether different content from the purely individual representations ...

So, given that religion is a collective phenomena with a cosmology originally anchored in religion, a society's worldview and its logical system of classification are both the product of generations of ancestral ideas and the living population. When viewed as the vital part of an organizational framework, these *collective representations* underlie the "essence" of a society, giving it an appearance of wholeness and unity.

Book 1: Preliminary Questions

The Elements of Religion

Durkheim divided *Elementary Forms* into three books. In Book One, his objective is (a) to provide a universal definition of religion, (b) dismiss the contending psychological theories of *animism* and *naturism* as elementary religions, (c) introduce *totemism* as elementary religion, and (d) describe his method of inquiry. By illustration (and to debunk the notion that Australian totemism is not a religion), Durkheim informs the reader of Frazer's grave error of neglecting to take the step of defining religion and, therefore, "failed to recognize the profoundly religious character of [Australian] . . . beliefs and rites . . . ([1912]1995: 21).[8] Then, adopting an exercise employed by Fustel De Coulanges and Robertson Smith,[9] Durkheim asks the reader to set aside all preconceived ideas about religion, including such widespread beliefs that gods, spiritual beings, or divine supernaturals are characteristic marks of religion as they only appear late in religious evolution. A meaningful definition must be constructed only from cognate traits common to all religions.

Another essential is to discard the usual image of religion as a single unit or "indivisible entity," and, instead, to conceptualize religion as divided up into parts, or segments that are constructed from established dogmas, myths, rites, and ceremonies. We need to first describe and characterize the distinctive nature of these "elementary phenomena" shared by all religions before we can characterize how they work together to form a unified, religious system ([1912]1995: 33). What concrete and external indicators can be used to identify these elementary phenomena?

All things religious, Durkheim said, are arranged into two natural universal categories—beliefs and rites. Beliefs are modes of thought or judgments composed of collective representations, whereas rituals are collective practices or fixed modes of action ([1912]1995: 34). What makes a rite religious? A religious practice can only be distinguished from a secular practice, Durkheim says, by the object to which it is addressed. So, the object of a rite must first be characterized. And, since beliefs are where the distinctive nature of a special object is conveyed, they too must be defined before the rite itself. What beliefs, then, are universal to all religions?

---

8 Durkheim's derogatory remarks are intended to discredit Frazer's theory that the Australian system of totemism is simply a primitive economic system designed to increase the fertility of a totem species. Throughout the book he tries to inflict damage on Frazer's ideas.

9 As Fustel De coulanges in *The Ancient City* informed his readers: "To understand the truth about the Greeks and Romans, it is wise to study them without thinking of ourselves, as if they were entirely foreign to us; with the same disinterestedness, and with the mind as free, as if we were studying ancient India or Arabia." To ignore this rule, "spring many errors," and "errors of this kind are not without danger" ([xx]1889: 10).

All religions, Durkheim said, share a paramount character—the classification of things into two spheres; a sacred domain and a profane domain (*profane, sacré*): "This division of the world into two domains, one containing all that is sacred, the other all that is profane, is the distinctive trait of religious thought..."([1912]1947: 37). What things are sacred? And what makes them sacred? According to Durkheim anything is eligible—a person, an animal, a cloth, a practice, a tree, a rock, a statue, a spring, a body movement, a dance, a sound, a song, a word. Anything, then, no matter what can be sacred. The list is boundless and endless because (a) all religious communities have their own collection of sacred things and (b) all things deemed sacred have this empirically undetectable attribute of *sacré* superadded or superimposed upon them. That is, the quality that marks something sacred is not built-in or inherent to the object itself.

How then do you recognize or distinguish the sacred from the profane? Are sacred things superior to profane things in the hierarchy of things? Status differences have a ring of truth, Durkheim says, but a purely hierarchic difference is *not* a defining characteristic. What truly separates the sacred from the profane is their *heterogeneity*—and one that is absolute: "... the sacred and profane have always and everywhere been conceived by the human mind as two distinct classes, as two worlds between which there is nothing in common ... But howsoever much the forms of the contrast may vary, the fact of the contrast is universal ..."([1912]1947: 38–39).

So the sacred is the essential and universal character of religious phenomena. It stands apart, indeed in absolute opposition to the profane realm with its common things and routines of daily life. Yet, Durkheim's definition is still vague and elliptical on what the *sacred is*. He relates that it has a creative power, an ability to inspire awe and reverence, an establishment by physical proximity to spread to nearby objects (as sacred contagion attracts and brings together unlike things), and a capacity to elicit special emotions ([1912]1947: 324). A source of Durkheim's ambiguity is that nothing starts out as inherently sacred and that sacredness is easily transmitted by close contact to any object simply by emotional contagion. Yet, a sacred character cannot be detected by observation or experience, and so, it cannot be verifiable by the normal senses ([1912]1947: 229). Instead, Durkheim attributes the ability to experience the sacred to the mind, a cognitive proclivity rooted in a special neurological process:

> Our whole social environment seems to us to be filled with forces which really exist only in our own minds. We know what the flag is for the soldier; in itself it is only a piece of cloth. Human blood is

only an organic liquid, but even to-day we cannot see it flowing without feeling a violent emotion which its physico-chemical properties cannot explain. From the physical point of view, a man is nothing more than a system of cells, or from the mental point of view, than a system of representations; in either case, he differs only in degree from animals.

([1912]1947: 227)

The mind then is predisposed to separate sacred things from profane things by channeling them into two opposed categories. Sacred things, Durkheim says, can be identified by anything guarded or isolated by authoritative interdictions, whereas profane things are everything else. The mind is also equipped by nature with special sensory properties for a transcending experience that raises the special emotions of sacredness. Religious beliefs are *collective representations* that express both the nature of sacred things and the relationships that they have with profane things and other sacred things. Finally, religious rites are rules of behavior when in the presence of a sacred thing. A religion is born once the sacred is distinguished from the profane. It then develops when corresponding rites evolve into an interdependent whole or a system of related parts.

Thus, a religion is not embodied within a single idea or one unique principle. Religion is always a complex, interdependent system of parts. Each part, in turn, can be individualized with an organizational center where single cults or groupings of beliefs and practices gravitate. This accounts for the existence of scattered fragments and floating parts of religious phenomena such as myths, ceremonies, or folklore that survive but no longer belong to any intact religious system. Sacred things are also complex phenomena because it is not by exceptional energy, status, or power that lead humans to conceive of sacred things. Instead, sacred things inspire religious sentiments because they are cognitively perceived to differ fundamentally from profane things by a qualitative essence or a difference in nature, generated by an inherent capacity in the mind.

What, then, leads humans to envision two such heterogeneous and incompatible phenomena, despite nothing in sensory input to project such a radical difference? How did this cleavage come about? Once again, Durkheim encourages readers to join him on an intellectual journey in the pages to follow to discover the source or origin of the sacred experience.

Durkheim completes his definition of religion by distinguishing magic from religion. Both have rites, beliefs, myths, and dogmas, and so, there is no clear separation. One bedrock distinction is that religious life commences when individuals assemble and experience an emotional feeling of unity:

> A society whose members are united by the fact that they think in the same way in regard to the sacred world . . . and by the fact that they translate these common ideas into common practices, is what is called a Church. In all history, we do not find a single religion without a Church . . . *There is no Church of magic.*
> ([1912]1947: 43–44; emphasis in original)

A Church or a "moral community" may be small, large, international, with or without authority by gods, priests or an explicit directing body. All that is required to make a Church is a unification under the banner of a common faith:

> *A religion is a unified system of beliefs and practices relative to sacred things, that is to say, things set apart and forbidden—beliefs and practices which unite into one single moral community called a Church, all those who adhere to them.*
> (p. 47: emphasis in original)[10]

Animism and Naturism as Elementary Religion

A definition of religion in hand, and one that embraces a sacred element requiring extrasensory perception for transcending reality, Durkheim turns to the search for the most elementary religion, inviting readers to come along on this journey. His theory is staked on the premise that religion is a collective phenomena, and thus, his next challenge is to show why the leading psychological theories of religion pale in the face of his social thesis.

In this pursuit, Durkheim highlights how the religions of today are richly complex, even the "primitive" ones; all contain a variety of principles, beliefs, and rites because all are developed from the same initial germ of religion and, therefore, all are the outcome of a long evolutionary history. So, to uncover the "truly original form of the religious life," the best

---

10 Durkheim notes that he originally defined religious beliefs solely by their obligatory character, but religious obligations exist in the first place because they are imposed on members. So, the old and new definitions are similar except that the new one places a much greater emphasis on the contents of collective representations (Durkheim [1912]1947: 47).

approach is to break down these religions into their essential and common elements and, then, to isolate out the original one from which the others are derived.

Leaving aside otherworldly approaches, the existing face-off is between two popular theories on the origin of religion: one is directed towards *visible* natural things (rivers, wind, plants, the sky, rocks, etc.) and is called *naturism*, whereas the other is directed towards *invisible* spiritual things (souls, spirits, divine entities, demons, etc.) and is called *animism*. The cardinal issue is whether animism is the elemental form (and naturism the derived form) or whether naturism is the elemental form (and animism the derived form). Or, possibly, whether they could have originally been combined in some fashion?[11]

The animist school of Edward Tylor and Herbert Spencer is focused on souls and spirits, and Durkheim discusses how the idea of the soul comes from the double life humans think they lead—during the day and another during dream-time at night. Is this the elementary religion, he asks? If so, it would be necessary to demonstrate how the soul came to exist without borrowing any components from an earlier religion; how the soul became a cult object and is later transformed into spirits; and how a cult of nature is derived from animism. Above all, Durkheim rejects animism on the grounds that it makes religious beliefs a pile of "hallucinatory representations" constructed by the human imagination (49ff).

After dismantling animism, Durkheim turns to naturism as elementary religion. In contrast to the animist school where no objective foundation exists, the naturist school of Max Müller and Albert Réville circumvents this problem by focusing on fire, thunderbolts, or any natural forces that arouse overpowering sensations to awaken the religious experience. The general idea is that the natural world stimulates ideas, and in a very direct way. Durkheim also dismisses naturism (which he endorsed as his elementary religion in *The Division of Labor*) on grounds that include: (a) the inability of natural forces to evoke enduring sentiments because nature cannot build up sufficiently strong emotions for the religious experience, (b) the inability to separate the sacred from the profane, and (c) the inability to explain how the bewitching action of language fosters the transcendence of natural forces into spiritual powers or gods. But, above all, Durkheim rejects naturism as the religious root because it only appears to rest on solid ground:

---

11 Durkheim cites Fustel de Coulanges who embraced both theories, by putting them both in his *The Ancient City* ([1864]1889 (see chapter 1).

> Only in appearance ... does naturism escape the objection I made against animism a short while ago. Since naturism reduces religion to nothing more than an immense metaphor without objective foundation, it too makes religion out to be a system of hallucinatory images ... if expressing the forces of nature is made out to be the principal object of religion, it is impossible to see religion as anything other than a system of deceiving fictions, the survival of which is incomprehensible.
>
> ([1912]1995: 78–79)

Summing up, Durkheim concludes that naturism and animism awaken sensations fashioned purely from common experiences. Yet, natural forces or dead ancestors do not by themselves possess a sacred character, and so, they cannot account for something outside common experience. As such, they cannot account for the grand opposition that separates the sacred from the profane. Thus far, then, Durkheim has provided:

- An introduction to the topic of religion
- A definition of religion
- A discussion and critique of other contenders for elementary religion

Totemism as Elementary Religion

Durkheim introduces totemism by sketching its history and the earliest and latest accounts of totemism. McLennan is credited with recognizing its religious character and place as a universal stage in human evolution, and Robertson Smith is credited as the first to effectively elaborate on the topic. What becomes evident is how well Durkheim is in command of the totem literature without actually going into the field. He knows the American tribes associated with totemism, ticking them off by name; he highlights mistakes by those reducing totemism to a mere plant or animal worship; and he elaborates further by adding nuanced facts about totems in footnotes. It was Smith, Durkheim says, who "realized more keenly than his predecessors how rich in seeds for the future this crude and confused religion is ... Smith set out to move beyond the letter of totemic beliefs in order to find the fundamental principles governing them" ([1912]1995: 86–87). Durkheim then shifts to Australia where he cites an extensive totem literature, although he stresses that despite the wealth of these data, the problem remained of finding an integrated, functioning totemic system in action. But all this changed, he said, with Spencer and Gillen's, *The Native*

Tribes of Central Australia and *The Northern Tribes of Central Australia*.[12] For this reason, the Central Australian aboriginals will be the focal group for his analysis of totemism.

Method of Analysis

Durkheim strongly disapproved of the popular nineteenth-century cross-cultural method used by Tylor, Frazer, and other social scientists where the traits of different societies were often ripped out of context, lumped together, and assumed to be congruent on surface similarities. It was essential, he felt, to consider both the geographical and social environment and, not to compare only societies or institutions of a single social type (or as he put it "varieties of the same species"). Robertson Smith in his *Religion of the Semites* (1889) had also rejected the general cross-cultural method, relying instead on the methodology of a biblical critic, albeit using this procedure in a path-breaking way to recreate ancient Semitic religion. This scientific method (also used in historical linguistics and biology [see Chapter 6]) seeks out relations among any phenomena believed to share the same origin, position, or structure.

Durkheim's procedure is in line with Smith's method coupled with his own enterprising approach. As Ivan Strenski (2006: 245–246) underscored, "If the Durkheimians sound like good classical Higher Critics of the biblical texts, it is because they descend intellectually from some of the founders of the so-called 'Higher Criticism' such as Julius Wellhausen, and more immediately, from Wellhausen's student, William Robertson Smith." In other words, as Gianfranco Poggi (2000: 142) expressed it, "a central plank of his theory is that religions are all, for their diversity, made of the same cloth. Thus, the essential features of all can be determined by analyzing closely the most elementary religion we know of, Australian totemism."

So, in lieu of the usual amorphous definition of religion or the cherry-picking of religious attributes, Durkheim constructed his definition by (1)

---

12 Durkheim cited other recent publications on Central Australians, notably by the missionary Carl Strehlow in his *Die Aranda-und Loritja-Stämme in Zentral Australien*, an ethnography published in installments between 1907 and 1920. Unlike Spencer and Gillen's ethnography, Strehlow's serial ethnography while rich in information especially on aboriginal social life, totemic mythology, and cosmology, is encased in compact, dense text and nearly impenetrable for anyone without an extensive background on aboriginal lifeways. Durkheim was up to this challenge as he used Strehlow's data to buttress the sacred character of aboriginal totemic beliefs and to poke holes in Spencer and Gillen's ideas on totemism by praising Strehlow's observations as more precise and by noting that Strehlow was far more fluent in the native tongue.

defining all religions as varieties (or subspecies) of a single species; (2) conceptualizing religion as a system of related parts; and (3) isolating out what he believed were shared, universal components of religion—beliefs, rites, the sacred, and a Church or community of believers. He also adopted Smith's method of largely confining his analysis of totemic religion to Australian aboriginals because they fulfilled his rigorous requirements: (a) The Australian aboriginals had (in his mind) the simplest form of *known* totemism; (b) the Australian aboriginal societies were all varieties of the same species or social type; and (c) the data were plentiful enough to ground his analysis in *facts*. It is said that *Elementary Forms* could have been written without the Australian system of totemism but this is improbable. Durkheim had already tried that tack with his essays on clans, exogamy, phratries, totemism, female descent, and sacredness with little success. He also had to convince skeptics with evidence of the religious character of totemism. He supplemented his analysis with American Indian materials to help explain the "function" and "importance" of totemism in Australia. In Book 2, he sets up totemism as the elementary religion by bringing into play his long-held assumptions as if they are long established facts.

Book 2: Elementary Beliefs

In a purely literal sense *Elementary Forms* is devoted to a richly detailed analysis of Australian beliefs and practices.[13] Yet, if that were really the case the book would be sitting on a library shelf consigned to obscurity. Instead, Durkheim fired up the human imagination by using the Australian aboriginals as *the* benchmark study to speculate on the dawn of religion and its elementary forms. And, by removing the mist clouding religion, he could proclaim that god is society itself. Moreover, as Ian Hamnett (1984: 203)

---

13 Durkheim's 1912 French edition is subtitled, *The Australian System of Totemism*. In the 1915 English transition by Joseph Swain the subtitle was dropped. At the time, Swain was a graduate student at Columbia University but he spent the years 1913–1915 enrolled at the Ecole Pratique des Hautes Etudes, Section des Science Religieuses in Paris, which is a famous place to study religion (Marcel Mauss was a professor there at the time). It is hard to imagine that Swain translated Durkheim's *Elementary Forms* (the first of his works to be translated into English) without consulting Durkheim. Indeed, he was translating it while he was there. As Karen Fields (2005: 61) remarked, "Presumably . . . Durkheim oversaw the work, and either proposed or agreed with dropping the original French subtitle *Le système totémique d'Australie* (replacing it with "A Study in Religious Sociology"— subsequently dropped." One reason may have to do with the negative reviews by anthropologists after the 1912 publication.

underscored: "In a real sense, the religious aspects of Durkheim's inquiry, while at a superficial level the most obvious and dominant theme, are secondary to his fundamental concerns. These were nothing less than to offer an account of the source of social solidarity itself and (beyond that) to propose an entire epistemology . . ." So, all we need do from our standpoint is to examine the book's core themes, especially Durkheim's radical thesis on the origin and nature of religion and society.

Totemic Organization

In Book 2, Durkheim's intent is to establish both the religious character of totemism and its evolutionary status as *the* elementary religion. This is no easy task; and so to set the scene, he starts by describing the two dominant traits that characterize Australian clans: (1) an affinity or "kinship" relation that is not based on blood-ties but on sharing a clan name, with kin-like obligations and rules of exogamy and (2) a clan name that is associated with an animal or plant species and called its *totem*. Clan recruitment will vary, he stressed, but in the majority of societies it is acquired by female descent at birth. In most clans, a marriage rule of exogamy also exists in which, even after females move to another clan after puberty, they keep their totemic identity and pass it on to their offspring. Thus, clan members can either live in propinquity on a homeland or apart but still keep their relations intact by virtue of sharing the same totem ([1912]1947: 102–103).

Another division in tribal societies is the *phratry*.[14] A phratry is a macro-organizational unit because it is composed of two or more clans. Clans making up a phratry perceive a historical unity among themselves or some sort of affiliative connection. A phratry often has a distinct name—an animal name. Durkheim asserts that an Australian phratry (composed of two or more clans) is an ancient institution. In Durkheim's scheme it was once a single clan—an ancestral "mother" clan. Given this assumption, all present-day clans making up a given phratry share a perceived unity because they are all descendants of an ancient single "mother" clan.

Durkheim's objective is to convince readers that the phratries of today are actually the *single clans* of yesterday or *hordes*, the primal formation

---

14 As discussed in Chapter 1, footnote 11 p.13 a phratry differs from a moiety (which means a half of something, splitting a social unit into two halves). A community or tribe than cannot have more than two moieties. Phratries also divide units but the term as used today refers to a community or tribe that is divided up into three or more subdivisions (each with several clans) or three or more phratries.

that he had long hypothesized.[15] To highlight the importance of the hypothesized ancient phratry (or single clan), *the* social formation crucial to his totemic thesis, Durkheim buttresses his argument with examples of phratries among American Indians to make clear the archaic nature of phratries and to demonstrate how they gradually subdivided into a certain number of clans. So, in Durkheim's scheme, clans are derived from phratries. Indeed, to preserve his theory of totemism as foundational religion, the phratry with its lack of blood-kinship ties *must be* the earliest social formation.

What then is characteristic of totemism? First, following Durkheim, a totem is a name and an emblem, a "coat-of-arms." As the group trademark or badge, totemic symbols are engraved on tombs, graves, trees, drawings, rocks, canoes, etc. and even stamped on the flesh of totem members. Members want an association with their totem, whether dead or alive. Second, above all, totemic symbols take on a sacred, religious character when they are engraved on Australian aboriginal objects such as the *churinga's* (or Tjurunga), which are pieces of wood or polished stones employed in religious ceremonies. The word itself, Durkheim says, means sacred and these sacred objects are so exceptionally precious that they are kept in caves or other special places where women or uninitiated males cannot touch them. As Durkheim expressed it, "'every churinga ... is counted among the eminently sacred things: there are none which surpass it in religious dignity" ([1912]1947: 120). Where does its religious nature come from? For Durkheim, sacredness is derived from the sacred emblem; it is the material symbol of the totem. Durkheim then provides a very detailed analysis of different Australian sacred artifacts associated with the totem. The totem is sacred and, so, any objects associated with the totem are sacred by contagion. They are made sacred because of some enigmatic property of the mind and the natives feel an emotional need to represent these collective representations in a material way.

The Totemic Animal and Humans

In addition to the ultra-sacred totemic images on tools, canoes, weapons, bodies etc., Durkheim highlights two other special categories of sacred things: the totem species and the totem members. A clan's totem is usually

---

15 Durkheim emphasized that when all members of the same totem do not share a phratry, the totemic system has undergone a breakdown due to a disturbing influence. He has used this argument before to justify why some clan members do not follow the rules of exogamy.

an edible plant or animal, which is taboo for eating or killing except under special circumstances.[16] Even clans found in the same phratry often refrain from eating the totems of sister clans, Durkheim said, because a phratry is nothing less than the original mother clan of all clans in the present-day phratry. Hence, in some phratries, the warm sentiments generated by common ancestry still linger on with this special relationship, marked by honoring the food taboos of other clans ([1912]1947: 130–131). Here, Durkheim reinforces his hypothesis that the original social organization was a horde (or single original clan).

A second survival in support of an ancient phratry is a taboo on the consumption of the mother's totem. All totems, following Durkheim, were originally inherited by a maternal descent rule. Yet, in clans that practice a rule of female exogamy, offspring inherit their mother's totem at birth but grow up in and, for males, remain permanently in their father's territorial group. So, under a female-biased marriage rule, the members of a matri-totem are never concentrated in a locality, but scattered among a variety of clans in different localities. Over time, Durkheim noted, a shift to a patrilineal line of descent may happen so that offspring inherit their father's totem. Still, in some clans, sacred interdictions forbidding the eating of the mother's totem are still observed as an ancestral survival.

Totem species are sacred for members but they are visible and can be seen and touched by everyone. In contrast, objects engraved with sacred, totemic emblems such as the Arrernte *churinga* are so revered they must be hidden from view. This limiting of access to totemic symbols testifies to the highest degree of sacredness, leading him to conclude that *"the images of totemic beings are more sacred than the beings themselves"* ([1912]1947: 133, original emphasis). And, this means that "representations of the totem are therefore more actively powerful than the totem itself" (p. 133). Thus, totemism is *not* the worship of animals or plants because what is exceptionally sacred is its symbolic representation—and not the totem itself. He continues to build his case that totemism is the elementary religion.

After emphasizing the utmost sacred qualities of totemic representations (and not the totem species), Durkheim turns to human relations with their

---

16 To address why Spencer and Gillen reported no rigorous interdictions against eating your totem and to refute Frazer's claim that totemism is not a religion but a "primitive" economic system to increase the food supply, Durkheim claims that these relaxations are simply due to a breaking down of the Arrernte totemic system itself, citing many references to support this assumption. Despite his confident manner, Durkheim is on the defensive, picking at the assumptions of Spencer/Gillen and Frazer by demonstrating why their ideas do not stand up. His position here is essentially the same as in his 1902 paper "On Totemism."

totems. Humans fit mostly in the category of profane or secular beings (as they must deal with practical matters), but they still possess in privileged places a personal sacredness (i.e. a soul) by virtue of their identification with their totemic species. They share a totem name, represent their totem symbolically in public and private ways, and practice rituals that simulate their totem species (i.e. a kangaroo), leading humans to reveal a coexisting nature—a human and a totem nature. For this reason myths and legends were invented in support of this common origin with this duality by affirming a genealogical affinity between a human and his totem. Human blood also has a holy nature, with blood from the genital organs especially sacred. Thus, the worship of an animal or plant totem as an all-powerful supernatural being, deity, or god-figure has no place in totemic religion. Instead, although totems are endowed with slightly more degrees of sacredness than human beings, both are part of the sacred world, and both stand largely on the same plane of equal value and equality. Their relationship is essentially one of friendly, kindhearted associates (p.134ff).

The Cosmological System of Totemism and the Idea of Class

After elaborating on the three cardinal classes of sacred things—totem species, clan members, and, above all, totemic emblems—and providing reams of examples and references in support, Durkheim shifts in a conversational way to the system of ideas inherent in totemic religion:

> [A] religion is not merely a collection of fragmentary beliefs in regard to special objects . . . To a greater or lesser extent, all known religions have been systems of ideas which tend to embrace the universality of things, and to give us a complete representation of the world. If totemism is to be considered as a religion comparable to the others, it too should offer us a conception of the universe. As a matter of fact, it does satisfy this condition.
>
> ([1912]1947: 141)

Drawing from *Primitive Classification* (1903), Durkheim discusses how the religious life of totemism is the touchstone for the original system of logical classification and thought. While acknowledging that humans are naturally predisposed to arrange things into types and hierarchies, the classification process itself needs a model. As totemic religion is at the root of social organization and sociality, it provides the template for classifying by placing corresponding things into a general organizational scheme for society. When clans are organized into phratries, for example, everything else in the universe is distributed among the clans in each phratry. Thus, a conception of the universe and model for the first logical classifications are independent of climate, ethnicity, or geography; instead they are modeled after totemic beliefs. As Durkheim expressed it

> All known things will thus be arranged in a sort of tableau or systematic classification embracing the whole of nature ... It is because men were organized that they have been able to organize things, for in classifying these latter, they limited themselves to giving them places in the groups they formed themselves ... The unity of these first logical systems merely reproduces the unity of the society.
> ([1912]1947: 142–145)

A religious character then can be extended to some degree throughout the entire universe of totemic society—from symbolic emblems, clan members, totem species—to all things because everything is classified under the totem umbrella. Then, once the first gods appear later in time, each divinity will rule over parts of the natural world that were once organized on the basis of affinitive cults who fit into each other as parts of a complex totemic unity or "a community of belief" (p. 155). Totemism, then, like all religions has a cosmology.

Origin of Totemic Beliefs

The Horde or Primary Clan

Durkheim argued that totemism is *the* elementary religion and it is inseparable from a *clan-based organization.*

> A religion so closely allied with the social system that is simpler than all others can be regarded as the most elementary religion we can know. If we can find out the origin of the beliefs just analyzed, we may well discover by the same stroke what kindled religious feeling in humanity.
> ([1912]1995: 167–168)

Why would Durkheim argue that a clan-based organization was the simplest social system? Let me emphasize here that during Durkheim's time, there was a considerable amount of sematic confusion over kinship and organizational nomenclature (a problem Durkheim complained about in his writings). And, some usage differs from conventional usage today. The hunter-gatherer nomatic *band*, for example, is the foundational society, whereas a clan-based or tribal society is considered far more complex given a sedentary population (except for pastoralists).[17]

Durkheim's usage of *clan* harks back to the traditional European meaning and refers to *any* collection of individuals, whether scattered or concentrated, where individuals are linked by actual or fictive kinship by sharing a name, or a totem. This afforded him license to conceptualize the primal grouping as an undivided, promiscuous *horde* (or a free-standing, single clan) without kinship ties or a totem. Once a horde morphed into two hordes (or two primary clans) Durkheim called it a true clan, although unity was still not necessarily based on consanguinity but on sharing the same name or emblem. Seen in this light it was a legitimate usage to consider the earliest human grouping a horde with totemism inseparable from a clan formation (for kinship definitions see Chapter 1, footnote 11).

The Totemic Principle or Mana

The religious sentiment begins, Durkheim said, once the sacred is set apart from the profane. And in his eyes, totemism has a vast array of sacred things. By definition, things stamped sacred are *all* permeated with a sacred character; what differs is the degree of sacredness, with symbolic or figurative representations of the totem ranked first in importance, followed by the plant or animal totem, and last by the clan-mates. If all sacred things evoke identical sentiments that differ only by degree, these very special emotions cannot be inherent in the sacred things themselves. Instead, what evokes the sacred experience must come from somewhere else:

---

17 The Australian aboriginals were also an atypical food collecting society. Nomadic hunter-gatherers usually have a simple band-level organization with a bilateral descent system (i.e. descent is traced through both sexes). Instead, the Australian aboriginals had the traditional band-level territorial unit but with a unilineal descent system. They also had totemic groups where individuals were lifelong members of their totem. Thus, with female exogamy, a wife left her homeland but retained her totemic affiliation and given matrilineal descent passed it on to her children. So while she moved to the territorial unit of her husband and his relatives, her home, so to speak, was still in the territorial unit of her totem. Totem cults also called for lots of ceremonies, especially elaborate and complex initiation rites (uncommon for nomadic food collectors but common for horticultural clan-based societies). In the case of Central aboriginals, totemic ceremonies and such seemingly served to integrate a widely scattered population who had to forage long distances for food in a dry bushland ecology.

The similar sentiments inspired by these different sorts of things in the mind of the believer . . . come only from some common principle . . . In reality, it is to this common principle that the cult is addressed. In other words, totemism is the religion, not of such and such animals or men or images, but of an anonymous and impersonal force . . . It is so completely independent of the particular objects in whom it incarnates itself, that it precedes them and survives them. Individuals die, generations pass and are replaced by others; but this force always remains actual, living and the same. It animates the generations of today as it animated those of yesterday and as it will animate those of tomorrow.

([1912]1947: 188–189, emphasis added)

In clan societies, a totem is simply how the human imagination represents this impersonal, mysterious force under the concrete form of a plant or animal species. It is how clan members form a relationship with this source of energy. The *totemic principle* (or god) is also a moral force since it embodies the beliefs and values of the community. In traditional societies around the globe, the totemic principle goes by other names—"wakan," "pokunt,"or "orenda" (among American aboriginals) or "mana" (among Melanesia aboriginals) and its incarnation is so relative that it can be diffused into almost anything. In totemic religion, the form taken is linked with a social system of clans, each represented by a particular totem species. While clans share a sense of a tribal unity, the tribe itself has no single totem because totemism is a "federative religion" that cannot survive beyond a certain degree of centralized control.

As societies develop, however, the anonymous force or *totemic principle* will get cloaked in a wide variety of new configurations because the type of persona projected will be determined by (a) the social environment and (b) the interplay of collective representations among themselves. In 1924 Bouglé (1965: xxxvii–xxxviii) sought to clarify Durkheim's often misunderstood position on the dynamics of collective representations:

There is no doubt that in his earlier works Durkheim [insisted] upon the close relationship . . . between the beliefs and the actual form of their social milieu . . . Once formed [however] collective representations combine, attract, and repel each other according to their own particular psychological laws. Durkheim is very concerned to point out that men's religious ideas, and all the more their scientific notions, are very far from being simple reflections of the social forms themselves.

(see Durkheim [1898]1965: 23)

Thus, Durkheim argued that the energy force inherent in religion is born with totemism, but after totemism disappears with social change, the force itself will live on—but this time in the guise of another external form. The manner or persona it assumes is a function of two variables (a) the social mileau and (b) the interplay or reciprocal dynamics *among* the collective representatives themselves. As Durkheim characterized this energy force:

> This is the original matter out of which have been constructed those beings of every sort which the religions of all times have consecrated and adored. The spirits, demons, genii and gods of every sort are only the concrete forms taken by this energy . . . If the sun, the moon and the stars have been adored, they have not owed this honour to their intrinsic nature or their distinctive properties, but to the fact that they are thought to participate in this force which alone is able to give things a sacred character . . .If the souls of the dead have been the object of rites, it is not because they are believed to be made out of some fluid and impalpable substance, nor is it because they resemble the shadow cast by a body or its reflection on a surface of water . . . they have been invested with this dignity only in so far as they contained within them something of this same force, the source of all religiosity.
>
> ([1912]1947: 199–200)

The Origin of the Totemic Principle

Totemic cults are forged by an intimate relation between a human group and a plant or animal species. How and why does the mind make such a connection? By themselves, Durkheim argued, animals or vegetables have no intrinsic or inherent sacredness and, so, the source of these special religious emotions must reside elsewhere. Instead of tangible plants and animals, the "center of the cult" for these religious sensations is found in the *symbolic representations* of a totem species. The totem, then, must be representing something else in tangible form. What? Above all, the totem symbolizes two things: (1) it is the concrete and visible form of the totemic principle (or god); and (2) it is the distinctive emblem or "coat-of-arms" for a clan. Given this dual symbolic role leads to only one conclusion—that the totem god and society are the same:

> The god of the clan, the totemic principle, can therefore be nothing else than the clan itself, personified and represented to the imagination under the visible form of the animal or vegetable which serves as totem . . . it is unquestionable that a society has all that is necessary to arouse

the sensation of the divine in minds, merely by the power it has over them; for to its members, it is what a god is to his worshippers.

([1912]1947: 206)

Following Durkheim, this is the reason why society has the power to arouse a sense of the divine and eventually of gods:

- A god and society are seen as superior to individuals and both elicit a sense of dependence.
- A god and a society have rules of conduct and both have the moral authority to demand a particular way of behaving, while making individuals feel good when they follow the rules.
- A god and society awakens in humans a moral power, fueled by special emotions.
- A god and society evoke sensations that something is far greater than individuals; it elevates and provides energy and strength to carry on and this force is penetrating and an essential part of our being.

When humans assemble there is a "general effervescence" where society itself is felt, and this emotional arousal keeps the sentiments elevated until the next collective renewal. In fact, most of what makes us human is what we get from society:

We speak a language we did not create; we use instruments we did not invent; we claim rights that we did not establish; each generation inherits a treasure of knowledge ... We owe these varied benefits of civilization to society, and although in general we do not see where they come from, we know at least that they are not of our own making.

([1912]1995: 214)

While all societies and religions share these attributes, it is important, Durkheim said, to determine how these collective forces in Australian clans awaken sacredness and the religious experience. So, in a colorful narrative, Durkheim describes two contrasting phrases of Australian aboriginal life ways, a dispersed, dull phase when society is separated into little wandering families, and a concentrated phase when clan members are assembled, awakening passions full of life and energy:

An event of any importance immediately puts him outside himself. Does he receive happy news? There are transports of enthusiasm.

If the opposite happens, he is seen running hither and yon like a madman, giving way to all sorts of chaotic movements: shouting, screaming, gathering dusk and throwing it in all directions, biting himself, brandishing his weapons furiously, and so on. The very act of congregating is an exceptionally powerful stimulant. Once the individuals are gathered together, a sort of electricity is generated from their closeness and quickly launches them to an extraordinary height of exaltation ... Probably because a collective emotion cannot be expressed collectively without some order that permits harmony and unison of movement, these gestures and cries tend to fall into rhythm and regularity, and from there into songs and dances.
([1912]1995: 217–218)

The embellished point is that the stimulus for a collective effervescence is the sheer act of assembling. And, when such experiences are repeated again and again, they generate beliefs that two contrasting worlds exist, a life of profane/daily relations and a life of relations with supernatural forces and sacred things:

It is in these effervescent social milieux, and indeed from that very effervescence, that the religious idea seems to have been born ... Indeed, we may well ask whether this starkness of contrast may have been necessary to release the experience of the sacred in its first form.
([1912]1995: 220–221 emphasis added)

Why does the foundational religion take on the form of a plant or animal totem? Durkheim's explanation is a bit vague but the general idea is this: (1) an animal or plant species is the flag of a clan, its symbolic representation; (2) the clan (when it assembles) is the source that awakens strong emotions that are perceived as external forces; (3) clan members, however, find these effervescent emotions bewildering and excessively abstract; (4) an understanding comes when these sentiments are linked to a visible object, the totem species, and, above all, to the many totemic symbolic images. As food collectors, it would be natural for hunter-gatherers to put a transcendental collective force onto a local plant or animal and treat it and its images as the reality itself:

[A] religious force is nothing other than the collective and anonymous force of the clan, and since this can be represented in the mind only in the form of the totem, the totemic emblem is like the visible body of the god ... this is ... why it holds the first place in the series of sacred things.

([1912]1947: 221)

With totemism religion takes root in reality. A religion is not the creation of a fanciful imagination, a hallucination, or an illusion but a part of the real world, a symbolic marker of the living reality that is society. Its chief task is not to provide either an explanation or a representation of the natural world. Above all else, it evolved to provide a focus and material grounding for "a system of ideas" for individuals to represent their society within themselves, and the intimate but little understood expressed relations they have with it.

> Religious force is only the sentiment inspired by the group in its members, but projected outside of the consciousnesses that experience them, and objectified. To be objectified, they are fixed upon some object which thus becomes sacred; but any object might fulfill this function ... the sacred character assumed by an object is not implied in the intrinsic properties of this latter: *it is added to them*. The world of religious things is not one particular aspect of empirical nature; *it is superimposed upon it.*
>
> ([1912]1947: 229, emphasis in original)

A society can only live through the consciousness of its members. But if a society is to become conscious of itself, minds must act and react upon each other to experience a communal reality. Far from trivial practices or fancy movements, collective rituals serve to attach members closer to their god by serving to bind members to each other, with god being only a "figurative expression" of society. Collective representations have the power to make minds rise beyond the normal senses. And, while a collective effervescence is detrimental to the organism if it lasts too long as it is "a kind of delirium," its renewal is essential. For when the group is no longer assembled and distinctive human temperaments quickly return, the forces generating the sacred will run down as they are solely a product of the human brain.

> ... if we give the name delirious to every state in which the mind adds to the immediate data given by the senses and projects its own sentiments and feelings into things, then nearly every collective representation is in a sense delirious; *religious beliefs are only one particular case of a very general law* ... But collective representations

very frequently attribute to the things to which they are attached qualities which do not exist under any form or to any degree. Out of the commonest object, they can make a most powerful sacred being. Yet the powers which are thus conferred, though purely ideal, act as through they were real; they determine the conduct of men with the same degree of necessity as physical forces.

([1912]1947: 227–228, emphasis added)

Book 3: Rites[18]

The Negative Cult

As important as beliefs are to a cult, they cannot be maintained without religious rites. So, all religious cults have positive and negative rituals that play an important part in religious life. The sacred and profane must be kept separate; so, negative rites or interdictions are first to appear. These special rites do not facilitate or dictate acts but just their opposite: they make certain acts forbidden or *taboo*. Some interdicts separate incompatible sacred things, whereas others separate the sacred from the profane. These latter taboos are what Durkheim calls "interdicts *par excellence*" (p.302, original emphasis). Thus, the negative cult is a system of abstentions, a barrier that forbids but has positive effects by making cult members rid themselves of profane relations before becoming intimate with sacred relations.

How did the system of negative taboos arise? Durkheim answer is vague, although he believes it is related to how the sacred and profane are channeled in our minds into two different domains. Following Durkheim, the sacred and profane worlds are housed in two distinctive cognitive domains that exclude each another. One reason they must be kept apart is the extraordinary contagiousness of a sacred character; for even superficial contact enables the sacred to spread from one object to another. And anything, of course, can be made sacred. The character of sacredness is what charges up the emotions and elicits intensive respect for a sacred object.

---

18 An important theme in *Elementary Forms* ([1912]1995: 242ff) that is not covered in this overview is Durkheim's idea of the soul, which he treats as a thing or substance that is part of the body and yet independent of it (as it is society internalized in humans). I did not include it because Durkheim did not include the soul in his universal definition of religion or as a core component in totemic religion, and in any case it could not be evaluated within the context of the primate data set in Part 2 of this book. But see W.Watts Miller (1998) for an enlightening discussion on this salient Durkhemian theme.

This contagion brings together unlike things—rocks, plants, waterfalls, humans, totems and they all become sacred things. Durkheim places great importance on the distinction between the profane and sacred because religious life starts with a neurological cognizance of the sacred domain. And, Durkheim believed (as did Robertson Smith) that taboos are what jumpstarted the sacred domain by generating the special emotions drawing individuals to the religious life.

The Positive Cult

Positive rituals are different from negative rituals in that they are celebratory and performed in a state of joy, happiness, and enthusiasm. Individuals assemble, emotions are intensified, and a shared faith is restored or is invigorated in the reawakening of communal sentiments. Yet these emotions can dissipate and, thus, must be periodically recharged through collective rituals. Hence, humans must come together at regular intervals and enter into relations with each other and with the sacred being. If not, once cult members lose faith in their god, and the sacred, collective representations of this force of god withers away. And the only way to renew these collective representations is to keep the sentiments flowing, because passionate emotions are the very source of religious life. So the faithful must assemble because a divinity is real only to the extent that it has a place in the consciousness of humans. Neither can do without the other; individuals and god (i.e. society) need each other.

Now, if we are to see in rites anything more than the product of a chronic delirium, Durkheim said, "we must show that the effect of the cult really is to recreate periodically a moral being upon which we depend, as it depends upon us. Now this being does exist: it is society. Howsoever little importance the religious ceremonies may have, they put the group into action; the groups assemble to celebrate them. So their first effect is to bring individuals together, to multiply the relations between them and to make them more intimate with one another" ([1912]1947: 348).

So, the purpose of rites is to reaffirm the cult on a regular basis. Community members assemble and become conscious of their unity. In totemism, they represent this unity by uniting around a plant or animal species. A way they do this is to imitate the movement of their totem species and, for this reason, Durkheim believed that imitative practices are an essential ingredient of early rituals by laying the foundation blocks for totemic cult structures that bring individuals together. It is the concentration of humans moving into stable groups and performing rites that lead to the elementary religion and the origin of society itself.

Finally, Durkheim discusses the forlorn celebrations or what he calls "piacular" rites where humans assemble but in sadness. Mourning rituals are piacular practices but instead of happy dances and relaxed moods, there are tears, groans and anxiety, the experience of sorrow over a sickness or death, or other horrors. Individuals gather in a sort of collective pity that generates shared emotions of sadness. The community is upset but the participation in a single affective state of empathy or pity is also a catalyst that serves to eventually restore positive energy among group members. So, no matter how diverse the rites are in a given religion, there is a continuity as they overlap with one another into a system of collective practices that charge up the positive emotions:

> Thus, the practices no more fall into two separate genera than the beliefs do. However complex the outward manifestations of religious life may be, its inner essence is simple, and one and the same. Everywhere it fulfills the same need and derives from the same state of mind. In all its forms, its object is to lift man above himself and to make him live a higher life than he would if he obeyed only his individual impulses. The beliefs express this life in terms of representations; the rites organize and regulate its functioning.
> ([1912]1995: 417)

12
Under the Microscope

> *Rationalism does not at all suppose that science can ever reach the limits of knowledge . . . we might say that this principle is demonstrated by the history of science itself. The manner in which it has progressed shows that it is impossible to mark a point beyond which scientific explanation will become impossible . . . Whenever people thought that science had reached its ultimate limit, it resumed . . . its forward march and penetrated regions thought to be forbidden to it.*
>
> Emile Durkheim [1903]1973: 5) *Moral Education*

Introduction

Durkheim wanted his theory of religion and society to be tested. In a closing sentence in *Elementary Forms he asked us to* follow his lead: "What must be done is to try out the hypothesis and test it against the facts as methodically as possible. This is what I have tried to do" [1912]1995: 448]. The problem here is the same one Durkheim faced as he struggled to find evidence to support his thesis. What facts do we use to *try out* the hypothesis? Durkheim's method was to start with what he viewed as the most "primitive" form of the religious life but he well knew that Central Australian aboriginals were not the "primitives" that he needed to support his totemic thesis. Not only did they violate long established canons on totemism but they also overturned his connections among totemism, exogamy, and female descent as the earliest kinship system. By the time he settled on Spencer and Gillen's ethnography, he had run out of options. The Arrernte were the only known population with a relatively intact totemic system. He then faced an uphill battle to reinterpret Spencer and Gillen's findings and explain away Frazers's theory that totemism was not a religion but a system of magical practices to increase the food supply.

To make the facts fit his theory, Durkheim argued that Arrernte's totemism was in an advanced stage and had undergone a series of profound shocks to the institution and, hence, was slowly transitioning into another social form. This alternative explanation was essential for the science-minded Durkheim as he needed at least one case study to support his thesis. Until the very end, he surely hoped that support could be found for his hypothesized archetype, the single clan or horde. By the time *Elementary Forms* was published in 1912, interest in totemism was fading, which only exacerbated Durkheim's problems. It was "now or never," and Durkheim—the empiricist to the core—knew his thesis sat on a very shaky foundation. Still, he was sure that he was right—that religion was the symbolic representation of society and totemism was the primal religion.

A century has passed since Durkheim's death and little has been done with his *totemic principle*. It is true, that in 1960, Guy Swanson attempted to validate parts of Durkheim's thesis with a cross-cultural study of societies and found many associations that exist between religion and social structure, especially with regard to notions of god-like figures, their types and numbers (see Bergesen 1984 for an analysis).[1] In 2003, Michael Hammond also found support, this time for Durkheim's claim that religion serves to symbolize a collective, utilizing data suggestive of neural "enhanced arousers" that serve to facilitate the human capacity to move beyond direct tie-by-tie social networks and to seek out wider circles of ties using religion as an early framing device. And, of course, generations of scholars have taken up Durkheim's rich ideas, building upon them as foundation blocks or for generating their own theories. For example, Erving Goffman (1967), Randall Collins (1975, 2004), Robert Bellah (1967), Mark Cladis (1992), Radcliffe-Brown (1977), Jonathan Turner (1988, 2002, 2007), W. Loyd Warner (1949), Robert Merton (1968), Hans-Peter Müller (1993), Kenneth Thompson (1998), Ivan Strenski, 2006), Seth Abrutyn and Anna Mueller (2014), Mustafa Emirbayer (2003), N.J. Allen (1998), W. Watts Miller (1998), Alexander Riley (2014), Mary Douglas (2002), Talcott Parsons (1937), Sondra Hausner (2013), Edward Tiryakian (2009), and see Smith and Alexander (1996), to name only a few scholars who have drawn upon Durkheim's ideas to build modern-day theories on interpersonal processes revolving around rituals, arousal of emotions, symbolizations, deviance, education, and other dynamic processes outside of Durkheim's focus on religion, *per se*.

---

1 Guy Swanson's provocative work, *The Birth of the Gods: The Origin of Primitive Beliefs* (1960) was a pioneering effort to test parts of Durkheim's theory of religion. Durkheim's *Elementary Forms*, Swanson said, is "one of the most stimulating in all the literature about society." As I saw myself following in Swanson's footsteps in my effort to evaluate Durkheim's totemic theory, I thought it was appropriate to adapt the title of my book to reflect this affiliation.

In fact, the consensus today is that religion is a collective phenomena that does roughly correspond to the structural features of a society[2] and that religious rituals and other processes endemic to religion are fundamental to how humans interact more generally (see also, Turner et al. 2017 for an analysis on religion as yet another form of interpersonal interaction with others in the supernatural realm). And, so, much has been done with Durkheim's ideas, but almost nothing has been done with his core origin theory that religion had its genesis in totemism or that it is a natural byproduct of a collective awakening of a sense of society.

Many reasons exist for why Durkheim's origin thesis has been ignored, but they boil down to these problems:

- The theory is encased in flawed nineteenth-century social evolutionary thinking.
- The nineteenth century's simple to complex scale of societal progressions has been discredited.
- The historical reality of totemism is dismissed on the grounds that totemic systems are not uniform in composition or structure, are not universal, and are not necessarily a religion or, for some, not even real.
- The existence of Durkheim's hypothesized single clan or horde has never been observed in any human population.
- The belief that religion originated with the rise of the sacred and the sheer assembly of individuals cannot be refuted or supported.
- The relationship among exogamy, totemism, and the incest taboo is still an open question.
- The proposal that kinship began with a female descent system is questionable.
- The classification proposed by Durkheim of a universal division of things by the mind into sacred and profane is questionable.

---

2 As discussed earlier, Durkheim felt that while "collective representations" start out with an intimate connection with a social structure, once created they reveal a partial degree of independence. As Durkheim expressed it: "[O]nce a basic number of representations has been thus created, they become . . . partially autonomous realities . . . They have the power to attract and repel each other and to form amongst themselves various syntheses, which are determined by their natural affinities and not by the condition of their matrix. As a consequence, the new representations born of these syntheses have the same nature; they are immediately caused by other collective representations and not by this or that characteristic of the social structure. The evolution of religion provides us with the most striking examples of this phenomenon" ([1898]1965: 31).

- The proposal that the horde is the elementary human formation is an open question.
- The belief that the nuclear family is not a natural unit or the baseline human organization is an open question.

All these problems or questions tell us why Durkheim's thesis needs to be evaluated with facts. Do any of his core assumptions have scientific merit? The answer depends on what one is trying to support or refute—the existence of the primal horde, matriliny as the first kinship, the origin thesis, the connection between religion as society, etc. And, it depends on what can be subjected to scientific inquiry.

So, how do we begin? On this score, Durkheim left us instructions in his "Method of Sociology" ([1908]1982: 245). As to method, he said it must be *historical* and *objective* (see Bellah 1959). For Durkheim, history held the key to understanding present-day institutions, their reasons for existence, and the elements and causes upon which they depend. We cannot understand the nature of a social institution until we examine its underlying components. So he wanted to use historical methods as a microscopic instrument for stripping down an institution into its distinctive and essential elements. He began with religion rather than kinship because he believed it was the first institution. Later, as he told us in *Elementary Forms*, he would take up the kinship institution.[3]

The second instruction is objectivity. Social scientists must proceed by adopting the mind-set of biologists, physicists, and chemists who often work in uncharted and even unseen domains. When applied to the social sphere, scientific detachment is difficult, he said, because we are all products of society and naturally biased towards particular beliefs and values. Yet, only objectivity can reveal the truth and have scientific value. In Durkheim's eyes, then, uncovering the original causes and significance of present-day institutions entails using historical methods, suspending our preconceptions and taking up an impartial lens to lead us where it may.

---

[3] As Bellah underscored (1959: 448–449) "Almost all of ... [Durkheim's] ... own researches draw heavily from historical and ethnological sources and are in fact organized in an historical framework. This is true, for example, of his sociology of the family, his treatment of the division of labor, his theory of punishment, his discussion of property and contract, his sociology of education, his sociology of religion, of his study of socialism. Even *Suicide* which depends more on contemporary data than almost any other of his studies, derives its conceptual scheme in part at least from hypotheses about very long-term changes in the structure of solidarity in society."

So, let us begin our scientific expedition by starting with the fossil and archaeological records and searching for *any* empirical traces of religious sentiments or even signs of a proto-religion in *hominin* evolution (i.e. humans, human ancestors, and near ancestors). This way, we can be faithful to Durkheim's guidelines of taking an institution as far back as we can in *hominin* evolution, which is much further back then Durkheim proposed to go. Yet, he did not have the 100 years of accumulated data on hominin evolution, on primate origins of humans, and on archeological findings. If he had, I suspect that he would have pursued these empirical fields, especially given the early influence of Espinas on his thinking.

Moving into this uncharted religious turf will also make it easier to free our minds of customary notions we might have about what religion is, or is not. All we need to take along is Durkheim's definition of religion, which is generic enough to be applicable to any class of religious phenomena ([1912]1995: 44).

> *A religion is a unified system of beliefs and practices relative to sacred things, that is to say, things set apart and forbidden–beliefs and practices which unite into one single moral community called a Church, all those who adhere to them.*

The Fossil, Molecular, and Archaeological Records to 300,000 BCE

The fossil, molecular, and archeological records are our only sources of first-hand evidence on the biological and social evolution of humans. The steady accumulation of these materials over the last 200 years provides enough data to paint with broad strokes a portrait of *hominin* evolution (i.e. modern humans and their direct and near ancestors).[4] The molecular and fossil data document that basal hominins evolved in tropical Africa between 5 and 7 million years ago, after branching away from a *last common ancestor* (LCA) with present-day chimpanzees (*Pan*). During the Pliocene epoch (which began about 5 million years ago), a variety of early hominin species appear in the fossil record. Collectivity known as *Australopithecines*, their dentition points to a diet of soft foods such as ripe fruits (with a trend

---

4 Hominins include all members of the human family in the past or present. A hominin status also includes all fossils on the sideline (e.g. Austrapithecines) or on the direct line to *Homo sapiens* (e.g. *Homo erectus*). By definition, a fossil primate is labeled a hominin if it had an upright posture and a habitual bipedal gait. So, any upright walking primate (no matter how ancient) is considered a hominin if it has this defining characteristic. (Note: The term hominin replaces the traditional former term hominid.)

toward harder, grittier foods), while a reconstruction of their habitats points to a preference for heavily wooded forests, woodlands, or in some cases, open, park-like environments.

A recent chemical analysis of Austrapithecine male and female dentition dated between 1.8 and 2 million years ago provides a tantalizing clue into their social arrangements. What they discovered is a distinctive difference in the kinds of mineral deposits between male and female teeth, indicating that females (but not males) grew up in one locality and moved to another locality as adults (Copeland et al. 2011 and see Foley and Gamble 2009). A female-biased dispersal by Austrapithecines perhaps such as "Mrs Ples," a famous hominin fossil, lends support to Durkheim's premise that female "exogamy" played a pivotal role in early human organization (see later chapters on hominoids). In addition, while the australopiths (their informal name) closely resemble contemporary chimpanzees with their ape-like jaws and faces, skeletal features, body size, and brain size (from 420 to 550 cc's), they differ in appearance from apes in two stand-out features—smaller canines and a habitual bipedal gait. Walking on two limbs is rare for mammals and so when selection favored a hominin upright posture, it set in motion further structural changes for a wholly different lifestyle from our ape cousins. One evolutionary edge was early stone tool technology, with direct evidence for the earliest modification of stones dating back to 3.3 million years ago (Harmand et al. 2015; for discussions see Bolus 2015; Antón, Potts and Aiello 2014).

Between the late Pliocene and early Pleistocene (i.e. the Plio-Pleistocene, circa 2.8 million years ago), basal *Homo* species appear in the fossil record (Gibbons 2015a; Villmoare et al. 2015; Spoor et al. 2015). Although species of early *Homo* resembled their austrapithecine ancestors and co-existed with them for several million years until all austrapith taxa went extinct about a million years ago, *Homo* had on average a larger body size with a more human-like anatomy. Cranial capacity in *Homo* is also larger on average with brain size ranging between 510 and 750 cc's (the human range is 1200 to 1600 cc's), with some species evidencing a differently shaped skull vault with more modern frontal lobes. Facial features are more human-like (jaws take on the more modern form of a parabola), and the stride is fully human. In habitat reconstruction, paleogeography points to climatic change as a spur for *Homo* evolution with a shift in some African regions from a forest/open woodland ecology to a seasonal dryer bushland and grassland ecology—for discussions see Robinson and Rowan et al. 2017; DiMaggio et al. 2015; Gibbons 2015a; Stanford et al. 2013; Relethford 2010; Maryanski 2013; Wood and Lonergan 2008.

Climate and habitat change are linked, in turn, with advances in stone tool technology, with a shift towards sharp-edged flakes that appear in the fossil record about 2.6 million years ago.[5] Thousands of stone tools in assemblies called the *Oldowan* industrial complex, have been uncovered in African localities. Microscopic examinations of wear patterns on these simple core and flake assemblages, along with experimental tryouts for possible functions, tell us they were used for a variety of splitting and cutting functions, offering clues into dietary and living habits. In particular, recent evidence of cut marks on the bones of butchered mammals in association with Oldowan tools now points to "a clear causal link between Oldowan stone technology and processing of large animal carcasses" (e.g. for extracting bone marrow and cutting soft tissue) (Sahnouni et al. 2013: 148; Yravedra et al. 2017). This activity seemingly involved a collective strategy. Yet, aside from a consensus that early Homo taxa were consuming animal flesh (either by scavenging leftovers or hunting practices) and that they moved about in small groups from one site to the next, little is known about their behavioral or social activities because little else is found with these stone assemblages. Nor do artifacts reveal markings that even hint of proto-religious symbols.

The next hominin grade was early *Homo erectus* who appeared about 1.8 million years ago. This ancestor had smaller jaws and teeth, a larger average body size, and a human-like appearance from the neck down, although they were far more robust than modern humans. Early *H. erectus* also differed from early *Homo* in a brain volume closer to the human range with a range of 850 to 1200 cc's. During the Pleistocene epoch (beginning about 1.8 MYA), the earth grew cooler with a looming ice age in the forecast, shrinking the forests and expanding the grasslands. Population waves of *Homo* responded by leaving Africa and moving into diverse ecosystems in Europe, Asia, and as far as China.

The archaeological record also documents that by 1.7 MYA technological innovations are introduced by toolmakers—a stone assemblage called the *Acheulian* Industrial Complex. The hand axe represents this tradition, along with a variety of bifacial tool designs such as scrapers and cleavers used for specialized purposes—signaling the first technological leap in cultural evolution. Roughly a million years ago, the archaeological record also confirms that *Homo erectus* populations not only used fire but a strong

---

[5] Early hominins may have made tools from bone or wood that were not preserved. All we can say given the evidence is that the first *documented production* of stone tools are dated to 3.3 million years ago with early hominins. And, early *Homo* tools with stone flake assemblies for making finer cuts seemingly built on this technology.

possibility exists that they also controlled fire, seemingly for cooking foods, keeping warm, seeing at night, and for keeping predators at bay (Berna et al. 2012). Tool kits and fire are hallmarks of human behavior, lending clues into the lifeways of *H. erectus* who left remains of their material culture all over the African, Asian, and European continents. Their tool chests also stayed rather uniform over time, indicating the passing on of collective traditions from generation to generation. For example, the hand axe remained an essential tool from 1.5 million years ago to 250,000 years ago, marking a longstanding cultural tradition.

As food collectors, *Homo erectus* populations were eating wild plants but their occupation sites were also utilized for the butchering of *big* game animals. Indeed, the migration cycles of animal herds may account, in part, for the dispersal of *Homo erectus* all over the Old World. Moreover, given the large body size of *erectus* with some males over six feet tall, they probably had a "fission-fusion" social structure, characteristic of studied nomadic hunter-gatherers who forage in small parties when resources are scarce and concentrate in bands or even at the regional population level (or big band-level) when resources are plentiful or for ceremonial occasions. Did a social structure with fission-fusion cycles set the stage for the origin of religion, as Durkheim argued? The evidence from the home bases of *Homo erectus* strongly hint at *collective representations* but we can only document the existence of creative minds pursuing an adaptive lifestyle by using stone tools. Still, the accumulating piles of artifacts do establish that cognitive enhancements in the *Homo* line were well underway, and in all likelihood, it was a *Homo erectus* population that became the ancestral stock for the rise of *Homo sapiens*.

By the Middle Pleistocene (circa 780,000 to 300,000 years ago), *Homo* fossils are increasingly more human-like in facial appearance and cranial features, signaling a gradual transition from *Homo erectus* to *Homo sapiens*. At present, the hominin nomenclature is in flux in the assigning of categories representing this transition with fossils labeled "advanced *Homo erectus*" and "archaic *Homo sapiens*," to *Homo heidelbergensis* and *Homo rhodesiensis*. And, while the evidence strongly points to an African homeland for the origin of *Homo sapiens*, the exact time and place is still unknown (Hublin et al. 2017).

In technology, Middle Stone Age tool kits resemble those of H. *erectus*, but they show creative variations, again representing an intelligence for fashioning new technologies. Archaeological sites place hominin living arrangements in open-air sites, rock shelters, or caves with hunting and butchering game now involving tracking herds of animals, seemingly by parties of hunting males. Among the archaeological finds are cut marks on hominin bones, suggestive of some sort of ritualized ceremony, or ritualized cannibalism. There is even a shell from an assemblage of freshwater mussels with a zigzag pattern or some sort of abstract engraving dated to 500,000 years ago (Joordens 2015 et al.). It was intentionally done so is it the earliest abstract artwork? It is tempting to speculate that during this time there was some sort of proto-religious or even religious activity but the archaeological record is mostly silent on this question. Still, the huge expansion in *Homo* neurobiology during the long Pleistocene epoch surely reflects a gradual heightening of cognition, even without a wisp of evidence on underlying symbolic realms of collective representations.[6] To date little can be supported or refuted. The absence of evidence could simply be a lack of preservation.

The Fossil, Molecular, and Archaelogical Record of *Homo Sapiens* and Neanderthals

The earliest phrase of *Homo sapiens* was ushered in about 300,000 years ago, documented by a mosaic of human features that include big brains (albeit with less rounded and more elongated skull shapes), dental morphology and delicate cheekbones (Hublin et al. 2017; Stringer and Galway-Witham 2017). In origin, the first *Homo sapiens* are surely the descendants of Middle Pleistocene African hominins because the *earliest H. sapiens* (looking similar to humans today) and *early modern* H. *sapiens* (looking just like humans today) with their fossil remains dated to about 200,000 years ago are found in African fossil beds (see Richter et al. 2017). One astonishing finding by paleogeneticists (based on maternally inherited mitochondrial DNA and Y-chromosome markers) is that all humans alive today are descendants of a small African mother population (setting the stage for a founder's effect).[7] Just when modern looking *Homo sapiens* moved outside of Africa is currently in flux (with some new fossil finds

---

[6] Humans lived as hunter-gatherers for 99 percent of their time on earth. Nomadic populations have few material possessions so evidence of their cultural traditions would be a rare find at any time. In fact, we would be hard pressed to find traces of recent food collecting populations if ethnographers had not gone into the field to observe their lifeways.

[7] Founders effect is a type of genetic drift in population genetics. It refers to the migration of a subset population from a parent population. As the founder population is usually small, its genetic makeup is not representative of the parent population. Because of this loss of genetic variation, the founder's effect population may soon become distinctively different from the original population (or deme), sometimes resulting in speciation and the origin of a new species.

in Israel dated to about 180,000 years ago), and while the number of dispersions is still debated, thus far, many scholars contend that in the main roughly between 70,000 and 50,000 years ago humans migrated out of Africa into Asia and Europe in a widespread single wave (Stringer and Galway-Witham 2018; Culotta 2012; Disotell 2012; Lambert and Tishkoff 2009; Gibbons 2015b).

In these new habitats, early humans were prolific and prospered, eventually spreading their genes around the globe. But it is telling that all humanity originated from a single ancestral population—consisting of, at best, a few thousand individuals because it helps to explain the small amount of variation now present in the *Homo sapiens* gene pool. In fact, levels of human genetic variation are so small that even chimpanzees (*Pan*), gorillas (*Gorillas*), and orangutans (*Pongo*) with contemporary gene pools of less than a million individuals have more diversity than does the human genome. Indeed, despite the seven billion humans alive today, *Homo sapiens* evidence the *least* genetic variability of any living primate species (Barbujani et al. 2013: 156). This finding collaborates the long-standing observation among social scientists that more diversity exists within a single human population than between populations. It also lends credibility to Durkheim's strong conviction that differences in human cognition are mostly a product of different experiences and different environmental conditions. To his credit, Durkheim was always a strong proponent of a shared human neurobiology.

The emergence of early modern humans ushered in new levels of craftsmanship, especially the deft use of bone technology. Bone was used for making weapons such as knives and harpoons, for putting holes in materials such as leather skins, for making eyed needles for sewing garments, and for fashioning bone ornaments. And, while hominins continued to live in caves and cliff-shelters, they started to construct framed dwellings built from bone, wood, and animal skins with regional architectural variations. Evidence of hominin communal activities is also introduced into the archaeological record, thus marking not only symbolic behaviors, but also clear signs of *collective representations*. Of special significance are two cognitive domains associated with two object-linked social activities: (1) intentional burial of the dead and (2) artistic expressions.

Burial of the Dead

Signs of collective representations are evident in gravesite practices. One could argue that burials are often by chance or intentional to avoid spreading disease but when a corpse is gently placed underground with body parts in a fixed, standardized direction, and accompanied by grave goods, a ritualized burial is difficult to dismiss. Yet, whether a purposeful burial represents a belief in the afterlife, a secular rite, or an act to prevent predators from devouring a loved one is unknown. Traces of intentional burials are found as early as 160,000 years ago for early modern *Homo sapiens* (see Geertz 2013 for a review), but sites with "mortuary patterns" truly suggestive of ritualistic burials are found about 70,000 years ago, notably in Europe and, surprisingly, among Neanderthals (*Homo neanderthalensis*) where at least seventeen sites in Asia and Europe point to intentional burials with some skeletal remains laid to rest with colorful wildflowers (Akazawa and Muhesen 2003; Steadman 2009; Haviland et al. 2014; Condemi and Gerd-Christian Weniger 2011; Harvati 2015; Winzeler 2008: 50). Recent evidence indicates that La Chapelle-aux-Saints (a famous male Neanderthal fossil) was deliberately buried after a reanalysis of his burial pit (Zorich 2014 and see Gamble 2013 for a review).

Neanderthal mortality patterns also include the burials of infants, juveniles, and adolescents whose remains are carefully positioned and found in association with burnt horse bones, reindeer teeth, goat horns, and other animal remains (Spikins et al. 2014). Neanderthals went extinct about 30,000 years ago, but DNA analysis has confirmed the presence of Neanderthal genes in contemporary European and Asian populations, greatly enhancing their status as a subpopulation of *Homo sapiens (*Wall et al. 2013; Meyer et al. 2012; Simonti et al. 2016). Of note, is that Neanderthal female dentition also bears signs of the same Austrapith pattern of females growing up in one locality and moving to another locality after puberty (a dispersal pattern also found in our closest living relatives). Thus, in the Upper Pleistocene, hard evidence exists of female dispersal or "exogamy" as well as symbolic activities that include communities engaged in elaborate burials by carefully positioning the dead before burial and embellishing grave pits with decorated stones, bones, shells, and canine teeth, perhaps to ensure some future destiny (Cleyet-Merle 2007; Holt and Formicola 2008; Pettitt 2011). But the archeological record is silent on whether or not these *collective representations* can be extended to include beliefs and practices of a sacred nature.

The Late Pleistocene Artistic Explosion

About 100,000 years ago, new mixtures of artifacts are introduced into the archaeological record, the earliest in Africa and the Middle East. Categorized as mobility art (because of its easy portability), these pleasing objects include drilled sea shells and bone parts, often painted with colorful ochre (a brownish, yellow pigment) and decorated with intentional surface marks (Cooke et al. 2014: 529, 533ff). Soon, this "state-of-the-art" human activity explodes throughout Europe, Asia, and Australia with portable art made from stone, bone, and ivory. Fixed artistic creations of images, engravings, and often-mysterious abstract designs are also found on the face of rocks in open-air sites or on caves walls, ceilings, and cave floors. Artistic expression is associated with the widespread migration of *Homo sapiens* out of Africa in the late Pleistocene, with the creation of Upper Paleolithic art in Europe overlapping with indigenous Neanderthal populations, suggesting that Neanderthals also pursued this rich cultural activity (Pike et al. 2012: 1409; Callaway 2014, 2015). In fact, the very recent dating of some simple European cave drawings made more than 64,000 years ago leaves little doubt that the Neanderthals were Europe's first artists (Appenzeller 2018).

While magnificent Pleistocene art collections are found throughout the Old World, including Australia, the archaeological sites from Spain to the Soviet Union have received the most attention because they yield precise dates, have exceptionally preserved collections, and well-established funding. By the Upper Paleolithic, European tool kits reveal a new sophistication with the innovative use of such raw materials as stone, ivory (e.g. from deer antlers), sea shells, and flint (a form of mineral quartz) to craft weapons such as blades, spears, bows and arrows and harpoons as well as household items that include knives and needles for making jewelry and elegant finery from animal skins. The diffusion of "imported" goods from outside local encampments also speaks to the existence of extensive trading networks from the flatlands to the mountains to the Atlantic and Mediterranean shores.

Upper Paleolithic European hunter-gatherers also left behind truly monumental parietal art. Only in 1902 were these awe-inspiring cave drawings and paintings formally recognized, in part because nineteenth-century scholars could not believe that "savage minds" were capable of such skill and imagination that their artistry would be considered outstanding at any age (Abadía and Morales 2004, 2013). Indeed, they rival paintings in today's art galleries. But prehistoric galleries were situated in rock shelters or deep inside caves, with towering high arches, hence the name parietal or cave art. But why decorate a cave? In 1866, Felix Garrigou, an Ariège archaeologist visiting caves on the border of the French Pyrenees wrote in his notes, "Walls with curious drawings of oxen and horses ... Amateur artists have drawn animals. Why?"(quoted in Sesta 2005: 6). Researchers are still asking this question: Was it art for art's sake, was it art with religious significance or something else? (see Dickson 1990).

What was Painted and How?

The majority of cave paintings are clusters of animals in a mastery of perspective. The artists often favored particular animals, with horses or animals with "horsey like features" popular among the 350 cave interiors with ornate cavities (Pruvost et al. 2011; Fanlac 1984). Other represented species on cave walls are reindeers, mammoths, foxes, bisons, ibex (i.e. goats), aurochs (or oxen ancestral to domestic cattle), lions, rhinoceros, and brown bears. Fish (especially trout and salmon) are occasionally portrayed, while insects, reptiles, birds, and rodents are rare. Human figures in parietal art are also surprisingly rare, although stick figures and part animal/part human hybrids are occasionally drawn. For example, in the Trois-Fréres cave in Southwestern France is an engraved mythical creation named *The Sorcerer*. Situated near the ceiling of a chamber, it sports large deer antlers, stag ears, a horsey tail, paws and feet with primate-like fingers and toes, a long beard, forward facing eyes, and an implicit bipedal gait. While the engraving is concocted by using parts of different animal species, the overall effect in the mind's eye is to "see" a hybrid animal-human creature or a human dressed up in animal garb and dancing—a Paleolithic shaman or sorcerer? (Hodgson 2008; Balter 2000; Curtis 2006).

While the human figure is, strangely enough, rarely drawn in parietal art, big and little hand impressions are left behind after palms are firmly pressed against rock surfaces. Paleolithic galleries are also accented with dots, dashes, lineal lines, circles, and bars with some geometrical shapes specific to a given locality and some that appear to be associated with the decorative paintings in a locality. To create these stunning murals, the artists used a variety of natural pigments, especially black charcoal and red ochre for coloring. As parietal art is often found in the inner recesses of dark caverns, some spanning well over two kilometers, one puzzle was how such realistic and outstanding work was done without natural light. This enigma was solved with the recovery of hand-held torches and attractive hallowed out bowls with handles made of sandstone, limestone, or stone. Even the fat-burning portable lamps were decorated with animal imagery or geometrical etchings that in some localities were found to match the geometrical etchings on nearby cave walls (Cleyet-Merle 2007: 106–107).

The Nature of the Art

It can be said that "art is in the eyes of the beholder," but there is no question that art of outstanding quality was being done during the Upper Paleolithic and for at least 20,000 years. Yet, the artwork itself does not follow a progression of simple to complex, although precise dates for some early caves are not yet confirmed (Pettitt 2008). In each cultural phase, some artists painted exceptionally well, with no indication that paintings in any generation were done by a single individual. In shape, size, style, and presentation, the painted animals are lifelike in appearance and are typically represented towards the side or side-on in a state of suspension without any background or ground lines. To create such realistic images was challenging because the artists had to first gauge the precise contours of cave walls to see if they conformed to the dimensions necessary to play up or down prominent anatomical features of their subjects. Knowledge of the composition and properties of the rocks themselves was also necessary for accenting their subjects with proper lines, shading, and color mixtures. Any mistake would be difficult to correct for a mural drawn on the chamber of a rough and bumpy cave.

What Motivated the Artists?

Scholars for generations have studied the inventory, and placement of animal themes, while comparing similarities and differences among caves and their geographical locations. Did the artists paint simply for creative expression? Was it art for spiritual inspiration, art for sheer pleasure, or art for its visual beauty and for engaging the emotions? But the artists never signed their paintings; we cannot interpret the many geometrical symbols; and we cannot reconstruct the emotions and behaviors. Still, the art and artifact collections, the symbols left behind, the underground chambers and exhibition rooms are still informative and tell us the following:

- The hundreds of caves with art works were not used as living quarters.
- The artists were traditionally depicted as adult males, but recent analysis of human handprints pressed against walls, suggest females, adolescents, and even children (who etched near ground level) were involved in cave drawings and graphics.
- The discovery of flutes made of bone in some caves were surely used for harmonious sounds produced by the vibrations of air blowing into these wind instruments. It was possibly accompanied by a chorus of voices, lending itself to an afternoon or evening of musical entertainment and an effervescent experience. Can it be accidental that the most awe-inspiring art is found in the most acoustically sonorous parts of a cavern and accentuated by glowing lamps?
- The parietal art can be viewed as a form of visual communication from the anonymous artists of long ago. It can also be viewed as an early

example of Durkheim's *collective representations*; for despite the varied techniques, phases, motifs and structural changes here and there, it has a stylistic unity that was passed on from generation to generation by prehistoric communities for at least 20,000 years (see Fritz and Tosello 2007 for a discussion).

Commentary

Paleolithic caverns with their cathedral-like ceilings are sometimes characterized as open-air structures for religious cults or magical ceremonies but there is no solid evidence they were used for such purposes. Durkheim was surely aware of prehistoric cave art because nineteenth-century tourists were already exploring caves in the Southwest of France near to the University of Bordeaux where he taught until 1902. Spencer and Gillen also roused public curiosity about painted caves after they published *Native Tribes of Central Australia* in 1899. And, early on, Frazer was second-guessing on what they represented. One of Durkheim's colleagues, Solomon Reinach, even gave a "magico-religious" interpretation of cave art based on the work of Spencer, Gillen and Frazer.

The caves can now be radiocarbon dated testifying to their prehistoric age with provocative clues accumulating, but no one has yet decoded what the symbols mean; why particular animals were chosen over other animals and painted over and over again; and why human figures are so rare. Seemingly, the art has meaningful symbolic value—but only for the Upper Paleolithic people of long ago.

Could the animals in frieze patterns be totemic emblems? The caves were not used for shelters or domestic activities so it is possible they were local totemic centers and used for religious-like ceremonial gatherings. Some scholars have even speculated that cave art may depict legendary scenes of kinship relations between bands, perhaps inspired by totemic mythologies or sacred ancestral narratives to reinforce communal solidarity. Or, the extended mural art may have served as secular "picture books" to accompany storytelling and intended purely for community entertainment. But how do we distinguish between secular art and sacred art with religious overtones? Sacred-ness following Durkheim is not detectable by the known senses or even inherent in an object itself. It is superimposed upon objects by a transcendental "sixth" sense in the human brain. And, as Alexander Riley (2005: 274) underscored, "the sacred is of course the key to the Durkheimian definition of religion." Yet, the sacred is so arbitrary that what is sacred to one population may not be sacred to another population.

Thus, while speculations abound it is difficult to draw any firm conclusions about the origin of religion from the fossil and archaeological records. Many tourists and scholars visiting the caves (including myself) sense an aura of the sacred or an arousing thrill generated by the exhilarating atmosphere of the great caverns but the beliefs and practices of Upper Paleolithic people are anyone's guess. Yet, the burial customs and painted caves of Upper Paleolithic communities are of stellar importance because they represent the first wide-scale evidence of ritualized collective symbolism and creativity. This type of activity, *per se*, has major implications because until recently most social science research has focused on the cultural relativity among human populations. Major cultural differences do exist, of course, although they can be viewed as simply reflections of the range of cultural variation intrinsic to *Homo sapiens*. Now if we also open the door to the notion of a shared human nature, in light of the small degree of variation in the human genome, it should not be surprising that when humans are placed in the same environment, they tend to behave in similar ways because the same emotions are triggered in the subcortical areas of the brain.

There is, then, every reason to believe that prehistoric populations reacted exactly as we do today to the incredibly beautiful images and aesthetically pleasing colors, lines, forms, and patterns in eye-catching cave art. It is plausible that the painted caves served as centers of social life for communities. For example, the ways in which some animals are configured and positioned in painted caves such as Lascaux in Southwestern France creates the impression of a Paleolithic style cinema because the animals appear to be in motion. In the semi-darkness with soft, shimmering lamps burning on the gallery walls and ceilings, the handsome animals with their fine, easy gaits can easily be perceived as galloping around the painted walls. Now if we introduce the gentle sounds of flutes and a chorus of melodious voices floating in the air, it is easy to imagine an emotionally powerful collective experience that would take on a life of its own. Indeed, artistic expression is common to all human populations and is clearly an invariant component of human cognition and emotional arousal. As Aubarbier and Binet (1987: 10–11) commented, "We can simply conclude that the emotions aroused in us by these cave paintings must have also been felt by prehistoric man. Our sensitivity brings us very close to him" (and her as well).

Thus, the fossil, molecular, and archaeological records are invaluable because they supply our only first-hand data on human evolution and culture. We now know that *Homo sapiens* originated about 300,000 years ago and that early modern looking humans evolved about 200,000 years ago from a small ancestral population. Humans have thus a long pre-history to slowly develop their technologies and cultural traditions. Yet, the origin and nature of the first social institutions are still unknown as are the meanings of symbolic activities because no Rosetta stone exists to interpret these cultural packages.

Still, we have prima facie evidence for some of Durkheim's hypotheses: the existence of female biased dispersal after puberty (with additional evidence in the next chapters); the ritual use of objects in burials; the possible existence of totems in artifacts and cave paintings; the possibility of emotion-arousing rituals around campfires and inside caves and the strong potential for rhythmic synchronization of these rituals in caves with flutes and singing to heighten these emotions to a higher level of effervescence. Is the origin of religion to be found in these activities? We cannot know at present. Still, as Gamble (2013: 139) reminds us, "Religious behaviour, as Durkheim argued, comes in many forms and has a social origin. It should never be seen as separate, and there is no reason to restrict its analysis to the genealogy of material symbols." In the next chapter, we will follow this advice by trying another tack that will cast more light on these early human populations and on Durkheim's theory of religion. These data will enable us to see back in time—much like the Hubble space telescope in search of clues into the origin and nature of the sacred, religion and society.

13
The Hominoid Social Legacy

> ... [T]he greatest obstacle to ... [the] ... joining of minds in a common consciousness, is the individual personality. The more decided that personality is ... the more difficult for it to merge into something other than itself. To experience the pleasure of saying "we," it is important not to enjoy saying "I" too much.
>
> Emile Durkheim ([1902–03]1973: 240) in *Moral Education*

For Émile Durkheim, sociology is the "science of social institutions" with religion its cornerstone institution. To understand present-day institutions, he insisted, we must go back in history and seek the causes for how and why religion emerged from a non-institutional environment. Durkheim's quest is similar to present-day astronomers who focus their high-powered lenses on distant galaxies for clues on the formation of the early universe. And, just like astronomers peeking through telescopes, Durkheim focused his lens on hunter-gatherers for clues on early institutions, even though he knew they were far removed from the earliest societies. The religious institution had to arise from a social environment of some sort, Durkheim reasoned, because as he liked to put it, only "nothing proceeds from nothing" ([1893]1984: 119). Yet, despite his best efforts, he had little choice in the end but to propose a daring conjecture on the origins of religion and society.

Durkheim was convinced that religious sentiments originated when nomadic food collectors met up on occasion and detected an intangible aura that seemed to surround them—an energy force that seemed to transcend all their individual selves. Reacting to this emanation, they responded by projecting these effervescing sensations onto visible, tangible things—plants and animals or their symbolic representations—resulting in the birth of religion and an *awareness of society* itself.

Is his narrative an improbable tale or an awakening reality? How can we evaluate his thesis given the limited first-hand data from the fossil and archaeological records? Fortunately, we now have rich secondary data on our closest living relatives along with scientific tools to appraise at least some of the core premises that underpin Durkheim's theory of religion and society. Such is our task in the next chapters.

An Alternative Approach

Durkheim's theory is embedded in a number of key assumptions that he fiercely defended throughout his academic career. So, despite the limited data on early human social formations, we can try another tack by stripping Durkheim's thesis down to its core components and then see what can be supported or refuted with data that was not available in his time. If his "articles of faith" are found to be erroneous in light of present-day research, his theory of religion and society is likely to be flawed or simply wrong.

A good starting point is Durkheim's overriding concern with social solidarity and the relationship between society and the individual. Recall that as early as 1885, he was sanctioning Albert Schaeffle for his naiveté that human reasoning alone will serve to promote social harmony in modern societies. Responding to Schaeffle's premise, Durkheim wrote, "But if society is a being which has a goal, then it may find the reasoning minds of individuals too independent and too mobile for the common destiny to be entrusted to them without fear" ([1885]1978: 112). By 1888, as a young assistant professor in Bordeaux, his first course was on "Social Solidarity" because, for him, it was the foremost problem of sociology. We need to know, "what ties bind men together, that is, what determines the formation of social aggregates" (1888: 257).

In his classic works, Durkheim echoed similar themes by addressing (a) the changing nature of societies, (b) the problematic relations between the individual and society, and (c) the recognition of an innate human individualism, writing of a "sphere of psychic life which, however, developed the collective type may be, varies from one man to another and remains peculiar with each ([1893]1938: 198). Durkheim also addressed the nature of sociality in *The Rules of Sociological Method* ([1895]1982: 132), noting that "It has not even been proved at all that the tendency to sociability was originally a congenital instinct of the human race. It is much more natural to see in it a product of social life which has slowly becomes organized in us . . ." And, in *Suicide* (1897) Durkheim linked individuals who commit suicide with deviations in social integration: (1) *Egoistic* Suicide—a minimal collective tendency, a slight integration; (2) *Altruistic* Suicide—a maximal collective tendency, an extreme state of integration with a loss of individuality; (3) *Anomic* Suicide—a minimal state or loss of regulation, stability or a disequilibrium and; (4) *Fatalistic* Suicide —a maximal state of regulation, an excessively high overregulation.

A concern with individualism was articulated even in his pedagogy lectures at the Sorbonne where he emphasized how important it is to educate the young into the values of the collective life by equipping a child with a "taste for this pleasure and to instill in him the need for it" ([1902–1903]1973: 240). Indeed, Durkheim's focus on how solidarity was to be created and sustained in contemporary societies was seemingly more important than any other consideration. If humans are naturally gregarious and collaborative, uncovering the laws of social cohesion would be far less problematic. But Durkheim clearly held to the opposite view and, hence, the necessity of educating the young into a collective spirit to curb potentially destructive individualism in complex societies.

In essence, Durkheim was asking: How "naturally social" are humans? And, how did this come to be so? If we can cast light on these elusive questions, we will be in a better position to understand how a religious institution could emerge from a non-institutional environment. But addressing this issue requires a shift to a more inclusive social universe. The key source of second-hand data on sociality collected over the last seventy years comes from field research on our close primate relatives, the Old World monkeys and apes. Primates do not have bona fide institutions but they are socially inclined as they live in year-round societies where members undergo a long period of socialization. Primates are also very intelligent, mature slowly, have enduring social relationships, and live a long time. To integrate and sustain a year-round society is truly a collective affair because it requires the cooperation of adult males and females, young adults, adolescents, juveniles, and even older infants. In a real sense, then, primate societies are ideal for accessing Durkheim's conjectures about the hominin pre-institutional environment but also, surprisingly, for insights into early hominin social formations. So, unlike Durkheim, we do not have to rely on conjecture to project back in time to the ultimate origins of human social history.

Monkeys and Apes: A Comparative Analysis

Anatomical Differences

The primate order has well over 200 living species. At least 70 percent of primate species are monkeys, 25 percent are prosimians (i.e. descendants of the earliest primates), and 5 percent are apes and humans (or *hominoids*). So, monkey species overwhelmingly dominate the primate order while *hominoid* species comprise a handful of apes (and one human species'. As Old World monkeys (e.g. baboons and macaques) and apes/humans (e.g. chimps, gorillas) shared a *last common primate ancestor* (LCA) about 28 million years ago, they naturally share many traits from this ancestral heritage, which include a sophisticated neuroanatomy for learning complex tasks, similar dentition (e.g. dental formulas), prehensile hands for gripping objects, delivery of a single infant at birth, and a nearly identical sensory system with a revolutionary visual modality that embodies such evolutionary novelties as 3-D stereoscopic vision, augmented by a three-cone color system for sharpened daytime acuity, and a fovea for fine-tuning the particulars of objects up close (for a discussion and analysis see Maryanski 2013).

Yet, despite this shared legacy, the brain sizes and skeletal features of monkeys and apes/humans are strikingly different. All monkeys are small-bodied (when compared to great apes and humans) with smaller brains, immobile shoulder joints, tails, narrow rib cages, small collarbones and front and rear limbs of near or *equal* length—reflecting a locomotor pattern adapted for *moving on the ground or on the tops of tree branches*. Great apes and humans are large bodied with much bigger brains, flexible shoulder joints, enlarged and developed collar bones, shorter spines, robust torsos, no tails, and limbs of *unequal* length (human legs are longer than arms; whereas ape arms are longer than legs) reflecting an *original* locomotor pattern adapted for *under-the-branch suspension using the hands alone* for maneuvering between branch levels or for navigating from tree to tree (see Campbell et al. 2011; Relethford 2010; and Conroy and Pontzer 2012 for discussions). But apes are not just strikingly different than monkeys in their physical appearance, locomotor patterns, and much longer life spans, they are also strikingly different in their organizational and social relations (Wood et al. 2017) And, oddly enough, these differences will lend support to Durkheim's conviction that human sociality is more a product of nurture than nature (Maryanski 2013; Turner and Maryanski 2008, 1992a, 1992b).

Organizational Differences

All primate species have the cognitive flexibility to adapt to changes in their environment, but species still mark a modal or species-typical group size, a stable mating pattern, and a characteristic sex and age class ratio. This regularity led primatologists to conclude that when organizational changes are necessary, primates respond with modifications in population size, diets, ranging habits, and the like. But some traits such as relational preferences are resistant to modification, and this *phylogenetic inertia* inherited from a past ancestry can be so inflexible and ingrained that it restricts the changes and elaborations possible no matter what the selection pressures (Shruhaker 1969: 113; Richard 1985: 349; Kummer 1971; Chalmers 1973). To tease apart the relative importance of phylogeny and ecology, a useful evolutionary rule is that traits shared by two or more closely related species that live and are adapted to diverse habitats are likely to reflect a shared phyletic heritage. The probability that they evolved independently is less likely, and this probability gets remote when there are three or more closely related species in different ecologies that share a characteristic trait.

All Old World monkey species (*Cercopithecoidea*) live in stable group-oriented societies that avoid contact with conspecifics in other groups. Group members move about in a rather synchronized way within a bounded ranging area (especially the ground-living monkeys) and, with rare exceptions, have either a single male/multiple female "polygamous" or harem breeding plan, or a multi-male-multi-female "promiscuous" breeding plan. To avoid inbreeding depression *males* (with rare exceptions) depart their natal group after puberty, whereas *females* stay home lodged in tight-knit matrilines, with up to four generations of blood-related females.[1]

In contrast, ape species (*Hominoidea*) live in societies that are strikingly idiosyncratic compared to the uniform stability of monkey societies. For unlike their highly prolific cousins who occupy ecologies ranging from forests through snow-capped mountains to dry and dusty savannas, apes live in loosely coupled societies and in ecological niches so narrow and specialized that some scholars refer to apes as "atypical relict forms" and "evolutionary failures" (Corruccini and Ciochon 1983: 14; Andrews 1981: 25; Temerin and Cant 1983). And, unlike Old World monkeys where only males depart, all ape *females* or both sexes disperse their natal unit after puberty (for general discussions of monkey and ape societies see Fleagle 2013; Campbell et al. 2011; Mitani et al. 2012).

To evaluate Durkheim's assumption on whether or not humans are highly social by nature or nurture, we need to compare the social structures of apes and a control sample of Old World monkey species. In this way we can determine if Durkheim was correct about the individualistic nature of humans (as evolved apes in the hominoid family). By using the theory and

---

1 Primates follow the pattern of higher vertebrates by dispersing one or both sexes at puberty (See Greenwood 1980 for a discussion).

tools of social network analysis coupled with the scientific procedures of cladistic analysis (to be discussed) we can look back to deep time in ways not possible with nineteenth-century evolutionary analysis. We can, almost literally, see what Durkheim could only speculate about.

Methods

The Social Network Approach

In primate research, an *attribute approach* is used for describing the personal characteristics of primates such as age, sex, body size, personality, and social rank, or for highlighting the general characteristics of specific classes of individuals (e.g. cycling and lactating females, alpha and beta males). In comparison, a *relational approach* is used for describing occasional or stable patterns of primate social relations with the unit of analysis not individuals or classes *per se* but the ties or lack of ties among members of a society. A relational approach is especially valuable for highlighting the foundational *forms of relations,* for mapping the configuration of these linkages, and for uncovering the underlying structure of a society that is not easily seen when the focus is on individual attributes or classes of individuals (for discussions of network analysis see Hinde 1983; Wellman and Berkowitz 1988; Borgatti, Everett and Johnson 2013). So our first step is to conduct a comparative network analysis of the social ties among our closest living primate relatives, an analysis that can provide essential clues into what early proto-human societies were like at least in their relational layout.

In this network analysis, our focus will be on the unifying blocks of Old World monkey and ape societies by considering just one crucial relational property—the strength of ties and the effect of dispersal (or migration) on these ties. To simplify this procedure, we will assume that all affect ties are positive and symmetrical interactions. While asymmetric and negative interactions are a facet of primate relations, an emphasis on affect relations will allow us to focus on what Durkheim emphasized: positive emotional arousal as a source of social ties and the building block of social solidarity. Such mutually reinforcing sentiments between dyads include social grooming, embracing, spending time together, sharing of food, protecting each other, cooperating, and providing mutual assistance. These actions signal positive emotions that increase the potency and endurance of social bonds.

As the data on free-ranging primates covers well over seventy years, it can be best arrayed for our purposes on a simple ordinal scale summing up modal tie strength: null ties, weak ties, moderate ties, and strong ties. In assigning graduations, individuals whose ties are unknown (e.g. father–daughter in promiscuous mating patterns) or for individuals who rarely or never interact will be scored as having *null or weak ties*; those who interact on occasion have *weak ties*; those who affiliate closely for a time but with little emotion or endurance over time (at least for adults) have *moderate ties*; and those who evidence close propinquity with extensive physical contact, with many observable episodes of positive emotions and arousal (as in mutual grooming bouts), with very high rates of interaction, and with relations that endure over time and often for a lifetime have *strong ties*. The spectrum of tie strength ranges then from no affect to expressed intimacies.

While all age and sex classes have proclivities for particular bonding patterns, we need only to compare the core social ties: adult-male/adult male ties; adult-female/adult- female ties; adult male/adult female ties; mother/child daughter ties; mother/child son ties; father/child daughter ties; father/child son ties; mother/adult daughter ties; mother/adult son ties; father/adult daughter ties; father/adult son ties. Using network analysis, a social structure will be conceptualized as a network of habitual and typical patterned social relationships for a given species. I should add that assessing tie strength for primates is a straightforward process as "who likes to be with whom" is easily observed by researchers.

We can now evaluate Durkheim's thesis on the nature of human sociality *if* we are willing to entertain the premise that the shared *relational* features of great apes with whom we share 97 percent to more than 99 percent of our genetic material can inform us about the ultimate social history of humans, which is another more precise way to explore what Durkheim loosely portrayed as the primordial, pre-kinship, and pre-religious *horde*. This supposition is feasible given that molecular analysis using ape and human DNA has documented that living orangutans, gorillas, chimpanzees, and humans comprise a monophyletic unit or *clade* and that each taxa gradually branched away from this single ancestral lineage or last common ancestor (LCA) (for discussions see Varki and Altheide 2005; Varki and Nelson 2007; Chatterjee et al. 2009; Bradley 2008). And, while this mother lineage is long extinct, we can use the shared relational ties of its living ape descendants to reconstruct the LCA social structure *from the inside out*.

The results of this network research will be shown to support the following particulars: (a) a strong "Founder's Effect" of nested proclivities in all LCA descendants has served to constrain the kinds of social structures possible and (b) a predisposition exists in the LCA heritage for weak- and low-density networks and, surprisingly, rather low levels of sociality when compared to species of monkeys. To support these conclusions, I need to begin by summarizing the relational data on: (1) present-day non-human great apes [that is, orangutans (Pongo), gorillas (Gorilla), and chimpanzees (Pan)]; and (2) a representative sample of terrestrial Old World monkeys [as our control sister population]. Then I will summarize the networks evident in the data and employ the tools of cladistic analysis to get our first look at what Durkheim believed to be the foundational proto-society or what he called—the single clan or *horde*.

Historical Comparative Reconstruction

The second step in our evaluation is to use the historical comparative methodology, the scientific tool with a long-established history of general use in linguistics and textual criticism and, more recently, in biogeography and biology where it is called *cladistics*. This procedure starts by identifying entities known to be descendants or end points of an evolutionary or developmental process. For example, as discussed earlier, it is used in historical linguistics to compare words in related languages in search of "sound correspondences." Then, once these cognates are identified from these daughter languages, they are used to reconstruct the *speech* forms of the extinct mother language from which the daughter languages were derived. In comparative biology, cladistics is used to identity related organisms in the same way on the basis of shared or derived diagnostic characters. Cladistics also incorporates a control group, usually a closely related sister lineage or "outgroup population" to precisely identify measurable "evolutionary novelties" or unique "derived characters" retained by related descendants (here great ape taxa) after they branched away from a *last common hominoid population* (LCA).

While the relationships themselves are not always testable, this scientific tool builds-in two testable assumptions: (1) a "relatedness hypothesis" that holds that a class of derived characters or evolutionary novelties are the result of descent from a stem LCA and not by chance, and (2) a "regularity hypothesis," that holds that the modifications from the ancestral to descendant entities are systematically biased by evidencing a "founders effect" (See Jeffers and Lehiste 1979, p. 6; Forey et al.1994; Maas 1958). It is assumed that the more novelties or derived characters entities share the more closely related are the entities. This straightforward but powerful methodology thus offers a means to reconstruct ancestral patterns for a proto-language, an ancient text, or any set of related entities including an ancestral social structure. Below is a brief synopsis of the findings on extant

The Organizational Profiles of Great Apes[3]

Orangutan (Pongo)

Orangutans are native to the Southwestern Asian islands of Sumatra and Borneo where they occupy a tropical rainforest niche. The orangutan (which means "forest person") is a large bodied mostly tree-dwelling great ape (females average 85 pounds and males average 150 pounds) that relies on a dietary stable of soft, ripe fruits. Orangutans are unique among higher primates because they are semi-solitary, although fifty or more orangutans share a solid block of rainforest about two miles square. While typically found alone when observed (aside from a mother and her dependents), the red-haired apes will occasionally mingle in short encounters that average about 1.8 individuals. A male and female will also socialize when the female is sexually receptive, and the male will sometimes remain with her for a time, even weeks. Adolescent males and females are the most socially inclined as they congregate occasionally for brief encounters, especially near trees packed with succulent fruits.

This sporadic gregariousness has led researchers to suggest that despite their reclusive ways, orangutan locals are co-residents of a widely dispersed community-level of organization by virtue of their joint ownership of a regional locality. How communal life is sustained given their aloof lifestyle is still a mystery. The emerging picture is that mothers and dependents forage in ranges that overlap with other females, although females appear to actively avoid each other and only occasionally interact (Knott et al.

---

2 This network analysis of Old World monkey and ape societies is based on a comprehensive review of the field literature. Reported here are the normative and well-documented age and sex class attachments for ape taxa and a sample of well-studied Old World monkey taxa and their structural implications. See Maryanski 1992; Maryanski and Turner 1992; Turner and Maryanski 2005, 2008 for a detailed analyses.

3 Gibbons (*Hylobates*) and related species such as siamangs (*Symphalangus*) are also apes, but they are small arboreal hominoids (15 to 30 lbs.) inhabiting Asian forests. They share propensities with their great ape cousins (e.g. female and male dispersal, an idiosyncratic social structure) but are very far removed from the LCA of the great apes. Above all, gibbon/siamangs lack the revolutionary great ape neurobiology (e.g. a self-identity) that is essential for this analysis so there was no need to include them. To see a cladistic analysis that does include gibbons, see Maryanski and Turner 1992; Turner and Maryanski 2008; and for recent field studies of gibbons see: Barlet 2011; Reichard and Barelli 2008; Barelli et al. 2013; Watts 2012; Huang et al. 2013; Reichard et al. 2016).

2008). In turn, several adult female ranges are organized around a single dominant male, although a number of other males are also in the vicinity of local female ranges. While the dominant male in a given locality is seemingly a favored sexual partner, female choice is the rule because females are free to mate with any male. Relations among adult males are null to very weak as they actively avoid each other, although adolescent males occasionally show some affiliation with each other.

Overall, cooperation is minimal, adult social grooming is very rare, and attachments between adults are uncommon, although it is reported that "individualized relationships do exist" (Knott and Kahlenberg 2011). Even the maternal bonds between a mother and her dependents weaken once offspring mature and leave the matri-focal unit (at between 10 and 12 years). Although both adolescent males and females disperse from their mother and establish independent ranges, some settle within the surrounding area while others move to another regional locality. Visits with their mothers by adult offspring occur occasionally. This rare social structure composed of self-contained conspecifics who socialize only occasionally is reflected in the social network patterns arrayed in the third column of Table 13.1 (for discussions of orangutans see Atmoko et al. 2008; Noordwijk et al. 2008; Russon 2009; Setia et al. 2009; Knott et al. 2008; Knott and Kahlenbert 2011; Nater et al. 2017).

Gorilla (Gorilla)

Gorillas are native to the forests of Western and Central Africa. They are the "King Kong" of primates (females average 185 pounds and males average 335 pounds). Gorillas are mostly ground-living, spending their days on the forest floor, and when observed they are typically found sitting about, dozing off for an afternoon nap, or foraging for plants and fruits that grow in lowland secondary (i.e. regenerating) forests and high-altitude forests or along ravines. Unlike orangutans, gorillas are organized into loose-knit heterosexual groupings composed of a lead "silverback" male, a number of adult females with dependents, adolescent males and females, and up to four adult males with an average group size of fifteen individuals. Four or more gorilla *bands* (as these groupings are called) and unattached single males are residents of a regional population with some neighboring bands day-resting, feeding, and even bedding down together overnight (Robbins 2011). Resident adult females in a band typically favor the lead silverback for sexual activity but females can mate with resident males, migrate to another band, or join an unattached, solitary male (Harcourt and Stewart 2007; Bradley et al. 2005).

TABLE 13.1 Strength of Social Ties** among Extant Species of Great Apes and the Last Common Ancestor to Great Apes and Humans

	Species of Apes			
	Gorillas (Gorilla)	Chimpanzees (Pan)	Orangutans (Pongo)	Last Common Ancestor
Adult-to-Adult Ties:				
Male–Male:	0	0/+	0	0*
Female–Female	0	0	0	0*
Male–Female	0/+	0	0	0*
Adult-to-Adult Offspring Procreation Ties:				
Mother–Daughter	0	0	0	0*
Father–Daughter	0	0	0	0*
Mother–Son	0	+	0	0*
Father–Son	0	0	0	0*
Adult-to-Pre-Adolescent Offspring Ties:				
Mother–Daughter	+	+	+	+*
Father–Daughter	0	0	0	0*
Mother–Son	+	+	+	+*
Father–Son	0	0	0	0*

0 = null to weak ties
0/+ = weak to moderate ties
+ = strong ties
* = is used to denote a reconstructed social structure, in this case the likely structure, of the last common ancestor to humans and extant great apes. As is evident, this structure is most like that of contemporary orangutans.
** All primate species have preferential relationships within and between age and sex categories (Cheney, Seyfarth, and Smuts 1986; Hinde 1983). For primates, the strength of ties is assessed on the basis of social grooming, food sharing, adding and protecting, continual close proximity, embracing (excluding sexual contact), and the length and intensity of social relationships. The table summarizes the emergent properties—the modal network ties of varying strength—that result from these kinds of relations. For detailed analyses see Maryanski 1986, 1987, 1992a, 1992b.

Daily life in a gorilla band is casual and relaxed with adult males highly tolerant of each other, but ties are weak as they engage in few overt interactions. Gorilla bands are anchored in a male-female bond between a lead silverback and a number of adult females (Harcourt and Stewart 2007a). The association is unusual, however, as it is seemingly linked to the degree of attention the silverback gives to a mother's dependent offspring.

Females with young dependents have moderate ties with the lead male, whereas females with older offspring (or with the sudden death of an offspring) have much weaker ties. This may be why a lead male will often assist a mother by playing with and "baby-sitting" her offspring and by assuming full parental care when she is ill or dies. Adult females in a band are very tolerant of each other, but ties are weak with few social interactions. Indeed, some researchers have literally classified gorilla females as "non-female bonded" and "dispersal egalitarian" (quoted in Robbins 2011: 335).

Male-male ties are also weak but individual friendships do exist. Mothers and dependent offspring have strong ties until puberty (between 9 and 15 years), but then adolescent females disperse to another band or to another regional population, whereas adolescent sons depart to become lone males or visiting guests in neighboring gorilla bands. Bands may be stable for years but over time residents can be capricious (with the exception of the lead male) as adult and adolescent males and females are free to slip away on impulse at any time. This easy relocation, along with evidence that four or more bands and a number of lone males co-occupy a 12-mile square block of forest suggests that gorilla bands are not wholly discrete units but segments of a local "big band" community.[4] This band-level arrangement with both males and females leaving after puberty is reflected in the social network patterns in column 1 of Table 13.1 (Rosenbaum, Maldonado-Chapparo and T.S. Stoinski 2016; Harcourt and Stewart 2007b; Schaller 1964; Robbins 2011).

Chimpanzees (Pan)

Chimpanzees are native to the Eastern, Central, and Western belts of equatorial Africa. They are large-bodied primates (females average about 85 pounds and males average 100–135 pounds) who subsist on a dietary stable of soft, ripe fruits, although they eat many plant foods, insects and red meat (especially young monkeys). In their rainforest habitat, chimpanzees move easily between the canopy and forest floor with up to 150 individuals moving about individually *within* a definable block of forest that can vary in size from 8 square miles in primary forest to more than 70 square miles in a mixed savanna-woodland habitat (Watts 2002).

---

4 For example, A. Goodall and C. Groves (1977) drew a line separating the home ranges of a number of bands over a wide area. They found that the bands that interacted with each other also shared a common home range with weak ties connecting members of bands and lone males. In one regional area, they proposed a resident community of at least sixty-eight members and an eastern community with seventy-seven members.

Yet, despite their free mobility in space, chimpanzees are far more socially inclined than orangutans, or gorillas because each day a diverse number of residents will gather in varied impromptu social parties that can last a few minutes, a few hours or, occasionally, a day within the boundaries of a clearly defined community-level of organization. In chimpanzee society, adult male-male ties are weak to moderate, whereas ties between male siblings and special friends are strong; adult female-female ties are absent to weak; adult male-female bonds are also weak, for unless a female is sexually receptive she usually does not seek male companionship. One exception is mother-adult son ties that remain strong even *after* puberty. In contrast, all females usually disperse after puberty to another community (at about 10–13 years of age). This rare arrangement where females disperse after puberty and males remain lifelong locals is connected to the pattern of social relationships in column two of Table 13.1 (Lukas et al. 2005; Watts 2002; Goodall 1986, 1990; Nishida 1990; Stumpf et al. 2009; Boesch and Boesch-Achermann 2000).

Monkey and Ape Social Structure Compared

What generalizations can be drawn if we compare ape and Old World monkey societies? First, Old World monkey societies are all organized into stable groups with one of two equally stable and rather uniform mating plans—the one-male/multiple female arrangement (i.e. harem plan) and the multiple-male/multiple female arrangement (promiscuous plan). Second, in Old World monkey societies *only* males are dispersed after puberty (with rare exceptions), while females are lifelong locals and remain embedded in blood-tied matrilineal cliques with mothers, daughters, sisters, aunts, and female cousins. Old World Monkey societies are called "female-bonded societies" because matrilines are the core and stable integrating force for recruitment and for intergenerational continuity over time.

In contrast, great-ape societies are not anchored by matrilineal bonds. Adult orangutans are self-contained with only occasional ties and with no generational continuity as both sexes leave mother after puberty. Gorilla bands are organized around weak and moderate ties with a superficial resemblance to monkey harem groups, but bands can have up to four adult males and adult females can disperse (usually alone) at any time. Moreover, if we drop our traditional image of a group as a tight-knit cluster of individuals (as in monkey kinship-based matrilineages), an unusual social structure emerges for gorillas: daughters at puberty often move to another regional population, whereas sons become solitary travelers, leaders of other bands, or transient visitors to other bands within their homeland. Adult male-male ties are weak; adult male and female ties are also weak, although lead silverbacks and young mothers with dependent offspring are moderately tied, but this tie is conditional because it depends on a mother's success in raising offspring.

Hence, despite the appearance of a relatively tight-knit social structure, gorilla bands resemble more a shifting collection of individuals over time. The core supporting ties are between a lead silverback and mothers with dependent offspring, a star-shaped configuration because females only occasionally engage in any form of sociality with each other. While the high proportion of weak ties in a gorilla band may seem surprising given that gorillas live in groups, it does help to account for why gorilla groups differ from monkeys in nature and quality. In monkey groups, females *never* leave their female relatives until they die. Even when a large monkey group splits into two smaller groups, matrilines stay intact as single entities. This is why adult males in monkey societies compete for access to matrilines—and not to individual females. In contrast, gorilla females spontaneously and easily leave one band for another or transfer to liaisons with lone males. The only exception is the leader silverback male who remains with his band until death but then, all members disperse. So gorilla bands also lack intergenerational continuity, fueling speculation that gorillas are organized at a more macro-level or community level of organization.

Chimpanzees are socially inclined but only mothers with dependent offspring form stable groups until offspring leave to live on their own. Mother-daughter strong ties are broken after daughters move to another community, never to return. Mother-son strong ties are permanent because sons *never* leave their community. Male siblings are strongly tied but, otherwise, males-male relations vary from a few intimate "friends" to weak or moderate relations. Female-female ties are weak as incoming females are mutual strangers and adult females usually forage alone with dependent offspring. Jane Goodall refers to adult female-female ties as "neutral relationships" or ones she characterizes as neither friendly nor unfriendly (Goodall 1986: 17). Chimpanzees are promiscuous and so, father-offspring ties are non-existent. Thus, at the natal group-level, chimpanzees also lack intergenerational continuity as both sexes leave their mother after puberty. Males however, stay tied to their community and often visit with their mothers, although on a day-to-day basis males move about alone or join small social gatherings.

The Relatedness Hypothesis and the LCA Social Structure

If we now apply the procedures of cladistic analysis to the patterns of great-ape ties, we can sketch a blueprint of the social structure of the last common ancestor (LCA) population, as is outlined in the far-right column in Table 13.1 on page 221. In line with the *Relatedness Hypothesis*, we need to initially consider the *null* hypothesis that all the patterns in the ties of each of the three non-human great apes were acquired after each hominoid separated from the LCA. The null hypothesis cannot be ruled out, but the close ape phyletic ancestry, the strong contrasts with monkey ties, the finding that primate relational ties are conservative and resistant to change, and the results of the *Regularity Hypothesis* (to be discussed) strongly minimize this probability. We can assume then that the tie patterns shared by orangutans, gorillas, and chimpanzees were also present in the LCA population from which all three great ape lineages split at varying points in time. And, the variations in tie patterns reflect adaptive changes due to varying selection pressures on the great apes in diverse niches (e.g. arboreal or forest floor, degree of predation pressures, concentrated or dispersed resources).

So, to reconstruct by cladistic analysis the pattern of social ties of the last common ancestor (LCA) to great apes and hominins/humans, we need to collate the data on the affect ties they share. In this way, we can see how the conclusions outlined in the far-right column of Table 13.1 were reached. First, and most important, are the *ties jointly* held (whether the bonds are null, weak or strong) by *all* three great apes or a correspondence of 3/3: so across the board we get these matches: adult female/female ties are null to weak ties (orangutan, gorilla and chimpanzee); mother/child daughter ties are strong (orangutan, gorilla and chimpanzee); mother/child son ties are strong (orangutan, gorilla and chimpanzee); mother/adult daughter are weak ties (orangutan, gorilla and chimpanzee); father/child daughter ties are null (orangutan, gorilla and chimpanzee); father/child son ties are null (orangutan, gorilla and chimpanzee); father/adult daughter are null ties (orangutan, gorilla and chimpanzee); and father/adult son are null ties (orangutan, gorilla and chimpanzee).

Second, if we tally the number of ties jointly held by two of the three great apes, or a correspondence of 2/3, we get the following matches: adult-male/adult male are null to weak ties (orangutan and gorilla); mother/adult son are weak ties (orangutan and gorilla) and male-female ties are weak ties (orangutan and chimpanzee). The split-ties here are the chimpanzee adult mother/adult son strong ties; the chimpanzee adult male/adult male weak-to-moderate (with some strong) ties; and gorilla adult male/adult female weak-to-moderate ties. For the gorilla the male/female moderate ties are unusual in that they are linked to the maternal status of the female with non-maternal ties between male and female gorillas otherwise weak. Thus, it is likely that weak ties prevailed between adult males and females in the LCA population of all great apes, with the gorilla pattern being a more recent adaptation. This is also highly probable for the chimpanzee adult mother-adult son ties and the adult male/adult male ties as both are rare among primates.

The next step in cladistic analysis is to compare the control group of representative species of monkeys to those outlined above and arrayed in Table 13.1. If we begin with adult male monkeys, most affect ties are null-to-weak. This pattern is common to Old World monkeys and to great apes as well (except for chimpanzees); and it is linked to male dispersal at puberty. Monkeys and great apes also share the strong ties between a mother and her *dependent* offspring (a nearly universal mammalian trait), along with the null-to-weak ties of father/young sons and daughters since paternal care is very rare among primates. One *striking* difference between great apes and monkeys is the adult female-female ties. Monkey adult female ties are strong among maternal kin throughout the life cycle and across generations, whereas ties among adult ape females are usually weak. On top of that, monkey mother/daughter adult ties remain strong for a lifetime, while great ape mother/adult daughter ties become weak to non-existent after puberty. Taking into account that both Old World monkeys and apes shared a LCA in the not too distant past (in evolutionary terms) and that most adult females in Old World monkey societies are connected by strong ties within matrilines (and this is the case for most social mammals as well), the null-to-weak ties among adult ape females was likely also present in their last common hominoid ancestor. Given that this pattern is coupled to a rare female dispersal pattern, it is highly improbable that such traits would have evolved independently in each ape genera. Instead, both the breakdown in mother/daughter bonds and adolescent female dispersal was an evolutionary novelty in the LCA mother population and subsequently passed on to its descendants. Given that male dispersal is also found in two of the three great-ape genera, we can safety assume that in the LCA population, both males and females dispersed after puberty.

Of note: what is essential here is the *strength of ties* and *not* their absolute number and, of equal importance, whether or not these ties can be employed for constructing generations of high-density networks. Well studied representative species of monkey societies as varied as those organizing patas (*Erythrocebus*), gelada (*Theropithecus*), macaque (*Macaca*), and baboon societies (*Papio*) are called *female-bonded societies* because their kin-based matrilineal networks promote stability, and unbroken female recruitment over intergenerational time. In contrast, orangutan, gorilla, and chimpanzee societies all break the bonds between mothers and daughters at puberty, thus also breaking the capacity to construct matrilines, which is the major unifying force among monkeys. Orangutan mother and offspring units dissolve with the dispersal of adolescent offspring; gorilla bands breakup with the death of the lead male (as the adult females and even males disperse), and chimpanzee adolescent females depart from their mother's community after puberty. Chimpanzees differ dramatically, however, in that males *never* leave their *natal community*. Yet, chimpanzee *patrilineal kinship* networks cannot be compared with monkey *matrilineal kinship* networks because patrilineality cannot exist in a promiscuous mating system so paternity is *always unknown*. Instead, adult males are lifelong locals at-large within their community.

Next, if we look over great-ape reproductive patterns, we can deduce the LCA mating arrangement. Orangutans and chimpanzees are promiscuous, which, as noted above, eliminates the capacity to know who the biological father of offspring is (without drawing blood for testing in laboratories) and, in any case, adult males and females do not form permanent sexual bonds. Even gorillas who nominally have a one-male/multiple female arrangement lean toward more promiscuity, since an adult female can exercise her sexual freedom by mating with other adult males in her band, moving to another band, or joining a lone male in the vicinity. Such female sexual freedom also fits nicely with female dispersal where a single female will seemingly on whim decide to take herself elsewhere as reflected in the weak and fluid ape tie patterns shown in Table 13.1. Thus, it is probable that the LCA population of all contemporary great apes had a promiscuous mating system and a social structure of mostly weak ties as is reported in the LCA cladistic reconstruction in Table 13.1 in the far-right column.

The Regularity Hypothesis and the Swing to Sociality During Hominoid Evolution

Our next step is to validate the LCA blueprint by applying the *regularity hypothesis* and searching for systematic biases or regularities still present in all living apes that will connect them to each other and to the LCA population. I need to mention that great apes (and humans) share a bundle of derived, cognitive traits to be discussed in the next chapters. But in this chapter, the *regularity* hypothesis will be used to highlight *organizational biases* that are traceable to their LCA. Since all living ape genera are the end points of ancestral lineages that split from their LCA long ago, resulting in the idiosyncratic nature of each ape society, one might question whether an organizational bias or a "founder's effect" is still detectable given the length of time and the many modifications needed to adapt to diverse ecological niches. On this score, one standout organizational feature is female-biased dispersal because it eliminates the possibility for a permanent mother-daughter bond and, hence, recursive group formations. Given its rarity in Old World monkeys (and in mammals more generally), *while being the key regularity among all apes*, it is surely an evolutionary novelty handed down by the LCA population to great apes and hominins.

In order to address this hypothesis, a comparison of the LCA blueprint and modern ape social structure points to LCA ties that were very fluid and weak, whereas for descendent taxa there is a clear upward trend favoring a heightened sociality after branching away from the ancestral population. Yet, in this adaptation for greater support networks, selection did not act to promote "monkey-like" matrilineal networks. Instead, in the wake of retaining female dispersal, selected worked to build a heightened sociality by strengthening other potential ties. And so, sets of truly novel ties were forged for each ape genera depending on environmental demands, which is why their organizations stand apart from monkeys and from each other as well.

Now, if we consider ape social arrangements using this lens, what becomes evident is that the social structure of each great ape taxa is configured around female dispersal after puberty. For gorillas, the core network is a leader male and several females in a band, but unlike monkey networks, where related females are clustered into high-density networks comprising matrilines, a gorilla social structure is star-shaped as female social bonds are only with the lead male, with all adult female-female bonds being weak. For chimpanzees, the social structure pivots on a communal structure with strong ties limited to male siblings, mother and adult sons, and a few personal friendships. For orangutans, the core network is the mother-dependent offspring bond (common to mammals), but among orangutans a bond that is broken, thus destroying the capacity to form any lineage-level structures. Indeed, because orangutans are semi-solitary, they are the least modified from the LCA social structure and it is probably no coincidence that the "red apes" are the least successful ape, given their very restricted habitats on the islands of Borneo and Sumatra.

In contrast, chimpanzees and gorillas have heighted their benchmark sociality for survival in new ecological zones. While each ape has its own idiosyncratic arrangements, they are consistent with selection dancing around a female dispersal pattern by fashioning peculiar ties for members of the primate order. Still, why not jump-start sociality simply by keeping blood-tied females in their natal group? One explanation is that great apes need more space and food than little monkeys so an enduring mother-daughter bond to secure monkey-style matrilines would limit the foraging freedom needed for such large-bodied primates. Yet, this explanation does not account for why *all* living apes—even the little 15-pound gibbon ape (see footnote 3) retained female dispersal. A more likely explanation is that this trait harbors a strong phylogenetic inertia. And, given that selection usually takes the most convenient pathway, the best option when environmental pressures favored greater sociality was for apes to forge a motley collection of alternative ties. The anchoring effect of phylogenetic inertia is best conveyed by the renowned primate ethologist Hans Kummer (1971:117):

> Our ultimate aim is a thorough understanding of the inherited potential of primate species and genera ... We may then understand why an adaptation may be less than ideal, why it is the best solution of which the species was capable, and how much the species has to pay even for this next-best design. A way of life will then appear as a compromise, first between the conflicting requirements of the environment, and then between these requirements and the limitations of the animal's own behavioral resources as they emerged from its phylogenetic past.

Today, the orangutan, gorilla, and chimpanzee remain self-reliant and independent with some strong ties but with social structures built mostly around weak ties.[5]

What can we conclude about Durkheim's assumptions on human individuality and sociality? First, humans are primates; and despite our

---

5 The extreme case of idiosyncratic ape ties is found among bonobo chimpanzees (Pan paniscus), a small population of relatively rare chimpanzees who, like common chimps, live in communities with female biased-dispersal. Yet, their niche is one where foods are so highly concentrated that immigrating females must feed close together (in contrast to common female chimpanzees). So, when environmental pressures favored an adaptation for female propinquity, it acted on the subcortical parts of the bonobo brain to greatly heighten sexuality. One result is a strengthening of adult female/female ties—but not affect ties—sexual ties. This is evident when bonobo females meet up and perform a unique and truly bizarre "greeting ritual" of grabbing each other and mutually rubbing their genitals together (i.e. GG rubbing), which results in sexual pleasure and seemingly an orgasmic experience. White (1989: 162) considers it an erotic contact "to reduce tensions among unrelated females" (and see Stevens et al. 2006). As GG rubbing is unique to bonobos and is more an activity to release tension and ease conflict rather than a traditional affect tie, only relational data from the widespread common chimpanzee was included in this analysis. Moreover, as Rice and Moloney (2005: 205) expressed it, "This kind of sexuality was not found in the LCA either." This kind of sexuality, however, is a tribute to how selection acted to heighten sociality by fostering GG rubbing between bonobo females.

current reproductive success, we are still one of the few remaining species on the hominoid family tree. And, let me add, we also have atypical social arrangements for a primate species. A longstanding assumption in sociology is that humans are "naturally" gregarious, seeking out high levels of collective solidarity. But Durkheim did not buy into this generalization. At the level of the genome, humans may be far less social and more individualistic, as Durkheim surmised. Early on, he recognized the constant tension between the individual and the collective, and this tension is probably the result of enduring degrees of human' derived individualistic heritage from the LCA.

So, it seems that Durkheim had good reason to worry about the relationship between the needs of society and the problem of egoistic individualism. For despite the dearth of information on humans' evolutionary history during Durkheim's time, his assumptions on human sociality were on the mark—as the data summarized in Table 13.1 document, particularly the reconstruction of the last common ancestor (LCA) to all great apes and hominins, including humans. He made a brilliant deduction that humans were more individualistic than collectivistic. And, given this deduction, he reasoned that solidarity had to come from somewhere else, *somewhere outside of the individual.* Hence, the importance he placed on collective rituals for maintaining social solidarity in human groups. His insistence that ritualized activity be reinstituted frequently or the collective emotions would wither away, stem from his belief that humans were social more by nurture than by nature except to the extent that a large brain makes culture and collective beliefs possible. In the next chapters we will continue our evaluation of Durkheim's core assumptions by turning to the community relations and shared cognitive traits of our closest hominoid relative with some very surprising findings.

14
A Sense of Community

Before we can engage for collective purposes, we must above all have a sense and affection for the community.
   Émile Durkheim (1902–1903:166) *Moral Education*

The last common ancestor (LCA) of great apes and humans lived a long time ago. Yet, a cladistic analysis tells us that this ancestral population imparted to its living descendants strong individualism, relatively low sociality (compared to monkeys), and propensities for social structures built from weak ties. With this background in mind, we can now focus our evolutionary lens on Durkheim's quest to uncover the roots of religion and society, or the birth of sacred "collective representations," his essential condition for society to become aware of itself.

With the withering away of both traditional family life and long-established religions, Durkheim's sought new sources of solidarity such as the occupational groups he mentions in *Suicide* (1897), the first edition of *The Division of Labor* (1893) and elaborates upon in the Preface to the second edition of *The Division of Labor* (1902). In this pursuit he reasoned that only "nothing comes from nothing" so to understand any social phenomena it must be taken back to its earliest possible beginnings. So, to glimpse the birth of society and religion, he started with the simplest social formation he could imagine, *the horde*, or a loose human aggregation without stable internal parts. This meant, of course, that kinship relations and the nuclear family itself were *invented* later. He truly wished for the discovery of this proto-totemic formation, or, at least, a clan with primeval totemism—in Durkheim's eyes the "perfect type of primitive civilization" ([1902]1985: 107). Then, the essential qualities of these aggregates could be observed first-hand along with a chance to simultaneously uncover the causes that made the religious sentiment. All he needed was an ongoing arrangement with such a way of living.

Yet, no human population then or now even remotely resembles Durkheim's horde, so an assessment of his origin thesis is not possible—

unless we again cross species lines and look through the lens provided by cladistic analysis to glimpse the lifeways of proto-human or early hominin ancestors. If we do, the lifeways of great apes are obviously our best candidates for this exercise. Free-ranging orangutans with whom humans shared a LCA between 13 and 16 million years ago approach Durkheim's description of a horde. While adult orangutans live a reclusive life as they are usually found alone, adult males and receptive females do partner up for intimate *consortships,* sometimes for weeks; mothers gather on occasion in "nursery parties;" and a few orangutans do aggregate when trees are laden with ripe fruits, although they arrive and leave independently. Orangutan locals also make up a relatively stable regional population, which, as noted, recent findings suggest that orangutans may be organized into a very loose-knit community (Setia et al. 2008). Yet, the red apes tend to avoid social encounters as they typically ignore one another even when they meet up by chance. Nor do they *ever* assemble as a bounded social formation even in a disorganized way. While habituated orangutans living in captive conditions demonstrate a greater potential for sociality, the lifeways of free-ranging orangutans appear as an antecedent formation to Durkheim's more *effervescent* primitive horde.

Gorillas (Gorilla) are also candidates as they shared with humans a LCA about 8 million years ago, and they too seem to be organized into a community composed of a number of loosely woven bands, but our best model for clues into proto-human society are chimpanzees because *they are humans closest living relatives.* As Gagneux and Varki (2001: 2) highlighted, "if taxonomic classification were based solely upon genomic DNA sequence similarity, the nearly 99% identity of human, chimpanzee and bonobo genomes would require a reclassification of the latter two into the genus *Homo.*"

Chimpanzees are not living fossils but the end products of their own ancestral lineage that split from the LCA with humans about 5 or 6 million years ago. Yet, chimps never left the forest zones with its stable resources, and so with little environmental change or an ecological shift, evolutionary theory would predict population stabilization on trait values.[1] As species typically build on the social structure that they inherit, proto-humans or

---

1 A species is adapted to particular resources in a given environment or a niche (where it lives, eats and mates) and this adaptation includes all the interactions it has with the organic and the inorganic world. In a stable habitat like a forest zone, *stabilizing selection* will be favored and fitness will be higher for individuals with the average or mean for character traits. So if the status quo has a higher fitness for survival and reproductive success, little change in a species will take place. This is the most common type of selection. Should the

early hominins likely started out with an organizational arrangement much like chimpanzees, opening up a path of inquiry for evaluating the core assumptions underlying Durkheim's theory on the origins of society and religion.

A Bird's Eye View of Chimpanzee Organization

A Promiscuous Horde?

If we start by taking an aerial view of chimpanzee daily movements and activities, what would we see? A first impression is that chimpanzees are like the reclusive orangutans—self-contained nomads. One would probably conclude as did early primatologists that chimpanzees have a fancy-free and foot-loose lifestyle with no apparent organization but, over time, you would see individuals engaged in fleeting interactional mixing and co-mingling within a ranging area of 8 miles to 70 miles square (in less heavily forested areas). For chimpanzees have a rare *fission-fusion* organizational structure, composed of up to 150 members who freely move about alone or join brief social gatherings or "parties" throughout the day staying, a few minutes, hours, or occasionally a day. This intangible "commonwealth" *is their only stable formation* (aside from a mother and dependent offspring). An entire population may assemble in propinquity but, rarely, and on a day-to-day basis, members may not see a fellow resident for weeks or months, with ranging size dependent on available resources. For large-bodied primates dependent on scattered, seasonal resources (especially ripe fruits), this hang-loose adaptation is seemingly the best strategy for survival and reproductive success (for discussion see Mitani and Amsler 2003; Lehmann, Korstjens and Dunbar 2007).

What kind of social form is evident here? Is it (1) an undivided large aggregate that cannot be broken down into smaller, stable units? Is it (2) a *fission-fusion* system where individuals travel on their own and come together on a temporary basis. Or, is it (3) a social formation of mostly voluntary relations instead of kinship relations? In structural features, it resembles Durkheim's whimsical and loosely structured *horde*. Yet, it has

---

ecosystem change or a species moves to a different ecosystem as did *Homo* species, selection is likely to favor either *directional change* (e.g. strong selection pressures say for an increase in body size) or *disruptive selection* where either extremes of the population bell curve has a higher fitness and is favored over the population mean. So natural selection can be a stabilizing, directional or a disruptive force.

a post-horde feature: it is anchored by lifetime local males and adult kinship bonds, but they are limited to mothers, adult sons, and male siblings. So, this social form has some potential for being structured into more stable sub-formations but, in actual fact, all chimpanzee clusters are unstable or at least constantly coming together and then breaking apart in a fission-fusion pattern throughout the day (Lukas, Reynolds, Boesch and Vigilant 2005; Mitani, Merriwether and Zhang 2000; Boesch and Boesch-Achermann 2000; Goodall 1986; Luncz and Boesch 2014).

What Forces, Then, Hold Chimpanzee Society Together?

How then do you connect a large aggregate of individuals without stable groupings or lots of kinship ties? Durkheim asked this very question in *The Division of Labor* (1893) and then proposed a *mechanical solidarity* based on everyone thinking and acting precisely alike. In the case of chimpanzees, a "group-think" image can be ruled out because chimps are staunch individualists who differ in personality traits, habits, choice of friends, ranging patterns and even sociality.

One source of integration is geographical because males grow up, forage, mate, sleep and socialize within their homeland for a lifetime. But a shared homeland is probably not enough to counter the fragmenting effects of a widely scattered conglomeration of individualistic apes, and it could easily dissolve into acrimony. Another source of integration is emotive because the fission-fusion system of parting and uniting in diverse combinations often evokes in chimpanzees spontaneous and visceral emotions. Early in his career, Durkheim ([1887]1975: 36) distinguished between two types of human sentiments: (1) emotions that connect individuals to individuals; and (2) emotions that connect individuals to the collective whole. The emotions linking individuals to the collective whole, he said, were the ones that are essential for social integration.

In chimpanzee societies, emotions connecting individuals to individuals are spontaneously expressed with behaviors that Jane Goodall called greetings (especially among friends) that include vocalizations, hugs, touching and holding hands, kissing, brief social grooming, and other warm personal exchanges. They are also all too familiar. As Goodall underscored, "In fact, many of the greeting gestures described for chimpanzees have striking parallels in the greeting behaviour of man" (1968: 284). Emotions connecting individuals to the social whole are difficult to quantify but, as she (1986) relates, chimpanzees behave as though they have a cognizance of belonging to something that transcends personal relationships—a sense of community. A community organization is a rare social formation because it requires a sensitized awareness, or an extra-sensory perception that such a macro-level of reality exists. It must also be inferred, especially among chimpanzees because the entire community rarely acts as a collective unit nor for that matter do they congregate in one place.

A sense of community obviously springs from meaningful interactions, although it cannot be reduced down to their sums or their differences. Like all "emergents," it shares the property of a coherence or wholeness, a dynamic that is not precisely measurable or verifiable by direct observation, but can, nonetheless, be cognitively perceived. The primatologists who first claimed that chimpanzees had no social organization gradually detected a social synergy and its emergent effects—even though they had no evidence of it. But over the last seventy years, researchers have deduced its reality by long-term studies on the behaviors and interactions of free-ranging chimpanzees in a wide variety of locations in Africa.

What they documented is an active participation by chimpanzees in a wide-assortment of communal-like activities. Each chimpanzee community stakes off the exact boundaries of a homeland using an invisible fence-line, with voluntary "patrol-parties" on hand to guard the parameters looking for trespassers. Immigrating females are usually (but not always) given a neighborly welcome, whereas adult males are warned away, attacked or killed. As Mitani and Watts (2005: 1079–1080) relate:

> During patrols, chimpanzees move to the periphery of their territory, where they search for signs of members of other communities . . . Patrols include 8–13 individuals on average and are primarily a male activity . . . In some encounters, patrollers launch coalitionary attacks on individuals of neighbouring communities. Such attacks can be lethal . . .

The strict enforcement of this *taboo* on male immigration to another community curbs male mobility, but it serves the collective good by anchoring a community with cohorts of lifetime local males. And, by growing up, establishing friendship bonds, and remaining with peers, self-reliant males are more likely to carry out activities in the pursuit of common goals (Mitani et al. 2002; William et al. 2004).

Adult chimpanzees are also active in organizing frequent "hunting parties" where a team of male friends will plot a strategy for capturing and killing a young monkey (with a preference for Colobus monkeys) and then sharing the carcass among themselves or occasionally with non-participating males and females (Boesch and Boesch-Achermann 2000; Mitani and Watts 2002; Fahy et al. 2013). Chimpanzees also routinely engage in "grooming parties" where preferred friends gather to rub, brush, and clean each other's fur, although in general great apes groom far less than monkeys (Nakamura 2003). Communal living is also expressed in erotic "sexual parties" when a female decides to invite the local males to engage in carefree sexual intercourse. Rather than compete for her attentions, they patiently wait in line for the opportunity to enjoy her sexual favors. Chimpanzee mothers also participate in "nursery parties," seemingly to assure that their infants and juveniles have regular playmates. Serendipitous "fruit-eating parties" also elicit a "spirit of community" upon the discovery of a jam-packed fruit tree followed by loud calling inviting residents to an impromptu feast.

Above all, chimpanzee "cultural traditions" embody commonwealth phenomena. These collective customs differ by community and include distinctive tool-making techniques, gestural communications, hunting techniques, rituals, herbal medicine treatments, and the like. These traditions are not genetically derived but, like human traditions, rely on the imagination, creativity, and inventiveness of community members and the transmission of cultural knowledge to the next generation. As Luncz et al. (2012: 924) noted:

> [C]ultural differences in chimpanzees can be found over a very small spatial scale and between neighboring communities. In this regard, chimpanzees show a strong similarity to humans, for whom ecology, genes, and cultural inheritance interact to produce a variety of different cultural solutions. It has generally been assumed that in humans, culture overwrites ecological and genetic influence on behavior, and that once it has evolved, it allows for more independence from ecological constraints ... in wild chimpanzees, cultural practices can also to some extent overwrite ecological pressures, and that their cultural systems can be resilient.

In addition, Luncz and Boesch (2014: 656) found that "chimpanzee communities have long-lived cultures that are passed on conservatively throughout time." Indeed, research now indicates that cultural stability and "great time depths" characterize chimpanzee communities (Langergraber et al. 2014: 5). Whiten et al. (2007: 1042) even suggests that "humans' prodigious capacity for culture is likely to have evolved from a foundation in the common ancestor we share with chimpanzees that in these respects already represented the most developed cultural abilities among animals."

Thus, chimpanzees are linked by a regional homeland, networks of social relations, a richness and longevity of cultural traditions, and a strong "sense of community," which is elusive but a very real force (for reviews and discussions see McGrew 1992; Matani 2009; Boesch and Boesch-Achermann 2000; Lycett, Collard and McGrew 2009; Whiten 2011 et al.; and Langergraber et al. 2014).[2] Yet, chimpanzees are also fancy-free nomads who travel about their homeland alone, with a friend or two, or voluntarily join or leave impromptu gatherings that are sustained by no particular individuals. The fluidity of this social system is reflected in the ties that make up chimpanzee social structure.

As discussed, a mother and her dependents are the only stable grouping until offspring reach puberty and daughters move to another community; whereas mother-son ties and male sibling ties are enduring as males settle within the boundaries of their community. Adult male-male ties are voluntary, ranging in strength from strong ties among good friends to weak or occasional ties among community residents. Adult male-female ties are weak, in part because of promiscuous mating and because mothers are occupied full-time with their dependent offspring. Adult female-female ties are also weak or what Jane Goodall (1986: 17) calls a "neutral relationship" being neither friendly nor unfriendly, in part because immigrant females are strangers to each other. A chimpanzee community is thus configured around some strong ties and lots of weak ties. Now if we imagine a field of social relations with strong ties representing high-density interactional patterns and weak ties sparse interactional patterns, a chimpanzee social structure can be characterized as a low-density social network.

Given that a social formation of weak ties is intuitively viewed as tenuous and easily broken, what kind of integration accounts for the enduring stability and deep longevity of chimpanzee communities? One explanation proposed by Mark Granovetter (1973; 1983) on the workings of both strong and weak tie structures is that both types can serve as supportive networks, but each type generates a different basis of social integration. Granovetter's hypothesis is consistent with the following proposition: the higher the level of density (or number of strong ties) at the micro-group level, the less the level of integration at the macro-level. And the lower the level of density (or number of weak ties) at the micro-group level, the greater the level of integration at the macro-level. If we apply this proposition to chimpanzee society, chimpanzee integration clearly rests on a weakly tied support network. Consanguinity (see Chapter 1, p. 13 footnote 11) is limited to mothers and sons/brothers because female emigration

---

[2] Let me emphasize that there are scores of publications from chimpanzee sites all over Africa documenting the communal lifeways of free-ranging chimpanzees and their strong "sense of community."

disrupts the formation of maternal lineages. And, female promiscuity disrupts the formation of paternal lineages. For paternity as Henry Maine (1883: 9) once quipped, is a "matter of inference, as opposed to maternity, which is matter of observation." The result is a social structure built primarily on voluntary relations.

A social structure organized around weak ties is noticeably different than one organized around strong ties because the latter are important regulators of social support, reciprocal obligations, and cohesion. As a consequence, when individuals are embedded in tight-knit cliques, solidarity is fostered within groups *but* fragmentation is created between groups through the restriction of the flow of interactions. Weakly tied networks, in contrast, promote a greater independence because they place few constraints or obligations on members. As individuals are not locked into high-density cliques, there is less restriction on movement, allowing for a much larger number of interactions in a population. Thus, with few extended kinship anchors, chimpanzees freely move about their community as they jolly well please. So, for chimps there is a strength in having weak ties because they foster interactions among residents in a widely scattered "fission-fusion" population, giving chimpanzees a "sense of community" in lieu of a strong sense of group affiliation. Yet, since individuals can maintain many more weak ties than strong ties on average, the end result is a stable structural integrity that would be very difficult to obtain on the basis of strong ties alone. A weakly tied network also provides the needed "breathing space" for large-sized apes who often need to forage alone for widely scattered and seasonal resources while providing at the same time a sense of belonging to something greater than self.

The Nature of Community

Chimpanzees live in a rare social formation that Jane Goodall called a community rather than a group or troop. She obviously borrowed the term but do chimpanzees truly share with humans a communal type of integration, albeit in its elementary form? If so, it would lend support to Durkheim's long-standing claim that the original social formation for humans was a macro-unit or a single clan characterized by a lack of internal divisions until the kinship institution was invented later in time. Answering this question is critical to our analysis, but it is not easy to do. Humans and chimps, however, shared a LCA for millions of years before they split into different lineages between 5 and 7 millions years ago so we can tackle this question by considering (1) the features that define a human community and, (2) the neurological building blocks that make such a rare social formation possible.

According to George Murdock (1949) there are only two human social formations that are "genuinely universal," the *nuclear family* and the *community*.[3] The community concept in Western Civilization is so old that it can be found in the writings of Aristotle and in Plato who defined community as "a having-in-common (*koinonia*) of pleasures and pain" (quoted in Catlin 1959: 117). Yet, whether it is called *gemeinschaft*, *communauté hapari*, or *koinonia*, this universal concept is riddled with ambiguities over what it is meant to entail or even what it is. In a classic literature review, Hillery (1955) found ninety-four definitions of community, although few definitions had clearly defined characteristics—even when community was the subject matter. A majority of scholars did agree that a community is associated with people who live in a defined space, socially interact and have shared ties. Lee and Newby (1983: 57) emphasized, however, that physical propinquity alone is not enough for a feeling of unity, but, rather, it was in the nature and types of social interactions that characterize a community. Yet, despite the lack of consensus on a clear-cut definition of community, it is a long-standing core concept in the social sciences and is typically defined (when it is defined) on some combination of the following attributes. A community is:

- A defined geographical/space area where members interact with each other
- A social unit where more than one center exists
- A social form where a conscious "sense of belonging" is the criterion of membership
- A social arrangement where genealogical relations are not essential
- A place for meaningful types of human associations, families, neighborhoods, institutions, and voluntary associations
- A felt emotional dynamic—a feeling, a sensation, a perception, an awareness, a recognition of something
- A response by the sensory system to some conscious or unconscious phenomena
- A cognitive unity; an emotional connection, a spiritual harmony that transcends individuals

---

3 Murdock (1949: 1–2) considers the micro *nuclear* family as one universal basic form—mother, father, and offspring. It can be combined into larger aggregates such as the *polygamous* family, which is two or more nuclear families with one parent in common, usually the father under *polygyny*. The community is a macro-universal form.

- A dynamic entity that is not a group or a society
- The formation of a cognitive pleasing social whole
- An essential component of religiosity.

Why should the concept of community be so elusive and inexplicable? Why do people universally embrace the term, as though it has special or even sacred properties? Indeed, it is commonplace today for individuals to speak of the "loss of community" or wanting to "build community," "support community," "experience community" or to live where there is a "sense of community." Moreover, the concept usually generates such positive sentiments that localities with a "sense of community" are intuitively viewed as places with fellowship, connection, and exchange. One might assume that a "sense of community" brings forth such inclinations as collectivism, intimacy, and strong-ties. Yet, family relations are not essential properties of a community nor is a deep-seated collectivist intimacy; and while the term can evoke such emotions, it is the fluid, voluntary ties that account for why the concept gets generalized to all sorts of voluntary associations, even virtual communities on the internet without face-to-face relations or spatial boundaries. Elizabeth Frazer (1999: 83) writing on the *experience* of community best captures why the community concept remains such an enigmatic and ill-understood human universal:

> On occasion . . . members experience a centred and bounded entity that includes the self as such; they engage in exchanges and sharing that are personalized; the orientation to each and to the whole engages the person and, as some are tempted to put it, his or her soul. It is from such occasions that 'the spirit of community' or 'the sense of community' is achieved. Here I think we have the . . . 'pay-off' of community . . . In the relation of community concrete patterns of material social relations are felt to be transcended . . . the aspiration to community is an aspiration to a kind of connectedness that transcends the mundane and concrete tangle of social relations.

The early primatologists who first detected a "sense of community" among chimpanzees likely did so because they intuitively perceived as Frazer put it, "a kind of connectedness" that transcends concrete social relations. For chimpanzees, a *community spirit* is the touchstone for integrating a social structure erected mostly on voluntary associations. If humans and chimpanzees do share a "sense of community" and evidence exists that gorillas and orangutans do so as well, this trait is likely derived from the LCA we shared with the great apes. Supposedly, given the right triggers, great apes and humans are primed to experience an emotionally-driven extramundane entity—a property of *the social mind*. This takes us to the next phase of our enquiry: what are the sensory building blocks of this shared cognitive property? Then, in light of this analysis we can turn to the dynamics of a chimpanzee community to uncover the elementary forms of this emergent property, and to access its possible relationship to Durkheim's theory on the origin of society and religion. Because chimpanzee communities are rudimentary compared to human ones, it will fulfill Durkheim's essential guideline of taking a social phenomenom back to its earliest possible beginnings.

The Sensory Reality of Higher Primates

The primate order began about 65 million years ago during the Paleocene epoch when a shrew-like mammal took up life in the trees. The first true primates, or *prosimians* (i.e. pre-monkeys and apes) evolved about 55 million years ago during the Eocene epoch. Natural selection favored these early tree-huggers with a cluster of traits that included nails instead of claws, soft finger pads for improved tactile perception, forward-facing eyes, bigger brains, (compared to ground-living mammals), an enhanced neuroanatomy for balance and muscular movement, and an uptick in visual acuity for moving about in a three-dimensional environment.

About 33 million years ago in the Oligocene epoch, *early anthropoid* primates evolved—the stem ancestors of today's Old World monkeys, apes, and humans. Selection favored these early anthropoids with a cluster of elaborate traits over prosimians that included finely tuned prehensile hands and feet, a larger brain, and a signature dentition shared today by all Old World monkeys, apes, and humans. But the hallmark of anthropoid evolution was increased brain size, with vast new tracks of cortical tissue for more flexible and purposeful responses to the physical and social environment. As the sensory modalities are the gateway to human cognition and even effect the brain's "functional architecture" (Kirk 2004, 2006, Purvis et al. 1996), a little background on anthropoid sensory software is essential for our analysis, especially the central role played by the visual system in coordinating what information is received and how it is perceived.

The Anthropoid Sense Modalities

To detect the physical world, all species receive sensory impressions through some body parts with the degree of sophistication dependent on perceptual demands. Yet, no matter how complex the sensory equipment, all organisms are limited in their perceptual abilities because it is physically impossible to pick up and signal all possible qualities of objects in space (Werblin 1976: 21). For this reason, the organ favored by selection to be the dominant modality depends upon what kinds of information are crucial to an animal's survival. For ground-living mammals, the olfactory organ is usually dominant for object recognition because smell is automatically alerting, superior for long distance communication and for detecting the lingering cues of both predators and prey, whereas for tree-living primates vision is dominant for object recognition because sight is superior for arboreal foraging and generally moving about in a three-dimensional world. The dominance of cortically-based vision over the sub-cortical olfactory organ and the elaboration of the other cortical senses marked a turning point in primate evolution because it set into motion the capacity for flexible and purposeful cortically-based responses to environmental stimuli.

Contemporary Old World monkeys, apes, and humans are a group of related species (or a clade) with virtually the same sensory equipment.[4] Both the molecular clock and cladistics point to an early anthropoid ancestor (LCA) who lived about 28 million years ago and bequeathed to her descendants a cluster of traits that included a redrafting of the sensory organs. Because this enhancement culminated in the ability of apes and humans to represent the world symbolically, a little information follows on the contents of this extraordinary package of sensory traits.

The Chemical Modalities

Olfactory perception underwent a major reduction in primate evolution. Located in sub-cortical tissue, the primate olfactory bulb is still essential for detecting toxic chemicals, for sexual functions, for triggering taste sensations, and for generating strong visceral sensations as it is close to emotional centers in the subcortical portions of the mammalian brain, but smell is rarely used by contemporary Old World monkeys, apes, and humans for locating objects in space, detecting predators, or for communication by urine marking. Moreover, as the gustatory and olfactory systems act in combination, when selection downgraded the olfactory system it upgraded the gustatory system with greatly enhanced "sweetness receptors" for the detection of energy-rich foods, particularly

---

4 A clade is a compact related set of species. Clades are monophyletic in that they contain one last common ancestor (LCA) and descendants.

soft, ripe fruits. We can thank or blame our Oligocene ancestor for such an innovative sweet-tasting receptor that having originally evolved for detecting the delicious tastes of sweet fruits now seeks out sugar-heavy processed desserts and "junk foods" made with refined sugars (for discussions see Rouquier and Giorgi 2007; Preuschoft and Preuschoft 1994; Stein and Rowe 2011; Maryanski 1997; Nofre et al. 1996; Glaser et al. 1995).

The Haptic Modality

Tactile perception underwent a dramatic heightening in primate evolution. Located in neocortical tissue, the touch modality is highly sophisticated in Old World monkeys, apes, and humans, especially for grasping and manipulating objects by using the prehensile hands. In fact, haptic or "active touch" is so complex that, in blind humans (such as Helen Keller), it serves as a surrogate for sight by recognizing objects in space using the prehensile hands for gaining impressions and, then, cognitively processing these patterns in a temporal sequential realm (Preuss 2007; Kass and Pons 1988; Hamrick 2001).

The Auditory Modality

Sound perception underwent a progressive fine-tuning in primate evolution. Located in neocortical tissue, the auditory modality in Old World monkeys, apes, and humans has receptors for both high and low frequencies (unlike ground-living mammals whose hearing is usually in the higher frequencies). Selection for these frequencies is surely linked to a multi-canopied rainforest where higher frequencies are less valuable because they have a directional flow and fade quickly, whereas lower frequencies travel better *around* physical objects such as trees and are perceived for longer distances. While the primary function of the primate auditory system is its utility as a wide-ranging early warning system, it also serves as a rich repertoire for close and long-range vocal communication.

It is important to point out that all monkey, ape, and human *sound inputs* and *perceptions* are under cortical control for higher order flexible processing. In contrast, monkey and ape *vocal production* is largely under limbic or sub-cortical control for the emission of mostly emotionally laden vocalizations. Humans alone have the capacity for cortically controlled vocal sounds for voluntary, open-ended responses. But human speech rests on these early anthropoid precursors—the perception of low-sensitive sounds and the placement of sound *perception* (but not production) under cortical or voluntary control. As Hackett (2008: 775) expressed it, "there is both direct and indirect evidence that the major features of nonhuman primary auditory cortex organization are conserved in humans" (Heffner 2004, 2008; Coleman 2009: 88; Heidegard et al. 2009; Glendenning and Masterton 1998).

The Visual Modality

Visual perception underwent an overhaul in primate evolution. Located in neocortical tissue, the visual modality in Old World monkeys, apes, and humans is rich in neurological enhancements that include stereoscopic or depth perception to pick up information as a three-dimensional representation, a finely tuned fovea with exceptional clarity to see objects up close, and trichromatic or a three-coned color system with perception so sensitive that it detects even slight color variations. All the sense modalities are integrated to prevent sensory disharmony, but vision is considered dominant because it is the major integrator of most environmental stimuli, and it is dominant for transmitting information about objects in space and for primate communication. This change from smelling the world to seeing the world was truly revolutionary because it involved not just a shift from a chemically-based sensory mode but a shift from a limbic-based olfactory domain to a cortically-based visual domain. And, in contrast to the subcortical senses that are tuned largely to the monitoring of the internal well-being of an organism for preservative and protective responses, the cortical modalities—haptic, auditory, and vision monitor the outside environment for general information about the external world. The visual system also differs fundamentally from the haptic and auditory systems in how it transmits information to the brain. The tactile and auditory systems are coded by a linear time-sequenced pattern of integration, whereas the visual system is specialized to transmit information coded by a simultaneous spatial pattern or "gestalt" integration (Jacobs 1999, 2007; Conroy 2012; Lyon 2007; Kirk 2004, 2006).

All these "avant-garde" endowments courtesy of a still to be identified Oligocene anthropoid ancestor are still intact in Old World monkeys, apes, and humans today and provided the neurological platform for further brain elaborations.[5] Yet, when the monkey lineage and ape/human lineage went

---

5 A fossil of interest for the LCA is a late Oligocene/early Miocene anthropoid by the name of *Saadanius hijazesis* (i.e. a collective name for a monkey-ape) who lived in Afro-Arabia between 28 and 30 million years ago. It points to a split between ancestral monkeys and apes between 28 and 24 million years ago, which is congruent with the molecular clock (Zalmout et al. 2010).

their separate ways (between 28 and 24 MYA), the monkey lineage and the ape/human lineage took different evolutionary paths. In the next chapter we will turn to an analysis of a living brain close to our own to see how the ape/human sensory features underwent selection for further groundbreaking capacities in an evolutionary stair-step process that paved the way for the neurological structures of the human mind.

15
The Hominoid Mind and the Self

> [S]ociety can exist only if it penetrates the consciousness of individuals and fashions it in "its image and resemblance." We can say, therefore, with assurance . . . that a great number of our mental states, including the most important ones, are of social origin.
>
> Émile Durkheim [1914]1960 *The Dualism of Human Nature and its Social Conditions*

Three Kinds of Identities

The brains of Old World monkeys, apes, and humans are built according to the same plan (a legacy of their Last Common Ancestor), but the hominoid brain (ape and human) is much bigger than that of monkeys. The cortical sheet of the hominoid brain is also far more convoluted with much of the surface buried in the fissures, allowing for greater neuron densities in a limited space and more complex networks among circuits (Semendeferi and Damasio 2000; Clowry 2014: 223). The outcome of these stepped up cortical enhancements allowed for more adept prehensile hands for gripping objects, a heightened sensitivity for touch using the soft pads under the fingertips, augmented cortical tissue in specialized association zones, notably in multimodal regions for the convergence of sensory modalities, and novel enhancements in neurochemistry and neurocircuitry for learning, memory, and other higher-level cognitive functioning (Sherwood and Hof 2007; Napier and Napier 1985; Holloway 1978).[1]

---

1 Monkeys are highly intelligent and possess a wide range of sophisticated cognitive skills (e.g. tool-using, solving problems with creative solutions). I can personally testify to the high intelligence of stumptail macaques (*Macaca*), whom I studied for several years. Monkey and ape abilities overlap in some domains as would be expected given their shared LCA heritage. Yet, the LCA of great apes (and humans as an evolved ape) bequeathed to its descendants a bundle of evolutionary novelties that set apes qualitatively apart from monkeys as this chapter and the two that follow will document (for a discussion of some monkey abilities see, Amici, Aureli and Call 2010).

Apes and humans thus reveal a cognitive leap to a radically distinctive mind with a suite of revolutionary features. Of great importance was the appearance of a personal or a *self-identity*. All primates have a *species identity*, an inborn trait that is activated by early exposure to conspecifics. Identifying with your own kind is crucial for mating and reproduction and for avoiding hybridization. In simple organisms, a species identity is activated by a passive imprinting process, but for primates early ongoing interactions with conspecifics are essential for the formation of a species identity (for discussions of species identities in animals, see Roy 1980).

All primate species have a *social identity*. In a series of classic deprivation studies on young primates, Harry Harlow and his associates (1971, 1965) discovered that the circuits for a social identity are hard-wired, but their activation requires a nurturing social environment. Primates isolated at birth lack a social identity and have only a *place identity*. A social identity is crucial for the coordination, interaction, and integration of primate age and sex classes who live together in societies all year long.

A handful of primate species have a *self-identity*. Among the 200+ species of primates, only great apes and humans evolved the complex neural circuits for a *species identity, a social identity, and a rare self-identity*. A personal self is constructed slowly over time but its activation and progressive development are contingent upon social experiences.[2] Charles Horton Cooley (1902) (influenced by William James) introduced the concept of the "looking glass self" as a metaphor to describe a process whereby a self arises in children from reading the gestures and responses of closely connected persons or *significant others* that, in turn, reflect back on an individual such as a mirror, leading to the acquisition of a self-identity and self-consciousness. George Herbert Mead ([1934]1974), building on Cooley, also viewed self as a social object and provided a detailed and systematic explanation for how the self develops. For Mead, a *mind* is not an entity but a behavioral capacity whereby a *self* or what Mead called a "mental content" (p. 149) is constructed by assessing experiences (about oneself) in a social milieu. Acquiring a self, then, is wholly dependent on social interactions with others. Mead especially wanted to bring out the character of the self as reflexive by giving it the quality of being both a subject and an object to itself. That is, metaphorically speaking, a self is present once individuals can step outside of themselves and view themselves as an object in relation to other selves in a social setting.

---

[2] Species of dolphins, whales, and elephants also have very large and convoluted cortical sheets. They too are reported to have a self-identity as well as agency and self-awareness (see for example, Herman 2011; Whitehead and Rendell 2015; Plotnik et al. 2006).

A self is also present when one can take on the psychological attitudes and beliefs of others towards oneself, when one can take on the statuses, roles, and psychological states of other selves, and when one can understand that other individuals can also be objects to themselves in the same reflective way. So from Mead's standpoint, the activation and subsequent development of self is triggered by adjusting one's behaviors to the responses of others. And once an organism can be both subject and object to itself, this organism can see itself as separate from its body, and as an object implicated in social structures filled with other distinctive selves. A self-identity, then, is a truly liberating force that reaches far beyond a species identity or a social identity. It plays a huge role in cognitive flexibility because the capacity to be both subject and object to oneself opens the door to self-awareness, self-reliance, self-consciousness, self-criticism, self-respect, self-centeredness, self-hatred, self-love, and self-agency—in fact, the open-ended personas of a distinctive inner self. A self also draws persons towards others and leads to taking on the roles, beliefs, and attitudes of other selves. Indeed, an ability to express happiness or empathy or to put oneself in the place of others, even fictional ones in plays, movies, and storybooks or to experience the passions and creativity inherent in figments of one's imagination rests on possessing a self.

So the self is a cognitive and emotional structure that affects every part of a person. It is concretized in a social structure where individuals can view themselves as an object and can take on the roles, beliefs, and attitudes of other selves as well as the culture of the situation. It is the social mind viewing and judging itself by acting on the perceptual data of the sensory modes (see Chapter 14). In the final stage of development, the self gradually acquires the capacity to generalize from concrete social fields to abstract social fields by internalizing the roles, beliefs, attributes, and reactions of multi-body formations such as an entire community, a society, or an otherworldly entity in supernatural realms. At this final stage, the maturing self transcends the range of immediate experiences by attaining the capacity to take on what Mead called "the generalized other" or "community of attitudes" among conspecifics. As Mead expressed it ([1934]1974: 154–155):

> The organized community or social group which gives to the individual his unity of self may be called "the generalized other." The attitude of the generalized other is the attitude of the whole community ... It is in the form of the generalized other that the social process influences the behavior of the individuals involved in it and carrying it on, i.e., that the community exercises control over the conduct of its individual members ... In abstract thought

the individual takes the attitude of the generalized other toward himself, without reference to its expression in any particular other individuals ...

Chimpanzees and the Self

Can chimpanzees infer the intentions, desires, and beliefs of others? Or, as David Premack and Woodruff phrased it in 1978, "Do chimpanzees possess a *theory of mind*?" The gold standard for testing the presence of a self-identity is to place an animal in front of a mirror-like reflecting object and then watch the response. As discussed in Chapter 14, the visual acuity of Old World monkeys, apes, and humans is virtually identical, and so higher primates all "see" the object in the mirror's shiny reflection. The difference is in what is being reflected. Monkeys "see" the image of a strange monkey; great apes and humans "see" themselves. Indeed, great apes recognize self whether the reflection is a realistic mirror image or a distorted curved "fun house" image or even a recorded image on a television screen. As Suddendorf and Collier-Baker (2009: 1676) put it, among primates it is "only the descendants of a hominoid that probably lived between 13.8 and 18 MYA ago [that] have so far reliably demonstrated that they know who it is that ... looks back at them when they look in the mirror." That great ape recognize their reflected self means they must already have a "mind's eye" image of themselves; the mirror test simply makes it possible for them to see an actual image or at least how others see them.[3] By comparison, chimpanzees reared in social isolation show no signs of self-recognition and fail the mirror test (see Gallup et al. 1971; and see Anderson and Gallup Jr. 2015).

---

3 When monkeys "see" another monkey in the mirror they respond in a social way. As Straumann and Anderson (1991: 125) noted, "most species of non-human primates do not possess a sufficiently well-integrated self-awareness to shift from social to self-directed responding." Recently, Chang et al. (2015) found that after elaborate and extensive training and reinforcement using visual-somatosensory association, rhesus monkeys (Macaca) evidenced "behaviors resembling mirror self-recognition." As macaques are "top of the trees" in monkey intelligence, it is not surprising that they would show some capacity for self-awareness. In a review article (and a critique of the macaque research), Anderson and Gallup (2015) pointed out that great ape and human self-recognition is spontaneous. Moreover, mirror self-recognition is only a marker for an underlying sense of self, allowing " individuals to engage in other emotional acts such as empathy, reconciliation, consolation, and perspective-taking." They concluded that "to date there is no compelling evidence that prosimians, monkeys, or lesser apes—gibbons and siamangs—are capable of mirror self-recognition." (p. 317)

Clues into how a self arises come from case studies of chimpanzees raised with humans. For example, Vicki, a female chimpanzee adopted as an infant by Keith and Catherine Hays and treated like their offspring, responded to her human-like socialization by behaving much like a normal child. When Vicki was three years old, the Hays documented the following:

> ... Vicki's development has closely paralleled that of a normal human child, her interests and abilities having appeared in roughly the same sequence, and at about the same rate. Her social behavior is that of an extrovert: she seeks the company and attention of people ... [And] Just as a human child copies its parent's routine chores, so Vicki dusts; washes dishes; sharpens pencils; saws, hammers, and sandpapers furniture; paints woodwork and presses photographs in books.
> (Hays and Hays 1951: 106)

Vicki's photo album also affords glimpses into her self-image. When she was asked to sort photographs into either a human or animal pile, Vicki placed the chimpanzee photos on the animal pile with dogs and horses but she placed her own picture on the top of the human pile (Hays 1951).

Another example is the chimpanzee Lucy who was raised in a human household and treated as a regular family member. She also elicited the behaviors of a normal human child. By the age of two, Lucy favored a little toy mirror, gazing into it for grooming and admiring herself, exploring her body parts, and practicing "play-faces" and other facial expressions. As adolescents, Vicki and Lucy both refused to approach, socialize, or mate with male chimpanzees because they were sexually attracted only to human males (Temerlin 1980). Having spent their formative years in the company of *human significant others*, Vicki and Lucy had seemingly acquired the self-identity of a human being. It also suggests that chimps and humans acquire a self-identity in much the same way (for discussions see Hays 1951 and Temerlin 1980).

The mirror test documents that chimpanzees (and gorillas and orangutans) have a consciousness of self, but a "theory of mind" also requires a capacity for human-like self-agency, the sense of being an independent agent with a feeling of control over events. It also demands the complex cognitive structure that Mead outlined—role-taking or an awareness of the beliefs, intentions, emotions, and desires of others and the capacity to evaluate themselves from the perspective of all of these properties of the external world. A growing body of research now strongly supports the hypothesis that chimpanzees possess the neural correlates for a human-like sense of self-agency that includes the ability to distinguish between events they generated, executed, and controlled by themselves from the actions generated by other individuals in the external environment. Chimpanzees can view themselves as an object and are even capable of "confidence movements" or a value-judgment of how successful they were at performing a current task (Beran et al. 2015). As Kaneko and Tomonaga (2011: 3701) concluded, ". . . chimpanzees and humans share fundamental cognitive processes underlying the sense of being an independent agent; that is self-agency."

Research also confirms chimpanzee perceptual skills for "taking the role of the other" (Mead [1934] 1974). Indeed, as Jay Meddin (1979) noted years ago, "chimpanzees nicely fit George Herbert Mead's general paradigm." Indeed, chimpanzees' perceptive skills are so fine-tuned and Machiavellian that they can remember what they observed at one point in time in the company of others and then exploit this knowledge later in time with the same others for their own benefit (MacLean and Hare 2012; Schmelz, Call and Tomasello 2011). They can also be kind-hearted by expressing empathy for a grieving member and even acting as though they understand what caused the sorrowful emotions expressed by another (Biro et al. 2010). They are equally good at monitoring how others perceive events and selectively informing them if they believe another individual is unaware of a dangerous situation (Crockford et al. 2012).

When making decisions, Rosati and Hare (2013) conclude that chimpanzee affective states and their motivational process closely resemble those of humans. In a literature review on the "theory of mind," Call and Tomasello (2008: 191) noted that, "All the evidence reviewed . . . suggests that chimpanzees understand both the goals and intentions of others as well as the perception and knowledge of others. . .the answer to Premack and Woodruff's pregnant question . . . is a definite yes, chimpanzees do have a theory of mind."

Communication and the Self

George Herbert Mead maintained that social contacts were crucial for acquiring a self-identity but he also included two other essential prerequisites: (1) an inherent potential for symbolic thought and (2) the company of significant others that meet the social and emotional needs of a child. For, it is from the company of familiar individuals and from the standpoint of their attitudes that a self-conception is constructed. In these social encounters, Mead emphasized the role of communication, especially with "significant symbols" or a communication directed to ego and others at the same time. This type of communication, Mead said, introduces the self.

One communicates and waits for a response and, in a sense an organism is responding to itself *vis-à-vis* the responses of others, thereby becoming an object to itself from the perspective of others. In these exchanges, one is also responding to oneself and in this way an individual becomes an object to itself. Mead was convinced that this way of interacting by seeing self in relation to the social environment was hard-wired for the potential but it was essentially dependent upon the cooperation of significant others. So a self is an emergent social behavioral capacity—not a physiological thing, although it rests on a neurological platform that needs to be activated by role taking with others.

And, once an organism has a self, it can be alone with itself, talk to itself, or even sanction itself by saying, "I'm not being myself today." Yet without social experience, the inherent potential for a self remains dormant, which is why Mead saw communication as playing such a crucial role in the acquisition of a personal identity.

Types of Chimpanzee Communication

Can chimpanzees represent the world symbolically? Do they communicate by using symbols? They live in a rare organization of mostly voluntary relations where individuals have preferred friendships, where self-reliant individuals travel about mostly in their own company, where social interactions occur in fleeting "parties," and where individuals sometimes remain apart from community members for weeks or even months. The image of early researchers that chimpanzees had no organization actually belied a social order of exceeding complexity. Given that chimps have a self-identity and its entailments, what forms of communication do they use to convey, share, or exchange information to sustain a "sense of community" in time and space?

Vocal Repertoire

The chimpanzee auditory cortex, which relies on moving sound waves for identifying and processing sounds in space, is an important medium for the input and comprehension of vocalizations and for their output or production. Specialized for both pitch and volume, the auditory system of chimpanzees is used for close and long-distance communication; and chimpanzees are endowed with a large stock of vocalizations that include spacing calls, alarm calls, localization calls, and general interactional grunts. *Of note*, the neural circuits in the chimpanzee auditory cortex are under cortical control for voluntary cognitive processing *but only* for *incoming* sounds and their *perception*. In contrast, the neural circuits for *sound production* are under subcortical or limbic control so vocalizations or vocal responses are mostly species-typical and largely emotion-based responses. Recent data indicates, however, that some types of acoustic sounds are open to social learning and content with some scholars now hypothesizing the existence of possible "cognitive building blocks" for the origins of human language (Watson et al. 2015).

Gestural Repertoires

Apes and humans possess exceptional visual systems and prehensile hands and feet with the capacity to grasp and manipulate objects. The haptic or touch modality is so extraordinary that it can identify objects in space by using the prehensile hands to sequentially string together the separate parts touched and to reconstruct a pattern or structure in the "mind's eye."

Chimpanzees engage in subtle and deft social exchanges with the aid of a rich repertoire of vocalizations, facial and body signals, and manual symbolic gestures. Their prehensile hands in particular are used extensively for intentional and flexible gestural communication. Much can be conveyed in gestures but it requires the active attention of vision (unlike smell or sound); therefore gesturing is restricted to daylight and face-to-face interactions between two or more individuals. To exchange information, chimpanzees rely on a large repertoire of symbolic gestures that are often combined with vocalizations, body movements, and facial gestures. The result is a highly efficient symbolic system for voluntary, intentional, flexible, meaningful, and goal-oriented communication that is open-ended enough to transmit a diverse range of information from simple requests (e.g. follow me, groom me, stop that), to commands (e.g. start play, change play, climb on me). Gesturing is also used extensively for denoting the location of objects, for negotiations between dyads, and for coordinating social relationships. Gestural symbolizing can be precise or general, concrete (e.g. alluding to a ripe fruit tree) or abstract (i.e. alluding to a mutual desire for sexual intimacy (Hobaiter and Byrne 2014). As Roberts et al. (2012a: 465–466) conclude:

> ... the manual gestures of wild chimpanzees are perceived semantically and manipulate the recipient's movements and attention, while recipients also infer the broader goal of the signaler from context.

While the gestural stock in a chimpanzee community is socially conditioned and familiar to all members, different age classes will often construct their gestural repertory in different ways. Juveniles and young adults, for example, favor some gestures not used by adults and the converse; some members sign with idiosyncratic gestures they simply make-up, and some gestures favored by adolescents are replaced later with adult gestures (Tomasello et al. 1985; Call and Tomasello 2007). According to Goodall (1986), chimpanzees simply invent new gestures when needed. Miscommunications are not problematic because a signal that receives no response, is repeated, substituted with another gesture, or combined with other signals until understood. These visual-tactile symbols are used to reference self and others (even an audience of others) and are inherently social because they coordinate behaviors and require responses. Such a flexible gestural system under cortical control works very effectively in a free-ranging community of 100 or more chimpanzees. And, not surprisingly, the neural structures underlying chimpanzee gestural communication are homologous with the language centers of the human brain. Indeed, an analysis of chimpanzee gestures by Roberts et al. (2012b: 588) noted the resemblance between chimpanzees and human gestures, and proposed that gestural communication "is likely to have also been pivotal in human language evolution" (also see Moore 2014; Call and Tomasello 2007; Parr et al. 2005; Blake 2004; Turner 2000).

Linguistic Repertoires

Chimpanzees are so genetically close to humans that scientists wondered if they could be taught to speak in a human way. So, teaching apes to "talk" became an intellectual challenge, with early attempts focused on home-raised chimpanzees such as Vicki Hayes who shared many social behaviors with human children of the same age. But a "talking chimp" was never forthcoming, and this line of research was dropped because of failure after failure (Kellogg and Kellogg 1933; Hayes 1952). One major problem stemmed from ape vocal tracts (the stretch between the vocal cords and lips). Although chimp and human vocal tracts work in the same way, such that chimp hoots are functionally produced in the same way as speech (allowing chimps to produce the rudiments of consonants and vowels), human vocal tracts underwent alterations and elaborations in the larynx, pharynx, and related neurological and muscular structures enabling them to modify sounds and to rapidly produce and sequence phonemes. Another major problem is that the ape auditory-vocal channel for sound production is still under control by limbic zones, although some calls (especially food calls) have some voluntary components. In contrast, the human vocal-auditory channel is under cortical control and adapted for voluntary, intentional sounds.

Yet, once the "oral bias" for producing speech was relaxed, researchers took another tack. What if the focus shifted to the visual and haptic modalities that *are* under voluntary control? And, once the visual-haptic channel was substituted, it became clear that apes could *linguistically* represent the world symbolically. The chimpanzee Washoe, for example, was raised in a human environment—but her "parents" (the Gardeners) treated Washoe like a deaf child by teaching her American Sign language (ASL). Washoe exceeded all expectations. Not only did she privately sign to herself, she later taught her offspring who then used linguistic signs to communicate with humans and other chimpanzees (Fouts and Fouts 1993). This line of research opened a door, they noted, to "the rich mental life of the chimpanzee."

Once chimpanzees were trained in a visual-gestural language, such as American sign-language (ASL), and were able to employ this system of communication with humans, they began to "talk" about events and things that they observed in their environment. Chimpanzees also asked about things not present or recalled past events. One chimpanzee, for example, signed "candy tree?" in anticipation of the upcoming Christmas holiday when a colorful decorated tree was put up filled with candy for the chimps (Fouts and Fouts 1993). The majority of visual-gestural signs fell into three categories: "play," "social interaction," and "reassurance," while others referred to grooming, feeding, private signing to self, cleaning, and discipline. When humans were not present, chimpanzees signed with each other, "talking" about social interactions or discussing favorite activities or favorite foods. Thus, chimpanzees can easily learn a sign language, pass it on to the next generation, and use it spontaneously to converse, think, and even talk to themselves (Gardner and Gardner 1969; Premack 1971; Fouts and Fouts 1993).

Artificial Languages

American sign language is a natural language but researchers also wanted to know if chimps could also learn a computer-based language by using geometric symbols or lexigrams imprinted on the surface of keys. Each key represented a word, and the keys were rotated from time to time so that linguistic expressions could not be memorized in any particular order. Lana (named after Lana Turner, the famous movie star) was the first chimpanzee to participate in this research, and she easily learned the rules and vocabulary of this artificial grammar by combining her lexigrams into meaningful sentences controlled by the computer (Rumbaugh 2015; Rumbaugh 2013). Other chimpanzees followed and learned an artificial language by using lexigrams in a broad context and in spontaneous ways to exchange information. What became clear is that apes have the neural circuitry to learn, produce, and comprehend complex, symbolically-based grammars (Gillespie-Lynch et al. 2013; Beran et al. 2000; Savage-Rumbaugh et al. 1978).

Human Speech Comprehension

Chimpanzees can be trained to use sign language and lexigrams, but what characterizes human language is that it is not formally taught to children. Then, by the irony of fortune, this difference was taken off the table when two unexpected events occurred: an adult female chimpanzee was being trained to use a computer-based language (with less than satisfactory results as she was a mature adult female). During her personalized lessons, her young son Kanzi sat nearby, quietly watching his mother interact with researchers and the keyboard. Then, in a stroke of serendipity, when Kanzi was 2 1/2 years old, he sat next to the desktop computer and typed a request for items along with a comment on activities. Kanzi had not been "trained" as they thought him too young; he had learned simply by exposure to a linguistic environment and just about the same time that human children begin to talk more fluently, he suddenly could do the same by using the keys on the computer (Savage-Rumbaugh et al. 1986; Savage-Rumbaugh and Lewin 1994).

A second astonishing discovery was Kanzi's ability to comprehend the "talk" of his caregivers. Kanzi cannot vocalize for the reasons discussed above, but the auditory system of young apes has an innate capacity to process human speech, a neurological process that requires isolating out phonemes, combining them into morphemes and applying the rules of grammar for the comprehension of sentences (Rumbaugh and Savage-Rumbaugh 1996). Kanzi was not trained to *comprehend* human speech—and, of all things, the rules of grammar linking words together. He did so spontaneously, again by mere exposure to a linguistic environment, a revelation for his caregivers when one day they realized that Kanzi had listened in on and responded in kind to their conversation.[4] Lieberman

---

[4] When I visited Kanzi years ago at Georgia State University research center where he was raised with his mother and siblings, one of his caregivers told me the amazing "apple" story of how she and another caregiver were babysitting Kanzi for the day and decided to take him for a picnic lunch in the woods. After lunch, one caregiver said to the other that she wanted an apple for dessert. Out of the blue, so to speak, Kanzi jumped up and rushed over to the picnic basket grabbed the fruit and then handed her a bright, red apple.

(2006: 45) concluded that the key finding in ape language research is that "apes have the biologic capacity to acquire and productively use human words and syntax at a reduced level equal to that of most three-year old children."

Other ape infants and juveniles have followed Kanzi's lead of listening to American English (or any human language) that, in turn, naturally triggers their auditory cortex (Wernicke's area in the brain) to start isolating out phonemes for speech comprehension that a normal three-year-old child would understand. Linguistic chimpanzees also use computer lexograms and manual gestures for multi-modal symbolic representation. In comparison with children, young apes make many of the same kinds of utterances about past events, future events, requests, declaratives, naming, and articulating what they would like to do. Indeed, ape statements went further back in the past then those of human children (Lyn et al. 2011: 73].

Chimpanzees (and other apes) have also shown a competence to use many dimensions of human language, albeit in simpler forms. And, like human children, young apes have a short open-window period for learning a first language. Thus, apes and humans have similar neurological structures that are primed to accept symbolic communications, whether in the form of a visual-gestural language used in a chimpanzee community, in the human world a computer language or the comprehension of a language used in language research centers. As our closest living relatives they offer an excellent template to meet the guidelines laid out by Durkheim. In the next chapter we will use the chimpanzee template (as well as data from the orangutan and chimpanzee) to evaluate Durkheim hypothesis on the origin of religion and society.

16
The Community Complex

> *In order to fully understand a practice or an institution, a judicial or moral rule, it is essential to go back as nearly as possible to its primary origin; for between the form it currently is and what it has been, there is a close relationship.*
>
> Émile Durkheim La Prohibition de l'inceste et ses origines. *L'Année sociologique* 1898: 1

Engaging Our Imagination

In the same way that Albert Einstein sought to explain the principle of relativity by asking us to imagine riding on a beam of light or the way that cosmologists sought to explain the birth of the universe by asking us to imagine a "big bang event" when energy, time, and matter took shape, Durkheim sought to explain the origin of religion and society by asking us to imagine a "veritable social protoplasm" or a free-standing aggregation as the pre-institutional stem from which all later social formations would evolve. To tackle this problem, he proposed two research guidelines: (1) a strict adherence to the scientific method and (2) a historical perspective by taking a phenomena as far back as possible to its origins.

Trying to account for the genesis of social institutions is an age-old question that has never really gone away because it arouses our curiosity about human and societal origins. After all, there must have been a time in human history when social institutions did not exist. In essence, Durkheim sought the fabled "Holy Grail" that for him was the fountainhead for social solidarity. And, he concluded that *totemism*, as it led to the emergence of religion, was this foundational institutional system— a controversial idea back in Durkheim's time and today. To evaluate Durkheim's theory in a fruitful, systematic way given that many of its underlying assumptions were shaped piecemeal over a long period of time, let us begin by reviewing his motley collection of premises, which he would eventually weave into a unifying synthesis in *The Elementary Forms*.

On the Individual and Society

Most scholars today believe that humans are by nature highly social. Taken at face value this assumption would seem to ring true because humans are primates and most primates are indeed very socially inclined. But most primates are monkeys; and so, the supposed inherent gregarious nature of humans rests on a monkey model of sociality. In contrast, the hominoid family tree (e.g. human and apes) represents but 5 percent of all primate species; and when compared with monkeys great apes are self-reliant individualists with rather low levels of sociality. Since humans by nature are evolved apes, we need to re-evaluate this long-standing presumption that humans are so highly social. Indeed, humans must work very hard to create and sustain high sociality, which suggests that interaction leading to enduring social bonds is not as "natural" as is generally presumed.

If we examine most models of interaction, such as Randall Collins (2004) theory of interaction rituals, we can see how much interpersonal effort goes into forming solidarities; and indeed, some solidarities are generated to forge conflict with other groups rather than to integrate large numbers of individuals (Collins 2009). And, if we look at other models of interaction, such as those by Jonathan Turner (1988, 2002, 2007, 2008, 2010), social interaction is a very complex and often exhausting process, suggesting that it is anything but "natural." Thus, Durkheim had a good sense that individualism and perhaps even low sociality posed a real barrier to societal-level integration. To his credit, from the outset, Durkheim took the self-centered nature of humans for granted, viewing human self-interest as a matter of "grave" concern and as a looming problem in large-scale industrial societies. As he expressed it in 1885, "How will you get . . . [the masses] . . . to devote themselves to the common interests . . . Individualism reasserts its hold over us . . . If I do not perceive the invisible bonds which link me to the rest of the society, I will think that I am independent of it and I will act accordingly" ([1885]1978: 112–114).

So, soon after he decided to become a sociologist, Durkheim was already laying the footings for the intellectual issues that would dominate his career: (1) the nature of the relationship between the individual and society and, (2) the question of how to generate and sustain solidarity in industrial societies in the face of inherent individualism. In 1902 he wrote: "By nature we are not inclined to curb ourselves and exercise constraint . . . If, in activities . . . we follow no rule save that of our own self-interest . . . how then can we acquire a taste for altruism, for forgetfulness of self and sacrifice?" ([1902]1984: xxxiv). Indeed, these overriding concerns were articulated even in his pedagogy lectures at the Sorbonne where he emphasized the importance of educating the young into the values of the collective life by equipping a child with a "taste for this pleasure and to instill in him the need for it" ([1902–1903] 1973: 240).

Thus, the essence and unifying theme in Durkheim's sociology was not his preoccupation with religion *per se*, but instead, it was his ideological commitment to the Third Republic and his intellectual commitment to discover the forces underlying social solidarity. This emphasis is understandable in light of the tumultuous political instability and social turmoil that followed the French Revolution, the rapid industrialization of France during his lifetime, and the widespread perception (whether or not correct) of the erosion of the morality and security of traditional family life. New sources of integration and a secular morality were urgently needed, Durkheim felt, to shore up the success of the Third Republic and the stability of all future societies.

While he greatly valued individualism and held strong liberal values, he argued for the priority of society over the individual, believing that a science of society was needed to uncover the laws of sociality and social unity. And, Durkheim went to great lengths to meet that goal by working tirelessly, even asking his nephew Marcel Mauss in ([1897] 1998: 86) to adopt the same work ethic:

> You need to teach yourself to get all your satisfaction and enjoyment from work rather than from anything else. You must make this an absolute rule. All else is contingent and consequently one should not attach any importance to it. I apply this rule to myself and I am well detached from all that used to fascinate me. All you need is to work with pleasure.

Having followed Durkheim's guidelines in Chapter 13 by taking his premises on human autonomy as back as they can be traced empirically using cladistics and contemporary apes as proxies for humans' hominin ancestors, it is clear that these ancestors were very weakly tied and highly individualistic. Indeed, orangutans today are so hermitic they are considered semi-solitary, a lifestyle unique among higher primates. Of course, humans are far more social than apes, but they are the descendants of a last common hominoid ancestor with weak-tie networks and individualism. So, compared to most thinkers of the nineteenth century, Durkheim was well ahead of his time in his recognition of human egoistic tendencies and in assuming that human sociality was far more a product of nurture than nature. And most particularly, Durkheim recognized how essential it was to seek a source of solidarity for larger-scale, differentiated societies.

In his early works he assumed that what he called the *mechanical* type of social solidarity would "naturally" transition into an *organic* type of solidarity, but by 1895, as has been noted, Durkheim abandoned this distinction because he realized that integration is not achieved naturally and that it is based on rituals, emotional arousal, and most controversial in his time, totemism. And, rather than two types of integration—one for small, undifferentiated societies, another for differentiated societies—he began the search for a fundamental basis for *all types of societies* after 1895.

The Horde

The *horde* or single "clan" is Durkheim cornerstone concept, a term he introduced in his 1887 lecture course on "Social Solidarity," depicting a horde as a free-standing aggregate or a macro-structure *without* kinship bonds or stable internal parts. It was the simplest formation imaginable and the foundation for his research on social solidarity. In *The Division of Labor* (1893), he proposed that once hordes transitioned into true clans, integration was rooted in the fusing of personal consciences into an overbearing "collective conscience," with *naturism* being the earliest basis of this collective conscience. But this form of solidarity was so rigid, surreal, and fragile that it could not, Durkheim felt, be sustained as societies became larger and more complex. By 1895 Durkheim dropped this line of argument with the first clue of a conversion to totemism evident in his review of Edward Westermarck's *History of Human Marriage* (1895) when, after rejecting Westermarck's theory of exogamy, he linked exogamy to totemic institutions. Yet, he never lost faith in the reality of the primitive horde because he was certain that clan-based totemic societies were derived from non-kin hordes and that the earliest human societies were not held together by kinship relations but, rather, by a macro-level network of communal relations.

Old World monkeys (and most social mammals) live in bounded micro-level groups with kin relations, whereas the great apes *all* appear to live in *macro*-level communities in which kinship is clearly not a dominant "force" of integration. Orangutans are "loners" but researchers are now documenting the existence of a proto-community or a loose sense of an inclusive community structure (Setia et al. 2008). Gorillas are organized into micro-level bands, but given (1) three or more bands and some lone males share joint proprietorship in foraging grounds and (2) the co-mingling and other affinities shown between bands are rather fluid, some researchers hypothesize that gorilla bands are not free-standing units but are instead internal divisions of a fluid, macro-level community (Goodall and Grover

1977 and see Schaller 1972: 111ff). Without question, chimpanzees live in a macro-level community organization; and since humans are so closely related to chimpanzees, it is likely that this same propensity to perceive community would also be at our genetic core.

Gorillas live on the forest floor where females with young are vulnerable to predation, which may account for why gorillas have a two-tier level of organization—relatively stable bands within a more inclusive community. But orangutans and chimpanzees fit Durkheim's hypothesized horde. Both are composed of stand-alone self-dependent food collectors. Stable groupings are unknown (except for mother with dependent offspring), and both apes evidence a fission-fusion pattern where individuals wander about by themselves or voluntarily join temporary parties (albeit, for orangutans sporadically). Indeed, chimpanzee communities mirror the quintessential horde hypothesized by Durkheim as his baseline formation for the origins of human society. Thus, if we are willing to entertain the assumption that chimpanzees and early hominins after branching away from their LCA were organized into horde-like macro-units of non-kin, Durkheim's hypothesized horde arrangement is supported by the data on chimpanzees. Since chimpanzees are so closely related to humans and, in fact, should be classified in a taxa closer to *Homo* because both are genetically closer to each other than either gorillas or orangutans, using chimpanzee data as a proxy for human hominin ancestors is not such a far reach. And, we can speculate that, given Durkheim's early interest in Espinal's *Animal Societies* declaring it "the first chapter of sociology" ([1888]1978), he would have pursued my line of inquiry if the data had been available in his time.

Exogamy and Matriliny

The origin and nature of exogamy is another of Durkheim's core assumptions. When Durkheim was a young agrégé teaching philosophy in *lycées* near Paris his lectures suggest that he supported the traditional view that the primal and natural group was the genealogical family and, hence, the starting point for society ([1883–1884]: 204). He later abandoned this assumption, replacing the family with the primitive horde where "incest was not forbidden" ([1898]1963) and where all humans lived in a kind of "promiscuous state of nature." This was an overstatement, to be sure, but it drove home the point that kinship was *not* the primal organizing principle of hominins.

In the beginning, Durkheim said, all humans lived in hordes (or single "clans") characterized by open sexual relations. But alliances would later form between hordes. And, once an alliance existed among two or more hordes, they morphed into clan-based societies, with each clan distinguished by a collective name taken from an animal or plant species. Clan unity, however, did not depend on genealogical blood-ties but on the emotional sentiments aroused by the sharing of a name, a totemic emblem, and a totemic ancestor. Totem members believed in the "kinship of the totem" because they were made from the same substance as their totem with this "substance" symbolized by blood.

In early totemism, following Durkheim, a mother passed on her totemic affiliation to her offspring or what Durkheim called descent by "the uterine line." As totem members all shared in the "familial blood" of their sacred totem, with the totem being the "divine blood" itself, a taboo was placed on all things connected with the blood of the totem. Then, given that totem membership is traced through females and that they are directly linked with menstrual blood, all females became taboo for males of their clan. But females in other clans were not taboo. And thus, the rule of exogamy was created so that females could be exchanged between different clans. The law of exogamy, then, was the vehicle by which the promiscuous horde moves to the first true clan. And, once this "primitive religiosity" of forbidding sexual unions within the "familial blood" of clans became institutionalized, it later evolved into the *incest taboo*. Thus, the prohibition of incest can be traced to the law of exogamy, which is a religious-inspired rule that takes root in totemism. And thereby, the law of exogamy not only served to integrate clan members, but also represented a very early expression of a religious-centered and emotional arousing taboo.

Durkheim's scenario on the origin of exogamy is, of course, a rather wild tale that for many scholars does not warrant serious consideration. Is there, however, some validity in this conjectural tale? To evaluate Durkheim's suppositions, we have to consider exogamy (a rule to marry out) and the incest taboo (a sexual avoidance rule among close kin) in a more inclusive context, or at least modify its customary usage in human societies.

A rule of "exogamy" or to outbreed is common to all social mammals with either one or both sexes departing their natal group at puberty. In most Old World monkey societies, males leave (as is the case with most mammals). In orangutan and gorilla societies, both males and females leave, although male gorillas typically stay within their natal ranging area, while females usually transfer to another ranging area. In chimpanzee society, both males and females leave their mother's side after puberty but males stay within their natal community, while females move to another community. Given open and promiscuous mating, mother and adult son could comfortably settle down, mate, and produce offspring, jumpstarting a genetically dense nuclear family with high rates of inbreeding. But, a *very* hard-wired trait blocks all sexual activity between mothers and their sons, despite their otherwise intimate, lifetime bonds. In fact, sexual avoidance or a biologically programmed "incest taboo" between mother and son is so ancient that it is common to *all* apes and Old World monkeys as well. As Allison Jolly (1985: 241) emphasized, "Adult sons seem to specifically avoid mating with their own mothers." Sexual avoidance has also been observed between chimpanzee brothers and sisters, despite the fact that females leave their community after puberty (for discussions on sexual avoidance among related dyads see, Demarest 1977; Turner and Maryanski 2005; Pusey and Packer 1987, Pusey 2005; Rhine and Maryanski 1996). On the human incest taboo Donald Sade (1968: 37) put forth this hypothesis:

> We may now speculate that a pre-existing condition became invested with symbolic content during hominization; the origin of at least the mother-son incest taboo may have been the elaboration of a phylogenetically older system, a system which can still be observed operating at the monkey level of organization.

So, while Durkheim's assumptions about kinship, exogamy, and incest taboos have obvious major problems, they may still have some utility in trying to understand human societies. Durkheim characterized his horde as a promiscuous freestanding aggregation that later morphed into a clan with an outbreeding rule that applied only to females. As noted earlier, "exogamy" or female-biased dispersal may have also operated in both *Australopithecine* and *Neanderthal* societies given the genetic evidence indicating that females grew up in one locality and later moved to another locality (Copeland et al. 2011; Lalueza-Fox et al. 2011). In fact, is it merely coincidental that 67 percent of all human societies in the cross-cultural ethnographic record also favor patrilocal residence where the bride moves near to or in with the groom's relatives after marriage? (see Ember, Ember and Peregrine 2009: 342).

Durkheim's premise that exogamy is rooted in totemic beliefs and rites with the incest taboo a derivative of exogamy cannot be evaluated, in part because he portrayed exogamy not so much as a rule to "marry out" but the first *sacred* taboo associated with totemism. In contrast, sexual avoidance among genetically close chimpanzees is not culturally derived but a biological propensity installed by natural selection to prevent inbreeding depression. Finally, Durkheim's premise that totemic membership was originally passed on through females is also difficult to evaluate, although in a purely technical sense, the only enduring blood-tie relations in a chimpanzee community are between a mother and her male offspring and between brothers. So, Durkheim is technically right that maternal bonds are the formative basis of genetic kinship because the mother-offspring dyad is truly the earliest elementary family. But it is an evolutionary dead end for producing offspring and it never leads to a lineal descent system over generations for chimpanzees (or humans). Nor do these tiny kinship units serve as the major source of integration in a chimpanzee community. While the idea may seem credible, researchers suggest that notwithstanding these lifelong attachments, "kinship plays an ancillary role in structuring patterns of wild chimpanzee behaviour within social groups" (Mitani et al. 2000: 885; Mitani et al. 2002; Lukas et al. 2005).

So Durkheim's colorful narrative linking the origins of exogamy with totemic cults and the exchange of females between clans cannot be "confirmed" using primate data, but of note is that (1) ape females leave at puberty and (2) a biologically-based "taboo" forbidding incest among close kin does operate with female-biased dispersal away from natal communities. He may also be technically right that the "incest taboo" is a derivative of "exogamy." Although an institutionalized rule of exogamy and an incest taboo are universals in human kinship systems (at least within the nuclear family), these cultural rules rest as Sade (1967) concluded on ancient biological foundations built up by natural selection. So, if we assume that early hominins initially organized like chimpanzees and the promiscuous horde was, in fact, real, Durkheim's presumption about its incestuous activity is incorrect, since these formations do not evidence sexual intercourse between mothers and adult sons or between opposite-sex siblings—as a consequence of their biological programming.

Durkheim was wrong on his notion of the incestuous horde, but he was right to reject kinship as the primal integrator of early hominin societies. If not consanguinity, it is reasonable to ask what other forces for integration exist? To address this question, we need to consider other components of chimpanzee society for clues into the underlying dynamics of their social cohesion. These data, I believe, can provide insights into the first building blocks of human societies.

The Forces Integrating Chimpanzee Society

Durkheim sought a scientific understanding of social solidarity. Without a true comprehension of what holds aggregates together, sociology would always be handicapped. This was his rationale for why he kept insisting that it was essential to go back as far as possible and uncover the forces of integration. So let us assume that, with chimpanzees, we are now looking at Durkheim's hypothesized horde. True, a chimpanzee horde is not quite what Durkheim imagined but he did say that he expected his theory to be modified over time. The only essentials, he mandated, was to "try out the hypothesis and test it against the facts . . ." ([1912]1995: 448) by seeking out the *simplest possible phenomenon with a scientific objectivity*.

While chimpanzees are not humans, they qualify for our assessment on these grounds: we are close cousins, indeed phyletically. Chimpanzees and humans are susceptible to the same parasites that bring diseases, and at the genome level we share 98.9 of our DNA, which means we are as genetically close as sibling species. As King and Wilson (1978: 91) phrased it: ". . . the chimpanzee-human difference is far smaller than that between species within a genus of mice, frogs or flies" (for discussions see Donaldson and Göttgens 2006; Polavarapu et al. 2011; Prüfer et al. 2012). Both humans and chimp brains also have the same cognitive template as well as the same sensory system. In fact, early *hominin* species for millions of years looked like upright walking chimpanzees. And, of importance here, chimpanzees provide our only opportunity to bring together data from the molecular, fossil, and archaeological records to evaluate Durkheim's thesis with scientific objectivity. Indeed, we are now in a good position to assess a theory that has largely lain dormant for a century. And, this analysis meets other criteria that Durkheim would have appreciated to consider his theory: there are no issues with diffusion of traits or wading through piles of secondary phenomena. So, then, what holds chimpanzee society together? If we can find this out—or even get a clouded glimpse into the forces underlying chimpanzee integration, we may also get a better understanding of the forces underlying human societies and even the forces underlying religious sentiments.

A Social Structure of Weak Ties

A chimpanzee society with 100 or more chimpanzees fits Durkheim's model of a stand-alone macro-aggregate, one with relatively few kinship bonds and a fission-fusion system that revolves around self-reliant individuals who move about alone or join temporary gatherings. This social structure is adaptive for such large-bodied primates whose dietary needs mandate the flexibility to forage independently in a forest environment with seasonal, scattered resources. So a weakly-tied network structure is an adaptation that fosters a self-governing freedom for individuals to forage largely unencumbered by the obligations inherent in tight-knit, stable cliques. And, field studies over the last seventy years have documented that chimpanzee communities (where members live on average fifty years) evidence long-term stability and intergenerational continuity over time. Indeed, Langergraber et al. (2014: 1) found in an analysis of eight chimpanzee communities that "community fissions are a very rare event."

How can integration spring from such self-reliant individualists who often forage and wander about by themselves with some members not seeing each other for weeks or months? Indeed, weak ties are usually viewed as serving best as an integrating bridge between two or more compact groups (Granovetter 1973, 1983). Moreover, a weakly-tied formation would seem to be inherently easily broken, and short-lived. Yet, a chimpanzee community is stable and long-lived. Some other forces of stability must underpin this social arrangement. We thus need to dig deeper into other possible anchors that foster social cohesion to keep this social system intact *despite* its weakly grounded social ties.

Self and Social Control

As discussed in Chapter 15, all primates have a species identify and a social identity but among the primates only apes and humans have a self-identity. The *potential* for a self-identity is hard-wired in humans and apes but its actuality is constructed slowly in stages. Because apes in social isolation fail to acquire a self-identity, the neurological circuitry that underpins a self must be activated by an external triggering process. And, following George Herbert Mead ([1934]1974), a self is activated only in a social environment by interactions with significant others and as a process.

In humans, this process starts when young children enter the *play stage* where they can assume the roles and attitudes of one concrete *other*. This is followed by a *game stage* when children can assume the roles and attitudes of a number of *concrete others* engaged in coordinated activities, such as varying positions in a sporting game. The last stage is reached when individuals acquire a consciousness of a *generalized other* by internalizing the roles, norms, and values of an entire community. As Mead ([1934]1974: 154) put it, "The attitude of the generalized other is the attitude of the whole community." That is, what goes to make up the mature self is the organization of the beliefs, values, and attitudes common to the social whole. Humans evidence a mature self when they take over the institutions of their community as a cognitive framework and adjust their conduct in accordance with the dictates of this framework. And, selves can only exist in precise relations with other selves in the context of a *generalized other* (Mead

[1934]1974: 164). Indeed, Mead's *generalized other* is very much in tune with Durkheim's notion of "collective representations" (see Turner 1982 for an analysis).

The foundational property of a *self*, Mead emphasized, is an ability to see oneself as a social object in an organizational and symbolic environment. A reflective self is truly a revolutionary behavioral capacity because it equips individuals with the cognitive facility to be both a private subject *and* a public object. And this capacity starts by taking the roles of significant others in the awakening process and this process, in turn, gives rise to the expansion of consciousness. It is a transcending process because it lets a person step outside oneself and become a thing in the external world and to become an object in a social field of selves. So, to participate in a community-based society built around a weakly-tied fission-fusion system, a sense of self is critical. This "theory of mind (TOM)," as it is called by those who have not read Mead, opens the door to a cognitive understanding of the thoughts and emotions of other selves in a social setting. Possessing an individual self then allows for forming different kinds of relationships, playing different roles, loving and hating, or changing oneself. And, with a self, persons can also talk and respond to themselves, enjoying themselves as a companion. And, by reorienting self towards the abstract generalized other, cognition is by nature a *transcending process linking dispersed individuals together* and, thereby, provides a basis for social integration and social control. As John Baldwin 2002: 113–114 emphasized:

> Mead's discussion of multiple selves reflects his structural view of the self. Taking the role of the generalized other and the larger community, people tend to perceive themselves as unified beings ... When we change from one set of social roles to another, different parts of our selves are emphasized ... It is because we can put ourselves into the roles of others and see their different points of view, that we can be different things for different people.

It is now well documented that chimpanzees possess a self-identity or a "theory of mind," an unfolding process that starts with role taking. Chimpanzee can take themselves as objects and take the roles and attitudes of other chimpanzees in specific social acts. They can also play different roles and have different relationships depending on whether someone is a relative, a good friend, or an occasional acquaintance. As a self is always activated outside the individual in a social milieu, it is by its very nature a social thing, a process triggered by interactions with significant others.

The organized self reaches its final phrase by acquiring the attitudes and values of the generalized other or the "community of attitudes" of the social whole that, in turn, facilitates the integration of the social whole.

We know that chimpanzees can recognize themselves in a mirror. And, they also possess a "theory of mind," because they can take themselves as an object, take others as an object, and take on the roles of other selves in a concrete setting. So we know that they can master Mead's *play* and *game stages* and these stages of self-identity are surely one indispensable cognitive pillar underpinning their weakly-tied social structure. But have chimpanzees mastered the last of Mead's stages leading to the mature self? Is there evidence of a capacity to generalize to a higher order abstract entity as in the *generalized other*? (for an excellent and lucid overview of Mead's ideas see Baldwin 2002).

Community

Let's imagine a chimpanzee society of 100 or so individuals moving about in a social universe of up to 30+ miles depending on the distribution of resources. Encountering community members by chance, chimpanzees usually elicit greeting rituals that vary from vocalizations, patting shoulders, and kissing hands to embracing good friends. During the day individual members pass time by joining others in a variety of social activities but, otherwise, stable groups do not exist outside of mother and dependent offspring.

While endowed by nature with a rugged individualism, it seems clear that chimpanzees have a dual identity—a personal self and a collective self. So they are individualists but not exclusive individuals because they experience and see themselves as part of a fluid and dispersed community of other selves. So in a concrete social setting, when chimpanzees engage in symbolic interactions, they can be both subject and object to themselves; and they can also role-take and, thereby, infer the desires, beliefs, and intentions of all the other selves present. While most animals have some capacity for symbolization, chimpanzees are clearly endowed with sophisticated symbolic abilities. Free-ranging chimpanzees have a large repertoire of shared symbolic gestures, affording them an ability to move ideas from one mind to another. Under experimental conditions, they also have the unusual ability to spontaneously understand human speech—even sentences—and then respond to these linguistic symbols by learning a human sign language or an arbitrary symbolic system associated with a computer-based keyboard.

Chimpanzees can also use numbers to count things and to understand the underpinning relations among objects that are otherwise distinctly different. That is, they have an ability to understand that the defining object properties might not lie in the object individually but in the relations of the properties of various objects to each other (Haun 2009). They also have a surprising capacity for cognitive organization and classification and, seemingly, share with humans a similar internal representation of the external world, albeit in a more simplified way. This largely covert cognitive power of chimpanzees points to the complexity of the chimpanzee mind (for discussions, see Beran et al. 2015; Melis, Hare and Tomasello 2009; Seyfarth and Cheney 2011; MacLean and Hare 2012; Proctor et al. 2012; Karg et al 2015; Yamamoto, Humle and Tanaka 2012; Whiten 2013). And, these covert talents extend to the following documented symbolic abilities:

- An ability to represent both abstract and concrete objects symbolically
- An ability to know which symbols are appropriate in a social milieu
- An ability to read the symbols of others and to reciprocate in kind
- An ability to acquire, use and read symbols in ways that allow for cooperation and mutual adjustment among individuals and promote interaction and solidarity.

We know that chimpanzees have a "theory of mind" when they engage in social interactions with others in concrete social environments. A mature self, however, also embodies the attitudes, beliefs, and values of *no specific other* or what Mead called the *generalized other* and what Durkheim called "collective representations." Does the chimpanzee self also embody a generalized other? A sense of something greater than the sum of individuals in the form of a collective whole is a cognitive leap to another level of reality in empirical terms, but Durkheim gave us a germinal clue on how to detect its reality. It entails deeply-felt emotions. As discussed earlier, Durkheim outlined two kinds of social sentiments (1) sentiments in daily life that link individuals in an interdependence that still keeps individuality and personality intact, and (2) sentiments that link individuals to a common collective entity, that integrates individuals into a social whole.

While the possession of a *generalized other* can only be inferred among chimpanzees (or humans for that matter), all researchers agree that chimpanzees share a "sense of community." A sense of community, by definition, is a transcendental thing that is not perceived as a specific or concrete other but as an emotionally-charged and generalized set of attitudes and expectations of the community.

What are the benefits of this sense of community? One social benefit is that a sense of the collective whole buttresses momentary face-to-face interactions, which, alone, are surely not enough to stabilize a society held together by mostly weak ties. If we consider a chimpanzee fission-fusion system where chimpanzees socialize and cooperate only part of the time, and where individuals do not see each other for weeks or months, another looping property is needed or social fragmentation could easily occur. How, then, are the interpersonal gaps filled with such free individualists who often forage for long distances and rarely assemble as a compact grouping in propinquity to become collectively integrated? What glue fills in the gaps and holes in such discontinuous face-to-face relations among community members?

When individuals are dispersed in large expansions of territory and interactions involving mutual role taking are sporadic and episodic, there appears to be a macro-level emergent force that provides a common reference for self-evaluations and guidance. This force has power in primates such as chimpanzees and humans that can role take, or assume the perspective of abstract symbolic frameworks that set an emotionally valenced sense of a shared community and the symbols denoting this community. As individuals can only loop in so many other selves and take in their attitudes, seeing self as not only an object to oneself and to others in situations but also *as a member of a community*, another force of social interaction is unleashed—a unity that does not rely directly on any concrete individuals; a force I would call "*the community complex.*"

It is well established that orangutans and gorillas possess a self—at least a "theory of mind," so it is likely that this trait was inherited from the LCA of apes and humans. But do all apes have a full-blown mature self in Mead's terms? After forty years studying orangutans, some researchers are convinced the red apes have a communal structure, but their reclusive habits suggest only a razor-thin "sense of community." But the precise emotions needed to generate the *community complex* in a social field are unknown. Gorillas live in distinct bands although interactions among three or more bands indicate a higher level of organization. Only our close cousins the chimpanzees have a well documented sense of community that points to a three-tiered mature self—a sense of self as a cognitive model in the brain, a sense of self in relation to specific others, and a sense of self in relation to the "generalized other" or the embodiment of the entire community. So once the capacity to see self exists, it can be built upon. Given that chimpanzees are the most social of all apes, they likely evolved a "generalized other" much like humans.

In chimpanzees, however, the *community complex* is one in which individuals live within a commonwealth, keeping male intruders out and otherwise protecting their homeland. And, a sense of community (as with humans) will surely vary in degree among age and sex classes. For example, chimpanzee adolescents, young adults and middle age males are far more social than adult females or older males. Thus, the long years of socialization for young chimpanzees are crucial because social cohesion rests on the transmission of social traditions and on the degree to which individuals internalize the sentiments or the "collective representations" of their community. Community is an emergent property, linked to social control and integration of a chimpanzee population by regulating a society of selves within a geographical space. For example, recent evidence that chimpanzee mothers forage in distinct forest pathways that they can eventually pass on to their sons after death means that males can inherit foraging rights (Mitani 2008), suggesting community rules over the allocation of such resources as a foraging area. This again is a collective awareness or a "sense of community," as Jane Goodall phrased it, and rights and obligations within this community. While a sense of community in humans is not always present, it can easily be triggered and expressed in the right social matrix. It is a transcending property of the social mind that cuts across regional space and rises above individual selves and goes far behind the limits of the senses. It is something abstract and yet it is emotionally felt within a conceptual field. Chimpanzee and human brains are seemingly adapted to seek out and perceive this transcendental sense of community.

Moreover, given that humans and chimpanzees shared a recent common ancestor, it would seem that individualism, self, and community are *all part of an inherited package* that has served as the underpinnings for integration in low-density networks among highly intelligent animals. Indeed, a community structure differs dramatically from strong-tie networks that are largely built from ties of consanguinity. If not kinship ties, how else is structure and continuity across large networks of individuals built before the rise of the state? A community organization allows for fields of selves to link up and feel a sense of belonging, a relational structure where more than one center exists. It is elusive, composed mostly of voluntary ties and, yet, it evokes a communal spirit. And, this perception exists in the mind and is not a tangible thing that you can touch, see, smell or hear but it is "there" as a sense of community. And, it evokes emotions, harmony, connections, and exchanges by creating a unity that does not belong to any specific set of individuals. Indeed, for some researchers (Mervin Verbit) a community is a key component of religiosity. In fact, it may be the *sine qua non* of the religious sentiment.

Thus, following Durkheim's guidelines, enough evidence is now on the table to reasonably consider chimpanzee societies as good models for evaluating the rest of Durkheim's core assumptions on the origin and nature of society. His premises on individualism, horde, lack of kinship in proto-human societies, and female-biased "exogamy" are overall supported, with some modifications to be sure (which he anticipated). Yet, it is one thing to find support for Durkheim's premises and another to see if this support helps us answer the next interesting question: do chimpanzees have the evolutionary precursors for a proto-religiosity that with subsequent selection pressures evolved into a religious institution in human communities? In the last chapter, we will take up this challenge.

17
Secrets of the Totem

> *It is impossible for men to live together and be in regular contact with one another without their acquiring some feeling for the group which they constitute through having united together, without their becoming attached to it, concerning themselves with its interests and taking it into account in their behaviour. And this attachment to something that transcends the individual . . . is the very wellspring of all moral activity.*
>
> Émile Durkheim ([1902]1984: xliii) Preface to the second edition of the *Division of Labor:* Some remarks on professional groups

Durkheim defined religion as beliefs and emotional-arousing practices revolving around sacred things in association with a community or a Church. His preoccupation with religion was important but secondary to his actual goal of uncovering the moral forces that underlie social solidarity or as he put it in 1888, "what holds aggregates together," which he considered the foremost problem of sociology. Durkheim hoped his focus on religion, which he viewed as social life itself in the earliest societies, would point the way toward a rewarding line of inquiry. In this regard, Durkheim made note of the centrality of rituals during the *formative* stage of religion.[1] Now if we use Durkheim's definition of religion, are their any practices or precursors of religiosity in chimpanzee societies?

Rituals and the Sacred

In the previous chapter, we viewed chimpanzee societies through the lens of Durkheim's portrayal of the horde. Are there any precursors in

---

[1] Durkheim's definition of religion has both beliefs and rites on an equal footing. But that one is more developed in the early stage of religion he had this to say: "there can be no ritual without myth, for a rite necessarily assumes that things are represented as being sacred and this *représentation* can only be mythical. On the other hand, one must recognize that in less advanced religions, rites are already developed and definite when myths are still very rudimentary." ([1899]1975: 99: footnote 25).

chimpanzee societies that also fit Durkheim's conception of religion? Religion starts with humans and nomadic hunter-gatherers, of course, but Durkheim's definition does not easily fit what has been recorded because, for him, it is sacred myths and rituals toward totems or their symbolic representations that is the original defining character of religion, whereas for many if not most religion theorists, there must also be some conception of a supernatural realm, set apart from the mundane realm of daily activity, even if this realm is a simple dream world or place where ancestors can be accessed. Durkheim pays less attention to this dimension of religion because his primary goal is not to explain religion, per se, but the original basis of integration among individualistic humans. So, with this qualification, let me focus on what Durkheim emphasized.

Rituals

Do chimpanzees engage in spiritual-like rituals? Jane Goodall (2005: 273) reflecting on her forty-four years of studying free-ranging chimpanzees answered this question in an illuminating way:

> [Chimpanzees] ... demonstrate, on scientific as well as intuitive grounds, that we humans are not ... the only living beings with personalities, minds capable of rational thought, and emotions similar to—and sometimes perhaps identical to—those that we call happiness, sadness, fear, anger, and so on. The great apes have brains more like ours than that of any other living creature. They demonstrate the ability to make as well as use tools. They are capable of intellectual performances that we once thought unique to ourselves, such as recognition of self, abstraction and generalization, cross-modal transfer of information, and theory of mind. They have a sense of humor ... Perhaps, after all, it is not so ridiculous to speculate as to whether chimpanzees might show precursors of religious behavior. In fact, it seems quite possible that they do.

As an example, Goodall (2005: 275–277) described the "waterfall dance" where chimpanzees face an ethereal and, yet, also roaring waterfall swaying in rhythmic movements with expressions of awe and wonder. Such humanlike ritualized behaviors prompted Goodall to emphasize that it was time to open our minds to the cognitive states of other intelligent beings, if only to better understand the underpinnings of human spirituality. While Goodall acknowledges that it cannot be proved one way or the other whether chimpanzees experience "spirituality," she thinks it possible they have the "precursors of religious behaviour" that undergird religion as a human institutional system.

In line with Goodall, N.J. Allen (1998: 158) notes that "effervescent assemblies" are not unique to humans because chimpanzees also engage in high-spirited gatherings, suggesting a proto-human origin that goes back millions of years. And, documented chimpanzee social rituals actually go back to the nineteenth century. In 1844, Thomas Savage described a gathering of chimpanzees:

> ... They occasionally assemble in large numbers in gambols ... not less than 50 engaged in hooting, screaming and drumming with sticks on old logs.
>
> (quoted in Reynolds 1965: 157)

In 1896, R.L. Garner, a self-trained zoologist in Gabor, described a sequence of events where a chimpanzee made a drum-like object out of clay obtained by a riverback of a stream. To intensify the sound, the clay object was put on a peat bed that seemingly served as a resonance cavity. When the drum was ready, Garner (1896: 59–60) described what in native tongue is called *Kanjo*, a kind of riotous gambol or a *carnival*:

> After the drum is quite dry, the chimpanzees assemble by night in great numbers, and the carnival begins. One or two will beat violently on this dry clay, while others jump up and down in a wild and grotesque manner. Some of them utter long, rolling sounds, as if trying to sing. When one tires of beating the drum, another relieves him, and the festivities continue ...

Henry Nissen, an early primatologist and world authority on chimpanzees (as well as past director of Yerkes Laboratory of Primate Biology) studied free-ranging chimpanzees in what was then Western French Guinea and wrote of their carnival activities (1931: 89):

> Most of the chimpanzee behavior which I observed is, perhaps, of a relatively unspectacular nature, but certainly their sound-production cannot be accused of lacking a melodramatic quality. Although the cries and drumming presaged no danger to human listeners, in fact such sound invariably ceased as soon as the apes became aware of our presence, their very intensity was sufficient to inspire, if not fear, than something akin to excited wonderment ... my guides and porters sometimes trembled perceptibly in spite of themselves.

Nissan (1931: 89) expressed regret over his inadequate verbal descriptions of chimpanzee sound-productions, wishing he had, in hand, phonographic discs to reproduce their " simultaneously vocalizing and drumming," but in his ears the drumming closely resembled the "dull beating of native drums."

In 1965, two anthropologists, Vernon and Frances Reynolds studying free-ranging chimpanzees in Uganda also observed a chimpanzee ritual using tree planks to create a bass drumming sound by beating their hands and feet on specific tree planks. They also observed party activities with lots of drumming, hooting, and screaming during the day and night. With all the carnival antics they documented, they reported an important regularity (1965: 158–159): "groups which had moved closer to each other slowly and noisily over a long period beforehand got into this wildly excited state when they finally met up." Oddly enough, chimpanzee highly emotional carnivals resemble Durkheim's conjectured account (drawn from Spencer and Gillen's *The Native Tribes of Central Australia* ([1899]1938) in *The Elementary Forms* ([1912]1995: 217) and how these collective actions might actuate religiosity:

> Gathering seeds or plants necessary for food, hunting and fishing are not occupations that can stir truly strong passions. The dispersed state in which the society finds itself makes life monotonous, slack, and humdrum. Everything changes when a corroboree takes place ... An event of any importance immediately put him outside himself. Does he receive happy news? There are transports of enthusiasm. If the opposite happens, he is seen running hither and yon like a madman, giving way to all sorts of chaotic movements: shouting, screaming, gathering dust and throwing it in all directions, biting himself, brandishing his weapons furiously, and so on. The very act of congregating is an exceptionally powerful stimulant. Once the individuals are gathered together, a sort of electricity is generated from their closeness and quickly launches them to an extraordinary height of exaltation.

Recently, chimpanzee researchers, Kühl, Kalan, and Boesch et al. (2016) documented on film another intriguing set of chimpanzee activities involving heaps of rocks deliberately thrown and stacked. Oddly enough, these stone assemblages resemble human cairns (or stone structures) on sites found around the globe. In the archaeological record, human cairns are found next to burials as grave markers, or in association with shrines, sign posts or to mark a pathway. So researchers were amazed to discover such rock piles in four chimpanzee communities in Western Africa during a sampling period of thirty-four months. Using remote video cameras, researchers recorded a sequence of events performed by mostly male chimpanzees who approached specific target trees and threw rocks against them and into the gaps inside the trees, constructing rock piles. The sixty-four filmed cases of stone throwing involved three common ritualized segments: (1) picking up a rock accompanied by Piloerection (N=48), Swaying (N=35), Bipedal stance (N=25), Leaf-clipping (N=1), (2) vocalizations (N=50/50) and (3) throwing stones at a particular tree trunk (N=63) by banging (N=15), hurling (N=36) or tossing it into the gap or hollow of the tree (N=12). This ritual was followed by pant hooting (N=24) and drumming (N=21).

Why keep visiting a site to throw rocks at trees? And, why accompany the rock throwing with ritualized displays of swaying, vocalizing, screaming, and drumming? The researchers emphasized that it had nothing to do with foraging behavior, or any practical function they could fathom (Kühl, Kalan and Boesch et al. 2016). Nor could they account for why the chimpanzees targeted particular trees in their community. Is it merely play—a fun game? Do the chimpanzees simply like the sound that rocks make? It appears to be a longstanding "cultural" tradition because the trees are worn down and the stone accumulations are conspicuously visible. Are the trees sacred? Could this be a precursor of early religious rituals? The emotions that accompany the displays are suggestive of some sort of spiritual ritual directed at forces perceived to exist, but we are not privy to what chimpanzees believe or don't believe. But they clearly display the ritual side of this equation marking religion, which means that as the hominin brain began to grow rapidly with later *Homo erectus* the other half of the equation —thoughts and cognitions about a supernatural realm, however simple— would make such ritual sacred and spiritual at the dawn of human evolution.

The Sacred

Durkheim formally defined the sacred as something forbidden, or anything set apart from common things. In his first essay on religion in 1898, he depicted how exogamy and the incest taboo (which he combined into a single entity for his essay), originated in the belief that because the totem was a sacred thing, symbolizing the "community of the blood," sexual intercourse between members of the same totem was forbidden or tabooed.

Durkheim's idea of the sacred is vague and ambiguous because the only way he could account for this intangible property was to consign it to an inborn proclivity of human cognition. Nothing is inherently sacred, he said, whether the object is a real entity or an imagined one. Individuals can have personal objects sacred to them alone but objects become sacred in a religious sense only when they are set aside by the community at large as sacred things. And, once charged emotionally with collective sacredness these objects are, by their nature, perceived in human minds as something other than common or profane things. A religion then is born, Durkheim said, once collective representations are perceived as sacred things in human cognition.

In Durkheim's theory, the genesis of religious sentiments is a product of occasional assemblies by nomadic hunter-gatherers whose heightened sociality over time eventually lead to a state of "effervescence," that ushered in boundless energies, deepening passions, high levels of emotional arousal, and a heightening of the senses. So, a sense of the sacred is a direct outcome of these collectively aroused emotions of high intensity. To perpetuate this sense of the sacred, however, this primal "effervescence," must be renewed periodically by the physical assembly of the faithful and the execution of emotional-arousing rituals.

So, for Durkheim, the sacred is the distinctive trait of religious thought and an inherent property of the social mind. It is driven by the opposing forces of "primitive classifications," and especially the separation of sacred things from profane things. As Durkheim (and Mauss) expressed it ([1903]1963: 86):

> Things are above all sacred or profane, pure or impure, friends or enemies, favourable or unfavourable; i.e. their most fundamental characteristics are only expressions of the way in which they affect social sensibility. The differences and resemblances which determine the fashion in which they are grouped are more affective than intellectual.

As the sacred is a cognitive phenomenon that is superimposed on objects, it is always a symbolic representation of something else. It is a special force beyond the normal senses because it cannot be detected empirically, but it is nevertheless real, evoking strong emotions associated with awe, reverence, and respect. The sacred is also a highly contagious emotion, which is another reason why sacred things must be kept apart from profane things. And, just as the sacred can be anything at all—a sound, an individual, a waterfall or even a tree—the rituals of a community can also be anything once they are charged with a sacred character.

A concentration of individuals in an emotional state can easily spread whether the emotions expressed are joy, pleasure, anger, fear, or hate.

Recent studies of human neuroimaging have revealed that this spontaneous sharing of emotions is triggered neurologically by mirror neurons as well as the centers of the brain responsible for mimicry and rhythmic synchronization of talk and body movements—all of which allow individuals to experience the world in similar ways. As Nummenmaa et al. (2012: 9599) noted, "It is well documented that observation of others in a particular emotional state rapidly and automatically triggers the corresponding behavioral and physiological representation of that emotional state in the observer." So the neural circuits of humans appear to be inherently primed for synchronization both in thoughts and behaviors during affective-laden social events. This well-supported area of research lends substantial support to Durkheim's longstanding assumption that it is the sheer face-to-face concentration of individuals that acts as a spontaneous trigger for shared emotional feelings and brings minds together for a collective effervescence (for discussions see Nummenmaa et al. 2012, 2014; Hari et al. 2013; and Lahnakoski et al. 2014). So the possibility exists that the sacred was born in collective rituals inflamed by a common passion. And, that religion, above all, is respect for a community or society carried to a superlative degree of symbolic intensity.

Totemism

Classic Totemism: Problems of Definition and Structure

Totemism has fascinated scholars for generations, perhaps so much that aside from Durkheim (and Robertson Smith) many missed its significance for the very existence and persistence of human societies. Part of this fascination is the deductive nature of the word itself. While its origin is linked with the Ojibway dialect of the Algonquin stock of American Indians, early ethnographers apparently mispronounced its phonemic components because the word "totem" does not exist in Ojibway native tongue (see Chapter 11, footnote 4). Among American Indians a "totem" signified a family or clan, but it took on a life of its own once scholars became fixated on learning about its origin, content, and function. It was McLennan who stirred the totemic pot in his classic essay on "The Worship of Plants and Animals" (1869–1870) by associating totems with similar things around the globe and, as a result, proposed that all societies, even "civilized" ones, had likely passed through a totem stage of evolution. McLennan not only awakened scholarly interest in totemism but the educated public as well. So instead of the early Americanist depiction of totemism as a family crest, or an emblem, it got confounded with animal worship and evolutionary stage models of progress and change.

Following in McLennan's footsteps, Robertson Smith drew further attention to totemism by arguing in *Kinship and Marriage in Early Arabia and in the Religion of the Semites* (1885, 1889) that the ancient Arabs had once passed through a totemic stage of development. But it was Frazer's worldwide survey and essay on Totemism published in the famous ninth edition of the Encyclopedia Britanna (and, later, in a short book version in 1887) that set totemism up as an "established fact." Frazer highlighted five distinctive features of totemism:

- Totems usually involve a plant or animal and a classification of sacred objects.
- Taboos exist against eating a life form totemized.
- Totem members always practice exogamy.
- Totem groups originated with female descent.
- Totemism has both a social and a religious side.

The sense that totemism constituted a distinctive complex of traits gave it a new and longer life inquiry about totems in general, and about its origins, in particular. As one scholar put it, "[s]ince 1887, when J. G. Frazer published his little monograph on totemism, no topic in the wide field of social anthropology has aroused greater speculation and controversy amongst English and continental scholars" (Webster 1911: 471).

So the reality of totemism steamed ahead although nobody had ever seen a society on its way to becoming totemic or a full-blown totemic system. Instead, by 1890 articles and books began documenting the bits and pieces or leftover survivals of totemic systems. Finally, in 1899 with the publication of *Native Tribes of Central Australia*, with its ethnographic account of a totemic system that failed to comply with Frazer's established "facts," a new phrase of totemism began, with Frazer, himself, proposing three distinctive theories of totemism. In 1910 when Frazer published his classic three volumes on *Totemism and Exogamy*, the debates and controversies over totems had grown into an enormous literature but with little agreement on exactly what totemism was supposed to constitute. During the great totemic debates, Durkheim kept a low profile until he published *Elementary Forms* ([1912]1995: 101) when he expressed deep regrets over being forced to use a name (given its universal designation) that was so provincial and so semantically simplistic that it failed to capture what was really behind such a pivotal and complex phenomena. Unfortunately, Durkheim never shared what nomenclature he would have substituted in place of totemism.

If we consider Bellah's 1973 query at the start of this book on why Durkheim would devote nearly fifteen years of his career to totemism and especially Australian aboriginal cults, the answer surely lies in his determination to uncover the origins of forces that hold social aggregates together. Having discarded his original conceptual scheme of a "mechanical solidarity" where personal consciences are swallowed up by an all powerful collective conscience, totemism was now the only way Durkheim could conceive of to enable human aggregations to form a unity without kinship-based blood ties—at least in the beginnings of human society. All that was needed was for food-collecting nomads to come together during an effervescent assembly and to perceive an invisible power force that had to be made concrete. This concretizing of a sense of an external power was then placed on everyday plants and animals so that individuals could share in the "community of the blood" symbolized by the totem. But instead of bonds that originate with consanguinity, totemic bonds originate with an attachment to an object. Clearly, it was the cognitive ability of humans to attach to a shared external object and especially its symbolic representation that was pivotal for his thesis on social solidarity. For as Durkheim's emphasized ([1902]1985: 91) "Everything that concerns totemism necessarily has repercussions extending into all the domains of sociology, for totemism lies at the root of a multitude of institutions."

Yet, whatever the attributes of totemism, Central Australian aboriginals could not tell anyone about the nature of early totemism because of (a) the major disruptions to their culture traditions for nearly thirty years, (b) the decimation of their fragile flora and fauna to support a food collecting economy, (c) the drastic reductions in the size of their populations, and (d) the forced dependence of aboriginals on government handouts (see Chapter 9). Indeed, if Francis Gillen had not requested and incentivized reenactment of these totemic ceremonies by local aboriginals with offers of needed provisions for anyone who participated, no pictorial or widely disseminated written record of these rituals would exist today. Given the importance of totemic rituals and the fact that they had not been performed for many years actually symbolized the extent of destruction of aboriginal lifeways. But, when seen by European scholars at the time, they drew the interest and attention of many diverse scholars—from Durkheim through Fraser to Freud, who all attempted to interpret their meanings.

So what did the ethnography in Spencer and Gillen's *The Native Tribes of Central Australia* (1899) mean for Durkheim's theory? Durkheim was well aware that the Arrernte were not the "primitives" of a pristine population that Frazer and others had portrayed. Long before he *wrote Elementary Forms*, Durkheim had read the corpus of literature on Central Australian aboriginals such as the famed 1896 Horn Scientific Expedition to Central

Australia describing the ongoing trauma and collapse of native Australian society.[2] Today, we even know that the commonly-held view that Australian aboriginals were isolated from the outside world before the arrival of Europeans is erroneous. A recent genetic analysis reveals that Australian populations had multiple waves of migrations, especially from India, with one wave about 114 generations ago associated with the arrival of the dingo [a close resemblance to Indian dogs] (Pugach et al. 2013). Durkheim was also correct that totemism in Central Australia did not even remotely resemble the formative stages of totemic cults. What Spencer and Gillen's ethnography provided, however, was a fascinating portrait of an actual totemic system, albeit an institution that was slowly teetering on collapse.

Yet, despite the many problems with Australian totemism, Durkheim was convinced that his entire theory would collapse without reference to these data; and it is important to remember that at this stage of Durkheim's career he was fighting for his intellectual life—even as he was also a living icon in French intellectual circles. But his thesis was under constant attack; and he knew that he had to offer a coherent explanation, focusing on religion and totemism as a way to isolate out the more general forces holding human societies together. And, he felt it essential to consider the point of departure, albeit his conjectured account, or what today is called in biology, "founder's effect." If he could cast light on the origins of totemism, he felt he had a chance to uncover the ultimate causes that made the religious sentiments holding the social universe together. At the conclusion to this chapter, we will appraise the magnitude and importance of Durkheim's insights into totemism. But first it is essential to bring to light some hidden secrets of the totem.

More Contemporary Problems in Conceptualizing Totemism

Why did a generation of nineteenth and early twentieth-century scholars become so fixated on totemism? Seemingly, it was simply a mystifying

---

2 In *Elementary Forms*, Durkheim cited many references on Australian aboriginals. One was the Horn anthropology report by E.C. Stirling ([1912]1915: 91). As Sterling (1896: 4) wrote, "The vices and diseases of Europeans have already borne their evil fruit, and the native population ... has diminished with painful rapidity; whole tribes have vanished from the scene ... Through the heart of the continent from Adelaide to Port Darwin the telegraph line, in its construction and maintenance, has made the presence of the white man a familiar feature over a large area. East and west of it, for a considerable distance and for some years, the country has been occupied for pastoral pursuits, while exploring parties have intersected much of the remainder in various directions."

puzzle to be solved. Frazer's initial survey of totemism established its global presence and its association with fixed, characteristic features that formed a "totemic complex." A few early scholars were skeptical about such characteristic traits but it was not until Spencer and Gillen's 1899 ethnography that questions began to be asked: Do established totemic traits really form a fixed complex? How many totemic systems can be linked to species of plants and animals, marriage regulations, exogamy, or to taboos against eating your totem? Were the first totems really linked with matriliny? Must totem members share a common ancestor? Is anything truly related? Is there such a thing as a totemic complex? Is the totem always symbolized? But since nobody knew how totemism originated or what event or circumstance lead to the creation of a totemic system, the controversy raged on throughout the late nineteenth century and into the early twentieth century.

Durkheim was busy finishing *Elementary Forms* when Frazer published *Totemism and Exogamy* ([1910]1968), a four-volume series of more than 1,700 pages devoted mostly to a comprehensive survey of both totemism and exogamy in Africa, America, Australia, and around the globe. Frazer concluded that (1) exogamy and totemism are found together in many traditional societies but they are independent institutions with different origins and, thus, exogamy is not a fixed feature of totemism and, (2) totemism is a "crude superstition," a democratic "imaginary brotherhood" between a grouping of people and a grouping of natural or artificial things called totems. It has both a social and a religious side although its status as a religion is greatly exaggerated. Frazer added that the thoughts of those in the totemic stage are "essentially vague, confused, and contradictory" ([1910]1968: 3–5).

In conjunction with Frazer's biting critique of totemism, Alexander Goldenweiser published "Totemism: An Analytical Study" (1910), a work that Robert Jones (2005: 294) stamped as a "watershed" moment in the history of totemism. Goldenweiser, a student of Franz Boas, also highlighted the lack of characteristic features in the makeup of a totemic institution:

> [No] particular set of features can be taken as characteristic of totemism, for the composition of the totemic complex is variable; nor can any feature be regarded as fundamental, for not one of the features does invariably occur in conjunction with others; nor is there any evidence to regard any one feature as primary in order of development, or as of necessity original, psychologically.
>
> (1910: 269–270)

While Goldenweiser agreed that some traits such as exogamy were typically found with totemism, they were the outcome of different origins and different historical traditions. Moreover, given the variability of totemic features, Goldenweiser concluded that even the notion of a totemic institution was lost to all scientific value when applied to a worldwide phenomena. At best, what is specific to totemism is an abstract expression of relations where variable combinations of traits get associated and fixed over time into a complex, creating a cognitive unity. What mattered was the relations among the elements that were brought together, an association usually linked with organizational units such as clans and phratries. The causes of these trait associations were "theoretically interesting" but unknown, he added, attributing the similar patterns found in totemic complexes in Australia, America and Africa to "convergent evolution" (1910: 273). The impact of Goldenweiser's paper was so epoch-making that Robert Lowie (1911: 207) dubbed it "the prolegomena to all positive attempts at a sane interpretation of 'totemic' institutions."[3]

Goldenweiser also dismissed totemism as a religion but agreed that the objects and symbols associated with totemism have strong emotional values for totem-mates. And, while the components of totemic complexes will vary from place to place and from time to time, the particular association of elements did create definite social units, and he regarded the social aspect of totemism as all important.

Having largely dismissed totemism as a religion, it is not surprising that two years later Goldenweiser (1912: 735) published a scathing critique of *Elementary Forms* (1912), attacking Durkheim on all fronts—his methods, his theory of social solidarity, his theory of ritual, his theory of knowledge, his gross misconception of the relationship between the individual and society and, above all, his unproved thesis "*that the fundamental reality underlying religion is society.*" Adding fuel to this firestorm, Goldenweiser also initiated a symposium on totemism by writing to the editor of *Anthropos* that "the appearance of Durkheim's brilliant but unconvincing treatise on religion brings home the fact that one of the phases of socio-religious thought, namely the problem of totemism, remains as replete with vagueness and mutual misunderstanding as ever" (quoted in Kuper 1988: 120).

---

3 During this period, other leading American anthropologists—even Franz Boas (1910) published similar views that totemism is not a motif of fixed traits nor is it essentially the same everywhere. But Lowie (1911: 206–207) said that Goldenweiser "has been the first to show at length, and with irrefragable logic, that totemism can not be treated as an integral datum . . ."

The *Anthropos* totem symposium remained an open forum for years, giving leading scholars around the globe every opportunity to express their disillusionment with totemism, with Durkheim's thesis often serving as a catalyst for unremitting attacks against totemism. Even in France, Arnold van Gennep ([1913]1975: 207–208), a fervent critic of Durkheim, called the foundation and construction of *Elementary Forms* "unstable" and "unsound," adding in a barbed wit that Durkheim "turns phenomena and living beings into those scientifically dried plants to be found in a herbarium."

So, despite Durkheim's effort to clarify his ideas and rebut earlier attacks on his totemic thesis, he was encircled with biting critiques. Indeed, as Roscoe Hinkle (1960: 267) noted, "During the period 1890–1917, few European sociologists were more generally disregarded and less enthusiastically received by American sociology than Durkheim." *Elementary Forms* is so large and complex because Durkheim was trying to address all his critics but, in the end, he seemed to have failed—miserably. These ongoing attacks are surely another reason for his early sudden death along with the utter dismay over the loss of his son, students, and colleagues in World War I, and near the end of his life, he may have begun to wonder if his iconic status in French intellectual circles was also in danger of being lost, forever.[4]

In 1917, Goldenweiser (p.321) wrote another devastating critique of *Elementary Forms*, this time by vilifying two themes central to Durkheim's thesis; (1) the individual and society and (2) the origin and nature of religion: "[O]ne closes the book [*Elementary Forms*] with a melancholy assurance that Durkheim has left these two perennial problems where he found them." Durkheim was surely aware of Goldenweiser's earlier critiques

---

[4] As a focus of controversy, *Elementary Forms* received an eclectic mix of reviews. See Edward Tiryakian 2012 for a truly delightful account of an American graduate student visiting Paris in 1914 writing to his mentor on Durkheim's "must-read" book. In England, Sidney Hartland (1913) gave the book a thoughtful positive review, calling it a "brilliant volume;" whereas Bronislaw Malinowski (1913) ended his otherwise negative review with faint praise. In Scotland, G.A. Johnston (1916) considered it an "important work" whether right or wrong because Durkheim at least tried to interpret facts and to understand the nature of religion. In America, Hutton Webster (1913) praised the book as "elaborate, scholarly, and well-reasoned" (having earlier in 1911 attacked Goldenweiser for his misguided study of totemism); A.B. Lewis (1917) and anonymous in *The Biblical World* (1916) gave the book a lukewarm review; Wilson Wallis (1914) apparently misunderstood Durkheim's thesis; and Ulysses Weatherly (1917: 563) noted that Durkheim's ideas have "at least the merit of consistency."

but given that this one was published in March of 1917, and Durkheim died shortly after in November of 1917, he probably never read it—which is just as well.[5]

Of all things, Goldenweiser began to reverse some of his earlier ideas on totemism by concluding in 1918 (and with shocked anti-totemists lamenting his dramatic reversal), that more restricted and concrete totemic complexes actually do exist, especially those associated with clan-based societies. Thus, despite the variability in totemic features, Goldweiser (1918: 289) proposed that tendencies exist for a common nucleus of traits, and he attributed these resemblances to the operation of similar mechanisms of a "general socio-psychological kind." In essence, Goldenweiser suggested (now in line with Durkheim) that the social environment creates particular demands and tendencies. While totemic complexes vary, such that no features are inherently totemic, they become so in given contexts. In clan-based societies, given the intimate association that aboriginals have with the natural environment, these spontaneous tendencies bring together certain features into a totemic complex. The first demand is to classify or identify subunits usually by name. Social units then project a communal spirit on to some plant or animal (and a hypothetical common ancestor) that symbolize clan unity, and these come to embody a spiritual crown or halo of sanctity.

While Goldenweiser danced around the notion of a deeply-rooted reason for totemism, by 1931 he was convinced that in totemic communities high emotions and ideological relations are universal components, that exogamy is nearly always present, and that relations between plants and animals are common as are taboos with a mystic affinity. He also called attention to the many totemic analogues in modern societies where complementary social units charged with intense emotions, adopt a mélange of animal mascots, emblems, banners, flags, buttons, tattoos and the like. As Goldenweiser (1931: 391) expressed it:

> In one form or another the mystic and social tendencies of totemic days linger on in modern society. But we miss them on its highways. Here and there, under specially favorable conditions, these tendencies may flare up in a sort of totemic glow . . .

---

5 Durkheim's son died in 1915 while fighting in Salonica although the Durkheim family did not receive official word of his death for some months. Despite his great sorrow, Durkheim continued to teach until he had a nervous breakdown in 1916; then, despite some recovery, he died, seemingly of a stroke.

Yet, despite Goldenweiser's change of heart, his satirical essays had set in motion a diminishing interest in totemism and the fire of curiosity faded, although the nature and origins of totemism remained an unsolved puzzle.

In 1962, Levi-Strauss in a little book called *Totemism* reviewed the English, French, and American literature and concluded that totemism as it had been theorized was simply an illusion and, thus, did not exist in its present understanding. In a novel approach, he broke the concept down and then recreated a model of its structure. Totemism, Levi-Strauss averred, is a system of classification created by grouping similar plant and animal species and selecting differences among these relatively similar phenomena. After assembling the contrasts among otherwise similar plant and animal species, these variations are then used to highlight and symbolize these differences. This results in a number of equivalent and homologous subgroups that serve, in turn, as a type of classification system. Thus, for Levi-Strauss, animals or plants are not chosen because they are good to eat but because they are easy to think about and use as markers of differences. What is real about totemism is (a) that it is a particular illustration of certain kinds of universal thinking and (b) that it is a part of human culture.

In a radical way, Levi-Strauss proposed that what was viewed as a totemic complex was really an example of universal thought processes and certain modes of binary oppositions by the perception not of similarities but of differences that served to generate a system—a position that is not radically different from Mauss and Durkheim's thesis in *Primitive Classification* (1903). So if one group called themselves the bear totem and another the fox totem, the differences between these species served as a symbolic metaphor to differentiate the groups. Levi-Strauss's intent was to uncover the properties underlying human cognition and in the case of totemism what was hidden behind totems as concrete objects. For Levi-Strauss, the features of totemism were arbitrarily assembled and so, scholars who sought to understand the origin and function of totemism were operating with a "totemic illusion."

Totemism then is not primitive nor a historical reality in any meaningful sense but an object of logic, a cognitive classification that is grounded in human neurology rather than any original form of organization. All minds are the same; what differs are the kinds of problems humans confront and how they are addressed. Yet, underlying all human classifications are deep structures that lay behind the veneer of surface phenomena. Thus, in Levi-Strauss's scheme, totem-mates sustain their society through unconscious logically ordered models lodged in the neurology of the brain. As all models are essentially products of human minds (which operate in the same way), all societal members must share these basic structures of the mind, or a universal "code of logic," with each culture resting on a variant of this code of logic. By isolating and observing models such as totemism, the rules that humans use to relate, perceive, and interpret their experiences can be discovered, with all societal models only variant expressions of this underlying universal structure.

A Totemic System from Scratch?

While Durkheim had long lamented that known totemic societies consisted only of fragmentary leftovers or ones in varying stages of decay, without anyone witnessing the birth of a totemic system, it is ironic that, in 1924, Ralph Linton published "Totemism and the A.E.F," a detailed account of nothing less than an empirical chronicle on the formation of totemic-like beliefs and practices. Linton's description might have spared the social sciences decades of time in search of the origins of totemism because if such systems were a natural force of social solidarity, it was likely that they would be constantly forming at many different levels of social organization in all organized societies—as Linton made clear in his descriptive analysis briefly summarized below. Ironically, it was the social environment during World War I that provided an intriguing portrait of just how totem-like structures might have originally developed in human societies. Much time and ink could have been saved.

In 1917, when the United States declared war on Germany, and an immediate call was issued for a build up of army forces, the National Guard Divisions were federalized. Some states lacked National Guard units, so Douglas MacArthur (at this time a major) proposed the creation of a single divisional organization that would "stretch over the whole country like a rainbow" (Gilbert 1994). To represent this country-wide diversity, the 42nd division or *Rainbow division* was created with recruits from twenty-six states and the District of Columbia. In line with other units, Ralph Linton and other enlisted men of the 42nd division were required to wear a shoulder patch icon with a singular crest that depicted the hues of a rainbow to symbolize the nickname. At first, Linton said, the *Rainbow* name was rarely used by the 42nd division but soon a "growth of a feeling of divisional solidarity" arose spontaneously and the namesake became a protected designation by Rainbow division members. So when members were asked who they were, nine out of ten members replied: "I'm a Rainbow." As Linton (1924: 297) described this transition:

> After six months, "A feeling of connection between the organization and its namesake was first noted . . . At this time it was first suggested

and then believed that the appearance of a rainbow was a good omen for the division. Three months later it had become an article of faith in the organization that there was always a rainbow in the sky when the division went into action. A rainbow over the enemy's lines was considered especially auspicious, and after a victory men would often insist that they had seen one in this position even when the weather conditions or direction of advance made it impossible. This belief was held by most of the officers and enlisted men, and anyone who expressed doubts was considered a heretic and overwhelmed with arguments.

At one point when the 42nd *Rainbow* division noticed that the 77th *Goddess of Liberty* division decorated their carts and other properties with the *Goddess* logo, the 42nd division began decorating their carts and items with the Rainbow logo. Soon, Rainbow members were so possessive of their "coat-of-arms" that anyone else who wore a symbol of a rainbow was resented—even punished. Even recruits sent in for replacements had to be formally recognized as rainbow members before they were entitled to wear the emblem (for more on insignias see Kauffmann 1919).

Veneration for names and representative symbols was commonplace, Linton emphasized, as "All the other army organizations which were in existence long enough to develop a feeling of group solidarity seem to have built up similar complexes centering about their group names." When the war ended, the A.E.F. had "well defined, and often mutually jealous groups each of which had its individual complex of ideas and observances." These complexes all conformed to the same military pattern but they all had different names, symbols and content. This, Linton said, served a dual purpose by linking members within divisions into tight-knit cliques for a united front, while a common military pattern provided a basis for tolerance and mutual understanding by creating a common conceptual framework and a united front against forces outside the system.

In his summary, Linton reported that once the "totem" complexes were developed the following conditions operated:

All personnel were divided into a number of groups with members of each group aware of their distinctness.

All groups were identified by a distinctive symbol associated with an object, an animal species or a natural phenomenon.

The divisional name was used as a personal identification by members when in company with outsiders.

A symbol of the group namesake was used to decorate group and personal adornments, with strong taboos forbidding use by outsiders.

A referential feeling existed towards both the group name and its symbolic representations.

In many cases, division members shared an unformulated but taken for granted belief that the group's namesake was a protector with prophetic, far-seeing powers.

Had such behaviors been found among aboriginals, Linton noted, most researchers would conclude they are part of a "totemic complex." And, while Australians aboriginals had a far more developed totemic complex, Linton thought the A.E.F. complexes as rich as some among North American aboriginals. Linton asked: Is there any real difference in cognition between an aboriginal who calls himself a Kangaroo, and a soldier who calls himself a Rainbow? Even when Rainbow members were asked about the emotions they felt between themselves and their namesake, they either had no idea, or their answers were emotionally elusive and mostly made-up. Instead, for the 42nd division, the Rainbow emblem took on a sacred quality.

The A.E.F. units differed in content from classic totemism in the lack of marriage regulations, beliefs associated with a common ancestor, and in special rituals to perpetuate the totems. But Linton (p. 299) believed that "both the A.E.F. complexes and primitive totemism are results of the same social and supernaturalistic tendencies" (he attributed the difference to the physical and social environments that shaped their expression). In aboriginal societies, these proclivities crystallized around a clan-based formation, whereas in the military they crystallized around a military formation. But they shared a structural similarity that aroused high emotions and induced a spiritual quality. And, for Durkheim, of course, once the sacred component exists, the potential is there for religious-like sentiments. True, the Rainbow namesake lacked a plant or animal totem. But Durkheim was adamant that totemism had nothing to do with animal worship, per se. For him, the essence of totemism was the relational attitude of individuals as a collective body to a reverential object of any sort whether it be artificial, natural, or organic phenomena.

The 42nd division was deactivated after World War I but was reconstructed again in 1943 with the same shoulder sleeve insignia worn in World War I. Out of respect for the older unit, the reconstituted unit in a celebration paid homage to the original unit as a past lineage of "ancient ancestors" who had "carried the blood."

The Origin of Totemic Complexes

Durkheim, Goldenweiser, Levi-Strauss, and Linton all viewed totemism in a broader perspective, but only Linton, as an enlisted soldier (and trained anthropologist), witnessed and participated in the origination of what appears to mirror the arrangement and relational features of a traditional totemic complex. In clan-based societies, a founding myth exists to justify a totem species. In the 42nd division, members lacked an origin myth and also initially lacked an emotional connection to their totem, but Durkheim had long ago proposed that to generate such an emotional connection took only the occasional meeting up of an aggregate—the sheer fact of association to generate an effervescence. What were the Rainbow men feeling? They didn't know; they simply experienced a special "feeling of connection." Given that the nickname was chosen by a ranking official because it represented volunteer recruits from different states, Rainbow members were strangers to each other. First, came the name symbolized by a shoulder patch of red, yellow and blue strips resembling a rainbow. After six months, recruits experienced an esprit de corps that involved a sense of solidarity, common perceptions, and loyalty. This was evident when a rainbow appearing in the sky was perceived as a good omen, indeed an article of faith after a successful battle when mates paid homage to the sighting of a rainbow despite weather conditions that made it impossible. And this belief, Linton said, was held by most officers and enlisted men and it was heresy to cast any doubts. Soon, the rainbow logo was painted on military equipment and personal items.

What underlies the emotions and unity expressed by Rainbow and other divisional complexes? Kinship or even friendship relations can be ruled out because the 42nd division represented a motley crew of newcomers. What looks familiar? What's behind the neurological propensity of humans to generate such complexes? Tracing the origin of the Rainbow division provides many clues to understanding what had for so long been a mysterious curious phenomenon but, in fact, was and is a rather common phenomenon because it is so fundamental to human social organization. Yet, it does not tell us about the origins of this cognitive capacity or the need humans have to totemize key social relations. Yet, as Linton (1924: 300) expressed it, "The ease and rapidity with which the army complexes were developed suggests that the tendencies underlying them were deep-seated and only awaited a chance for expression."

Totemism is, above all, a relational system that brings individuals together without genealogical blood ties. Totem-mates, however, must already have in place the neurobiology to attach themselves to an object of some sort—and then to experience collective relations of an emotionally charged affiliation with an external object. The object can be anything—organic, inorganic, or mythical. The novelty of a totemic connection is that totem-mates are able to attach to an external object or its symbolic representation rather than initially attaching directly to each other. It is what Durkheim ([1887]1975: 36) sought so long ago when he described two forms of social tendencies: (1) ones that link individuals within a community on a day-to-day basis; and (2) ones that link individuals to the social whole. The first, he said, leaves individuality mostly intact, whereas the second gives rise to obligations because individuals become a part of a greater social whole by adhering to its movements and its pressures. It is the latter one, Durkheim said, that has played a role in the genesis of religion.

What Underlies Totemism

By definition, classic totemism is a special emotional relation between a group and an external object—usually a plant, animal, or a cosmic object of some sort.

An association assumes a sharing of something but a totem connection does something special—it creates a sense of unity by entwining group members into a symbolic and emotional field, even without ongoing face-to-face social relations. What root cognitive process might underlie a phenomenon that connects emotions to a self-identity or to a collective-identity tied to a totem, with the mysterious ability to get individuals so charged emotionally that they develop strong commitments to a collectivity that is symbolized by a totem? In clan-based societies, totems are used to differentiate related clans, giving clan-mates an identity, an emotional identity that feels like blood-kinship. A clan then unites under the banner of collective interests that include mutual aid, obligations, inheritances, and other collective obligations. In clan-based societies, totems are usually associated with exogamy and other marriage regulations, often with taboos forbidding the killing and eating of your totem and a variety of rites and beliefs.

In industrial societies, as Linton emphasized, a totem can be used as a strategic device to anchor and unify strangers into a cohesive military unit. Indeed, as Goldenweiser highlighted, totemism is an important cognitive device that can be utilized in virtually all types of sociocultural formations. A recent case in point is Alexander Riley's (2014, 2015) ethnographic study of a small Chapel located near Shanksville, Pennsylvania that is dedicated to the memory of United Flight 93, the plane that crashed in a nearby field after being hijacked by terrorists on September 11, 2001. To commemorate the passengers who died after storming the cockpit and successfully foiling the intended attack on Washington, DC, the chapel is a hallowed memorial site to honor their collective memory. Utilizing what he calls "Durkheiman tools," Riley provides a detailed analysis of the elaborate web of beliefs, practices, and symbolic objects that spontaneously arose in association with the crash, and he offers a Durkheimian interpretation to account for the communal solidarity and regular attendance of congregants who now participate in yearly ritualized ceremonies and other occasions. It is also noteworthy of how the American flag came to symbolize the forty deceased patriots; how its totemization is coupled with a totemic myth; and how the flag and its symbolic representations are now the source of a collective identity for the totem-mates Riley calls the "Stars and Stripes clan." As these collective emotionally charged totemic-like formations occur with a high frequency in different times and places all over the globe, it is clearly a pan-human proclivity. It is nothing less than an evolutionary product of the social mind as it evolved along the hominin line from a common ancestor very much like present-day chimpanzees because they have much of the preliminary neurological wiring in place, thereby making it relatively easy for natural selection to make the final push to full-blown totemism among humans.

While a normal and constant occurrence, as Collins (1988, 2004) analysis of interaction rituals underscores, what is remarkable is the utility a totem has to underpin all sorts of diverse social formations. Totems usually serve to divide a population up into units of some sort, whether clans in traditional societies or corporate units, social categories of persons, or associations among individuals and different types of social units in modern, differentiated societies. But far more importantly, is its rare ability to integrate a population without familiar or blood-tied connections. Yet, as common as it is in human societies, it is exceedingly rare in the biotic world. For most social mammals, the sharing of blood-ties is the main source of social integration, although bioprogrammers for herding and other collective formations operate somewhat as a biologically based equivalent of what humans do when they totemize social relations. Still, for most animals, once members of a population move beyond one-to-one chain-linkages and direct ties or social formations beyond packs, pods, prides, and troops, much larger organizational structures become impossible to form. Indeed, the *in*ability of most social mammals to associate with strangers is the reason that large-scale societies are so rare among mammals (Machalek 1992). Indeed, only humans, insects, and micro-organisms reveal what Herbert Spencer (1874–1896) called superorganisms, or organization among organisms. And while Spencer and Durkheim in their early work emphasized structural interdependence and common culture (Spencer also stressed power as an integrative mechanism more than Durkheim), only Durkheim sensed the uniqueness of totemism as an underlying force in all human societies, whether very small and primal or large and complex. And, while the search for ultimate origins was somewhat obfuscating for him and all others so engaged in the nineteenth-century, his quest still raises the truly interesting and important question: How did a capacity to totemize evolve, and when did it evolve, in humans? Today, with new types of data and analytical tools, this question can no longer seem impossible to answer.

Let us immediately eliminate one type of argument that all too often appears in social science arguments invoking evolutionary biology: macro-mutations (or ones that fall well outside the range of normative variation) and especially mutations in neurological structures. As R.A. Fisher in *The Genetical Theory of Natural Selection* postulated long ago "... *favorable mutations* must ... be generally exceedingly minute in their somatic effects ..." (1930: 83 emphasis added). Or as G.L. Stebbins (1968: 105) emphasized, "Once a unit of action has been assembled at a lower level of the hierarchy of organization and performs an essential function in the development of organization at higher levels, mutations that might interfere with the activity of this unit are so strongly disadvantageous that they are rejected at the cellular level and never appear in the adult individual in which they occur."

Thus, to find the origins of totemism we can continue to follow Durkheim's guidelines by tracing its elementary forms, but we should not fall back on this gloss of assuming anything unique evolves solely through macro-mutations. While mutations are essential because they introduce new variation into a population, mutations are random or accidental so they constitute undirected variation (unlike natural selection which is a directed force). Mutations occur frequently, to be sure, but most are harmful or neutral and do not promote fitness, and large mutations in a complex brain would be especially harmful because of the intricate interconnections among very dynamic and multiplex systems in the mammalian brain. And Durkheim is correct in that a capacity and propensity for totemism did not arise from "nothing." It definitely came from something and that something is what we find in chimpanzees as reasonable surrogates for the last common ancestor of humans closest living relative. So, we need to focus on the "something" for which we now have new data not available to Durkheim or anyone in the first half of the twentieth century.

The Hominoid Self-Identity

As emphasized, one building block for social totemism is the possession of a self-identify, a cognitive trait with many facets, including the ability to take oneself as an external object in space. This bio-social capacity is hard-wired in humans but it is not manifest at birth because its maturation depends upon an ongoing interplay with significant others in a social milieu, a process that gets activated once a child can take the social role of another at Mead's "play" stage of development; and then with practice and biological maturation, young humans become able to role take at the level of "the game" stage. For Mead (1934), and implicitly for Durkheim coming from an entirely different intellectual tradition, the capacity to role take with the generalized other is the key ability that allows humans to build social structures using totemizing mechanics. The generalized other or any label that we might want to give to the human capacity to assume the perspective of collective actions—in Durkheim's case, "collective representations"—allows for a higher form of integration, a community of attitudes that as Durkheim said transcends the sum of individual representations. As he phrased it ". . . if one is to call the distinctive property of the individual representational life *spirituality*, one should say that social life is defined by its *hyper-spirituality*. By this we mean that all the constituent attributes of mental life are found in it, but elevated to a very much higher power and in such a manner as to constitute something entirely new" ([1897]1965: 34, original emphasis). Thus, cooperation and social cohesion is in large part dependent on the perspective of community attitudes.

In the case of Mead, as Paul Pfuetze remarked (1954: 86), "[S]ince [Mead] conceived of religion as the extension of social attitudes and relations to the universe at large, one may fairly raise the question as to why he did not see or why he was unwilling to grant the use of the Generalized Other as a religious equivalent for God." Pfuetze added that Mead's friends had encouraged—even urged him to extend the concept as a religious motif but given "Mead's secular bent" he kept it in a secular frame. Had Mead taken the advice of his friends, the convergence of his approach with Durkheim's would have been clearly evident.

As discussed in the last chapter, chimpanzees have a well-documented self, giving them a similar capacity to see themselves as an object and role take with others and, indeed, if need be, to use this information to manipulate others (as Erving Goffman would have argued if he knew about the strategic use of self presentations by chimpanzees to manipulate caretakers). A self has also been documented in gorillas and orangutans. Given that a self-identity is rare, but present in all living hominoids (i.e. great apes and humans), it was surely a derived trait passed on by their last common ancestor, with cladistic analysis placing its origin at least 13 million years ago in the Miocene epoch. Thus, if self is critical to being able to see oneself in a larger community, then it represents one of the "somethings" from which the propensity of humans to totemize relations evolved.

The Nature of Community

Community living is a rare form of organization among mammals because it integrates a population without direct linkages or with weak ties compared to social structures built from strong, kinship-based ties. Given the ongoing fission-fusion dynamics of communal living, how then, is integration achieved when most individuals are not in immediate propinquity and when they often do not interact for long periods of time, or in a large community, even at all? What transcendent force fills in the gaps that separate individuals? Without bioprogrammers for something such as herding or schooling, some of the gaps are filled in by a *self awareness* that one is part of a more inclusive social whole. Chimpanzees do not merely associate in transient social parties; they act as though they have a reflective awareness, a feeling of both self and community. We can speak empirically of a bounded regional space where a stable population of local chimpanzees move about independently because it can be observed. How they are integrated given the strong fission-fusion component to their sociality is subjective in that it is essentially a feeling—a sentiment—chimps are united by an enduring sentiment—a kind of social consciousness. So we can speak of chimpanzee society in that it is a durable social formation, a commonwealth. This orientation of a self-identity linked to a community, and indeed, perhaps the rudimentary capacity to build communal-level identities is probably an essential pre-adaptation for the capacity to totemize social relations and to form very large-scale social formations based upon common identification with, and emotional arousal toward, a shared totemic symbol.

Do Chimpanzees Totemize?

Something like religion is probably not needed in a chimpanzee community. A self-identity, a bounded and shared commonwealth, and a "sense of community" are enough to bridge the gaps needed for social cohesion and stability in a dynamic chimpanzee fission and fusion social structure.

Another level of abstract reference points would be superfluous and would require an energy sapping larger brain. Moreover, totemism in humans is mostly used to divide a micro-unit into sub-divisions or sections of some sort, whereas chimpanzee communities are at Durkheim's horde stage in that they are singular, undivided macro-units rather than societies with two or more interdependent hordes. In fact, between chimpanzee communities hostility reigns, even a documented case of "warfare" where one community systematically annihilated another community and took over its territory (Goodall 1986 and see Nishida et al. 1985 and Mitani et al. 2010).

Still, it is interesting to ask: What do they have that might be linked to totemism? What other social formations exist in chimpanzee societies that might also be at the root of institutional formations?

First, there is the stable grouping of a mother and dependent offspring. As discussed in Chapter 16, because a mother and her adult male offspring live for a lifetime in the same community, they could settle down and start a cozy kinship lineage. Yet, despite this intimacy, they comply with a biologically based "incest" taboo, or in reality, a dual propensity for mother and son to avoid each other as sexual partners. Adult males, however, are apt to visit their mother on a regular basis, sometimes for extended periods when food is in short supply. Also documented is that sons can eventually inherit the small, core foraging area of their maternal parent (Mitani 2008). Intriguingly, Robert Lowie (1966: 255) hypothesized years ago that a possible origin of human matriliny is connected to whether a woman can acquire possessive rights to a plot of land or locality, which is then shared with her offspring. In any case, a chimpanzee-like matri-focal unit of mother and offspring is the elementary formation for the later invention of the nuclear family in human evolution.

Second, there are fleeting chimpanzee gatherings or what researchers call "parties." These temporary gatherings are composed of community members who *choose* to associate with friends or acquaintances in a non-kinship based format. In human societies, these elective associations are called "sodalities." In Latin *sodalis* refers to "comrade, companion, bosom friend, associate, messmate, accomplice, the member of an organization . . ." (Lowie 1966: 14). They are voluntary associations and found in all societies . . . from hunting and gathering bands to horticultural, agrarian and industrial societies. These non-kinship entities defy classification for although they are associated with communities they are viewed as different phenomena. In essence, they are an association where some sort of social action takes place, and they can be composed of all males or all females, a mixed grouping, a secret society, or a book, bridge, knitting or any sort of club. Often they arise spontaneously, with marked degrees of fluidity to bring together individuals within or between bands or villages or cities. And, they vary so greatly that they can embody just about any theme—political, economic, social, military secular, or a sacred religious element. As Hammond (2003: 370) put it, "We are wired to seek more than close personal ties."

How, then, does totemism differ from a sodality? In surface features, they appear to operate under different formulas. But both are anchors for the creation of a novel type of social formation organized around voluntary ties, an arrangement that also facilitates the build-up of larger extensions of individuals into superorganisms. They arise in response to different motives and social needs, but totemic cults and sodalities also share an essential facet—both are broader entities beyond the narrow confines of genealogical kinship. They are also generated by the same cognitive process —a capacity to create an affect tie among a collective by utilizing some external object or a task-oriented sociality and by doing so, and with regular frequency to trigger a spontaneous emergent unity or "sense of community." I would venture to guess they are derived from the same neurological circuits that underlie and sustain what I termed *the community complex* in the last chapter. From sodalities and totems it is only a short adaptive step to add Durkheim's religious element—an aura of the sacred in the orientation of community members to a common emblem, image, figure or anything serving as a symbolic representation.

Humans and chimpanzees have the same brain architecture and share most of the same neural circuits. They share virtually the same sensory equipment to see, hear, touch, and smell (Maryanski 2013). They can symbolize; they have a gestural communication [and in a human linguistic environment can comprehend American English (see Chapter 15)]. The major difference is that chimpanzees (who have very large brains for mammals) have a brain that is only 1/3 the size of humans.

As discussed earlier, chimpanzees "parties" take place under many organizational guises—hunting parties, patrolling parties, nursery parties, sex parties, grooming parties, banquet fruiting parties and the like. Obviously, a chimpanzee sodality is an elementary formation compared to a human sodality, but even the concept of a sociality or to think in terms of such freely-formed "parties" for focused social action is a rare phenomenon. It can only occur in a fission-fusion society, and it occurs only in a handful of species. It requires agency, of course, as a sodality is a voluntary get-together.

Totems differ from sodalities in that they formally divide up a population into stable sub-groups such as clans, moieties, phratries or military divisions. But they overlap. Sport mascots such as USC Trojans, North Alabama Lions, LSU Tigers, Texas Longhorns, and Georgia Bulldogs can easily be put under the umbrella of totems serving as a vehicle for unity and identity. Sport fans eagerly wear their team logos (or its symbolic representation) on their person in tattoos; in fact, they place these symbols on just about everything from clothing, cars, bicycles to office staplers and coffee cups. Fans even undergo ceremonial rituals (e.g. face and torso painting and tattoos). Michael Serazio (2013: 2) assistant professor of communications at Boston College writing in *The Atlantic* asks: "Why exactly do we do this for our teams?" In Serazio's opinion, professional sport teams are a kind of civic religion, referring to the Super Bowl as "professional sports' highest holy day . . ." He then evokes Durkheim's totemic theory in *Elementary Forms* to address the "secret of fandom" in sports:

> . . . Our religious totems, while "officially" symbolizing deities, also implicitly offer vessels for fellowship; licenses to congregate together . . . there is something universal—and still enduring—in that tribal yearning . . . The totem, then, gives believers a physical representation of that need for identity and unity . . . Theological justifications are really just incidental; what matters is that through our faith in these common artifacts, community is forged . . . Yet community is often more abstract and imagined than concrete and identifiable.
> (Serazio 2013: 3, original emphasis)

Serazio adds that it is the aura of religion on a sports totem that gives totem-mates a license to communicate or to cherish the family team legacy over generations, treating those who switch over to a rival team as "heretics and apostates." It makes little difference, he says, if the team wins or loses a game: "As long as the totem survives, so do we" (2013: 5).

Some may scoff at such a comparison but given that all humans living today can be traced back to a small African mother population that lived about 200,000 years ago, we should not be surprised that humans behave in similar ways under similar conditions. Indeed, as Kenneth Thompson mused on tattoos, "The resurgence of tattooing in modern society suggests that it continues to bear witness to a shared moral identity . . . . Until recently it might have been assumed by sociologists that tattooing was simply part of a passing fashion . . . . But, as Durkheim perceived, it is still the case that tattooing is a mark of social membership within an urban "tribe" (1998: 99–100 original emphasis).

Scoring Durkheim

Durkheim has often been criticized for his superficial and dead wrong conclusions on the lifeways of Australian aboriginals, his stubbornness about totemism, his equating of religion with the social, and so on. Yet, as this book has hopefully demonstrated, assessing Durkheim's insights in light of newer data and analytical tools, allows us to emphasize his incredible success or high "score" for understanding the origins and operation of one of the key forces of human organization. Durkheim was devoted to the scientific method; he saturated himself with facts and he applied an inductive method to come up with captivating generalizations and theories that still inform social science. A comprehensive reading of all Durkheim's works and especially his more obscure writings can only reveal a scholar dedicated to sociology and a scholar committed to understanding how the world works.

The conclusion of this book is that Durkheim was far ahead of his time. Many of his suppositions, when taken back to their elementary forms, are supported by the hominoid, hominin, and especially the chimpanzee data. If we are willing to agree that the huge pile of data on our primate relations has validity, Durkheim's rather dogmatic belief that kinship (among hominins) was invented later in time is supported; his belief that the primal formation for humans was a more macro-structural unit is supported in light of the nature of communities among great apes and, hence, humans' hominin ancestors; his views that religion is a collective and, more importantly, an exemplar of an often hidden force of human organization are supported; his assertion that co-presence and rituals generate the emotions that move people to create totems is supported at the level of interpersonal encounters (Goffman 1967; Collins 2004), at the level of meso organization (Linton 1924), and at the macro-level of social organization (see Turner et al. 2018); his recognition that humans are highly individualistic and, by nature, less social than often hypothesized and that their social nature is a product of society is supported; and his argument that the first kinship was more like a chimpanzee type matriny unit—that is the initial *genetic* based family—is also supported by the data on great apes. So, Durkheim racked up a rather impressive score for a scholar working without the benefit of the accumulated data on hominin evolution and the ability to use cladistic analysis to look back millions of years in time to see the behavioral and organization features of the last common ancestor to great apes, hominins, and humans.

His conclusions on religion are given a mixed review. Neither society nor religion is likely to have originated quite as Durkheim described in his conjectured narrative, although he assumed his theory would undergo modifications. On this score he had no empirical data, and so, he relied mostly on conjecture although he did see the importance of the fission-fusion cycles of hunter-gatherers. The chimpanzee data also supports the hypothesis that early forest-living hominins were initially organized into a macro-organizational structure or a community-level of organization in the absence of strong kinship ties—an idea that was unpopular then and now but Durkheim's sense of what had to exist first was essentially correct. Indeed, modern humans seek out a sense of community. It was with early *Homo* populations and their shift from the forestlands to the bushlands and savannas that lead to the origin of the nuclear family and to the origin of religion as a social institution. But all this was made possible by two novel and rare neurological structures inherited from the last common ancestor of apes and humans: a self-identify and a feeling for or "sense of community." Both are primordial characteristics.

Finally, unless we wish to assert a heavenly influence, what can we conclude about his thesis on the origins of religion? First, self, community, and religion are all linked to a social environment. Like community, religion rests on special emotions, an effervescence generated by the sheer association of individuals. As Durkheim advised, always look behind the mask of a religion to see what is being symbolized. A sense of community is an emergent, transcendent property built from social interactions; and if religion is a phenomena generated from the same neuro-social processes in the human mind, then religion is not a mysterious property at all but simply a hyperbolic continuation of community and an early manifestation of one of the most fundamental integrative forces in human organization.

Indeed, a community and self are surely the pre-adaptations for religion. Both require a special kind of neurobiology that allows for attachments to the whole rather than the parts. If nothing else, a *sense of community* contains the seeds of religion. On the deification of society, Allen (2013: 119) recently concluded that despite the difficulty of validating Durkheim's premise, his "God-society relationship ... is ... still worth exploring." Hausner (2013a: 3) also noted that "Durkheim's model is as good or better than it ever was, insofar as he can help us explain new modes of religion, or ways of being religious (or social) ... that no one would have conceived of a century ago" (and see Hausner 2013b).

A system of beliefs and practices relative to sacred things is a human universal. Once invented, religion could then develop into all kinds of varieties and all kinds of conceptual schemes in the descendants of early hominins, especially in light of the enormous growth of the neocortex in human evolution. But if we travel back into deep time to religion's earliest beginnings, a phrase of religion that Durkheim equated with the social, it may be that the novel totemic-like star-shaped relational structure (outlined in Chapter 13) was evident in early hominins and could only but develop as the brain grew during hominin evolution. And, Durkheim's thesis on the origin of religion may be just what he thought it was . . . the first visible manifestation of the operative mechanism for the formation of solidarities in the sociocultural formations constructed by humans in the distant past, present, and future.

Bibliography

Abadía, O. and M. Morales. 2004. "Toward a Genealogy of the Concept of 'Paleolithic Mobiliary Art". *Journal of Anthropological Research*, 60: 321–339.

———. 2013. "Paleolithic Art: A Cultural History". *Journal of Archaeological Research*, 21: 269–306.

Abrutyn, S. and A. Mueller. 2014. "The Socioemotional Foundations of Suicide." *Sociological Theory*, 32(4): 327–351.

Ackerman, R. 1987. *J.G. Frazer: His Life and Work*. Cambridge: Cambridge University Press.

Akazawa, T. and S. Muhesen. 2003. "Neanderthal Burials: Excavations of the Dederiyeh Cave, Afrin, Syria". Auckland, NZ: KW Publications.

Alexander, J. 1982. *The Antinomies of Classical Thought: Marx and Durkheim* (Vol. 2). San Francisco, CA: University of California Press.

———. 2005. "The Inner Development of Durkheim's Sociological Theory: From Early Writings to Maturity". In J. Alexander and P. Smith (Eds.) *The Cambridge Companion to Durkheim* (pp. 136–159). Cambridge: Cambridge University Press.

Allen, N.J. 1994. "Primitive Classification: The Argument and Its Validity". In W.S.F. Pickering and H. Martins (Eds.) *Debating Durkheim* (pp. 40–65). London: Routledge.

———. 1998. "Effervescence and the Origins of Human Society". In N.J. Allen, W.S.F. Pickering and W. Watts Miller (Eds.) *On Durkheim's Elementary Forms of Religious Life* (pp. 149–161). London: Routledge.

———. 2013. "Durkheim's Sacred/Profane Opposition: What Should We Make of It?" In S. Hausner (Ed.) *Durkheim in Dialogue: A Centenary Celebration of the Elementary Forms of Religious Life* (pp. 109–123). New York: Berghahn.

Allen, N.J., W.S.F. Pickering and W. Watts Miller. 1998. *Durkheim's Elementary Forms of Religious Life*. London: Routledge.

Alpert, H. 1959. "Emile Durkheim: A Perspective and Appreciation". *American Sociological Review*, 24: 462–465.

———. 1961. *Emile Durkheim and His Sociology*. New York: Russell and Russell.

———. 1965. "Functional Theory of Ritual". In R. Nisbet (Ed.) *Emile Durkheim* (pp. 137–141). Upper Saddle River, NJ: Prentice-Hall.

Amici, F., F. Aureli and J. Call. 2010. "Monkeys and Apes: Are Their Cognitive Skills Really So Different?" *American Journal of Physical Anthropology*, 143: 188–197.

Anderson, J. and G. Gallup Jr. 2015. "Mirror Self-Recognition: A Review and Critique of Attempts to Promote and Engineer Self-Recognition in Primates". *Primates*, 56: 317–326.

Andrews, P. 1981. "Species Diversity and Diet in Monkeys and Apes During the Miocene". In C.B. Stringer (Ed.) *Aspects of Human Evolution* (pp. 24–61) London: Taylor and Francis.

Anonymous. 1893. "Comparative-Religious Notes". *The Biblical World*, 2(1): 62–69.

———. 1894. "Professor Robertson Smith". *Nature*, 49: 557.

———. 1897. "The Engwurra, or Fire Ceremony of Certain Central Australian Tribes". *Nature*, 1441(56): 136–139.

———. 1916. "The Elementary Forms of the Religious Life". *The Biblical World*, 47: 413.

Antón, S., R. Potts and L. Aiello. 2014. "Evolution of Early Homo an Integrated Biological Perspective". *Science*, 345(6192): 1–20.

Appenzeller, T. 2018. "Europe's First Artists Were Neandertals". *Science*, 359: 852–853.

Atmoko, S., S. Utami, I. Singleton, M. Noordwijk, C. van Schaik and T. Mitra Setia. 2008. "Male–Male Relationships in Orangutans". In *Orangutans: Geographic Variations in Behavioral Ecology and Conservation* (pp. 225–233). Oxford: Oxford University Press.

Aubarbier, J.-L. and M. Binet. 1987. *Prehistoric Sites in Périgord*. Rennes, France: Quest France (translated by A. Moyon).

Azouvi, F. 2007. *La Gloire de Bergson*. Paris: Gallimard.

Bachofen, J. "Das Mutterrecht." [1861]1931. In V.F. Calverton (Ed.) *The Making of Man: An Outline of Anthropology* (pp. 157–167). New York: The Modern Library.

Baldwin, J. 2002. *George Herbert Mead: A Unifying theory for Sociology*. Dubuque, IA: Kendall/Hunt Publishing.

Balter, M. 2000. "Paintings in Italian Cave May Be Oldest Yet". *Science*, 290: 419–421.

Barbujani, G., S. Shirotto and F. Tassi. 2013. "Nine things to Remember About Human Genome Diversity. *Tissue Antigens*, 82: 155–164.

Barlett, T. 2011. "The Hylobatidae". In C. Campbell, A. Fuenter, K. MacKinnon, S. Bearder and R. Stumpf (Eds.) *Primates in Perspective* (pp. 300–312). New York: Oxford University Press.

Bediako, G. 1995. "To Capture the Modern Universe of Thought, Religion of the Semites as an Attempt at a Christian Comparative Religion". In W. Johnstone (Ed.) *William Robertson Smith: Essays in Reassessment* (pp. 118–130). Sheffield, UK: Sheffield Academic Press.

———. 1999. *Primal Religions and the Bible. William Robertson Smith and his Heritage*. Sheffield, UK: Sheffield Academic Press.

Beidelman, T. 1974. *W. Robertson Smith and the Sociological Study of Religion*. Chicago, IL: University of Chicago Press.

Bellah, R. 1959. "Durkheim and History". *American Sociological Review*, 24: 447–461.

———. 1967. "Civil Religion in America". *Daedalus, Journal of the American Academy of Arts and Sciences*, 96: 1–21.

———. 1973. "Introduction". In R. Bellah (Eds.) *Emile Durkheim: On Morality and Society* (pp. ix–iv). Chicago, IL: University of Chicago Press.

Beran, M., B. Perdue, S. Futch, D. Smith and T. Evans. 2015. "Go When You Know: Chimpanzees' Confidence Movements Reflect their Responses in a Computerized Memory Task". *Cognition*, 142: 236–246.

Bergesen, A. 1984. "Swanson's Neo-Durkheimian Sociology of Religion". *Sociological Analysis*, 45: 179–184.

Berna, F., P. Goldberg, L.K. Horwitz, J. Brink, S. Holt, M. Bamford and M. Chazan. 2012. "Microstratigraphic Evidence of in Situ Fire in the Acheulean Strata of Wonderwerk Cave, Northern Cape Province, South Africa". *Proceedings National Academy Science*, 109: E1215–E1220.

Besnard, P. 1983. "The Année Sociologique Team". In P. Besnard (Ed.) *The Sociological Domain: The Durkheimians and the Founding of French Sociology* (pp. 11–70). Cambridge: Cambridge University Press.

———. 2005. "Durkheim's Squares: Types of Social Pathology and Types of Suicide". In J. Alexander and P. Smith (Eds.) *The Cambridge Companion to Durkheim* (pp. 70–79). New Haven, CT: Yale University.

Biro, D., T. Humle, K. Koops, C. Sousa, M. Hayashi and T. Matsuzawa. 2010. "Chimpanzee Mothers at Bossou, Guinea Carry the Mummified Remains of Their Dead Infants". *Current Biology*, 20: 351–352.

Black, J. Sutherland and G. Chrystal. 1912a. *The Life of William Robertson Smith*. London: Adam and Charles Black.

———. 1912b. *Lectures and Essays of William Robertson Smith*. London: Adam and Charles Black.

Blackwell, D. and D. Lockwood. 1965. *Alice on the Line*. Adelaide, Australia: Rigby Limited.

Blake, J. 2004. "Gestural Communication in the Great Apes". In *The Evolution of Thought: Evolutionary Origins of Great Ape Intelligence* (pp. 61–75). Cambridge: Cambridge University Press.

Boas, F. 1889. "On Alternating Sounds". *American Anthropologist*, 1–2 (old series): 47–54.

———. 1897. "The Social Organization and the Secret Societies of the Kwakiutl Indians: Based on Personal Observation and on Notes Made by Mr. George Hunt". *Annual Report of the Board of Regents of the Smithsonian Institution* (pp. 311–738). U.S. National Museum, Part 11. Washington, DC: Government Printing Office.

———. 1910. "The Origin of Totemism". *Journal of American Folklore*, 23: 392–393.

———. 1916. "The Origin of Totemism". *American Anthropologist*, 18: 319–326.

Bock, K. 1956. *The Acceptance of History*. Los Angeles, CA: University of California Press.

Boesch, C. and H. Boesch-Achermann. 2000. *The Chimpanzees of the Taï Forest*. Oxford: Oxford University Press.

Bolus, M. 2015. "Dispersals of Early Humans: Adaptations, Frontiers, and New Territories". In *Handbook of Paleoanthropology* (pp. 1–25). Berlin: Springer.

Borgatti, S., M. Everett and J. Johnson. 2013. *Analyzing Social Networks*. Los Angeles, CA: Sage.

Bouglé, C. [1924]1965. "Preface to the Original Edition". In Émile Durkheim (Ed.) *Sociology and Philosophy* (pp. xxxv–xli). London: Cohen & West.

Boutroux, É. [1879]1920. *The Contingency of the Laws of Nature*. Chicago, IL: The Open Court Publishing Company (translated by F. Rothwell).

———. [1912]1970. *Historical Studies in Philosophy*. New York: Kennikat Press.

Bradley, B. 2008. "Reconstructing Phylogenics and Phenotypes: A Molecular view of Human Evolution". *Journal of Human Anatomy*, 212: 337–353.

Bradley, B., M. Robbins, E. Williamson, H.D. Steklis, N. Steklis, N. Eckhardt, C. Boesch and L. Viglant. 2005. "Mountain Gorilla Tug-of-War: Silverbacks Have Limited Control Over Reproduction in Multimale Groups". *PNAS*, 102: 9418–9423.

Brooks III, J. 1998. *The Eclectic Legacy: Academic Philosophy and the Human Sciences in Nineteenth-Century France*. Newark, DE: University of Delaware Press.

Brooks, D. 1991. *The Arrernte Landscape: A Guide to the Dreaming Tracks and Sites in Alice Springs*. Alice Springs, Australia: IAD Press.

Brown, A.R. 1912. "Marriage and Descent in North and Central Australia." *Man*, 12: 123–124.

Bynder, H. 1969. "Emile Durkheim and the Sociology of the Family". *Journal of Marriage and The Family*, 31: 527–533.

Call, J. and M. Tomasello. 2007. *The Gestural Communication of Apes and Monkeys*. Mahwah, NJ: Lawrence Erlbaum Associates.

———. 2008. "Does the Chimpanzee Have a Theory of Mind? 30 Years Later". *Trends in Cognitive Science*, 12: 187–192.

Callaway, E. 2014. "Neanderthals Made Some of Europe's Oldest Art". *Nature*, 1 Sept: 15805.

———. 2015. "Neanderthals Had Outsize Effect on Human Biology". *Nature*, 523: 512–513.

Campbell, C., A. Fuentes, K. Mackinnon, S. Bearder and R. Stumpf. 2011. *Primates in Perspective*. New York: Oxford University Press.

Catlin, G. 1938. "Introduction to the Translation". In *The Rules of Sociological Method* (pp. xxviii). New York: Free Press.

———. 1959. "The Meaning of Community". In C. Friedrich (Ed.) *Community* (pp. 114–134). New York: The Liberal Arts Press.

Chalmers, N.R. 1971. "Difference in Behaviour Between Some Arboreal and Terrestrial Species of African Monkeys". In R. Michael and J. Crook (Eds.) *Comparative Ecology and Behaviour of Primates* (pp. 69–100). London: Academic Press.

Chang, L.Q., Q. Fang, S. Zhang, M. Poo and N. Gong. 2015. "Mirror-Induced Self-Directed Behaviors in Rhesus Monkeys after Visual-Somatosensory Training". *Current Biology*, 25: 212–217.

Charle, C. 1974. "Le beau mariage d'Émile Durkheim". *Actes de la Recherche en Sciences Sociales*, 55: 44–49.

Chatterjee, H., S. Ho, I. Barnes and C. Groves. 2009. "Estimating the Phylogeny and Divergence Times of Primates using a Supermatrix Approach". *BMC Evolutionary Biology*, 9: 259.

Cheney, D., R. Seyfarth and B. Smuts 1986. "Social Relationships and Social Cognition in Non-Human Primates". *Science*, 234: 1361–1366.

Cladis, M. 1992. *A Communitarian Defense of Liberalism: Emile Durkheim and Contemporary Theory*. Stanford, CA: Stanford University Press.

Clark, T. 1968. "The Structure and Functions of a Research Institute: The Année Sociologique". *European Journal of Sociology*, 9: 72–91.

———. 1973. *Prophets and Patrons: The French University and the Emergence of the Social Sciences*. Cambridge, MA: Harvard University Press.

———. 1979. "Emile Durkheim Today". In R. Jones and H. Kuklick (Eds.) *Research in the Sociology of Knowledge, Sciences and Art: A Research Annual 2* (pp. 123–153). Stamford, CT: JAI Press.

Cleyet-Merle, J.-J. 2007. *Musée National de Préhistoire, Les Eyzies-de-Tayac, Dordogne.* Évreux, France: Japp Lahure Jombart.

Clowry, G. 2014. "Seeking Clues in Brain Development to Explain the Extraordinary Evolution of Language in Humans". *Language Sciences*, 46: 220–231.

Coleman, M. and Colbert, M. 2009. "Correlation Between Auditory Structures and Hearing in Non-Human Primates". *Journal of Morphology*, 27: 511–532.

Collier, J. 1878. "Des societes animales: Etude de psychologie comparee". *Mind*, 3: 105–112.

Collins, R. 1975. *Conflict Sociology: Towards an Explanatory Science.* San Francisco, CA: Academic Press.

———. 1988. "Interaction Ritual". In *Theoretical Sociology* (pp. 187–228). San Diego, CA: Harcourt Brace Jovanovich.

———. 2004. *Interaction Ritual Chains.* Princeton, NJ: Princeton University Press.

———. 2005. "The Durkheimian Movement in France and in World Sociology". In J. Alexander and P. Smith (Eds.) *The Cambridge Companion to Durkheim* (pp. 101–135). Cambridge: Cambridge University Press.

———. 2008. *Violence: A Macro-sociological Theory.* Princeton, NJ: Princeton University Press.

Comte, A. [1830–1842]1998. *The Essential Writings – Auguste Comte and Positivism.* London: Transaction Publishers (edited by G. Lenzer).

———. 1853. *The Positive Philosophy of Auguste Comte.* London: Chapman (translated by H. Martineau).

Condemi, S. and G. Weniger. 2011. *Continuity and Discontinuity in the Peopling of Europe: One Hundred and Fifty Years of Neanderthal Study.* Heidelbert, The Netherlands: Springer.

Conroy, G. and H. Pontzer. 2012. *Reconstructing Human Origins: A Modern Synthesis.* New York: W.W. Norton and Company.

Cooke, A., A. Tripp and G. von Petzinger. 2014. "Art, Paleolithic." In Claire Smith (Ed.) *Encyclopedia of Archaeology* (pp. 529–539). New York: Springer.

Cooley, C. Horton. 1902. *Human Nature and the Social Order.* New York: Charles Schribner's Sons.

Copeland, S., M. Sponheimer, D. de Ruiter, J. Lee-Thorp, D. Codron, P. le Roux, V. Grimes and M. Richards. 2011. "Strontium Isotope Evidence for Landscape Use by Early Hominins". *Nature*, 474: 76–78.

Corruccini, R.S. and R.L. Ciochon. 1983. "Overview of Ape and Human Ancestry: Phyletic Relationships of Miocene and Later Hominoidea". In R.L. Ciochon and R.S. Corruccini (Eds.) *New Interpretations of Ape and Human Ancestry* (pp. 3–19). New York: Plenum.

Coser, L. 2003. *Masters of Sociological Thought: Ideas in Historical and Social Context.* Long Grove, IL: Waveland Press.

Cosman, C. 2001. *Émile Durkheim: The Elementary Forms of Religious Life.* Oxford: Oxford University Press.

Coughlan, F. 1991. "Aboriginal Town Camps and Tangentyere Council: The Battle for Self-Determination in Alice Springs". *MA Thesis.* Victoria, Australia: La Trobe University.

Crawford, L. 1924. *The Philosophy of Emile Boutroux as Representative of French Idealism in the Nineteenth Century.* New York: Longmans, Green and Company.

Crockford, C., R.M. Wittig, R. Mundry and K. Zuberbuhler. 2012. "Wild Chimpanzees Inform Ignorant Group Members of Danger". *Current Biology,* 22: 142–146.

Culotta, E. 2016. "A Single Wave of Migration from Africa Peopled the Globe". *Science,* 354: 1515–1523.

Curtis, G. 2006. *The Cave Painters.* New York: Anchor Books.

Darwin, C. 1859. *On the Origin of Species.* London: John Murray.

Davy, G. 1919 "Émile Durkheim: L' homme". *Revue de Métaphysique et de Morale,* 26(2): 181–198.

———. 1920. "Durkheim: 11 L'oeuvere". *Revue de Métaphysique et de Morale,* 27(1): 71–112.

———. 1923. L'oeuvre d'Espinas". *Revue Philosophique,* 96: 214–270.

De Coulanges, N.D. Fustel. [1864]1889. *The Ancient City* (Seventh Edition). Boston, MA: Lee and Shepard.

Demarest, W. 1977. "Incest-Avoidance Among Human and Non-Human Primates". In S. Chevalier-Skolnikoff and F. Poirier (Eds.) *Primate Bio-Social Development* (pp. 323–342. New York: Garland.

Deploige, S. 1912. *Le conflit de la morale et de la sociologie.* Louvain, France: Institut Supérieur de Philosophie.

Dickson, B. 1990. *The Dawn of Belief: Religion in the Upper Paleolithic of Southwestern France.* Tucson, AZ: The University of Arizona Press.

Disotell, T. R. 2012. "Archaic Human Genomes". *American Journal of Physical Anthropology (Yearbook),* Supp. 55: 24–39.

Dohlinow, P. and A. Fuenter. 1999. *The Non-Human Primates.* Mountain View, CA: Mayfield.

Donaldson, I. and B. Göttgens. 2006. "Evolution of Candidate Transcriptional Regulatory Motifs Since the Human-Chimpanzee Divergence". *Genome Biology,* 7: 52.

Donovan, P. 1988. *Alice Springs: Its History & The People Who Made It.* Alice Springs, Australia: Alice Springs Town Council.

Douglas, M. 1966. *Purity and Danger.* New York: Praeger.

———. 2002. *Mary Douglas: Collected Works.* London: Routledge.

Duncan, D. 1908. *The Life and Letters of Herbert Spencer.* London: Methuen and Company.

Durkheim, É. [1883]1973. "Address to the Lycéens of Sens". In R. Bellah (Ed.) *Emile Durkheim: On Morality and Society* (pp. 25–42). Chicago, IL: University of Chicago Press.

———. [1883–84]2004. *Durkheim's Philosophy Lectures: Notes from the Lycée de Sens Course.* Cambridge: Cambridge University Press (edited and translated by N. Gross and R. Jones).

———. [1885]1978. "Review of Albert Schaeffle Bau und Leben des Sozialen Körpers: Erster Band". In M. Traugott (Ed. and Trans.) *Emile Durkheim: On Institutional Analysis* (pp. 93–114). Chicago, IL: University of Chicago Press.

———. [1886]1975. "Review "Herbert Spencer–Ecclesiastical Institutions: Being Part VI of the Principles of Sociology". In W.S.F. Pickering (Ed.) *Durkheim on Religion* (pp. 13–23). London: Routledge and Kegan Paul.

———. [1887]1975a. "La science positive de la morale". In V. Karady (Ed.) *Émile Durkheim Textes* (Vol.1) (pp. 267–343). Paris: Editions de Minuit.

———. [1887]1975b. "Review Guyau-L'Irréligion de l'avenir, étude de sociologie". In W.S.F. Pickering (Ed.) *Durkheim on Religion* (pp. 24–38). London: Routledge and Kegan Paul.

———. [1888]1978a. "Course in Sociology: Opening Lecture". In M. Traugott (Ed. and Trans.) *Emile Durkheim: On Institutional Analysis* (pp. 43–87). Chicago, IL: University of Chicago Press.

———. [1888]1978b. "Introduction to the Sociology of the Family". In M. Traugott (Ed. and Trans.) *Emile Durkheim: On Institutional Analysis* (pp. 205–228). Chicago, IL: University of Chicago Press.

———. [1890]1973. "The Principles of 1789 and Sociology". In R. Bellah (Ed.) *Emile Durkheim: On Morality and Society* (pp. 34–42). Chicago, IL: University of Chicago Press.

———. [1892]1975. *Montesquieu and Rousseau: Forerunners of Sociology*. Ann Arbor, MI: University of Michigan Press.

———. 1893. *De La Division Du Travail Social: Étude Sur L'Organisation des Sociétés Supérieures*. Paris: Felix Alcan.

———. [1893]1984. *The Division of Labor in Society*. New York: Free Press (translated by W.D. Halls).

———. [1893]1938. *The Division of Labor in Society*. New York: The Free Press.

———. 1894. "Les Régles de la méthode sociologique". *Revue philosophique*, 37; 38: 14–39, 168–182, 465–498, 577–607.

———. [1895]1982. *The Rules of Sociological Method*. New York: Free Press.

———. 1895. "L'origine du mariage dans l'espéce humaine d'apres Westermarck". *Revue philosophique*, 40: 606–623.

———. [1895]1964. *The Rules of Sociological Method*. New York: Macmillan.

———. 1895. "L'Enseignement philosophique et l'agrégation de philosophie". *Revue philosophique*, 39: 121–147.

———. [1897]1978. "Review of Antonio Labriola, Essais sur la conception matérialiste de L'histoire". In M. Traugott (Ed.) *Emile Durkheim on Institutional Analysis* (pp. 123–130). Chicago, IL: University of Chicago Press.

———. 1897. *Le Suicide: étude de sociologie*. Paris: Alcan.

———. [1897]1951. *Suicide*. New York: Free Press.

———. [1897]1998. *Lettres à Marcel Mauss*. France: Presses Universitaires de France (edited by P. Besnard and M. Fournier).

———. [1898]1965. "Individual and Collective Representations". In D.F. Pocock (Trans.) *Sociology and Philosophy* (pp. 1–34). London: Cohen & West.

———. [1898]1963. *Incest: The Nature and Origin of the Taboo*. New York: Lye Stuart.

———. 1898. "La Prohibition de l'inceste et ses origines". *L'Année sociologique*, 1: 1–70.

———. [1898]1960. "Prefaces to *L'Année Sociologique*, Volumes I and II". In K. Wolff (Ed. and Trans.) *Emile Durkheim, 1858–1917* (pp. 341–375). Columbus, OH: The Ohio State University Press.

———. [1899]1984. "Concerning the Definition of Religious Phenomena". In W.S.F. Pickering (Ed.) *Durkheim on Religion* (pp. 74–99). London: Routledge and Kegan Paul.

———. [1900]1972a. "Lettres a Celestin Bougle". *Revue française de sociologie*, 17: 165–180.

———. [1900]1960. "Sociology and its Scientific Field". In K.H. Wolff (Ed. and Trans.) *Emile Durkheim, 1858–1917* (pp. 354–375). Columbus, OH: The Ohio State University.

———. 1900b. "Spencer, B. and F.J. Gillen, The Native Tribes of Central Australia, 1899". *L'Année sociologique*, 5(3): 330–336.

———. 1900c. "Boas, F., The Social Organization and the Secret Societies of the Kwakiutl Indians". *L'Année sociologique*, 3: 336–340.

———. [1902]1985. "On Totemism". *History of Sociology*, 5: 82–121 (translated by R.A. Jones).

———. [1902–1903 lecture]1973. *Moral Education: A Study in the Theory and Application of the Sociology of Education*. New York: The Free Press.

———. [1902–1903]1925. *L éducation morale*. Paris: Libraire Félix Alcan.

———. 1905. "Sur l'organisation matrimoniale des société australiennes." *L'Année sociologique*, 8: 118–147.

———. 1906. "Détermination Du Fait Moral". *Bulletin de la Sociéte Française de Philosophie*. Paris: Librairie Armand Colin.

———. [1907]1975. "Cours sur les origines de la vie religieuse". In V. Karady (Ed.) *Émile Durkheim Textes* (Vol. II) (pp. 65–122). Paris: Editions de Minuit.

———. [1907]1982. "Influences upon Durkheim's View of Sociology". In *The Rules of Sociological Method* (Two letters to the Director Revue néo-scolastique (Louvain) 14 (pp. 257–260). New York: Free Press.

———. [1908]1962. "The Method of Sociology". In S. Lukes (Ed.) *The Rules of Sociological Method* (pp. 245–247). New York: Free Press (translated by W.D. Halls).

———. [1912]1947. *The Elementary Forms of the Religious Life: A Study in Religious Sociology*. London: Free Press (translated by J. Swain).

———. [1912]1995. *The Elementary Forms of Religious Life*. New York: Free Press (translated by K. Fields).

———. 1913. "Deploige Simon. Le conflit de la morale et de la sociologie". *L'Année sociologique*, 12: 326–328.

———. [1914]1960. "The Dualism of Human Nature and its Social Conditions". In K.H. Wolff (Ed. and Trans.) *Emile Durkheim, 1858–1917* (pp. 325–340). Columbus, OH: The Ohio State University.

———. [1917]1920. "Introduction à la morale". *Revue Philosophique*, 89: 79–97.

———. 1972. *Émile Durkheim: Selected Writings*. London: Cambridge University Press (edited by A. Giddens).

———. 1975. *Textes V2*. Paris: Les éditions de Minuit (edited by V. Karady).

———. 1978. *Emile Durkheim on Institutional Analysis*. Chicago, IL: University of Chicago Press (edited and translated by M. Traugott).

———. 1980. *Emile Durkheim: Contributions to L'Année Sociologique*. London: Free Press (edited by Y. Nandan; translations by J. French, A.P. Lyons, Y. Nandan, J. Sweeney and K. Woody).

Durkheim, E. and M. Mauss. [1903]1963. *Primitive Classification*. Chicago, IL: University of Chicago Press (translated by R. Needam).

Ember, C., M. Ember and P. Peregrine. 2009. *Human Evolution and Culture: Highlights of Anthropology*. New York: Prentice Hall.

Emirbayer, M. 2003. "Introduction". In M. Emirbayer (Ed.) *Emile Durkheim: Sociologist of Modernity* (pp. 1–28). Oxford: Backwell Publishing.

Engels, F. 1972[1884]. *The Origin of the Family, Private Property and the State; in the Light of the Researches of Lewis Henry Morgan*. New York: International Publishers.

Espinas, A. [1877]1878. *Des Sociétes Animales*. Paris: Bailliére.

Evans-Pritchard, E. 1965. *Theories of Primitive Religion*. Glasgow, UK: Oxford University Press.

Fahy, G., M. Richards, J. Riedel, J. Hublin and C. Boesch. 2013. "Stable Isotope Evidence of Meat Eating and Hunting Specialization in Adult Male Chimpanzees". *PNAS*, 110: 5829–5833.

Fanlac, P. 1984. *La Grotte De Font-De-Gaume*. Périgueux, France: Lo Trebuc.

Fauconnet, P. 1923. "The Pedagogical Work of Emile Durkheim". *American Journal of Sociology*, 28: 529–553.

Faysal, B., M. Lewis, A. Slouron, D. Garello, L. Werdelin, K. Reed and J. Ramón. 2015. "Late Pliocene Fossiliferous Sedimentary Record and the Environmental Context of Early Homo from Afar, Ethiopia". *Science*, 347: 1355–1359.

Fenton, S. 1984. *Durkheim and Modern Sociology* (with R. Reinet and I. Hamnett). Cambridge: Cambridge University Press.

Fields, K. 2005. "Translating Durkheim on Religion". In T. Godlove Jr. (Ed.) *Teaching Durkheim* (pp. 53–86). Oxford: Oxford University Press.

Fisher, R. 1930. *The Genetical Theory of Natural Selection*. Oxford: Clarendon Press.

Fison, L. and A.W. Howitt. [1880]1991. *Kamilaroi and Kurnai*. Australia: Aboriginal Studies Press.

Fleagle, J. 2013. *Primate Adaptation & Evolution*. Amsterdam: Elsevier.

Foley, R. and C. Gamble. 2009. "The Ecology of Social Transitions in Human Evolution". *Philosophical Transactions of the Royal Society B*, 364: 3267–3279.

Forey, P.L., C.J. Humphries, I.L. Kitching, R.W. Scotland, D.J. Siebert and D.M. Williams. 1994. *Cladistics: A Practical Course in Systematics*. Oxford: Clarendon Press.

Fournier, M. 2006. *Marcel Mauss: A Biography*. Princeton, NJ: Princeton University Press (translated by J.M. Todd).

———. 2013. *Émile Durkheim: A Biography*. Cambridge: Polity Press (translated by D. Macey).

Fouts, R. 1972. "Use of Guidance in Teaching Sign Language to a Chimpanzee (*Pan Troglodytes*)". *Journal of Comparative Psychology*, 80: 515–522.

Fouts, R.S. and D.H. Fouts. 1993. "Chimpanzees' Use of Sign Language". In P. Cavalieri and P. Singer (Eds.) *The Great Ape Project: Equality Beyond Humanity* (pp. 28–41). New York: St. Martin's Press.

Fox, R. 1967. *Kinship and Marriage*. London: Penguin.

Frazer, E. 1999. *The Problems of Communitarian Politics: Unity and Conflict*. Oxford: Oxford University Press.

Frazer, J. [1887]. *Totemism*. Edinburgh, UK: Adam and Charles Black.

———. 1890. *The Golden Bough: A Study in Comparative Religion* (2 volumes). New York Macmillan & Company (enlarged to three volumes in 1900; 12 v in 1911–1915 and a supplement in 1937).

———. [1898]2005. *Selected Letters of Sir. J. G. Frazer*. Oxford: Oxford University Press (edited by Robert Ackerman).

———. 1899. "Observations on Central Australian Totemism". *Journal of the Anthropological Institute of Great Britain and Ireland*, 28: 281–286.

———. 1899. "The Origin of Totemism". *The Fortnightly Review*, LXV (new series): 647–665, 835–852.

———. 1905. "The Beginnings of Religion and Totemism among the Australian Aborigines". *Fortnightly Review*: 151–162, 452–467.

———. 1909. "Beliefs and Customs of the Australian Aborigines". *Man*, 9: 145–147.

———. [1910]1968. *Totemism and Exogamy: A Treatise on Certain Early Forms of Superstition and Society* (4 volumes). London: Dawsons of Pall Mall.

———. 1912. "Anthropological Research in Northern Australia". *Man*, 39: 72–73.

Fritz, C. and G. Tosello. 2007. "The Hidden Meaning of Forms: Methods of Recording Paleolithic Parietal Art". *Journal of Archaeological Method and Theory*, 14: 48–71.

Fuentes, A. 2000. "Hylobatid Communities: Changing Views on Pair Bonding and Social Organization in Hominoids". *Yearbook of Physical Anthropology*, 43: 33–60.

Gagneux, P. and A. Varki. 2001. "Genetic Differences Between Humans and Great Apes". *Molecular Phylogenetics and Evolution*, 18: 2–13.

Gallatin, A. 1836. "A Synopsis of the Indian Tribes of North America". *American Antiquarian Society, Worcester, Massachusetts, Transactions & Collections*, (Archaeologia Americana), 2 :1–422.

Gallup. G.G. Jr., M.K. McClure, S.D. Hill and R.A. Bundy. 1971. "Capacity for Self-recognition in Differentially Reared Chimpanzees". *The Psychological Record*, 21: 69–74.

Gamble, C. 2013. "Durkheim and the Primitive Mind: An Archaeological Retrospective". In S. Hausner (Ed.) *Durkheim in Dialogue: A Centenary Celebration of The Elementary Forms of Religious Life* (pp. 124–142). New York: Berghahn.

Gardner, R.A. and B.T. Gardner. 1969. "Teaching Language to a Chimpanzee". *Science*, 165: 664–672.

Garner. R.L. 1896. *Gorillas and Chimpanzees*. London: Osgood, McIlaine and Company.

Geertz, A. 2013. "Whence Religion? How the Brain Constructs the World and What This Might Tell Us About the Origins of Religion, Cognition and Culture". In A. Geertz (Ed.) *Origins of Religion, Cognition and Culture* (pp. 17–70). Denmark: Acumen.

Gehlke, C. [1915]1938. *Emile Durkheim's Contributions to Sociological Theory*. New York: AMS Press.

Geiger, R. 1972. *The Development of French Sociology 1871–1905*. Dissertation: University of Michigan.

Genty, E. and K. Zeberbühler. 2014. "Spatial Reference in A Bonobo Gesture". *Current Biology*, 24: 1601–1605.

Gephart, W. 1998. "Memory and the Sacred: The Cult of Anniversaries and Commemorative Rituals in the Light of the *Elementary Forms*". In N.J. Allen, W.S.F. Pickering and W. Watts Miller (Eds.) *On Durkheim's Elementary Forms of Religious Life* (pp. 127–135). London: Routledge.

Gibbons, A. 2015a. "Deep Roots for the Genus *Homo*". *Science*, 347: 1056–1057.

———. 2015b. "Ancient DNA Pinpoints Paleolithic Liaison in Europe". *Science*, 348: 847.

Giddens, A. 1970. "Durkheim as a Review Critic". *Sociological Review*, 18: 171–196.

———. 1979. *Emile Durkheim: Selected Writings*. London: Cambridge University Press.

———. 1981. *Durkheim*. Glasgow: William Collins Sons & Company.

Gilbert, M. 1994. *The First World War: A Complete History*. New York: Henry Holt.

Gillen, F. [1896]2001. *My Dear Spencer: The Letters of F.J. Gillen to Baldwin Spencer*. Melbourne: Hyland House (edited by J. Mulvaney, H. Morphy and A. Petch).

Gillespie-Lynch, P., M. Greenfield, Y. Feng, S. Savage-Rumbaugh and H. Lyn. 2013. "A Cross-Species Study of Gesture and its Role in Symbolic Development: Implications for the Gestural Theory of Language Evolution". *Frontiers in Psychology*, 4: 1–15.

Glaser, D. (2007). "The Evolution of the Sweetness Receptor in Primates". In J. Kaas and T. Press (Ed.) *Evolution of Nervous Systems: A Comprehensive Reference*, volume 4 (pp. 121–128). Amsterdam: Elsevier.

Glaser, D., J.M. Tinti and C. Nofre. 1995. "Evolution of the sweetness receptor in primates. I. Why does Alitame Taste Sweet in all Prosimians and Simians, and Aspartame only in Old World Simians?" *Chemical Senses*, 20: 573–584.

Glazko, G.V. and M. Nei. 2003. "Estimation of Divergence Times for Major Lineages of Primate Species". *Molecular Biology and Evolution*, 424–434.

Glendenning, K.K. and R.B. Masterton. 1998. "Comparative Morphometry of Mammalian Central Auditory Systems: Variation in Nuclei and Form of the Ascending System". *Brain, Behavior and Evolution*, 51: 59–89.

Goffman, E. 1967. *Interaction Ritual*. New York: Anchor Books.

Goldenweiser, A. 1910. "Totemism, An Analytical Study". *The Journal of American Folk-Lore*: xxiii, 179–293.

———. 1912. "The Origin of Totemism". *American Anthropologist*, 14: 600–607.

———. 1915. "Les Formes élémentaires de la vie religieuse: Le système totémique en Australie". *American Anthropologist*, 17: 719–735.

———. 1917. "Religion and Society: A Critique of Emile Durkheim's Theory of the Origin and Nature of Religion". *The Journal of Philosophy, Psychology, and Scientific Methods*, 14: 113–125.

———. 1918. "Form and Content in Totemism". *American Anthropologist*, 20: 280–295.

———. 1931. "Totemism, An Essay on Religion and Society". In V.F. Calverton (Ed.) *The Making of Man* (pp. 363–392). New York: The Modern Library.

Goodall, A. and C. Groves. 1977. "The Conservation of Eastern Gorillas". In Prince Rainier III of Monaco and G. Bourne (Eds.) *Primate Conservation* (pp. 599–637). New York: Academic Press.

Goodall, J. 1986. *The Chimpanzees of Gombe: Patterns of Behavior*. Harvard, MA: Harvard University Press.

———. 1990. *Through a Window: My Thirty Years with the Chimpanzees of Gombe*. Boston, MA: Houghton Mifflin.

———. 2005. "Do Chimpanzees Have Souls? Possible Precursors of Religious behavior in Animals?" In C. Harper Jr (Ed.) *Spiritual Information: 100 Perspectives on Science and Religion* (pp. 275–278). Philadelphia, PA: Templeton Foundation Press.

Gould, S. 2002. *The Structure of Evolutionary Theory*. Cambridge, MA: The Belknap Press of Harvard University Press.

Granovetter, M. 1973. "The Strength of Weak Ties". *American Journal of Sociology*, 78: 1360–1380.

———. 1983. "The Strength of Weak Ties: A Network Theory Revisited". In R. Collins (Ed.) *Sociological Theory* (pp. 201–233). San Francisco, CA: Jossey-Bass Publishers.

Greenberg, L. 1976. "Bergson and Durkheim as Sons and Assimilators: The Early Years". *French Historical Studies*, 9: 619–634.

———. 1981. "Architects of the New Sorbonne: Liard's Purpose and Durkheim's Role". *History of Education Quarterly*, 21: 77–94.

Greenwalk, D. 1973. "Durkheim on Society, Thought and Ritual". *Sociological Analysis*, 34: 157–168.

Greenwood, P. 1980. "Mating Systems, Philopatry, and Dispersal in Birds and Mammals". *Animal Behaviour*, 28: 1140–1162.

Gross, N. 2004. "Introduction". In N. Gross and R. Jones (Eds.) *Durkheim's Philosophy Lectures: Notes from the Lycée de Sens Course, 1883–1884* (pp. 1–30). Cambridge: Cambridge University Press.

Gross, N. and R. Jones. 2004. *Durkheim's Philosophy Lectures. Notes from the Lycée de Sens Course, 1883–1884*. Cambridge: Cambridge University Press.

Gunn, A. 1922. *Modern French Philosophy: A Study of the Development Since Comte*. New York: Dodd, Mead and Company.

Guyau, J.M. [1887]1962. *The Non-Religion of the Future: A Sociological Study*. New York: Henry Holt.

Hackett, T. 2008. "Anatomical Organization of the Auditory Cortex". *Journal of the American Academy of Audiology*, 19: 774–779.

Haddon, A. 1902. "Opening Address". *Nature*: 561–567.

Haddon, A. and A. Hingston Quiggin. 1910. *The History of Anthropology*. London: Watts and Company.

Hammond, M. 2003. "The Enchancement Imperative: The Evolutionary Neurophysiology of Durkhemian Solidarity". *Sociological Theory*, 21: 359–374.

Hamnett, I. 1984. "Durkheim and the Study of Religion". In S. Fenton with R. Reiner and I. Hamnett (Eds.) *Durkheim and Modern Sociology* (pp. 202–218). Cambridge: Cambridge University Press.

Hamrick, M. 2001. "Primate Origins: Evolutionary Change in Digital Ray Patterning and Segmentation". *Journal of Human Evolution*, 40: 339–351.

Harcourt, A. and K.J. Stewart. 2007a. "Gorilla Society: What We Know and Don't Know". *Evolutionary Anthropology*, 16: 147–158.

———. 2007b. *Gorilla Society*. Chicago, IL: University of Chicago Press.

Hari, R., T. Himberg, L. Nummenmaa, M. Hämäläinen and L. Parkkonen. 2013. "Synchrony of Brains and Bodies During Implicit Interpersonal Interaction". *Trends in Cognitive Sciences*, 17: 105–106.

Harlow, H.F., M.K. Harlow, K.A. Schiltz and D.J. Mohr. 1971. "The Effect of Early Adverse and Enriched Environments on the Learning Ability of Rhesus Monkeys". In L.E. Jarrard (Ed.) *Cognitive Processes of Non-Human Primates* (pp. 121–148). New York: Academic Press.

Harmand, S., J. Lewis, C. Feibel, C. Lepre, S. Prat et al. 2015. "3.3-Million-Year-Old Stone Tools from Lomekwi 3, West Turkana, Kenya". *Nature*, 521: 310–315.

Harris, M. 1968. *The Rise of Anthropological Theory*. New York: Thomas Y. Crowell Company.

Hartland, S. 1900. "L'Année Sociologique". *Folklore*, 11: 92–96.

———. 1901. "The Golden Bough: A Study in Magic and Religion". *Man*: 57–60.

———. 1902. "L'Année Sociologique". *Folklore*, 15: 314–323.

———. 1904. "The Northern Tribes of Central Australia by B. Spencer and F.J. Gillen". Review. *Folklore*, 15: 465–474.

———. 1905. "L'Année Sociologique". *Folklore*, 16: 468–475.

———. 1906. "The Secret of the Totem, by Andrew Lang". *Man*, 16–17: 27–28.

———. 1913. "Les Formes Élémentaires de la Vie Religieuse: Le Système Totémique en Australie". *Man*, 53–54: 91–96.

Hartwig, N.C. 1965. "The Progress of White Settlement in the Alice Springs District and its Effects upon the Aboriginal Inhabitants, 1860–1894". *Doctoral Dissertation*, University of Adelaide.

Harvati, K. 2015. "Neanderthals and Their Contemporaries". In W. Henke and I. Tattersall (Eds.) *Handbook of Paleoanthropology* (pp. 2244–2266). Berlin: Springer-Verlag.

Haun, D.B.M. and J. Call. 2009. "Great Apes' Capacities to Recognize Relational Similarity". *Cognition*, 110: 147–159.

Hausner, S. 2013a. "Introduction". In S. Hausner (Ed.) *Durkheim in Dialogue: A Centenary Celebration of the Elementary Forms of Religious Life* (pp. 3). New York: Berghahn.

———. 2013b. "Is Individual to Collective as Freud Is to Durkheim?" In S. Hausner (Ed.) *Durkheim in Dialogue: A Centenary Celebration of The Elementary Forms of Religious Life* (pp. 167–179). New York: Berghahn.

———. 2013. *Durkheim in Dialogue*. New York: Berghahn.

Haviland, W. 2014. *Evolution and Prehistory: The Human Challenge*. Belmont, CA: Wadsworth/Cengage.

Hayes, C. 1951. *The Ape in Our House*. New York: Harper.

Hayes, K. and C. Hayes. 1951. "The Intellectual Development of a Home-Raised Chimpanzee". *Proceedings of the American Philosophical Society*, 95: 105–109.

Hays, H.R. 1958. *From Ape to Angel: An Informal History of Social Anthropology*. New York: Knopf.

Heffner, R. 2004. "Primate Hearing from A Mammalian Perspective". *The Anatomical Record*, 281A: 1111–1122.

Heffner, H. and Heffner, R. 2008. "High Frequency Hearing". In P. Dallos, D. Oertel, and R. Hoy (Eds.) *Handbook of the Senses: Audition* (pp. 55–60). New York: Elsevier.

Heidegard, H., B. Beil, H. Hilbig, J. Call and H. Bidmon. 2009. "Superior Olivary Complex Organization and Cytoarchitecture may be Correlated with Function and Catarrhine Primate Phylogeny". *Brain Structure and Function*, 213: 489–497.

Heppell, M. and J.J. Wigley. 1981. *Black Out in Alice: A History of the Establishment and Development of Town Camps in Alice Springs*. Australia: The Australian National University.

Herman, L. 2012. "Body and Self in Dolphins". *Consciousness and Cognition*, 21: 526–545.

Herrick, J. 1954. *The Historical Thought of Fustel de Coulanges*. Washington, DC: The Catholic University of America Press.

Heyek, F.A. 1941. "The Counter-Revolution of Science". *Economica*, 8 (new series): 281–320.

Harlow, H.F., R.O. Dodsworth and M.K. Harlow. 1965. "Total Social Isolation in Monkeys". *PNAS*, 54: 90–97.

Hill-Tout, C. 1904. "Totemism: A Consideration of its Origin and Import". *Man*, 46–48, 74–78.

Hillery, G. 1955. "Definitions of Community: Areas of Agreement". *Rural Sociology*, 20: 111–123.

Hinde, R. 1983. *Primate Social Relationships*. Oxford: Blackwell.

Hinkle, R. 1960. "Durkheim in American Sociology". In K. Wolff (Ed.) *Emile Durkheim 1858–1917: A Collection of Essays, with Translations and a Biography* (pp. 267–295). Columbus: Ohio State University.

Hobaiter, C. and R. Byrne. 2014. "The Meanings of Chimpanzee Gestures". *Current Biology*, 24: 1596–1600.

Hoblin, J., A. Ben-Ncer, S. Bailey, S. Freidline, S. Neubauer et al. 2017. "New Fossils from Jebel Irhoud, Morocco and the Pan-African Origin of Homo Sapiens". *Nature*, 546: 289–292.

Hodgson, D. 2008. "The Visual Dynamics of Upper Palaeolithic Cave Art". *Cambridge Archaeological Journal*, 18: 341–353.

Holloway, R. 1978. The Relevance of Endocasts for Studying Primate Brain Evolution". In C.R. Noback (Ed.) *Sensory Systems of Primates* (pp. 181–200). New York: Plenum.

Holt, B. and V. Formicola. 2008. "Hunters of the Ice Age: The Biology of Upper Paleolithic People". *Yearbook of Physical Anthropology*, 51: 70–99.

House, F.N. 1936. *The Development of Sociology*. New York: McGraw-Hill.

Howard, G.E. 1904. *A History of Matrimonial Institutions Chiefly in England and the United States, with an Introductory Analysis of the Literature and the Theories of Primitive Marriage and the Family.* Volume 1. London: Fisher Unwin Paternoster Square.

Howitt, A.W. 1904. *The Native Tribes of South-East Australia.* London: Macmillan and Company.

———. 1907. "Australian Group Relationships". *Journal of the Royal Anthropological Institute of Great Britain and Ireland*, 37: 279–289.

Huang, B., Z. Guan, Q. Ni, J. Orkin, P. Fan and Z. Jiang. 2013. "Observation of Intra-group and Extra-group copulation and Reproductive Characters in Free Ranging Groups of Western Black Crested Gibbon (Nomascus concolor jingdongensis)". *Integrative Zoology*, 8: 427–440.

Jacobs, G.H. and J.F. Deegan. 1999. "Uniformity of Colour Vision in Old World Monkeys". *Proceedings of the Royal Society London*, 266: 2023–2028.

Jacobs, G.H. 2007. "The Comparative Biology of Photopigments and Color Vision in Primates". In J. Kaas and T. Preuss (Eds.) *Evolution of Nervous Systems: A comprehensive Reference.* Volume 4 (pp. 80–85). Amsterdam: Elsevier.

James, W. and N.J. Allen. 1998. *Marcel Mauss: A Centenary Tribute.* New York: Berghahn.

Jeffers, R. and I. Lehiste. 1979. *Principles and Methods for Historical Linguistics.* Cambridge, MA: MIT Press.

Joas, H. 1993. "Durkheim's Intellectual Development". In S. Turner (Ed.) *Emile Durkheim: Sociologist and Moralist* (pp. 229–245). London: Routledge.

Johnston, G.A. "The Elementary Forms of the Religious Life: A Study in Religious Sociology". *International Journal of Ethics*, 26: 303–304.

Johnstone, W. 1995. *William Robertson Smith: Essays in Reassessment.* Sheffield, UK: Sheffield Academic Press.

Jolly, A. 1985. *The Evolution of Primate Behavior.* New York: Macmillan.

Jones, R.A. 1986. "Durkheim, Frazer, and Smith: The Role of Analogies and Exemplars in the Development of Durkheim's Sociology of Religion". *American Journal of Sociology*, 92: 596–627.

———. 1993. "Durkheim and La Cité Antique: An Essay on the Origins of Durkheim's Sociology of Religion". In S. Turner (Ed.) *Emile Durkheim: Sociologist and Moralist* (pp. 95–110). London: Routledge.

———. 2002. "Transaction Introduction". In R. Smith, *The Prophets of Israel and Their Place in History* (pp. viii-lxi). New Brunswick: Transaction Publishers.

———. 2005. *The Secret of the Totem.* New York: Columbia University Press.

Joordens, J., F. d'Errico, F. Wesselingh, S. Munro et al. 2015. "Homo erectus at Trinil on Java used Shells for Tool Production and Engraving". *Nature*, 518: 228–231.

Jullian, C. 1930. "Fustel de Coulanges. Revue des deux mondes". *LVI*: 257.

Kaneko, T. and M. Tomonaga. 2011. "The Perception of Self-Agency in Chimpanzees (Pan troglodytes)". *Proceedings of the Royal Society*, 278: 3694–3702.

Karady, V. 1968. *Oeuvres* (three vols) *on M. Mauss*. Paris: Editions de Minuit.

———. 1979. "Scientists and Class Structure: Social Recruitment of Students at the Parisian Ecole Normale Superieure in the Nineteenth Century". *History of Education*, 8: 99–108.

Kardiner, A. and E. Preble. 1961. *They Studied Man*. Cleveland, OH: World Publishing Company.

Karg, K., M. Schmelz, J. Call and M. Tomasello. 2015. "The Goggles Experiment: Can Chimpanzees Use Self-Experience to Infer What a Competitor Can See?" *Animal Behaviour*, 105: 211–221.

Kass, J. and T.P. Pons. 1988. "The Somatosensory System of Primates". In H.D. Steklis and J. Erwin, *Comparative Primate Biology, Neurosciences*. Volume 4 (pp.421–468). New York: A.R. Liss.

Kaufmann, R.M. 1919. "Shoulder Insignia of the American Expeditionary Force". In *Daughters of the American Revolution Magazine*, vliii, 7: 403–415. Philadelphia, PA: J.B. Lippincott.

Kellogg, W.N. and L. Kellogg. 1933. *The Ape and Child: A Study of Environmental Influence Upon Early Behaviour*. New York: Hafner Publications.

King, I. *The Development of Religion*. 1910. New York: Macmillan Company.

King, M. and A. Wilson. 1978. "Our Close Cousin the Chimpanzee". In N. Korn (Ed.) *Human Evolution* (pp. 88–94). New York: Holt, Rinehart and Winston.

Kirk, C. "Comparative Morphology of the Eye in Primates". 2004. *The Anatomical Record Part A*, 28IA: 1095–1103.

———. 2006. "Visual Influences on Primate Encephalization." *Journal of Human Evolution*, 51: 76–90.

Knott, C. and S. Kahlenberg. 2011. "Orangutans: Understanding Forced Copulations". In C. Campbell, A. Fuentes, K. Mackinnon, S. Bearder and R. Stumpf (Eds.) *Primates in Perspective* (pp. 313–326). New York: Oxford University Press.

Knott, C., L. Beaudrot, T. Snaith, S. White, H. Tschauner and G. Planansky. 2008. "Female-Female Competition in Bornean Orangutans". *International Journal of Primatology*, 29: 975–997.

Krubitzer, L. and Kaas, J. 2005. "The Evolution of Neocortex in Mammals: How is Phenotypic Diversity Generated?" *Current Opinion in Neurobiology*, 45: 444–453.

Kühl, H., A. Kalan, C. Boesch et al. 2016. "Chimpanzee Accumulative Stone Throwing". *Scientific Reports*, 6: 212–219.

Kummer, H. 1971. "Immediate Causes of Primate Social Structures". *Proc. 3rd International Conference. Primate*, 3: 1–11. Basel: Karger.

Kuper, A. 1985. "Durkheim's Theory of Primitive Kinship". *The British Journal of Sociology*, 36: 224–236.

———. 1988. *The Invention of Primitive Society: Transformations of an Illusion*. London: Routledge.

LaCapra, D. 1972. *Emile Durkheim: Sociologist and Philosopher*. Ithaca: Cornell University Press.

Lahnakoski, J., E. Glerean, I. Jääskeläinen, J. Hyönä, R. Hari, M. Sams and L. Nummenmaa. 2014. "Synchronous Brain Activity Across Individuals Underlies Shared Psychological Perspectives". *NeuroImage*, 100: 316–324.

LaLande, A. 1905. "Philosophy in France". *The Philosophical Review*, 14: 429–455.

———. 1906. "Philosophy in France (1905)". *The Philosophical Review*, 15: 241–266.

Lamanna, M. 2002. *Emile Durkheim on the Family*. Thousand Oaks, CA: Sage.

Lambert, C.A. and S.A. Tishkoff. 2009. "Genetic Structure in African Populations: Implications for Human Demographic History". *Cold Spring Harbor Symposia on Quantitative Biology*, 74: 395–402.

Lang, A. 1904a. "The Native Tribes of South-East Australia". *Man*, 183–186.

———. 1904b. "Dr Durkheim on 'Social Origins". *Folklore*, 15: 99–102.

———. 1904c. "A Theory of Arunta Totemism". *Man*, 4: 67–69.

———. 1905a. *The Secret of the Totem*. New York: Ams Press.

———. 1905b. "Misgivings of An Anthropologist." *Man*, 3–4: 7–10.

———. 1906. "Quæstiones Totemicæ: A Reply to M. Van Gennep". *Man*, 111–112: 180–182.

———. 1908. "Linked Totems". *Man*, 98–99: 178–179.

———. 1909a. "Totémisme et Méthode Comparative, Par A. van Gennep". *Man*, 33–34.

———. 1909b. "Exogamy". *Man*, 9: 137.

———. 1910. "Die Aranda und Loritja-Stämme by C. Strehlow". *Man*, 64–64: 110–111.

Lalueza-Fox, C., A. Rosas, A. Estalrrich, E. Grgli, et al. 2001. "Genetic Evidence for Patrilocal Mating Behaviour Among Neanderthal Groups". *PNAS*, 108: 250–253.

Langergraber, K., C. Rowney, G. Schubert, C. Crockford, C. Hobaiter, R. Wittig, R. Wrangham, K. Zuberbühler and L. Vigilant. 2014. "How Old are Chimpanzee Communities? Time to the Most Recent Common Ancestor of the Y-Chromosome in Highly Patrilocal Societies". *Journal of Human Evolution*, 69: 1–7.

Lavisse, E. 1918. "Louis Liard". *Revue internationale de l?enseignement*, 72: 81–99.

Leacock, S. 1954. "The Ethnological Theory of Marcel Mauss". *American Anthropologist*, 56: 58–73.

Lee, D. and H. Newby. 1983. *The Problem of Sociology: An Introduction to the Discipline*. London: Unwin Hyman.

Lehmann, J., A. Korstjens and R.I.M. Dunbar. 2007. "Fission-Fusion Social systems as a Strategy for Coping with Ecological Constraints: A Primate Case", *Evolutionary Ecology*, 21: 613–634.

Lessa, W. and E. Vogt. 1958. *Reader in Comparative Religion*. Illinois: Row, Peterson and Company.

Leví-Strauss, C. 1962. *Totemism*. Boston, MA: Beacon Press.

Levy-Bruhl, L. 1903. *The Philosophy of Auguste Comte*. New York: G.P. Putnam's Sons.

Lewis, A.B. "A Study in Religious Sociology". *American Journal of Theology*, 21: 143–148.

Lewis, G.H. 1897. *Comte's Philosophy of the Sciences*. London: George Bell and Sons.

Liberman, P. 2008. *Toward an Evolutionary Biology of Language*. Cambridge, MA: Harvard University Press.

Linton, R. 1924. "Totemism and the A.E.F.". *American Anthropologist*, 26(2): 296–300.

Logue, W. 1983. *From Philosophy to Sociology: The Evolution of French Liberalism, 1870–1914*. Illinois: Northern Illinois University Press.

Long, J. [1791]1904. *Voyages and Travels of an Indian Interpreter and Trader, Describing the Manners and Customs of the North American Indians*. London: Johnson Reprint Corporation.

Long, R. 1912. "Notes on Dr. J. G. Frazer's 'Totemism and Exogamy'". *Man*, 12: 107–110.

Lowie, R. 1911. "A New Conception of Totemism". *American Anthropologist*, 13: 189–207.

———. 1966. *Social Organization*. New York: Holt, Rinehart and Winston.

Lukas, D., V. Reynolds, C. Boesch and L. Vigilant. 2005. "To What Extent Does Living in a Group Mean Living with Kin?" *Molecular Ecology*, 14: 2181–2196.

Lukes, S. 1972. *Émile Durkheim: His Life and Work*. New York: Harper and Row.

———. 1982. "Introduction". In W.D. Halls (Trans.) *The Rules of Sociological Method and Selected Texts on Sociology and its Method* (pp. 1–27). New York: The Free Press.

Luncz, L. and C. Boesch. 2014. "Tradition Over Trend: Neighboring Chimpanzee Communities Maintain Differences in Cultural Behavior Despite Frequent Immigration of Adult Females". *American Journal of Primatology*, 76: 649–657.

Luncz, L., R. Mundry and C. Boesch. 2012. "Evidence for Cultural Differences Between Neighboring Chimpanzee Communities". *Current Biology*, 22: 922–926.

Lycett, S., M. Collard, W. McGrew. 2009. "Cladistic Analysis of Behavioral Variation in Wild *Pan troglodyes*: Exploring the Chimpanzee Culture Hypothesis". *Journal of Human Evolution*, 57: 337–349.

Lyell, C. 1830–1833. *The Principles of Geology; or, The Modern Changes of the Earth and its Inhabitants as Illustrative of Geology* (3 volumes). London: Murray.

Lyn, H., P.M. Greenfield, S. Savage-Rumbaugh, K. Gillespie-Lynch and W.D. Hopkins. 2011. "Non-Human Primates Do Declare! A Comparison of Declarative Symbol and Gesture Use in Two Children, two bonobos and a Chimpanzee". *Language & Communication*, 31: 61–34.

Lyon, D.C. 2007. "The Evolution of Visual Cortex and Visual Systems". In J. Kaas and L. Krubitzer (Eds.) *Evolution of Nervous Systems: A Comprehensive Reference*. Volume 3 (pp. 267–306). Amsterdam: Elsevier.

Maas, P. 1958. *Textual Criticism*. Oxford: Oxford University Press.

McGrew, W.C. 1992. *Chimpanzee Material Culture*. Cambridge: Cambridge University Press.

Machalek, R. 1992. "Why Are Large Societies so Rare?" *Advances in Human Ecology*, 1: 33–64.

McLennan, J. [1865]1970. *Primitive Marriage: An Inquiry Into the Origins of the Form of Capture in Marriage Ceremonies*. Chicago, IL: University of Chicago Press.

———. [1869–1870]1896. "The Worship of Animals and Plants". In Mrs McLennan and A. Platt. (Eds.) *Studies of Ancient History by the Late John Ferguson M'Lennan* (pp. 491–569). London: Macmillan and Company.

Maclean, E.L. and B. Hare. 2012. "Bonobos and Chimpanzees Infer the Target of Another's Attention". *Animal Behaviour*, 83: 345–353.

Maier, B. 2009. *William Robertson Smith, His Work and His Times*. Germany: Mohr Siebeck Publishers.

Maine, Sir H. Sumner. ([1861]1905). *Ancient Law: its Connection with the Early History of Society and Its Relation to Modern Ideas*. London: John Murray.

———. 1883. *Dissertations on Early Law and Custom, Chiefly Selected from Lectures Delivered to Oxford*. London: John Murray.

Malinowski, B. 1913. "Les Formes Élémentaires de la Vie Religieuse: Le Système Totémique en Australie". *Folklore*, 24: 525–531.

Mallery, G. 1879–1880. "Sign Language among North American Indians Compared with that Among Other Peoples and Deaf-Mutes". In J.W. Powell (Ed.) *First Annual Report of the U.S. Bureau of Ethnology to the Secretary of the Smithsonian Institution* (pp. 263–552). Washington: Government Printing Office, 1881.

Maryanski, A. 1986. "African Ape Social Structure: A Comparative Analysis". PhD dissertation, University of California.

———. 1987. "African Ape Social Structure: Is There Strength in Weak Ties?" *Social Networks*, 9: 191–215.

———. 1992 "The Last Ancestor: An Ecological Network Model on the Origins of Human Sociality". *Advances in Human Ecology*, 1: 1–32.

———. 1997. "Primate Communication and the Ecology of a Language Niche". In U. Segerstale and P. Molnar (Ed.) *Nonverbal Communication: Where Nature Meets Culture* (pp. 191–209). Mahwah, NJ: Lawrence Erlbaum.

———. 2013. "The Secret of the Hominin Mind: An Evolutionary Story". In D. Franks and J. Turner (Eds.) *Handbook of Neurosociology* (pp. 257–287). New York: Springer.

———. 2014. "The Birth of the Gods: Robertson Smith and Durkheim's Turn to Religion as the Basis of Social Integration". *Sociological Theory*, 32: 352–376.

Maryanski, A. and J. Turner. 1992. *The Social Cage: Human Nature and the Evolution of Society*. Stanford: Stanford University Press.

Mason, P. 1962. *Editor for Henry Schoolcraft's 'The Literary Voyager of Muzzeneigun'*. Michigan: Michigan State University.

Matani, J. 2009. "Male Chimpanzees Form Enduring and Equitable Social Bonds". *Animal Behaviour*, 77: 633–640.

Mathews, R.H. "Matrilineal Descent, Northern Territory". *Man*, 82–83: 150–152.

Mauss, M. 1900a. "B. Spencer & F. Gillen, The Native Tribes of Central Australia (London: Macmillan, 1899)". *L'Année Sociologique*, 5(3): 205–215.

———. 1900b. "J.G. Frazer, 'The Origins of Totemism' and 'Observations on Central Australian Totemism' 648–666, 835–853, 281 et suiv". *L' Année Sociologique*, 5(3): 217–220.

———. [1904–1905]1979. *Seasonal Variations of the Eskimo*. London: Routledge & Kegan Paul (translated by James Fox).

———. [1925]2000. *The Gift*. New York: Norton (translated by W.D. Halls).

———. 1983. "An Intellectual Self-Portrait". In P. Besnard (Ed.) *The Sociological Domain: The Durkheimians and the Founding of French Sociology* (pp. 139–151). London: Cambridge University Press.

Maybury-Lewis, D. 1990. "Durkheim on Relationship Systems". In P. Hamilton IV (Ed.) *Emile Durkheim: Critical Assessments* (pp. 278–286). London: Routledge.

Mead, G.H. [1934]1974. *Mind, Self, & Society*. Chicago, IL: University of Chicago Press.

Meddin, J. 1979. "Chimpanzees, Symbols, and the Reflective Self". *Social Psychology Quarterly*, 42: 99–109.

Melis, A., B. Hare and M. Tomasello. 2009. "Chimpanzees Coordinate in a Negotiation Game". *Evolution and Human Behavior*, 30: 381–392.

Merriam, C. Hart. 1908. "Totemism in California". *American Anthropologist*, 10: 558–562.

Merton, R. 1968. *Social Theory and Social Structure*. New York: Free Press.

Mestrovic, S. 1988. *Emile Durkheim and the Reformation of Sociology*. Totowa, NJ: Rowman and Littlefield.

Meyer, M., M. Kircher, M.T. Gansauge, H. Li, F. Racimo, et al. 2012. "A High-Coverage Genome Sequence from an Archaic Denisovan Individual". *Science*, 338: 222–226.

Middleton, J. and D. Tait. 1968. "The Lineage and the Lineage System". In P. Bohannan and J. Middleton (Eds.) *Kinship and Social Organization* (pp. 155–159). New York: The Natural History Press.

Mitani, J. 2008. "Chimpanzee Behavior: There's No Place Like Home". *Current Biology*, 18: 166.

Mitani, J. and D. Watts. 2001. "Why do Chimpanzees Hunt and Share Meat". *Animal Behaviour*, 61: 915–924.

Mitani, J. and S. Amsler. 2003. "Social and Spatial Aspects of Male Subgrouping in a Community of Wild Chimpanzees". *Behaviour*, 140: 869–884.

Mitani, J., A. Merriwether and C. Zhang. 2000. "Male Affiliation, Cooperation and Kinship in Wild Chimpanzees". *Animal Behaviour*, 59: 885–893.

Mitani, J., D. Watts and S. Amsler. 2010. "Lethal Intergroup Aggression Leads to Territorial Expansion in Wild Chimpanzees". *Current Biology*, 20: 507–508.

Mitani, J., D. Watts, J. Peppers and D. Merriwether. 2002. "Demographic and Social Constraints on Male Chimpanzee Behaviour". *Animal Behavior*, 64: 722–737.

———. 2005. "Correlates of Territorial Boundary Patrol Behaviour in Wild Chimpanzees". *Animal Behaviour*, 70: 1079–1086.

Mitani, J., J. Call, P. Kappeler, R. Palomit, and J. Silk. 2012. *The Evolution of Primate Societies*. Chicago, IL: University of Chicago Press.

Monod, G. 1876. "Du progrés des études historiques en France depuis le xvi siécle". *Revue Historique*, 1: 26–27.

Moore, B. 2014. "Differences in the Communicative Behavior and Neurobiology of Chimpanzees (*Pan* Troglodytes) and Bonobos (*Pan* Paniscus)". *Master of Science in Integrative Biology Theses*. 3.

Morgan, L. [1851]1954. *League of the Ho-De-No Sau-Nee or Iroquois*. New Haven, CT. Reprinted by Human Area Relations Files.

———. 1860. "The Welsh Indians". Correspondence. *The Cambrian Journal*, 2: 142–158.

———. [1871]1997. *Systems of Consanguinity and Affinity of the Human Family*. Lincoln, NE: University of Nebraska Press.

———. [1877]1985. *Ancient Society*. Tucson, AZ: University of Arizona Press.

———. 1937. *Extracts from the European Travel Journal of Lewis H. Morgan*. Volume XVI. New York: Rochester Historical Society Publications (edited by Leslie White).

Morphy, H. 1998. "Spencer and Gillen in Durkheim: The Theoretical Construction of Ethnography". In N.J. Allen, W.S.F. Pickering and W. Watts Miller (Eds.) *On Durkheim's Elementary Forms of Religious Life* (pp. 13–28). London: Routledge.

Müller, H-P. 1993. "Durkheim's Political Sociology". In S. Turner (Ed.) *Emile Durkheim: Sociologist and Moralist* (pp. 95–110). London: Routledge.

Mulvaney, J., H. Morphy and A. Petch. 2001. *My Dear Spencer: The Letters of F.J. Gillen to Baldwin Spencer.* Melbourne: Hyland House.

Mulvaney, J., A. Petch and H. Morphy. 2000. *From the Frontier.* Sydney: Allen and Unwin.

Murdock, G. 1949. *Social Structure.* New York: The Free Press.

Nakamura, M. 2003. "Gatherings of Social Grooming Among Wild Chimpanzees: Implications for Evolution of Sociality". *Journal of Human Evolution,* 44: 59–71.

Nandan, Y. 1977. *The Durkheimian School: A Systematic and Comprehensive Bibliography.* Westport, CT: Greenwood Press.

Nandan, Y. 1980. *Emile Durkheim: Contributions to L'Année Sociologique.* New York: Free Press.

Napier, J.R. and Napier, P.H. 1985. *The Natural History of the Primates.* Cambridge, MA: MIT Press.

Nater, A., M. Mattie-Greminger, A. Nurcahyo, M. Nowak, M. de Manuel (and others). 2017. "Morphometric, Behavioral, and Genomic Evidence for a New Orangutan Species". *Current Biology,* 27: 3576–3577.

Needham, R. 1966. "Comments on a Translation of Durkheim on Incest". *American Anthropologist,* 68 (New Series): 161–163.

Nichols, F. 1954. *Index to Schoolcraft's "Indian Tribes of the United States".* Washington, DC: United States Government Printing Office.

Nisbet, R. 1965. "Perspectives and Ideas". In R. Nisbet (Ed.) *Émile Durkheim* (pp. 29–102). New Jersey: Prentice-Hall.

———. 1966. *The Sociological Tradition.* New York: Basic Books.

Nishida, T. 1990. *The Chimpanzees of the Mahale Mountains: Sexual and Life History Strategies.* Tokyo: University of Tokyo Press.

Nishida, T., M. Hiraiwa-Hasegawa, T. Hasegawa and Y. Takahata. 1985. "Group Extinction and Female Transfer in Wild Chimpanzees in the Mahale National Park, Tanzania." *Z. Tierpsychology,* 67: 284–301.

Nissen, H. 1931. "A Field Study of the Chimpanzee: Observations of Chimpanzee Behavior and Environment in Western French Guinea". *Comparative Psychology Monographs,* 8: 1–122.

Nofre, C., J.M. Tinti, and D. Glaser. 1996. Evolution of the Sweetness Receptor in Primates. 11. "Gustatory Responses of Non-Human Primates to Nine Compounds Known to be Sweet in Man". *Chemical Senses,* 21: 747–762.

Noordwijk, M., S. Sauren, A. Abulani, H. Morrogh-Bernard, S. Suci, U. Atmoko and C. van Schaik. 2008. "Development of Independence: Sumatran and Bornean Orangutans Compared". In *Geographic Variations in Behavioral Ecology and Conservation* (pp. 189–203). Oxford: Oxford University Press.

Notes. 1894. "Professor Robertson Smith". *Nature,* 49: 557.

Nummenmaa, L., E. Glerean, M. Viinikainen, L. Jääskeläinen, R. Hari and M. Sams. 2012. "Emotions Promote Social Interaction by Synchronizing Brain Activity Across Individuals". *PNAS*, 109: 9599–9604.

Nummenmaa, L., H. Saarimäki, E. Glerean, A.Gotsopoulos, I. Jääskeläinen, R. Hari and M. Sams. 2014. "Emotional Speech Synchronizes Brains Across Listeners and Engages Large-scale Dynamic Brain Networks". *NeuroImage*, 102: 498–509.

Nye, M. 1979. "The Boutroux Circle and Poincare's Conventionalism". *Journal of the History of Ideas*, 40: 107–120.

O'Byrne, D. Undated. *Telegraph Stations of Central Australia*. Printed by the Northern Territory Government Printing Office.

Orru, M. 1983. "The Ethics of Anomie: Jean Marie Guyau and Emile Durkheim". *British Journal of Sociology*, 34: 499–518.

Parr, L., B. Waller and J. Fugate. 2005. "Emotional Communication in Primates: Implications for Neurobiology". *Current Opinion in Neurobiology*, 15: 716–720.

Parsons, T. 1937. *The Structure of Social Action*. New York: Free Press.

Penniman, T.K. 1965. *A Hundred Years of Anthropology*. London: Gerald Duckworth.

Pettitt, P. 2008. "Art and the Middle-to-Upper Paleolithic Transition in Europe: Comments on the Archaeological Arguments for an Early Upper Paleolithic Antiquity of the Grotte Chauvet Art". *Journal of Human Evolution*, 55: 908–917.

Peyre, H. 1960. "Durkheim: The Man, His Time, and His Intellectual Background". In K. Wolff (Ed.) *Emile Durkheim 1858–1917: A Collection of Essays, with Translations and a Biography* (pp. 3–31). Columbus, OH: Ohio State University.

———. 1975 "Foreword". In *Emile Durkheim's Montesquieu and Rousseau: pp. v–xvi in Forerunners of Sociology*. Ann Arbor, MI: University of Michigan Press.

Pfuetze, P. 1954. *The Social Self*. New York: Bookman Associates.

Pickering, M. 1993. *Auguste Comte: An Intellectual Biography* (Vol. 1). Cambridge: Cambridge University Press.

Pickering, W.S.F. 1979. *Durkheim: Essays on Morals and Education*. London: Routledge and Kegan Paul.

———. 1984. *Durkheim's Sociology of Religion: Themes and Theories*. London: Routledge and Kegan Paul.

———. 2000. *Durkheim and Representations*. London: Routledge.

Pickering, W.S.F. and H. Martins. 1994. "Introduction". In W.S.F. Pickering and H. Martins (Eds.) *Debating Durkheim*. London: Routledge.

Pike, A.W.G., D.L. Hoffmann, M. García, P.B. Pettitt, J. Alcolea, R.De Balbin, C. Gonzàex-Sainz, C. de las Heras, J.A. Lasheras, R. Nontes and J. Zilhão. 2012. "U.-Series Dating of Paleolithic Art in 11 Caves in Spain". *Science*, 336: 1409–1413.

Platnick, N. and H.D. Cameron. 1977. "Cladistic Methods in Textual, Linguistic, and Phylogenetic Analysis". *Systematic Zoology*, 26: 380–385.

Plotnik, J.M., F.B.M. de Waal and D. Reiss. 2006. "Self-recognition in an Asian Elephant". *Proceedings of the National Academy of Science, USA*, 103d: 53–57.

Poggi, G. 2000. *Durkheim*. Oxford: Oxford University Press.

Polavarapu, N., G. Arora, V. Mittal and J. McDonald. 2011. "Characterization and Potential Functional Significance of Human-Chimpanzee Large INDEL Variation". *Mobile DNA*, 2: 13.

Powell, J.W. 1881. "A Short Study of Tribal Society". *US Bureau of Ethnology*. Washington, DC: Government Printing Office.

———. 1902. "An American View of Totemism". *Man*, 75: 101–106.

Premack, D. and G. Woodruff. 1978. "Does the Chimpanzee have a Theory of Mind?" *Behavioral and Brain Sciences*, 1(4): 53–57.

Prendergast, C. 1983–1984. "The Impact of Fustel de Coulanges' La Cité antique on Durkheim's theories of Social Morphology and Social Solidarity". *Humboldt Journal of Social Relations*, 11: 53–73.

Preuschoft, S. and H. Preuschoft. 1994. "Primate Nonverbal Communication: Our Communication Heritage". In *Origins of Semosis* (pp. 66–100). Berlin: Mouton de Gruyter.

Preuss, T.M. 2007. "Primate Brain Evolution in Phylogenetic Context". In J. Kaas and T. Preuss (Eds.). *Evolution of Nervous Systems: A Comprehensive Reference* (Vol. 4) (pp. 1–34). Amsterdam: Elsevier.

Proctor, D., R. Williamson, F. de Waal and S. Brosnan. 2012. "Chimpanzees Play the Ultimatum Game". *PNAS*: 1–6.

Prüfer, K., K. Munch, I. Hellmann (and 35+ authors). 2012. "The Bonobo Genome Compared with the Chimpanzee and Human Genomes". *Nature*, 486: 529–531.

Pruvost, M, R. Bellone, N. Benecke, E. Sandoval-Castellanos, M. Cieslak, et al. 2013. "Genome-wide Data Substantiate Holocene Gene Flow from India to Australia". *Proceedings of the National Academy Science*, 110: 1803–1808.

Pugach, I., F. Delfin, E. Gunnarsdóttir, M. Kayer and M. Stoneking. 2013. "Genome-wide

Purvis, D., L. White, D. Zheng, T. Andrews and D. Driddle. 1996. "Brain Size, Behavior and the Allocation of Neural Space". In *The Lifespan Development of Individuals: Behavioral, Neurobiological, and Psycho-social Perspective*". Cambridge: Cambridge University Press.

Pusey, A.E. 2005. "Inbreeding Avoidance in Primates". In A.P. Wolf and W.H. Durham (Eds.) *Inbreeding, Incest and the Incest Taboo* (pp. 61–75). Stanford, CA: Stanford University Press.

Pusey, A.E. and C. Packer. 1987. "Dispersal and Philopatry". In B. Smuts, D. Cheney, R. Seyfarth, R. Wrangham and T. Struhsaker (Eds.) *Primate Societies* (pp. 250–265). Chicago, IL: University of Chicago Press.

Radcliffe-Brown, A.R. 1945. "Religion and Society". *Journal of the Royal Anthropological Institute of Great Britain and Ireland*, 75: 33–43.

———. 1977. *The Social Anthropology of Radcliffe-Brown*. London: Henley and Boston (edited by A. Kuper).

Radin, P. 1970. "Introduction". In E. Tylor (Ed.) *The Origin of Culture*. Gloucester, MA: Peter Smith.

Reichard, U.H. and C. Barelli. 2008. "Life History and Reproductive Strategies of Khao Yai Hylobates lar: Implications for Social Evolution in Apes". *International Journal of Primatology*, 29: 823–844.

Reichard, U., H. Hirai and C. Barelli. 2016. *Evolution of Gibbons and Siamang: Phylogeny, Morphology, and Cognition*. Canada: Springer.

Reinach, S. 1905. *Cultes, Mythes, et Religions*. Paris: E. Leroux.

Relethford, J. 2010. *The Human Species*. Boston, MA: McGraw Hill.

Réville, A. 1883. *Les religions Des Peuples Non-Civilisés*. Paris: Librairie Fischbacher.

Reynolds, V. 1965. *Budongo: An African Forest and its Chimpanzees*. New York: Natural History Press.

Rhine, R.J. and A. Maryanski. 1996. "A Twenty-One Year History of a Dominant Stumptail Matriline". In J. Fa and D. Lindburg (Eds.) *Evolution and Ecology of Macaque Societies* (pp. 473–499). Cambridge: Cambridge University Press.

Rice, P. and N. Moloney. 2005. *Biological Anthropology and Prehistory: Exploring Our Human Ancestry*. Boston, MA: Pearson.

Richard, A. 1985. *Primates in Nature*. New York: W.H. Freeman.

Richard, G. [1923]1975. "Dogmatic Atheism in the Sociology of Religion". In W.S.F. Pickering (Eds.) *Durkheim On Religion: A Selection of Readings with Bibliographies* (pp. 228–276). London: Routledge and Kegan Paul.

Richter, D., R. Grün, R. Joannes-Boyau, T. Steele, F. Amani, M. Rué, P. Fernandes, et al. 2017. "The Age of the Hominin Fossils from Jebel Irhoud, Morocco, and the Origins of the Middle Stone Age". *Nature*, 546: 293–296.

Riley, A. 2005. "Renegade Durkhemianism and the Transgressive Left Sacred". In J. Alexander and P. Smith (Eds.) *The Cambridge Companion to Durkheim* (pp. 274–301). Cambridge: Cambridge University Press.

———. 2014. "Flags, Totem Bodies, and the Meanings of 9/11: A Durkheimian Tour of a September 11th Ceremony at the Flight 93 Chapel". *Canadian Journal of Sociology*, 39: 719–740.

———. 2015. *Angel Patriots: The Crash of United Flight 93 and the Myth of America*. New York: New York University Press.

Rivers, W.H.R. 1907. "Kinship Organizations and Group Marriage in Australia by Northcote Thomas". *Man*: 55–56, 90–92.

———. 1908. "Totemism in Fiji". *Man*: 74–75, 133–136.

———. 1909. "Totemism in Polynesia and Melanesia". *JAI*, 39: 156–180.

Rivière, P. 1995. "William Robertson Smith and John Ferguson McLennan: The Aberdeen Roots of British Social Anthropology". In W. Johnstone (Ed.) *William Robertson Smith: Essays in Reassessment* (pp. 293–302). Sheffield, UK: Sheffield Academic Press.

Robbins, M. 2011. "Gorillas: Diversity in Ecology and Behavior". In C. Campbell, A. Fuenter, K. MacKinnon, S. Bearder and R. Stumpf (Eds.) *Primates in Perspective* (pp. 326–339). New York: Oxford University Press.

Roberts, S., J. Vick and H. Buchanan-Smith. 2012a. "Usage and Comprehension of Manual Gestures in Wild Chimpanzees". *Animal Behaviour*, 84: 459–470.

Roberts, A., J. Vick, S. Roberts, H. Buchannan-Smith and K. Zuberbühler. 2012b. "A Structure-Based Repertoire of Manual Gestures in Wild Chimpanzees: Statistical Analyses of a Graded Communication System". *Evolution and Human Behavior*, 33: 578–589.

Robinson, J., J. Rowan, C. Campisano, J. Wynn and K. Reed. 2017. "Late Pliocene Environmental Change During the Transition from Australopithecus to Homo". *Nature Ecology & Evolution*, 1: 1–7.

Rosati, A. and B. Hare. 2013. "Chimpanzees and Bonobos Exhibit Emotional Responses to Decision Outcomes". *Plos One*, 8: 1–14.

Rosenbaum, S., A.A. Maldonado-Chaparro and T.S. Stoinski. 2016. "Group Structure Predicts Variation in Proximity Relationships between Male-Female and Male-Infant Pairs of Mountain Gorillas (Gorilla Beringei beringei)". *Primates*, 57: 17–28.

Rothwell, F. 1922. "Emile Boutroux". *The Monist*, 22: 161–163.

Rouquier, S. and Giorgi, D. 2007. "The Loss of Olfactory Receptor Genes in Human Evolution". In *Evolution of Nervous Systems: A Comprehensive Reference* (pp. 129–139). Amsterdam: Elsevier.

Roy, A. 1980. *Species Identity and Attachment: A Phylogenetic Evaluation.* New York: Garland STPM Press.

Rumbaugh, D. 2013. *"With Apes in Mind: Emergents, Communication and Competence".* Georgia: Distributed by Amazon.com.

———. 2015. "A Salience Theory of Learning and Behavior and Rights of Apes". In J. Turner, R. Machalek and A. Maryanski (Eds.) *Handbook on Evolution and Society* (pp. 514–536). Boulder, CO: Paradigm.

Rumbaugh, D. and S. Savage-Rumbaugh. 1996. "Biobehavioral Roots of Language: Words, Apes, and a Child". In B. Velichkovsky and D. Rumbaugh (Eds.) *Communication Meaning* (pp. 257–274). Mahwah, NJ: Lawrence Erlbaum.

Russon, A. 2009. "Orangutans". *Current Biology*, 19: 295–297.

Sade, D.E. 1968. "Inhibition of Son-Mother Mating Among Free-ranging Rhesus Monkeys". *Science Psychoanalysis*, 12: 18–38.

Sahnouni, M., J. Rosell, J. van der Made, J. Vergés, A. Ollé, N. Kandi, Z. Harichane, A. Derradji and M. Medig. 2013. "The First Evidence of Cut Marks and Usewear Traces from the Plio-Pleistocene locality of El-Kherba (Ain Hanech), Algeria: Implications for Early Hominin Subsistence Activities circa 1.8 MA". *Journal of Human Evolution*, 64: 137–150.

Savage-Rumbaugh, D.R. and S. Boysen. 1978. "Symbolic Communication Between Two Chimpanzees (*Pan troglodytes*)". *Science*, 201: 641–644.

Savage-Rumbaugh, S., K. McDonald, R.A. Sevcik and E. Rubert. 1986. "Spontaneous Symbol Acquisition and Communicative Use by Pygmy Chimpanzees (*Pan paniscus*)". *Journal of experimental Psychology: General*, 115: 211–235.

Savage-Rumbaugh, S., and R. Lewin. 1994. *The Ape at the Brink of the Human Mind.* New York: Wiley.

Schaeffle, A. 1875. *Bau und Leben des Sozialen Körpers.* Tübingen, Germany: Laupp.

Schaller, G. 1963. *The Mountain Gorilla: Ecology and Behavior.* Chicago, IL: University of Chicago Press.

———. 1964. *The Year of the Gorilla.* Chicago, IL: University of Chicago Press.

Schmaus, W. 1998. "Durkheim on the Causes and Functions of the Categories". In N.J. Allen, W.S.F. Pickering and W. Watts Miller (Eds.) *On Durkheim's Elementary Forms of Religious Life* (pp. 176–188). London: Routledge.

Schmeltz, M., J. Calland, M. Tomasello. 2011. "Chimpanzees Know That Others Make Inferences". *Proceedings of the National Academy of Sciences U.S.A.*, 108: 3077–3079.

Schmidt, Father W. 1908. "Totemism in Fiji". *Man*: 83–84, 152–153.

———. [1931]1972. *The Origin and Growth of Religion: Facts and Theories*. New York: Cooper Squire Publishers (translated by H.J. Rose).

Schoolcraft, H. 1847. *Notes on the Iroquois or Contribution to American History, Antiquities and General Ethnography*. Albany, NY: Erastus H. Pease.

———. 1851–1857. *Historical and Statistical Information Respecting the History, Condition, and Prospects of the Indian Tribes of the United States*. Philadelphia, PA: Lippinlott, Grambo.

Schrift, A. 2008. "The Effects of the Agrégation de Philosophie on Twentieth-century French Philosophy". *Journal of the History of Philosophy*, 46: 449–474.

Seger, I. 1957. *Durkheim and His Critics on the Sociology of Religion*. Columbia University: Bureau of Applied Research.

Seligmann, C.G. 1908a. "Linked Totems: A Reply to Mr. Lang". *Man*: 99–100, 179–181.

———. 1908b. "Note on Totemism in New Guinea, with Reference to Man 75 and 84". *Man*, 8: 162–163.

Semendeferi, K. and H. Damasio 2000. "The Brain and its Main Anatomical Subdivisions in Living Hominoids Using Magnetic Resonance Imaging". *Journal of Human Evolution*, 38: 317–332.

Serazio, M. 2013. "Just How Much is Sports Fandom Like Religion?" *The Atlantic* (online): 1–6.

Service, E. 1962. *Primitive Social Organization*. New York: Random House.

SESTA. 2005. *Niaux Cave. Service D'Exploitation des Sites Touristiques de l'ariège*. European Union: APA Poux editions.

Setia, T.M., R. Delgado, S. Suci Utami Atmoko, I. Singleton and C.P. Van Schaik. 2008. "Social Organization and Male-Male Relationships". In *Orangutans: Geographical Variation in Behavioral Ecology and Conservation* (pp. 245–253). Oxford: Oxford University Press.

Seyfarth, R. and D. Cheney. 2011. "Animal Cognition: Chimpanzee Alarm Calls Depend on What Others Know". *Current Biology*, 22: 52.

Sherwood, C.C. and P.R. Hof. 2007. "The Evolution of Neuron Types and Cortical Histology in Apes and Humans". *Evolution of Nervous Systems: A Comprehensive Reference* (Vol. 4) (pp. 355–378). New York: Academic Press.

Simon, W.M. 1965. "The 'Two Cultures' in Nineteenth-century France: Victor Cousin and Auguste Comte". *Journal of the History of Ideas*, 26: 45–58.

Simonti, C., B. Vernot, L. Bastarache, E. Bottinger, D. Carrell, et al. 2016. "The Phenotypic Legacy of Admixture Between Modern Humans and Neanderthals". *Science*, 351: 737–741.

Slotkin, J.S. 1965. *Readings in Early Anthropology*. New York: Wenner-Gren Foundation.

Smend, R. 1995. "William Robertson Smith and Julius Wellhausen". In W. Johnstone (Ed.) *William Robertson Smith: Essays in Reassessment* (pp. 226–242). Sheffield, UK: Sheffield Academic Press.

Smith, P. and J. Alexander. 1996. "Durkheim's Religious Revival". *American Journal of Sociology*, 102: 585–592.

Smith, R. 1982. *The Ecole Normale Supérieure and the Third Republic*. Albany, NY: State University of New York Press.

Smith, R. [1869]1912a. "Hegel and the Metaphysics of the Fluxional Calculus". In J. Sutherland Black and G. Chrystal (Eds.) *Lectures and Essays of William Robertson Smith* (pp. 13–43). London: Adam and Charles Black.

———. [1869]1912b. "Theory of Geometrical Reasoning". In J. Sutherland Black and G. Chrystal (Eds.) *Lectures and Essays of William Robertson Smith* (pp. 3–12). London: Adam and Charles Black.

———. [1870]1912c. "On the Flow of Electricity in Conducting Surfaces". In J. Sutherland Black and G. Chrystal (Eds.) *Lectures and Essays of William Robertson Smith* (pp. 44–66). London: Adam and Charles Black.

———. [1875]1912d. "The Place of Theology in the Work and Growth of the Church". In J. Sutherland Black and G. Chrystal (Eds.) *Lectures and Essays of William Robertson Smith* (pp. 309–340). London: Adam and Charles Black.

———. 1880. "Animal Worship and Animal Tribes Among the Arabs and in the Old Testament". *Journal of Philology*, 9: 75–100.

———. [1882]2002. *The Prophets of Israel and Their Place in History*. New Brunswick, NJ: Transaction Publishers.

———. [1885]1907. *Kinship and Marriage in Early Arabia*. London: Adam and Charles Black.

———. 1889. *Lectures on the Religion of the Semites. First Series: The Fundamental Institutions*. New York: D. Appleton.

———. 1894. *Lectures on the Religion of the Semites: First Series, The Fundamental Institutions*. London: Adam and Charles Black.

———. 1995. *Lectures on the Religion of the Semites: Second and Third Series*. Sheffield, UK: Sheffield Academic Press (edited by J. Day).

Soressi, M., S. McPherron, M. Lenair, T. Dognandzic, et al. 2013. "Neanderthals Made the First Specialized Bone Tools in Europe". *Proceedings of the National Academy of Science, USA*, 110: 14186–14190.

Spencer, B. 1896. *Report on the Work of the Horn Scientific Expedition to Central Australia*. Four volumes. London: Dulau.

Spencer, B. and F.J. Gillen. 1938[1899]. *The Native Tribes of Central Australia*. London: Macmillan.

———. 1904. *The Northern Tribes of Central Australia*. London: Macmillan.

Spencer, H. 1873–1881. *Descriptive Sociology; or, Groups of Sociological Facts, Classified and Arranged by Herbert Spencer*. New York: Appleton (complied and abstracted by D. Duncan, R. Scheppig and J. Collier).

———. [1874–1896]1898. *Principles of Sociology*. Three volumes. New York: Appleton.

Spikins, P., G. Hitchens, A. Needham and H. Rutherford. 2014. "Growth, Learning, Play and Attachment in Neanderthal Children". *Oxford Journal of Archaeology*, 33: 111–134.

Spoor, F., P. Gunz, S. Neubauer, S. Stelzer, N. Scott, A. Kwekason and M.C. Dean. 2015. "Reconstructed *Homo Hablis* Type OH7 Suggests Deep-rooted Species Diversity in Early *Homo*". *Nature*, 519: 83–86.

Steadman, S. 2009. *Archaeology of Religion: Cultures and Their Beliefs in Worldwide Context.* Walnut Creek, CA: Left Coast Press.

Stebbins, G.L. 1969. *The Basis of Progressive Evolution.* Chapel Hill, NC: University of North Carolina Press.

Stein, P. and B. Rowe. 2011. *Physical Anthropology.* New York: McGraw Hill.

Stevens, J., H. Vervaecke, H. De Vries and L. Elsacker. 2006. "Social Structures in Pan Paniscus: Testing the Female Bonding Hypothesis". *Primates*, 47: 210–217.

Stirling, E.C. 1896. "Anthropology". In B. Spencer (Ed.) *Report on the Work of the Horn Scientific Expedition to Central Australia* (Part 4) (pp. 1–197). London: Dulau.

Stocking, Jr. G. 1968. *Race, Culture and Evolution: Essays in the History of Anthropology.* New York: Free Press.

Stokes, D. 2001. *Desert Dreaming.* Australia: Reed International Books.

Straumann, C. and J. Anderson. 1991. "Mirror-Induced Social Facilitation in Stumptailed Macaques (*Macaca* arctoides). *American Journal of Primatology*, 25: 125–132.

Strehlow, C. 1907–1908. *Die Aranda-und Loritja-stämme in Zentral-Australien.* Frankfurt, Germany: Joseph Baer.

Strenski, I. 1989. "Durkheim's Bourgeois Theory of Sacrifice". In N.J. Allen, W.S.F. Pickering and W. Watts Miller (Eds.) *On Durkheim's Elementary Forms of Religious Life* (pp. 116–126). London: Routledge.

Strenski, I. 2006. *The New Durkheim.* New Brunswick, NJ: Rutgers University Press.

Stringer, C. and J. Galway-Witham. 2017. "On the Origins of Our Species". *Nature*, 546: 212–214.

———. 2018. "When Did Modern Humans Leave Africa?" *Science*, 359: 389–390.

Struhsaker, T. 1969. "Correlates of Ecology and Social Organization Among African Cercopithecines". *Folia Primatologica*, 11: 80–118.

Sumpf, J. 1965. "Durkheim et le problème de l'étude sociologique de la religion". *Archives de sociologie des religions*, 20: 63–73.

Stumpf, R.M., M. Emery Thompson, M. Muller and R. Wrangham. 2009. "The Context of Female Dispersal in Kanyawara Chimpanzees". *Behaviour*, 146: 629–656.

Suddendorf, T. and E. Collier-Baker. 2009. "The Evolution of Primate Visual Self-recognition: Evidence of Absence in Lesser Apes". *Proceedings of the Royal Society B: Biological Sciences*, 276: 1671–1677.

Swanson, G. 1960. *Birth of the Gods: The Origin of Primitive Beliefs.* Ann Arbor, MI: University of Michigan.

Swanton, J. 1905. "The Social Organization of American Tribes". *American Anthropologist*, 7: 663–673.

———. 1906a. "Lectures on the Early History of the Kingship by J.G. Frazer". *American Anthropologist*, 8: 157–160.

———.1906b. "The Secret of the Totem by Andrew Lang". *American Anthropologist*, 8: 160–165.

Temerlin J. 1980. "The Self Concept of a Home-reared Chimpanzee". In A. Roy (Ed.) *Species Identity and Attachment: A Phylogenetic Evaluation* (pp. 245–264). New York: Garland STPM Press.

Temerin, J. and J. Cant. 1983. "The Evolutionary Divergence of Old World Monkeys and Apes". *The American Naturalist*, 122: 335–351.

Thomas, N.W. 1904a. "Arunta Totemism: A Note on Mr. Lang's Theory". *Man*, 68: 99–101.

———. 1904b. "Further Remarks on Mr. Hill-Tout's Views on Totemism". *Man*: 52–53, 82–85.

———. 1905. "Madagascar". *Man*, v35–36: 62–64.

Thompson, K. 1975. *August Comte: The Foundation of Sociology*. New York: Wiley.

———. 1998. "Durkheim and Sacred Identity". In N.J. Allen, W.S.F. Pickering and W. Watts Miller (Eds.). *On Durkheim's Elementary Forms of Religious Life* (pp. 92–104). London: Routledge.

———. 2002. *Emile Durkheim: Revised Edition*. New York: Routledge.

Tiryakian, E. 1964. "Introduction to a Bibliographical Focus on Emile Durkheim". *Journal for the Scientific Study of Religion*, 3: 247–254.

———. 1978. "Emile Durkheim". In T. Bottomore and R. Nisbet (Eds.) *A History of Sociological Analysis* (pp. 187–236). New York: Basic Books.

———. 1979. "L'École durkheimenne à la recherche de la société perdue; le debut de la sociologie et son milieu culturl". *Cahiers internationau.x de sociologie*, LXVI: 97–114.

———. 2009. *For Durkheim: Essays in Historical and Cultural Sociology. Rethinking Classical Sociology*. Aldershot, UK: Ashgate.

———. 2012. "Early Reviews of the Elementary Forms of Religious Life". *Journal of Classical Sociology*, 12: 513–525.

Tomasello, M., J. Call, and B. Hare. 2003. "Chimpanzees Understand Psychological States the Question is Which Ones and to What Extent?" *Trends Cognitive Science*, 7: 153–156.

Tomasello, M., B.L. George, A.C. Kruger, M.J. Farrar and A. Evans. 1985. "The Development of Gestural Communication in Young Chimpanzees". *Journal of Human Evolution*, 14: 175–186.

Tooker, E. 1997. "Introduction". In L.H. Morgan (Ed.) *Systems of Consanquinity and Affinity of the Human Family*. Lincoln, NE: University of Nebraska Press.

Toy, C. 1904. "Recent Discussions of Totemism". *Journal of the American Oriental Society*, 25: 146–161.

Traugott, M. 1978. *Emile Durkheim: On Institutional Analysis*. Chicago, IL: University of Chicago Press.

Trautmann, T. 1987. *Lewis Henry Morgan and the Invention of Kinship*. Berkeley, CA: University of California Press.

Trumbull, J.H. 1872. "Words Derived from Indian Languages of North America". *Transactions of the American Philological Association (1869–1896)*, 3: 19–32.

Turner, B. 1992. "Preface to the Second Edition". In *Professional Ethics and Civic Morals by Emile Durkheim* (pp. xiii-xlii). London: Routledge.

Turner, J. 1984. "Durkheim's and Spencer's Principles of Social Organization: A Theoretical Note". *Sociological Perspectives*, 27: 21–33.

———. 1985. *Herbert Spencer: A Renewed Appreciation*. Newbury Park, UK: Sage.

———. 1988. *A Theory of Social Interaction*. Stanford, CA: Stanford University Press.

———. 1990. "Durkheim's Theory of Social Organization". *Social Forces*, 68: 419–433.

———. 2002. *Face to Face: Towards a Sociological Theory of Interpersonal Behavior*. Stanford, CA: Stanford University Press.

———. 2010. *Theoretical Principles of Sociology* (Vol. 2 on Microdynamics). New York: Springer.

Turner, J. and A. Maryanski. 1979. *Functionalism*. Menlo Park, CA: Benjamin/Cummings.

———. 1988. "Sociology's Lost Human Relations Area Files". *Sociological Perspectives*, 31: 19–34.

———. 2005. *Incest: Origins of the Taboo*. Boulder, CO: Paradigm Publishers.

———. 2008. *On the Origin of Societies by Natural Selection*. Boulder, CO: Paradigm Publishers.

Turner, J., L. Beeghley and C. Powers. 2012. *The Emergence of Sociological Theory*. Los Angeles, CA: Sage.

Turner, J., A. Maryanski, A. Peterson and A. Geetz. 2018. *The Emergence and Evolution of Religion: By Means of Natural Selection*. London: Routledge.

Turner, S. 1993. *Sociologist and Moralist*. London: Routledge.

Tylor, E. 1865. *Researches into the Early History of Mankind and the Development of Civilization*. London: J. Murray.

———. 1871. *Primitive Culture: Researches into the Development of Mythology, Philosophy, Religion, Language, Art, and Custom*. 2 volumes. London: J. Murray.

Van Gennep, A. [1913]1975. "Review É. Durkheim—Les Formes élémentaires de la vie religieuse. Le système totémique en Australie". In W.S.F. Pickering (Ed.) *Durkheim on Religion* (pp. 206–208). London: Routledge and Kegan Paul.

Van Lawick-Goodall, J. 1968. "The Behaviour of Free-Living Chimpanzees in the Gombe Stream Reserve". *Animal Behaviour Monographs*: 161–311.

Varki, A. and T. Altheide. 2005. "Comparing the Human and Chimpanzee Genomes: Searching for Needles in a Haystack". *Genome Research*, 15: 1746–1758.

Varki, A. and D. Nelson. 2007. "Genomie Comparisons of Humans and Chimpanzees". *Annual Review of Anthropology*, 36: 161–209.

Villmoare, B., W. Kimbel, C. Seyoum, C. Campisano, E. Di Maggio, J. Rowan, D. Braun, J.R. Arrowsmith and K. Reed. 2015. "Early *Homo* at 2.8 Ma from Ledi-Geraru, Afar, Ethiopia". *Science*, 347: 1352–1354.

Wall, J. 2013. "Great Ape Genomics". *Lar Journal*, 1: 82–90.

Wall, J., M.A. Yang, F. Jay, S. Kim, E. Durand, L. Stevison, C. Gignoux, A. Woener, M. Hammer and M. Slatkin. 2013. "Higher Levels of Neanderthal Ancestry in East Asians than in Europeans". *Genetics*, 194: 199–209.

Wallis, W. 1914. "Durkheim's View of Religion". *Journal of Religious Psychology*, 7: 252–267.

Wallwork, E. 1972. *Durkheim: Morality and Milieu*. Cambridge, MA: Harvard University Press.

Warner, W.L. 1935. "Emile Durkheim on the Division of Labor in Society: Being a Translation of His *De la division du travail social* with an Estimate of his Work by George Simpson". *American Anthropologist*, New Series 37: 355.

———. 1949. *Democracy in Jonesville*. New York: Harper.

Watson, S., S. Townsend, A. Schel, C. Wilk, E. Wallace, L. Cheng, V.A West and K. Slocombe. 2015. "Vocal Learning in the Functionally Referential Food Grunts of Chimpanzees". *Current Biology*, 25: 495–499.

Watts, D.P. 2002. "Interchange of Grooming and Coalitionary Support by Wild Male Chimpanzees". *American Journal of Physical Anthropology*, Supp. 34: 162.

———. 2012. "The Apes: Taxonomy, Biogeography, Life Histories, and Behavioral Ecology". In J. Mitani, J. Call, P. Kappeler, R. Palombit and J. Silk (Eds.) *The Evolution of Primate Societies*. Chicago, IL: University of Chicago Press.

Watts Miller, W. 1998. "Durkheim, Kant, the immortal Soul and God." In N.J. Allen, W.S.F. Pickering and W. Watts Miller (Eds.) *On Durkheim's Elementary Forms of Religious Life* (pp. 66–77). London: Routledge.

———. 2012. *Solidarity and the Sacred*. New York: Berghahn.

———. 2013. "The Creation and Problematic Achievement of Les Formes Elémentaires". In S. Hausner (Ed.) *Durkheim in Dialogue: A Cententary Celebration of the Elementary Forms of Religious Life* (pp. 235–256). New York: Berghahn Books.

———. 2014. *Durkheim, Morals and Modernity*. Oxford: Routledge.

Weatherly, U. 1917. "The Elementary Forms of the Religious Life". *American Journal of Sociology*, 22: 561–563.

Webster, H. 1911. "Totemism: An Analytical Study by A.A. Goldenweiser". *Journal of Philosophy, Psychology and Scientific Methods*, 8(17): 471–473.

———. 1913 "Les formes élementaires de la vie religieuse. Le système totémique en Australie". *American Journal of Sociology*, 18: 843–846.

Wellman, B. and S.O. Berkowitz. 1988. *Social Structures: A Network Approach*. New York: Cambridge University Press.

Wendall, B. 1907. *The France of Today*. New York: C. Scribner.

Wentworth, W. 1976. "Heritage Review: A Prophet of the Scientific Study of Religion". *Journal for the Scientific Study of Religion*, 15(1): 103–106.

Werblin, F. 1976. "The Control of Sensitivity in the Retina." In *Recent Progress in Perception. Scientific American* (pp. 21–36). San Francisco, CA: W.H. Freeman.

Westermarck, E. 1891. *A History of Human Marriage*. London: Macmillan.

White, F.J. 1989. "Ecological Correlates of Pygmy Chimpanzee Social Structure". In V. Standen and R.A. Foley (Eds.) *Comparative Socioecology* (pp. 151–164). Oxford: Blackwell.

Whitehead, H. and L. Rendell. 2015. *The Cultural Lives of Whales and Dolphins*. Chicago, IL: University of Chicago Press.

Whiten, A. 2011. "The Scope of Culture in Chimpanzees, Humans and Ancestral Apes". *Philos. Trans. R. Soc. Lond. B. Biol. Sci.*, 366: 997–1007.

———. 2013. "Humans Are Not Alone in Computing How Others See the World". *Animal Behaviour*, 86: 213–221.

Whiten, A., A. Spiteri, V. Horner, K. Bonne, S. Lambeth, S. Schapiro and F. de Waal. 2007. "Transmission of Multiple Traditions Within and Between Chimpanzee Groups". *Current Biology*, 17: 1038–1043.

Williams, J., G. Oehlert, J. Carlis and A. Pusey. 2004. "Why Do Male Chimpanzees Defend a Group Range. *Animal Behaviour*, 68: 523–532.

Williams, K. 1997. *Ayers Rock of the Olgas*. Australia: Buscombe Vicprint.

Willshire, W.H. 1891. *The Aborigines of Central Australia*. Adelaide: By Authority: C.E. Bristow, Government Printer, North-Terrace.

Winzeler, R.L. 2008. *Anthropology and Religion*. New York: AltaMira Press.

Wood, B. and N. Lonergan. 2008. "The Hominin Fossil Record: Taxa, Grades and Clades". *Journal of Anatomy*, 212: 354–376.

Wood, B., D. Watts, J. Mitani and K. Langergraber. 2017. "Favorable Ecological Circumstances Promote Life Expectancy in Chimpanzees Similar to That of Human Hunter-Gatherers". *Journal of Human Evolution*, 105: 41–56.

Yamamoto, S., T. Humle and M. Tanaka. 2012. "Chimpanzee's Flexible Targeted Helping Based on an Understanding of Conspecifics' Goals". *PNAS*, 109: 3588–3592.

Yraveda, J., M.Á. Maté-González, J. Palomeque-González, J. Palomeque-González, J. Aramendi, V. Estaca-Gómez, M. Blazquez, E. Vargas, E. Organista, et al. 2017. " A New Approach to Raw Material Use in the Exploitation of Animal Carcasses at BK (Upper Bed 11, Olduvai Gorge, Tanzania): A Micro-photogrammetric and Geometric Morphometric Analysis of Fossil Cut Marks". *Boreas*, 46: 860–873.

Zalmout, L., W. Sanders, L. Maclatchy, L. Gunnell, et al. 2010. "New Oligocene Primate from Saudi Arabia and the Divergence of Apes and Old World Monkeys". *Nature*, 466: 360–365.

Zorich, Z. 2014. "Did Neanderthals Bury Their Dead?" *Archaeology*, 67(2): 19.

Index

Ackerman, R. 87–89, 135–137
Alexander, J. 79, 101, 110
Alice Springs 131–133, 157
Allen, N.J. 157, 195, 276, 302
Alpert, H. 26, 34, 51, 54, 56, 63, 141
Ancient City, The 21, 38, 40–51, 61
Ancient Society 15, 23, 61
animism *see* religious evolution
L'Année Sociologique 12, 24, 44, 62, 110, 111–114, 120, 127–128, 138–139, 142, 162, 164, 258
apes 199, 213–238, 240–249, 253–257, 259–264, 267, 271, 275, 297, 301–302
Arrernte 103, 117, 131–134, 136–139, 143–151, 157, 159–160, 164, 179, 181–182, 194, 282
Arunta *see* Arrernte
Aubarbier, J.-L. 209
Australian aboriginals *see* Arrernte
Australopithecines 198–199

Bachofen, J. 12, 14, 17–18, 21
Baldwin, J. 268–269
Beidelman, T. 84–85
Bellah, R. 27, 31–32, 79, 195, 197
Besnard, P. 104, 107, 112–13, 128
bilateral descent 21, 185n17
Binet, M. 209
Boas, F. 139–140, 167n4, 284
Boesch, C. 233–237, 236, 277–278
Bouglé, C. 103, 107–108, 112, 128, 186
Boutroux, É. 3, 35–40, 44, 65
bride capture 19–21
British Utilitarian Tradition 7
Brooks, J. 2, 44–45, 49–50, 53
Buchannan-Smith, H. 253–254

Cairns 277
carnival 276–277
Charle, C. 55, 161

chatada clan 153
chimpanzee communication: *Artificial Languages* 255–256; *Gestural Repertoires* 253–254; *Linguistic Repertoires* 254–255; *Vocal Repertoire* 252–253
churinga 131, 138, 181–182
cladistics: 218, 242, 260; (hypotheses of) Relatedness Hypothesis 218, 224–225; Regularity Hypothesis 218, 225, 227
clan *see* kinship forms
classes *see* kinship forms
collective conscience 4, 6, 9, 48, 50 73–75, 78, 105, 108–109, 261, 282
collective effervescence 189–190, 280
collective representations 4, 6, 9, 72, 106, 109, 126n12, 127, 165, 170–172, 174, 181, 186, 190, 192, 201, 203–204, 231, 268, 270, 272, 279, 296; *see also* individual representations 171, 296
Collège D'Épinal 29 *(Émile Durkheim stands in the last row, fourth student from left)*
Collier-Baker, E. 249
Collins, R. 1, 113, 195, 259, 294, 301
community complex, the 259–273, 299
community, definitions 238–241
community organization of chimpanzees 234–236, 262, 272
community, sense of 234–235, 237, 237n2, 238, 240, 270–272, 297, 299, 302
Comte, A. 2, 5–8, 10, 13, 25–26, 36–37, 40, 43–46, 48, 50, 57–58, 65–66, 73, 141–142
consanguinity 15, 158, 285, 237, 265, 272, 282
continuity thesis 39
Cooley, C.H. 247
Coser, L. 6–7, 31, 35
Crawford, L. 36–38

Darwin, C. 10, 13, 43, 53
Davy, G. 27, 30, 45, 55
De Coulanges, N.D. Fustel 12, 14, 21–24, 35, 38–42, 61, 67, 114, 172
Deploige, S. 65–66, 164
Division of Labor in Society, The 4–5, 7–8, 24, 40, 50, 54, 62, 72–73, 75, 78–79, 81–82, 100, 105–106, 108–109, 128–129, 142, 169, 176, 231, 234, 261, 274

eclectic spiritualism 48, 52
École Normale Supérieure 24, 29–32, 35–36, 39–40, 44–45, 49–51, 86, 112–113, 129n1
École Normale *see* École Normale Supérieure
Elementary Forms of Religious Life: The Australian System of Totemism, The 1–6, 13, 24, 41, 45, 53–54, 62, 93, 115, 130, 140, 162–166, 169–171, 179, 194–195, 197, 258, 277, 281–282, 284–286, 300
Encyclopaedia Britannica 83, 85, 88
endogamy 13–14, 14n11, 19, 86, 144, 147–148 *see* exogamy
English School of Social Anthropology 10–12
Engwura 133–134
Espinas, A. 2, 6, 25, 44–57, 64–65, 68, 198
Espinas' Societal types: Nutritive Societies 46; Relational Societies 47–48; Reproductive Societies 47
evolutionary continuity 47
exogamy 3–4, 13–14, 14n11, 19–21, 86, 89, 92, 98–99, 101, 116–120, 126–127, 129, 134–141, 143–146, 149, 158–161, 164, 166, 168, 179–182, 194, 196, 199, 204, 261–265, 278, 281, 284–285, 287, 293

female-bonded societies 223, 226
Fields, K. 165
Fisher, R.A. 295
Fison, L. 61, 133, 135, 137, 151
founders effect 202n7, 217–218, 227, 283
Fournier, M. 27–29, 39, 44, 55–56, 63, 64, 103, 108, 112, 129, 141–142, 149
Fox, R. 13–14n11, 16n14
Frazer, J. 4, 64, 67, 83–84, 87–89, 98, 130, 135–137, 141, 143–146, 148, 158, 160, 162, 164–166, 169, 178, 208, 281–282, 284

Gagneux, P. 232
Gallatin, A. 166
Gamble, C. 199, 204, 210
Garner, R.L. 276
Geiger, R. 33, 44–45, 48, 52, 56
Giddens, A. 111, 128–129
Gillen, F. 128, 130–140, 143–147, 157, 159–160, 164–165, 169, 177, 194, 208, 282–284
Glerean, E. 280
Goldenweiser, A. 162, 284–288, 292–293
Golden Bough, The 83, 87, 99, 135, 137
Goodall, J. 223–224, 234–235 237–238, 254, 261, 272, 275–276, 298
Granovetter, M. 237, 267
great heresy case 85–86
Greenberg, L. 28, 31
Guyau, J.M. 70–72, 78–79

Hackett, T. 243
Haddon, A. 142
Hammond, M. 195, 299
Hamnett, I. 179–180
Hari, R. 280
Harlow, H. 247
Hausner, S. 195, 302
Hays, H.R. 17, 250
Herrick, J. 21, 24, 38–39, 41
Hillery, G. 239
hominins 198, 198n4, 200, 200n5, 201–203, 213, 225, 228, 230, 232–233, 260, 262, 265–266, 278, 294, 301–303
Homo erectus 198n4, 200–201, 278
Homo sapiens 198n4, 201–205, 209
horde concept 4, 9, 15–17, 20–21, 25, 62, 74, 78, 86, 108–109, 116–117, 164, 168–169, 180, 182, 184–185, 195–197, 217–218, 231–234, 261–266, 272, 274, 298
Horn Scientific Expedition 132, 282

identity: place identity 247; self-identity 219, 247–252, 267–269, 293, 296–297; social identity 247–248, 267; species identity 247–248
individual representations 171, 296; *see also* collective representations 4, 6, 9, 72, 106, 109, 126n12, 127, 165, 170–172, 174, 181, 186, 190, 192, 201, 203–204, 231, 268, 270, 272, 279, 296

individualism 5, 6, 48, 51, 74n13, 79, 105n4, 109, 212–213, 230–231, 259–260, 269, 272
Intichiuma 135, 145

Jääskeläinen 280
Jolly, A. 264
Jones, R. 28n2, 67, 78, 99n16, 284

Kaneko, T. 251
Kawkiutl Indians 139
King, I. 266
Kinship and Marriage in Early Arabia 87, 91, 281
kinship forms: clan 13, 13–14n, 18, 21, 23, 41, 54, 62, 74, 74n13, 76–78, 81–82, 88–89, 99, 103, 109, 116–120, 123, 129, 140, 146–148, 151–153, 155–156, 158, 161, 164–169, 179–189, 195–196, 218, 231, 238, 261–265, 280, 285, 287–294, 299; classes 134, 138–139, 146–147, 151–152, 159–161; lineage 13, 13–14n11, 16, 16n15, 19, 217–218, 223, 225, 227–228, 238, 291, 298; moiety 13, 13–14n11, 146, 146n3, 151, 158, 180n14; nuclear family 13–15, 13–14n11, 105, 197, 231, 239, 239n3, 264–265, 298, 302; phratry 13–14, 13–14n11, 23, 89, 146n3, 146–148, 151, 153, 156, 158–159, 180n14, 180–182, 181, 181n15 184; pre-kinship horde 4, 9, 15–17, 20–21, 25, 62, 74, 78, 86, 108–109, 116–117, 164, 168–169, 180, 182, 184–185, 195–197, 217–218, 231–234, 261–266, 272, 274, 298; tribe 13, 13–14n11, 18–20, 23, 41, 89, 139–140, 152–153, 156–158, 160, 186, 300
Kühl, H. 277
Kummer, H. 215, 229
Kuper, A. 13, 101, 135, 285

last common ancestor (LCA) 198, 214, 217–218, 219n3, 221, 224–232, 238, 240, 242n4 244n5, 246, 262, 271, 295, 302
Lee, D. 239
Levi-Strauss, C. 288, 292
Lieberman, P. 256–257
Logue, W. 27, 48
Long, J. 165–166, 167n4
looking glass self 247

Lowie, R. 285, 298
Lukes, S. 1, 27, 29–30, 32–35, 39, 41–42, 44, 56, 67
Luncz, L. 234, 236
Lévy-Bruhl, L. 6, 142
Lycée de Sens 42–43, 53

McLennan, J. 12, 14, 16, 19–21, 84, 86–87, 98, 137, 177, 280
Maine, H. 12, 14, 16, 18–19, 238
matrilineal descent 160, 168, 179–180, 196, 199, 204, 224, 227–228; *see also* patrilineal descent 21, 23, 138, 140, 160
Marxian doctrine 107
matriliny *see* matrilineal descent
Mauss, M. 4, 28, 55, 62, 64–65, 111, 113–114, 138–139, 143, 149, 151–156, 164, 260, 279, 288
Mead, G.H. 247–248, 250–252, 267–271, 296
Mead's concepts of other, significant other: 247, 250–252, 267–268, 296; concrete other 267, 270; generalized other 249–249, 267–271, 296
Meddin, J. 251
Mémoires (Durkheim's) 114, 116, 121, 143, 149, 159
mirror neurons 280
modalities: auditory modality 243; chemical modalities 242; haptic modality 243; visual modality 214, 243
Morgan, L. 12, 14–17, 21, 137, 168
Müller, M. 176
Murdock, G. 239, 239n3

Nandan, Y. 66, 113, 128–129
Native American Tribes 152–153, 165–168, 179
Native Tribes of Central Australia, The 130, 134–136, 157, 159
naturism *see* religious evolution
Neanderthal 202, 204–205, 264
network analysis *see* social network theory and methods
Newby, H. 239
Nissen, H. 276–277
nuclear family *see* kinship forms
Nummenmaa, L. 280

Omaha 152–153
organic evolution 10, 53

patrilineal descent 21, 23, 138, 140, 160; *see also* matrilineal descent 160, 168, 179–180, 196, 199, 204, 224, 227–228
patrilineality *see* patrilineal descent
parietal art 205–207; Lascaux 209; Sorcerer, the 206
pedagogy 53, 55, 63, 113, 141, 213, 259
personal conscience 75, 78
Pfuetze, P. 296
phratry *see* kinship forms
phylogenetic inertia 215, 229
Pickering, W.S.F. 28, 65, 67, 79, 99, 102, 106, 110
Poggi, G. 178
Positive Philosophy 7
primates (ape case studies) Kanzi 256–257; Lana 265; Lucy 250; Viki 250; Washoe 255
primates, the apes: bonobos 229n5; common chimpanzees 198–199, 203, 217–218, 221, 222–228, 232, 233–238, 240, 249–257, 262, 264–266, 268–273, 275–278, 294–297, 299; gibbons 219n3, 249n3; gorillas 203, 214, 217–218, 220, 221, 223–225, 227–228, 232, 240, 250, 261–263, 271, 296; orangutans 203, 217–220, 221, 223, 225, 227–228, 232–233, 240, 260–262, 271, 296
primates, Old World monkeys 213–215, 218, 224, 226–228, 231, 236, 241–244, 244n5, 245–246, 246n1, 249, 249n3, 259, 261, 264
Primitive Classification 163, 169, 203, 308
Primitive Culture 11, 87
Primitive Marriage: An Inquiry into the Origin of the Form of Capture in Marriage Ceremonies 19, 86, 92, 99
profane (concept of) 95, 97–98, 101, 125–127, 173–174, 176–177, 183, 185, 189, 191–192, 196, 279; *see also* sacred 22–23, 67, 76, 89, 95, 98, 101, 123–127, 133–134, 136–138, 145, 147–148, 166, 173–177, 179, 181–183, 185, 187, 189–192, 196, 198, 204, 208–210, 231, 240, 263–264, 274–275, 278–281, 291, 299, 302

Radcliffe-Brown, A.R. 40, 195
Rainbow Division 152, 289–292
relational law of progress: 18; fixed status relations 19; fluid contract relations 19

religious anomy 71–72
religious evolution: 4, 68, 73, 146, 198; animism 2, 12, 41, 68, 76, 77–78, 98, 172, 175–177; naturism 2, 4–5, 23, 68–69, 75, 76, 77–79, 95, 98, 100, 100n17, 106, 108–109, 142, 163n1, 172, 175–177, 261
Revelation, The 54, 65, 66–68
Réville, A. 68–69, 77–79, 176
Riley, A. 293–294
rites: 4, 22, 79, 95–97, 120, 124–125, 127, 134, 137–138, 145, 149, 165, 172, 174–175, 179, 187, 191–193, 264, 293; negative cult 191; positive cult 192
rituals *see* rites
Roberts, A. 253–254
Rules of Sociological Method, The 7, 24, 54, 129, 141, 212

sacred (concept of) 22–23, 67, 76, 89, 95, 98, 101, 123–127, 133–134, 136–138, 145, 147–148, 166, 173–177, 179, 181–183, 185, 187, 189–192, 196, 198, 204, 208–210, 231, 240, 263–264, 274–275, 278–281, 291, 299, 302; *see also* profane 95, 97–98, 101, 125–127, 173–174, 176–177, 183, 185, 189, 191–192, 196, 279
Sade, D. 264–265
Sams, M. 280
Schoolcraft, H. 166–168
Serazio, M. 300
Sesta 205
Smith, R. 30–32, 39, 43, 113n3
Smith, Robertson 21, 41, 64, 66–68, 80, 83–91, 94–95, 97–98, 100–101, 106, 109, 116, 124, 126, 137, 164–165, 169, 172, 177–178, 192, 281
social facts 2, 7, 12, 25, 57–58, 60, 100, 120, 122
social network theory and methods: 216; attribute approach 216; relational approach 216
Sociology and the Social Sciences 142
sodalities 298–299
solidarity: mechanical solidarity 4–5, 8, 58–59, 73–74, 106, 108–109, 234, 261, 282; organic solidarity 4–5, 8–9, 58–59, 73–74, 78, 106, 108–109, 261; social solidarity 2, 27, 51, 56, 58–59, 61, 63, 72–73, 96, 142, 180, 212, 216, 230, 258, 260–261, 265, 274, 282, 285, 289

Spencer, B. 128, 130, 132–140, 143–147, 151, 157, 159–160, 164–165, 169, 177, 194, 208, 277, 282–284
Spencer, H. 2, 5, 7–10, 13, 25, 40, 43–46, 48–49, 50, 52, 57–58, 65–66, 68–69, 70, 73, 77–79, 176, 295
stage models: Bachofen 17, 18; Durkheim 75, 76, 77, 142, 153, 81–82; Espinas 46–48; Fustel de Coulanges 22, 23, 40, 41; McLennan 20, 21; Maine 18, 19; Morgan 15, 16
Stebbins, G.L. 295
Strenski, I. 28, 64, 178, 195
Suddendorf, T. 249
suicide (forms): Altruistic Suicide n4 105, 212; Anomic Suicide 105n4, 212; Egoistic Suicide 105n4, 212; Fatalistic Suicide 213
Suicide: A Study in Sociology 24–25, 63, 104, 106, 111–112, 114, 127, 129, 212, 231
Sur le totémisme see On Totemism
Swanson, G. 195, 195n1

taboo (forms): eating of totem 89, 144–145, 182, 281, 284, 293; incest taboo 20, 99, 115–119, 126, 143, 145, 160, 196, 263–265, 278, 298; male immigration 235
theory of mind 249–251, 268–271, 275
Thompson, K. 6, 67, 100, 195, 300
time revolution 9
Tiryakian, E. 56, 128, 195
Tomasello, M. 251, 254, 256, 270
Tomonaga, M. 251
tool usage: Acheulian Industrial Complex 200; Oldowan industrial complex 200
totemic principle 185–187, 195 *see* totems

Totemism (Frazer) 88–89, 99, 135, 141, 159–160
On Totemism 163, 177, 180
Totemism and Exogamy 161, 179–180, 301, 304
totems (theories of): Durkheim 75–77, 108–110, 116–120, 123, 129, 138–139, 144, 147–149, 151, 153, 160, 165, 177, 180–187, 189, 192, 263, 278, 282, 288; Frazer 88–89, 135, 139, 145–146, 160, 165, 281, 291–293; Gallatin 166; Gillan and Spencer 128, 133–134, 137, 139, 159–160, 165; Goldenweiser 284–285, 293; Fields 165; Lang 162; Levi-Strauss 288; Linton 290–293; McLennan 19, 86, 280; Riley 293–294; Schoolcraft 167–168; Serazio 300; Smith 92, 95–96, 98, 108–110; Toy 158
tribe *see* kinship forms
Turner, J. 195–196, 214, 219, 254, 259, 264, 268
Tylor, E. 10–11, 13, 176, 178

Urabbuna 138

Van Gennep, A. 286
Varki, A. 217, 232
Vick, S.J. 253–254
Viinikainen, M. 280
visual-haptic channel 255

Watts Miller, W. 77, 164, 191
Westermarck, E. 101, 115, 126, 261
Wilson, A. 266
Worship of Plants and Animals, The 21, 86, 280
Wundt, W. 52, 65–66

Zuberbühler, K. 253–254
Zuñi 152–153

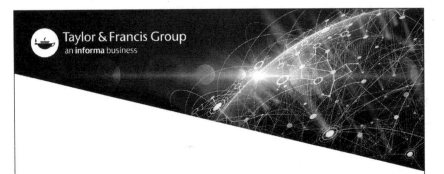